SWORD OF
ISLAM

"You will not enter paradise until you believe,
and you will not believe
until you love one another.
Let me guide you to something
in the doing of which you will love one another.
Give a greeting to everyone among you."

❀ ❀ ❀

"Inscribed on the Prophet's sword:
forgive him who wrongs you;
join him who cuts you off;
do good to him who does evil to you;
and speak the truth even if it be against yourself."

from Kabir Helminski, *The Knowing Heart:
A Sufi Path of Transformation*
(Boston: Shambhala Publications, 1999), pp. 178–80.

SWORD OF
ISLAM

*Muslim Extremism
from the Arab Conquests
to the Attack on America*

JOHN F. MURPHY JR.

 **Prometheus Books**

59 John Glenn Drive
Amherst, New York 14228-2197

Published 2002 by Prometheus Books

Inquiries should be addressed to
Prometheus Books
59 John Glenn Drive
Amherst, New York 14228–2197
VOICE: 716–691–0133, ext. 207
FAX: 716–564–2711
WWW.PROMETHEUSBOOKS.COM

06 05 04 03 02   5 4 3 2 1

Library of Congress Cataloging-in-Publication Data

Murphy, John Francis, 1937–
    Sword of Islam : Muslim extremism from the Arab conquests to the attack on
America / John F. Murphy, Jr.
       p. cm.
    Includes bibliographical references (p.) and index.
    ISBN 1–59102–010–7 (alk. paper)
    1. Panislamism. 2. Violence—Religious aspects—Islam. 3. September 11
Terrorist Attacks, 2001. 4. Islamic countries—Politics and government—20th century.
I. Title.

DS35.7 .M87 2002
303.6'25'0882971—dc21   2002018918

Printed in the United States of America on acid-free paper

Dedication

To the memory of John O'Neill, Federal Bureau of Investigation; Specialist John C. Edmunds and Pvt. Kristofor Stonesifer, 75th U.S. Army Rangers, "Rangers lead the way!"; Johnny Michael Spann, Central Intelligence Agency; Daniel Pearl, reporter for the *Wall Street Journal*; and the firemen and policemen of New York City, ordinary Americans, extraordinary heroes.

"May you be in heaven a half-hour before the devil knows you are gone!"

> "Our hearts so stout have got us fame,
> For soon 'tis known from whence we came,
> Where'er we go they fear the name,
> Of Garryown in glory!"

From "Garry Owen," Regimental March of the
Fighting 69th Regiment, New York National Guard

And in memory of those who have died in the struggle against terrorism and for peace in the Middle East: His Majesty Abdullah I, King of Jordan (1951); Count Folkke Bernadotte, UN Peace Negotiator (1948); Yitzhak Rabin, prime minister of Israel (1995); and Anwar Sadat, president of Egypt (1981).

The tumult and the shouting dies;
The captains and the kings depart;
Still stand Thine ancient sacrifice,
An humble and contrite heart,
Lord God of Hosts—be with us yet,
Lest we forget—lest we forget!

—Rudyard Kipling, "Recessional"

Contents

Acknowledgments

To my dear wife Janet, all my love; to my father, Capt. John F. Murphy Sr., U.S. Navy (Retired), of the first Greatest Generation;

to John Waller and Rosanne Klass, perhaps the only two Americans who have realized the importance of central Asia, India, Pakistan, and Afghanistan to the United States, all hail;

to the memory of Lawrence of Arabia, Mickey Markus, Golda Meir, Orde Wingate, David Ben-Gurion, Gertrude Bell, and John Bagot Glubb, who also fell in love with that beautiful and stark corner of the world, the Middle East, the land of God and prophets;

to Marechal Marcel Bigeard, whose autographed photo adorns my desk, and to Col. Roger Trinquier, de l'Armee de la France, and my honored friend, Col. Jean Martel, former Curator of the French Musee de l'Armee, *peres de la doctrine de la guerre contre-revolutionaire, veterans des guerres d'Indochine et d'Algerie, bon barodours, et grands heroes de la belle France! Toujours a vous, la gloire!*;

to Dr. Albert J. Dorley Jr. of Villanova University, Villanova, Pennsylvania, for leading me down the path of military history, and to Mr. Kevin Keeley, formerly an English teacher at Holy Spirit High School, Absecon, New Jersey, for teaching me to love poetry;

to Rep. Curt Weldon (R-Penn.) and U.S. District Attorney for Eastern Pennsylvania Patrick L. Meehan, for their encouragement;

and to the memory of Bernard B. Fall, whose writing and whose life have been my inspiration, and who now sleeps with the heroes.

Thanks also to John O'Neill, Ph.D., and Joseph A. Morinelli for their supportive influence through friendship.

I thank R. Don Green, Ph.D., for his friendship, counsel, and inestimable support.

And a special note of thanks to Madam Kamal Abu-Jaber, for her friendship and insight into the Israeli-Palestinian conflict.

"These are the times that try men's souls. The summer soldier and the sunshine patriot will, in this crisis, shrink from the service of their country; but he that stands it now deserves the love and thanks of man and woman. Tyranny, like hell, is not easily conquered; yet we have this consolation with us, that the harder the sacrifice, the more glorious the triumph."

—Thomas Paine, *Common Sense*, 1776

"But as the love of liberty and attachment to the real interests and just rights of America outweigh any other consideration, we resolve that we will exert every power within us for the defense of American liberty."

—*Fort Gower Resolves*, Virginia Gazette, 1775

A Note on Arabic Spelling

As those who have studied the region know all too well, the ways of spelling Arabic names and words seem to be as varied as the sands of the Nejd Desert. Several different ways of transliterating Arabic into English have passed over the desert like the winds of the *khamsin*. I have done my best to follow modern orthography in this book. However, some well-known names have remained in the traditional spelling, for instance, Tewfik was the Khedive of Egypt, and not Tawfif; King Farouk was deposed by the Free Officers Movement in Egypt, not King Farouq. The holy city is Mecca, not Makka. For this vexing question, I have retreated to an "appeal to authority," as it is called in logic. When a publisher brought out *Revolt in the Desert*, an abridged edition of Lawrence of Arabia's *Seven Pillars of Wisdom*, the publisher was perplexed by the different spellings of Arabic words that Lawrence gave. In response, Lawrence wrote, "Arab names won't go into English, exactly, for their consonants are not the same as ours, and their vowels, like ours, vary from district to district." I am vindicated.

J. F. M.

Introduction

T hrough its various revisions, to keep up with the rapid pace of events in the Middle East, this book has taken three years to finish. It has been a beautiful but demanding mistress. It has been a labor of love. Its genesis lies many years ago when I saw two motion pictures, *Lawrence of Arabia*, starring Peter O'Toole, about the famous Englishman who went to the Middle East to help lead the Arab revolt against the Ottoman Turks in the First World War, and *Cast a Giant Shadow*, starring Kurt Douglas, about Mickey Marcus, the famous American who went to the Middle East to help the Israelis gain their homeland in the War of 1948 against the Arabs. When I saw these films, I fell in love with the Middle East, with the Arabs and the Jews, their good humor, their grace, their maddening and fascinating complexities. In a sense then, this book is really nearly thirty years in the making.

The Arab and the Jew, both descendants of Abraham, both worship the same God of the desert, as do Christians. It is perhaps that they are both so much the same that the hostility between them has been so great. They are brothers—but so were Cain and Abel. It is the nature of the land in which they live that they be hard and uncompromising toward each other. It took an uncompromising and hard nature for the Arab nomad to make a home for himself and his family in the desert and the sun. It took an uncompromising and hard nature for the early Jewish settler to make home for himself and his family in the desert and the sun. It is a climate that fosters extreme points of view, since compromise seems so alien beneath such a harsh and demanding sun.

15

The spirit born of this climate gave birth to the Islamic extremism, which is the subject of this book. This book is not an indictment of Islam, one of the three beautiful religions which bloomed in this desert land. It is an indictment of those who took from Islam its most uncompromising tenets, forgetting the message of love that accompanies them. Extremism is a part of all three religions born of this land. If the modern Muslims have their extremism in terrorism, Christianity had its during the Crusades, and the Hebrews in the killing of all those who opposed them when they made their march to the Promised Land. Yet I have chosen to write about Islamic extremism because it represents the most clear and present danger today. Islamic extremists like the Hizbollah and the organization of Osama bin Laden have the financial resources and the ability to obtain the most sophisticated of weaponry, a generation ago reserved for only the great powers of the world. Atomic, chemical, and biological warfare are three of the lightning bolts they can hurl at their enemies like modern incarnations of the Greek gods on Mount Olympus. It is for this reason that these groups must be studied and explored.

Tragically, the words written here bore bitter fruit on Black Tuesday, September 11, 2001. On that new day of infamy, suicide bombers of Osama bin Laden hijacked four American commercial jets and flew them like bombs into the World Trade Center in New York City and the Pentagon in Washington, D.C. In less than two hours, nearly 4,000 Americans died, more than have been killed by terror attacks since the modern age of terrorism began with the Arab defeat by Israel in the Six Day War of June 1967. No adult who was alive on September 11 will ever forget the images of the burning buildings, the second jet flying into the World Trade Center, or the horrible sight of people jumping from windows to certain death on the street below rather than perish in the flames. September 11 reminded us that Islamic terrorists, like Osama bin Laden and his al-Qaeda group, in their desire to recreate a harsh Muslim world that never really existed have declared war on every American. In fact, they have declared war on everybody, Christian, Muslim, or Jew, who does not agree with their view of a fascistic, theologic Utopia. In doing so, they have hijacked Islam, one of our great desert faiths, as surely as the bin Laden terrorists hijacked the four jetliners on that desperate Tuesday. When reading of bin Laden and al-Qaeda, we are reminded of what the British author Joseph Conrad wrote in *Heart of Darkness* when his character Marlow recalled entering the interior of the Congo to find the demonic Kurtz: "the tranquil waterway leading to the uttermost ends of the earth flowed sombre under an overcast sky—seemed to lead into the heart of an immense darkness."[1]

After the atrocity of the assault on the Pentagon and the World Trade Center, we are indeed "at war with terrorism," as President George W. Bush has said. However, it is a war we did not declare, but one that Osama bin Laden declared against us as far back as 1998, the year he attacked the American embassies in Tanzania and Kenya in East Africa. As with the generation that faced the attack on Pearl Harbor in 1941, we are faced with a war against a cruel and relentless enemy. Like those before us, we must be steadfast in prosecuting the war to its ultimate victory, for against a ruthless and barbaric foe, either the Nazis of Hitler's Germany and the militarists of Japan, or the terrorists of Osama bin Laden and his like, there is no substitute for victory. But in our struggle, as President Franklin D. Roosevelt proclaimed in World War II, and as President Bush has proclaimed in the new war against terror, our fight is not against a people or a religion but against a twisted and perverted ideology whose supporters only offer death to those who oppose it. To those of good will of all faiths who stand with us in this battle against a new totalitarianism, there is no better answer to these terrorists than to quote the Quran, the book of the religion that they have perverted to serve their own evil ends: "Hold together the Rope of God, and hold it fast. Be not divided among yourselves. And be grateful for His favor. You were enemies before, but he has made you brethren in faith. You were on the brink of disaster and he has rescued you. He has shown you His signs so that you may be rightly guided" (Surah III, Ali Imran [The Family of Imran], *The Holy Quran*).

As used here, the terms *extremism* and *fundamentalism* are interchangeable. However, more emphasis is laid on *extremism* than on *fundamentalism*. This is because the term *fundamentalism* is in itself a misnomer. It was the American traveler William B. Seabrook who perhaps coined *fundamentalism* first when writing about Islam in the 1920s. Here he used the term to mean an uncompromising, fanatical belief in Islam that would permit its adherents to commit any act to further their beliefs. Of course, such extremist behavior is found in followers of all religions. However, many people are religious "fundamentalists" in the sense that they believe fundamentally and completely in the truths about God as revealed in their own religion. But none of them would think of casting a stone at a another human being, let alone blowing him or her up. Therefore, in this book, the term *extremism* is used to describe in the majority of cases those believers who have no qualms about killing or maiming in the name of religion. And when the term *fundamentalism* is used here, it has the same meaning. Nowhere in this book is the term meant to apply to those who have a simple, *a fundamental*, belief in the teachings of their religion.

John F. Murphy Jr.
October 25, 2001

1

A *Bloody Day* on the *Barren Rocks of Aden*

A United States Navy presence in Aden harbor, a rocky outcropping in Yemen on the southern edge of the Arabian Peninsula, on the morning of October 12, 2000, was a classic example of the theories of U.S. Navy Admiral Alfred Thayer Mahan, whose work Navy Secretary Theodore Roosevelt would make required reading for the captains, the commodores, and the flag officers of the U.S. fleet. Mahan, in seminal works like *The Influence of Seapower upon History*, had, with the enthusiastic support of soon-to-be-president Teddy Roosevelt, dragged the United States Navy from its slumber since the end of the American Civil War in 1865. According to Mahan, the purpose of the navy and its far-flung squadrons was not just for commodores to host on-board *soirées* for commodores from other countries' navies in exotic ports of call like Papeete in Tahiti or Rio de Janeiro in Brazil. In Mahan's revolutionary view, the squadrons of the fleet were the cutting edge of the American sword, the projection of naked force in the protection of American foreign interests. On this day, the USS *Cole* and her sisters in the fleet had dropped anchor in the faraway port of Aden for the same reason that the USS *Oregon* had sailed around South America to take part in the naval battle of Santiago de Cuba against the Spanish fleet, in the Spanish-American War a century ago in 1898. It was a clear demonstration that the United States, through its navy, could project brute power anytime, anywhere in the world, in pursuit of what it believed were its vital interests.

On this trip, the skipper of the *Cole* was Commander Kirk S. Lippold, a career navy officer. Lippold knew he was sailing the *Cole* into troubled waters. On July 18, 2001, the State Department had issued a warning against the possibility of imminent terrorist attack in the region of the Arabian Sea. The alert read in part, "The United States has strong indications that individuals may be planning imminent terrorist actions against U.S. interests in the Arabian Penuinsula. In the past, such individuals have not distinguished between official and civilian targets." As he was bringing his ship into "harm's way," Commander Lippold was celebrating his twentieth year in the service, having received his commission in 1981. Commander Lippold, as he sailed the *Cole* into Aden harbor, could look ahead to a fine career in the navy, one that would probably earn him an admiral's rank. Before taking command of the *Cole*, he had been the administrative aide to the secretary of the navy at the Pentagon. The Arleigh Burke class of destroyer, to which Lippold's ship belonged, was as well armed as the fighting admiral it was named after could ever hope. The *Cole* and her sister ships in the Burke class, like the *Arleigh Burke*, the *Barry*, and the *John Paul Jones* (John Barry and John Paul Jones being two heroes of the American navy in the Revolutionary War), were truly "loaded for bear." When the USS *Arleigh Burke* was commissioned on July 4, 1991, according to the U.S. Navy Web page on destroyers from which this information is taken, it "was the most powerful surface combatant ever put to sea." Each carried in its armament eight Harpoon missiles; Tomahawk cruise missiles, like those that U.S. forces have used against Saddam Hussein's Iraq; vertical launch ASROC (anti-submarine) missiles; six Mark-46 torpedoes; two 5"54 Mark-45 deck guns; and two 20 mm Photon gun mounts, with M-60 machine guns for close action.[1]

Yet in spite of the proud heritage of Arleigh Burke, who had made his name as a destroyer leader in the Second World War, the U.S. Navy no longer had the power to project American influence that it once had. Since 1992, with the official end of the Cold War and the demise of the former Soviet Union (FSU), the navy had been the subject of drastic budget cuts. According to the conservative Heritage Foundation, the number of ships afloat had plummeted from 393 in 1992 to a current low of 316. Not only has this reduced the number of combat ships (gone are the days when the 16-inch guns of the battleship USS *New Jersey* terrified the Palestinian Liberation Organization in Lebanon in 1982), but a *decrease* in the number of support ships has meant an *increase* in the number of times a ship like the *Cole* has to stop at a port to take on needed supplies. And, in the Persian Gulf region, especially after the U.S. and British bombing raids on Iraqi radar in February 2001, this had meant increased exposure to anti-American terror activity.

Aden, where the *Cole* was headed, was a hot fly speck on the Horn of Arabia. Beyond it to the north lay what was called the Republic of Yemen, really a country where the federal government at S'ana could claim control only as far as its biggest artillery piece could fire. This was tribal territory, where Arab warriors carried on feuds as they have done for thousands of years. Although Yemen's president Ali Abdullah Salah made a point to eradicate Islamic terrorism from his country, the U.S. State Department has admitted candidly that the situation is handicapped by "lax and inefficient enforcement of security procedures and the government's inability to exercise authority over remote areas of the country." This is the region where Osama bin Laden was drawing his strength. Osama's father, Mohammed bin Laden, although he made his fortune in construction in Saudi Arabia (he runs the Bin Laden Group), was born in the desolate tribal region of Yemen known as the Hadramaut. There, as centuries ago, tribes control their small fiefdoms and carry on the age-old ritual of inter-tribal warfare. If indeed this is the location bin Laden has established as his base in the Yemen, then the members of his clan can be expected to provide fiercely loyal, and absolutely ruthless, foot soldiers for al-Qaeda. It is believed that it was in Yemen that bin Laden's organization carried out its first bombing in 1992, when an explosive device tore apart a hotel that was being used by American personnel supporting the humanitarian effort then occurring in Somalia. However, in a *Time* magazine article, reporter Douglas Waller had some interesting revelations about bin Laden's early terrorist career. Using CIA and FBI sources, Waller wrote how bin Laden's terrorist apparatus, al-Qaeda, "the base," had attacked "American soldiers in Somalia, Yemen, and Saudi Arabia. They had plans to kidnap U.S. military personnel in the Persian Gulf, and they might have U.S.-made Stinger missiles left over from the Afghan War."[2]

Before the *Cole* episode, bin Laden was taking unusual steps to solidify his ties to Yemen, unusual for the fact that he had identified with the Taliban movement in Afghanistan. Bin Laden had often appeared in Yemeni tribal dress and had even wed a Yemeni woman, which did much to strengthen his position, since now he could call on the manpower of the woman's clan, if she were not a member of his father's tribe.[3]

As the investigation developed in the aftermath of the October 12 *Cole* bombing, bin Laden's fingerprints began to appear all over the case. Vincent

Cannistrano, a former operational chief at the CIA's Counterterrorist Center, told the *Washington Post* that bin Laden had been cultivating ties with the fundamentalist tribal chief Abdel Majid Zandani. Zandani, like bin Laden, was a veteran of the war in Afghanistan, and may very well have met Osama bin Laden in that country.

During the good old days of the Cold War, when Washington and Moscow competed for every hot spot all over the globe, Yemen had been divided into a northern, Marxist statelet and a southern one which had a pro-American orientation. This situation meant that these tribal lords of the desert were showered with aid as the Eastern and the Western power blocs funneled every type of modern weapon to the knife-carrying Yemenis in the hope of winning their dubious loyalty. The two Yemens became a veritable F. A. O. Schwartz of high-technology killing toys. The old Yemeni proverb, "my fist is in his mouth, his fist is in my eye" was never more true! Yemen was such a popular spot during the Cold War years that even President Gamal Abdel Nasser of Egypt, in a bid to extend Egypt's influence, had for years deployed there battalions of Egyptian combat engineers and special forces. When I interviewed one of these Egyptian Cold Warriors in a Philadelphia coffee shop, this urbane gentleman summed up his tour of duty in Yemen in roughly two words: hot and unpleasant. His comments conjured up images of a desert sand dune where safe drinking water was as rare as water for a fresh shower.

Had it not been for the port of Aden, to which the Arleigh Burke class destroyer *Cole* was now steaming at cruise speed, nobody—not Egyptians, Americans, or Russians—would have given Yemen a second thought. But there was Aden, and that was what had changed the entire strategic equation for Yemen. Frank Richards was a British soldier who had served in the Royal Welch Fusiliers regiment around 1905. Returning from his tour of duty in British India, the troop transport in which he was sailing home to England stopped at Aden. Writing years later, Richards recalled, "Aden is known as one of the most dead-alive and dreary stations that troops can be sent to; it has great strategic value. That is all."[4] Aden was quite simply one of the best natural harbors in the Arab world. Even Marco Polo, in his account of his travels, wrote about the great harbor. For over three thousand years, Arab sailors in their wind-powered *dhows* would stop at Aden to take on fresh water and provisions, as well as slaves for sale later, as they traversed the maritime trade route from what became Mombasa and Zanzibar in East Africa to the west coast of India at Calicut. Vasco da Gama, the Portuguese navigator, would follow much the same nautical path when he became the first European to circumnavigate Africa to reach the rajah's court at Calicut in 1494.

It would be Aden, too, that would draw the British to Yemen in the heyday of the great Victorian Empire. When British Prime Minister Benjamin Disraeli bought the Suez Canal in 1869, the importance of Aden stood out starkly to the strategic planners in Whitehall. It was not enough that the warships of the British Royal Navy could patrol the waters off the northern entrance to the Canal at Suez and Port Said. Why? Because any potential political enemy, like tsarist Russia or France of the Third Republic, which could gain control of Aden would be able to bottle up the British fleet in the canal. Fortunately in 1839, Captain Haines and the Royal Navy had already landed and laid claim to Aden for the British Union Jack. With the acquisition of the Suez Canal, however, the British were more determined than ever that Aden and the Yemen hinterland beyond it remain under their absolute rule.

All through the rest of the nineteenth century and the first half of the twentieth, a snarling British lion kept Aden firmly in its clenched teeth. Holding Aden was all the more important in that it became the main stopover point on the sea voyage to the most precious jewel in England's imperial crown: India. The importance of Aden and the Suez Canal was made brutally clear during the First and Second World Wars, when the British dominion in the Middle East was under rude attack by Germany and her allies. This was especially true in World War I, when the Turkish Ottoman Empire, allied to Imperial Germany and ruler of most of the Middle East (including northern Yemen), furiously tried to seize control of the Suez Canal from the British. It took ferocious fighting by the British garrison in Egypt under the command of Gen. Archibald Murray to throw back the Turkish threat.

It was after the end of World War II that Great Britain, drained of men and treasure after five years of the most terrible war in its history, had painfully realized that it could no longer afford to pay the price of empire. This had become poignantly clear when in 1947 the old Indian Empire was divided into the new countries of India and Pakistan, both of which won their independence from England. It was after this that prime ministers Anthony Eden (1955–1957) and Harold Macmillan (1957–1963) began the traumatic policy of pulling back British power and influence from "east of Suez." This was only made more painful when in 1956 England and the new state of Israel seized the Suez Canal from Gamal Abdel Nasser of Egypt (who had taken it from the British-owned Suez Canal Company), only to see the

United States force them to return it to Egypt for fear of precipitating war with Egypt's main supporter, the Soviet Union.

Yet the British were not quite through with Aden and Yemen. During the painful process of imperial withdrawal, their last years in Aden were marred by the beginning of a vicious Communist-backed insurgency which began in 1965. What resulted for the long-suffering British "squaddies," or soldiers, was what they would face several years later in Belfast and Londonderry in Northern Ireland, only without public houses serving Guinness Stout, cheery Irish music, and the company of lovely Irish colleens. Yemen and Aden became a squalid hell for the soldiers on duty, like the Highlanders of the Argyll and Sutherland Regiment. Derek Rose, a civilian friend of Oliver Miles, one of the British officers of the Foreign Service which governed Aden, was simply shot and killed when his car broke down one day, as Miles recorded in his memoir for the British-Yemeni Society.[5]

It had become a tradition among the regimental pipe and drum bands of the British Army's Highland Division to compose a march to commemorate the leaving of an overseas posting. When the 79th Regiment departed from Gibraltar, which has been the favorite foreign duty spot for British soldiers and sailors since Admiral Rooke took it from Spain in 1703, the 79th's Pipe or Drum Major (a pipe and drum band has both) composed the jaunty "The 79th Regiment's Farewell to Gibraltar." No doubt the Highland composer was thinking of the Gibraltarian females, some of the most exotic ladies in the Mediterranean. However, when the British finally decided to shake the sand of Yemen from their shoes and withdraw in 1967, the pipes and drums of the Argyll and Sutherland Highlanders played the dour "Barren Rocks of Aden." Ever since pipes had accompanied highlanders to war, pipe tunes had been written to show how the men had felt about where they had served. The paen to Aden reflected the troop's utter disgust at the sun-blasted colony.

With the final retreat of Great Britain from "east of Suez," it was the turn of the United States, in the middle of the Cold War, to keep the peace in "faraway places with strange-sounding names." It has been the greatest public relations achievement in history that the federal government in Washington has been actually administering since 1945 an American empire, a Pax Americana, and so majestic has been this public relations campaign that the American people still do not realize it! It was as part of the U.S. Navy's battle group intended to keep the peace in the Persian Gulf that the *Cole* had dropped anchor in Aden in October 2000. The *Cole* was not intended to remain long on the Persian Gulf station. The destroyer was expected to leave the region on December 21, so that the crew could be back home with their families for Christmas.

Sailing into Aden's waters, the *Cole* was entering the twilight world between war and peace in which the United States has lived in the Middle East for over thirty years. Although there had been warnings of possible anti-American activity in Yemen (such diplomatic notices are almost a daily occurrence in that part of the world), the crew of the *Cole* was not permitted to take the protective measures that would have guarded the ship in known hostile waters. According to Kenneth Katzman, an analyst with the Congressional Research Service, the former Marxist state of North Yemen had been listed as a state sponsor of terrorism from 1979 to 1990. But when North Yemen and South Yemen merged in 1990, the country was dropped from the watch list.

In short, the men on board the destroyer were restricted by what have come to be known (and often loathed) by members of our armed forces as the "rules of engagement." These rules govern under what circumstances force can be used to defend American lives, property, or ships. In the navy, the captain of the ship has the privilege of modifying these rules of engagement if it is deemed necessary.

In the case of the good ship *Cole*, these rules were to have catastrophic effects. Sentries were patrolling the deck of the destroyer on October 12, 2000, the day the bombing took place. They were carrying their service side arms, most likely the 9-mm Beretta semi-automatic pistol that first saw service in the Gulf War of 1990–91. Each sailor, according to an extensive *Washington Post* investigation, was issued two magazines of ammunition for his side arm but, following the rules of engagement, was not permitted to have a magazine loaded into the butt of his pistol! Even if the magazines were in their Berettas, the sailors on guard would not be allowed to fire until after they had received permission from the captain commanding their ship.

But all seemed well that Aden afternoon, when a fiberglass boat approached the man of war. The *Cole* was undergoing refueling and small boats had been going back and forth all day from the harbor quay to carry on the project. On this particular boat, as it approached the destroyer, sailors on the deck of the *Cole* saw the two men aboard it salute, as if saluting the American flag hanging from its mast. Then, seconds later, those crewmen were dead, and the two in the boat incinerated in the blast. A boatload of C-4 explosives, later said by experts to have been in the range of hundreds of pounds, had erupted in a ball of heat and flame right next to the side of the ship. A 40-by-40-foot hole was blown into the *Cole*, disemboweling it. Even worse, on the deck above where the explosion hit, a party of crewmen, men and women, had just sat down in the galley to eat. The force of the blast pushed the ceiling of the compartment that received the impact up and into them, crushing them between the floor of their deck and the ceiling of that above them. Seventeen caught in that horrible carnage were killed. In seconds, the ship was transformed into a broken and smoking wreck. The blast was so intense that parts of the ship on the side hit by the bomb were blown clear over to the other side of the sixty-six-foot deck. Alarms went off all over the ship as the crew went into the damage and fire control roles they had learned so well—only this time they were acting in earnest, it was no drill. The ship was suddenly transformed into a potential gasoline bomb. There were twenty-one fuel tanks aboard the ship, each threatened by any fire, electrical or otherwise, that resulted from the initial explosion. Luckily, the hours of drill spent on fire control proved their worth. The ship was saved.

After the explosion, the port of Aden became a hornet's nest of counterterrorist activity. An initial Federal Bureau of Investigation (FBI) force of forty agents was flown into Aden to begin the investigation. John O'Neill, who had been instrumental in the FBI's investigation into the bombings at the American embassies in East Africa in 1998, would take overall command of the *Cole* inquiry. It was a case right out of *Casablanca*, where Claude Raines's French policeman calls out in the casbah to "round up the usual suspects!" In spite of the Yemeni president's avowed intention to eradicate terrorism from united Yemen, the country was an alphabet soup of all the Islamic terror groups known to the FBI or to the CIA. The Middle Eastern terror group Hamas and the Palestinian Islamic *Jihad* have representatives in the country. However, these groups might soon have a more relentless opponent than the United States. In January and February 2001, the Israeli government admitted to a policy of deliberately targeting for assassination any leaders of the armed *Intifidah*, or Palestinian uprising in the West Bank and the Gaza Strip. On February 20, 2001, a leader of Hamas was killed from an Israeli army guard post, most likely by sniper. Remembering how Israel's intelligence unit, Mossad, hunted down those responsible for the massacre of the Israeli athletes at the 1972 Olympic Games in Munich, Germany, it would not be unlikely for Mossad *katsas*, or agents, to begin targeting leaders of terror groups in Yemen as well. Also to be counted as possible Mossad targets are members of the Egyptian Islamic *Jihad*, which was responsible some years ago for the massacre of a tourist group at the famed archaeological site in Egypt at Luxor, the site of the ancient ruins of Karnak and Thebes from the time of the pharaohs; the Islamic Group; and even the Algerian Armed Islamic Group. The Algerian Armed Islamic Group, which will figure prominently later in this book, has been responsible for an insurgency in Algeria that since 1992 has claimed nearly 100,000 Algerian lives. Even though Yemen's President Salah in 1998 had executed the leader of the Islamic Army of Aden, an indigenous Yemeni terror group, for kidnapping sixteen Western tourists, his country still appealed to Islamic terrorists as a happy hunting ground. Soon the FBI team and Yemeni investigators had homed in on likely identities for the suicide bombers. The terror operation showed all the signs of the infrastructure that Osama bin Laden had apparently carefully crafted throughout Yemen. On October 21 local Yemeni security agents detained employees of a government registration office in charge of issuing identification cards for those employed in Aden harbor. One card was issued to a resident of the Lahej region of Yemen, which is next to Aden province. The name on the card was one Abdullah Ahmed Khaled Musawab. More evidence of complicity in the registration office surfaced when it became known that all supporting documents for the issuing of the card to Musawab had conveniently disappeared. By October 21, a small army of American investigators had descended on the port city to pursue the hunt for the identity of the bombers and their supporters.

After the force of the C-4 explosion, there was certainly little if any physical evidence left from Musawab and his accomplice. All that investigators seem to have uncovered was a pair of glasses that matched a pair worn by one of the two bombers in a fake ID photo that accompanied his registration card.

Yet it was not just the incident in the registration office that pointed to Musawab and a compatriot as the two possible suicide commandos. In a closely packed city with some of the world's oldest surviving multilevel dwellings, like Marrakech in Morocco, people watched their neighbors with an intense interest that has long since departed our Western megacities. The duo had simply, to the discernment of their neighbors, not "fit in." They professed to be Muslims, like the majority of Yemenis are today. However, in a city where the mosque was not only the center of spiritual life, but cultural life as well, these two professed Muslims never went there, not even for the traditional prayers every Friday. In a city where people enjoyed the warm environment of a closely knit community, the two remained aloof from their neighbors. Considering their mission in Aden, this was the worst thing that they could

have done. Investigators soon had reason to believe that the two were operatives of al-Qaeda, the Afghanistan-based terror network of Osama bin Laden,
who had been indicted by the United States for his role in the embassy bombings in 1998 in East Africa, in Dar-es-Salaam in Tanzania and in Nairobi,
Kenya. The United States posted a $5 million reward on bin Laden's head in
1998, wanting him presumably alive, but it is a reward that has yet to be
claimed. The fundamentalist government of the Taliban in Afghanistan continued to shield bin Laden, asserting that he was only a visitor there. In spite of
the threat of United Nations' sanctions, the Taliban still harbored bin Laden. It
did so even after its mission to the United Nations was closed in New York City
because of its defiance of that international body. Meanwhile, Osama bin
Laden felt strong enough in Afghanistan to host in early 2001 a large wedding
feast for his son, Mohammed, who married the daughter of Mullah
Mohammed Omar, the former leader of the radical Taliban in Afghanistan.

Not only had the deceased murder team belonged to bin Laden's al-
Qaeda, roughly translated from Arabic as "The Center," American intelligence
sources had unearthed that, like Osama himself, they had served in the ranks
of the U.S. proxy army of the *mujahidin*, "the soldiers of the faith," in the war
against the Russian Soviets in Afghanistan (1979–89). It had been a bitter
struggle, which received limited coverage in the Western media, except perhaps in the pages of *Soldier of Fortune* magazine. (Whatever you may think
of the politics of Col. Robert Brown, the publisher and founder, his reporting
team has certainly been intrepid. Several of his correspondents have been
killed in the wars that they covered.) In the *Afghansti voina*, as the Russians
called the Afghan war, the CIA had tried to follow the operational template
that had been successfully used in Tibet against the Chinese Communists, and
in Laos against the combined forces of the Communist Pathet Lao and the
North Vietnamese "main force" army. They had attempted to form and to fund
a mercenary army to do the fighting that Congress and the American people
would not want American soldiers to do. Indeed, the same strategic scenario
had been used by President Ronald Reagan and William Casey, the director of
the Central Intelligence Agency, to put into the field the controversial *contras*
in the war against the Communist Sandinistas in Nicaragua.

However, while the game plan had been carried out in varying degrees of
success in Tibet, Laos, and Nicaragua, it did not in Afghanistan. The Afghans
were not pragmatic fighters like the Laotians of General Vang Pao. They were,
instead, fundamentalist Islamic tribal warriors whose outlook on life had

changed little since Mahmud of Ghazni had come riding through the Khyber Pass to convert their ancestors to Islam at the point of a scimitar in the eleventh century. The Afghanis possessed an uncompromising, simple commitment to Islam coupled with a savagery in war that had compelled England's poet Rudyard Kipling to warn Victorian-era British soldiers left wounded on the Afghan "plain" to save their last bullet for themselves. For what the Afghans' *jezail* muskets had not finished, their grim Khyber knives would.

It was in this war that Musawab and his comrade had been converted to the Islamic struggle and had likely joined al-Qaeda. Since the war, the two had been in and out of Yemen, presumably on errands tied to the bin Laden organization. Fears that they had a network of supporters in Yemen were confirmed by the work of the joint American and Yemeni team. The support network appeared to be a closely knit group of individual cells, each one numbering some one to three members who were sympathetic to bin Laden's call to drive the Americans out of the Persian Gulf. The two suicide bombers fitted the profile of the other human bombs that bin Laden would employ: They were fanatical believers in the rightness of their cause. Their psychology was very similar to that of the ideologically motivated spy: "Ideologies are stern task-masters; they demand constant service and sacrifice. The true believer is only too ready to pay the price, whatever it might be."[6]

By the middle of November 2000, the Yemeni and United States investigators, who were led by John O'Neill of the FBI, had combed through the information that they could gather about the covert terror group. Finally, some fifty of those held in custody were identified as core members of the group, with "less than 10" being among the inner circle. The Associated Press gave six as the number of men that the Yemenis thought were at the heart of the plot against the destroyer. More information also came in about Musawab and his accomplice. Before their return to Aden, where they had stirred up unwanted attention among the citizens, they had been abroad. It would be a safe assumption to make that they had been in Afghanistan, getting last-minute instruction from bin Laden's al-Qaeda network. This makes sense for another reason. The Yemen *Observer* noted that security officials had uncovered details of a previous plot slated for January 2000 to blow up an American warship in Aden harbor. Whether that attack date was chosen to have significance for the new millennium was not learned. The first attack failed when the small boat to be used took on too much sea water and sank before it reached its target, which was not disclosed in the newspaper.

There was evidence piling up that the brains behind the operation were not among the barren rocks of Aden. Interest centered around a length of red towing rope that was found still attached to the remains of the small boat after the explosion. Investigators soon theorized that the fiberglass boat had been towed into Yemen from outside the country specifically for the assault on the *Cole*. Moreover, the type of explosive used also piqued the interest of the FBI explosive authorities, who were now, sadly, becoming accustomed to deployment overseas in such crises. Indeed, they noticed a sophistication similar to the explosives used in the summer 1998 bombings of the United States embassies in Dar-es-Salaam in Tanzania and in Nairobi, Kenya. The bomb used against the *Cole* was made from military style C-4 plastique, or plastic explosive, a type known to the United States armed forces. It was a "shaped-charge," in other words, placed inside a metal housing to intensify the force of the blast. Indeed, if the explosion had taken place a few feet lower, below the *Cole*'s water line, the ship would have sunk to the bottom of the harbor according to FBI agents. The bomb-maker on the Tanzania and Kenya jobs was an expert, one Fazul Abdullah Mohammed, a native of the Comoro Islands. Investigators in Aden learned that an expert had been secretly brought into Yemen for the *Cole* job after the fiasco in January. Whether this was Fazul or not was not known. (In the current Palestinian *Intifida* against Israel, Israeli security forces have made killing such bomb experts among Palestinian extremists a high priority. In February 2001, the Israelis chased one Palestinian on their kill list for twenty-two minutes by helicopter and ground vehicles before they brought him to ground and finally killed him.) As of January 2002, Fazul has still eluded death or capture. Yemeni Prime Minister Abdel Karim Ali Iryani confirmed that his government believed the bombing of the *Cole* was the product of a widespread conspiracy. Iryani said, "the picture inside the country should be very clear soon. The question is outside. Who was involved outside the country?"

The investigation would continue. Osama bin Laden would deny involvement in the bombing, but with a several million dollar reward already placed on his head by the United States for his role in the East African catastrophes this is not unlikely behavior. The Yemenis arrested denied they were part of al-Qaeda, a denial probably motivated by the same consideration. Some of those questioned would even claim that they acted simply because they wanted the United States out of Yemen. As Muhammed Al-Masyabi of the British-Yemeni Society would write in the *Proceedings* of the society, they felt "they were therefore justified in inflicting as much harm as possible on the 'infidel forces.'" Even Iraq and Iran would be mentioned as possible suspects of "state-supported terrorism." But meanwhile, for the men and women of the navy, the most important things were the burying of their dead, the saving of the wounded, and salvaging the *Cole*, still afloat after the October 12 onslaught.

Those who were killed were brought home to the United States, where they were received with honor by the secretary of defense and high-ranking officers of the navy. There were the guards of honor to carry in quiet ceremony the flag-draped caskets of the slain off the transport plane and then to honored burial. Each family would receive a flag, carefully folded into the traditional triangle by the white-gloved guard of honor. Those who had been wounded were taken away by ambulance plane to navy hospital facilities for treatment. Some of them might receive psychiatric counseling to help them find their way through the ordeal they had just experienced.

On November 3, the remaining crew of 216 arrived home at the Norfolk, Virginia, naval station after a trans-Atlantic flight from a U.S. military base in Germany. A day before they arrived, U.S. Army general William W. Crouch, who had been picked by Defense Secretary William S. Cohen to help chair an inquiry into the bombing, had praised the crew since "the actions of the commanding officer and the crew, following the attack, saved the ship and several of their shipmates," according to the Navy Office of Information. By early November, two sailors were still under medical care at the Naval Medical Center at Portsmouth, Virginia, while another was at the National Naval Medical Center in Bethesda, Maryland. Most of the crew would remain in Norfolk pending reassignment to other vessels or the repair of their own ship. The *Cole* itself was unable to make the return trip to the United States under its own power. The navy contracted for the Norweigian big ship *Blue Marlin* to bring the *Cole* home, after the wounded destroyer was brought out of Aden harbor by the navy tug *Catawba*. As an honor to the ship and those who had perished, a crew made up of various commands would staff the *Cole* on its journey home and the destroyer *Donald Cook* would provide the escort of honor.

The sad saga of the *Cole* was over. But it wrote a new chapter in the history of the United States Navy. The USS *Cole* was the first U.S. Navy ship to be a direct casualty of the sword of Islam, the *jihad*, or holy war, being waged against the infidel nations of the world by the extremists of fundamentalist Islam.[7]

2

The 100th Birthday of the Modern Jihad

The terrorist bomb explosions that destroyed the American embassies in Kenya and Tanzania and the Planet Hollywood club in South Africa in August 1998, two years before the *Cole* was struck, occurred on the hundredth anniversary of the end of the first of the Muslim holy wars, or *jihads*, of modern times. On September 2, 1998, the date I first began work on this book, the centennial took place of the defeat of the first mass Islamic fundamentalist, or extremist, movement of our era. On September 2, 1898, while Americans were celebrating our victory in the Spanish-American War, an Anglo-Egyptian-Sudanese army led by British Sir Horatio Herbert Kitchener defeated the Mahdist Army under the Khalifa Abdullahi at Omdurman, is just outside Khartoum, the capital of the Sudan, where a century later in 1998 U.S. Tomahawk missiles destroyed a factory believed to be controlled by the Islamic terrorist entrepeneur Osama bin Laden.

Half a world away, another centennial went unnoticed. One hundred years ago, British forces under Lt. Gen. Sir William Lockhart finally recaptured the strategic Khyber Pass, the fabled gateway to British India, which had been captured by Islamic fundamentalist Pathan (Pashtun) tribesmen, supported by their brethren in Afghanistan, months earlier. One hundred years later, at the same time that Tomahawk missiles crashed into Khartoum on the Nile, other missiles destroyed bin Laden's fundamentalist terrorist training camp at Khost in Afghanistan, partly identified by satellite imagery.

The genesis of the Battle of Omdurman lay in the rise of a militant Islamic holy man, or *mullah*,* in what was then the Anglo-Egyptian Sudan. The *mullah* was Mohammed Ahmed, who styled himself the Mahdi, or the Expected Leader of all Islam. Appearing in about 1881, the Mahdi's goal was to liberate the Muslim world, especially the holy cities of Mecca and Medina, from Western influence and corrupt, Western-oriented regimes.

This was September 1882, a time when England occupied Egypt and with it the Sudan. At the same time, the twin holy cities of Mecca and Medina in Arabia were ruled as part of the decrepit Ottoman Empire (c. 1300–1922), which was desperately trying to modernize itself through the use of Western means. Sultan Abdul Hamid imported advisers throughout Western Europe to help his empire, and also to offset the power of tsarist Russia, which had attempted to conquer the empire in the Crimean War of 1854–56 and most recently in 1878. Egypt shared the underdevelopment with the Ottoman Empire; the sultan in Constantinople was still titular ruler of Egypt. Yet under the rule of the Khedive Ismail, Egypt had taken great strides toward entering the modern world, not the least of which had been Ismail's opening of the Suez Canal in 1869. For the first time since the Egypt of the pharaohs, a waterway now cut across the Isthmus of Suez to join the Mediterranean with the Red Sea and India beyond.

When the Mahdi became a serious threat to Egyptian rule in the Sudan, the British government refused to send troops. Therefore, the Khedive Tewfik of Egypt, the nominal ruler, who had succeeded his father, Ismail, sent an expedition of some 10,000 men in 1883 under Hicks Pasha, formerly Col. W. Hicks of the Indian Army, into the vastness of the Sudan to subdue the Mahdist forces. Mohammed Ahmed used the same tactics that Saladin, the leader of Islam at the time of the Third Crusade, had used against the army of the Crusader Kingdom of Jerusalem in 1187. Leading Hicks's disorganized army ever deeper into the wilderness of Kordofan, the Mahdi surprised the Egyptians at El Obeid in November and destroyed the force under Hicks the same way that Saladin had crushed the Crusaders at the Horns of Hattin. Exhausted and weakened from lack of water, the crusading army had been virtually annihilated, as were the Egyptians at El Obeid.

The Hicks debacle at El Obeid led to a rescue operation to save the situation in the Sudan, much like the ill-fated American expedition to Somalia in

---

*Terms for Muslim religious leaders are as varied as the spellings of Arab names, a fact noted in Lawrence of Arabia's *Seven Pillars of Wisdom*.

1992–93. The British effort was mismanaged by the reluctance of the Liberal party government of Prime Minister William Gladstone to become further enmeshed in Egyptian affairs. Meanwhile, Charles Gordon, the British emissary in the Sudan, had become besieged in Khartoum on the Nile River in April 1884 by the Mahdist army, called the *Ansar*, after the first followers of Mohammed, who had helped him recapture Mecca, subsequent to his historic flight, or *hegira*, from that city to Medina in 630 C.E. A relief expedition up the Nile River under Sir Garnet Wolseley failed to reach Gordon in time. The advance river boat, the *Bordein*, did not reach Khartoum until January 28, 1885, two days after the city fell and Gordon was killed. A second British operation, under Lt. Gen. Sir Gerald Graham, returned to the Red Sea port of Suakim on April 4, abandoning any further attempt at reconquest, after defeating the *Ansar* at Hasin and Tofrik in March.

Retribution did not come until the Conservative Prime Minister Marquess Salisbury began the reconquest of the Sudan in March 1896. The Anglo-Egyptian army was led by Kitchener, who commanded as the Sirdar of the army, nominally under the leadership of the ruling Khedive. With victories at Firket, Abu Hamed, and at the Atbara River, Kitchener steadily pushed back the *Ansar* so that by mid-1898 much of the Sudan had been retaken. Finally, as Winston Churchill vividly wrote in his *River War*, Kitchener decisively crushed the forces of the Khalifa Abdullahi at Omdurman on September 2, 1898, a triumph Churchill took part in while attached to the 21st Lancers. Escaping from Omdurman, the Khalifa was finally cornered and killed in battle in November 1899, where a British photographer photographed the dead Abdullahi surrounded by his slain brothers.[1]

The influence of the Crusades and their Muslim spirit of *jihad*, or holy war against unbelievers, was still manifest in the reconquest of the Sudan. The Haddendowah black warriors, Rudyard Kipling's "Fuzzy-Wuzzies" (named so after their tribal hair style), who "broke a British square" at Abu Klea in January 1885, carried Crusader-style swords with cruciform hilts. As Kipling wrote in "Fuzzy-Wuzzy,"

An 'ere's to you, Fuzzy Wuzzy, with your 'ayrick 'head of air—
You big black boundin' beggar—for you broke a British square!

The *amirs* of the *Ansar* rode into battle wearing Islamic armor unchanged since the time of Saladin, the greatest Muslim champion of the Crusades.

One of these Muslim paladins can be seen in a painting of the charge of the 21st Lancers at Omdurman by George Delville Rowlandson in the Museum of the 17th/21st Lancers in Lebanon's Belvoir Castle today.

At the same time that Kitchener was fighting the fundamentalist forces of the *Ansar* in the Sudan, a critical rebellion broke out against the British raj along the North-West Frontier of British India, fueled by militant Islamic preaching by *mullahs* like Najb-ud-din and Sayyid Akhbar, who were most prominent of the holy men. The clerics were strongly supported by Abdur Rahman, the ruling emir of Afghanistan. Soon, all the Pathan tribes along the frontier rose up against the British in a religious-inspired revolt. It would be interesting to know if the fiery clerics among the Pathans were in fact influenced by the Mahdi's brand of militant Islam. Although the risings in the Sudan and on the North-West Frontier have never been causally linked, it is likely that one could have influenced the other, if only because frontier pilgrims on their yearly *hajj*, pilgrimage, to Mecca would have heard of the Mahdist success from coreligionists coming from the Sudan.

When British border militia, the Khyber Rifles, went over to the rebels, the way was open for the fall of the Khyber Pass to the tribesmen, on September 12, 1897, when the last loyal Sikh garrison was overrun. It would take months of hard campaigning before the Pathan tribes were subdued and the pass regained by the British. The North-West Frontier rising saw the British mount the largest expedition seen since the Crimean War, the Tirah Field Force, under Sir William Lockhart, which numbered some 40,000 men. Beginning on October 18, Lockhart took on a tribal army of Orakzai and Afridi Pathans that easily equaled his own force in number. It would not be until November 1, 1897, that Lockhart would be able to reach the Tirah Valley, the tribes' main homeland. Even after the Orakzais surrendered, the Afridis kept up their guerrilla war. It would not be until March 1898 that the Khyber Pass would be safely back in British hands, and the last of the Afridis make their submissions in tribal *jirgas*, or councils.

Thus, one hundred years ago, Western interests were dealt severe blows in the very regions from which blows were struck on the United States by militant Islam in 1998, Afghanistan, from which Osama bin Laden planned his attacks, and East Africa, where his bombs exploded. Two years later, the USS *Cole* would be bombed in Aden harbor which, ironically, had been used by the British as a staging center for their reconquest of the Sudan in 1898. The religious fervor of the Mahdi in the Sudan, the tribes on the Khyber Pass, and the modern warriors of Osama bin Laden's al-Qaeda one hundred years later is different from what we have experienced in the ongoing struggle between Israel and the Palestinians, which has dominated the Middle East since the birth of Israel in 1948.

The battle between Israeli and Palestinian stems from the approximately 500,000 Palestinian Arabs who left the new state of Israel in the months after its founding. Not accepted by other Arab countries like Syria, Egypt, or Jordan, they were forced to live in United Nations refugee camps. Eventually, the refugee camps became permanent cities, as the Palestinians' hope of returning to their former homes grew ever fainter with the passage of time. It was these refugee camps which gave birth to the Palestine Liberation Organization (PLO) of Yassir Arafat after the Israeli victory in the Six Day War against the Arab countries in June 1967, the same year the British Highland Division gladly departed "the barren rocks of Aden." With the defeat of the Arab armies in traditional warfare against the superior army of Israel, the PLO began a campaign of terror against Israel through its paramilitary army, known as *Al-Fatah*. Other Palestinian terror groups followed, like the Popular Front for the Liberation of Palestinine, led by Lebanese physician Dr. George Habash. Habash was emblematic of the Palestinian Christians who joined the Palestinian liberation movement. There are more than a few Palestinian Christians, including the wife of Yassir Arafat himself. Explaining the role of the Christian Palestinians, Robert Kaplan in his book *The Arabists: The Romance of an American Elite*, suggested that

> Arab nationalism, on account of its emphasis on Arab nation-building, constituted a secular alternative to the Moslem fundamentalism threatening non-Moslems. Arab Christians, therefore, tended to support the Arab nationalist movement with special fervor in order to protect themselves against the politics of Islam and to establish their bona fides in the larger Arab community. An unflinching stand against Zionism was often the most effective way for a Christian to show his Moslem neighbors that he, indeed, was an Arab.[2]

The following years of terrorism between the Palestinian organizations and the state of Israel echo so greatly what the great English poet Rudyard Kipling called "the savage wars of peace." The Palestinian cause attracted, during the period of the Cold War, the covert support of the Soviet Union and other Warsaw Bloc nations (those allied to the Soviets), as well as other Muslim nations like Syria, who had fought Israel in the wars, and the Libya of Col. Muammar Quaddafi, who began to see himself as inspired to lead the Arab world against Israel (and also insure that Libya could supplant Egypt as the traditional leader of the Arab countries). The Soviet Union saw the fight against Israel as a way to undermine the power of the United States in the Middle East, since the United States had emerged as Israel's main supporter, both through economic and military aid and as a trusted advocate in the United Nations' Security Council, where the United States—like the Soviets—had absolute veto power over any decisions made by the council.* Time and again, U.S. support within the Security Council would prove critical to Israel's survival.[3]

The fight between Israel and the Palestinians also attracted the attention of left-wing terrorist groups throughout Europe and even into Asia, some of which also received covert backing from the Soviet KGB or intelligence service, the Russian counterpart of our Central Intelligence Agency (CIA). The scope of the terror operations mounted against Israel in the 1960s through the 1970s have filled many a book, and thus trying to retell the history of this tumultuous era would be far beyond the scope of this volume.[4]

The first blows of the terror war were struck by the *Al-Fatah* paramilitaries of Arafat's PLO, including the first known hijacking of an airplane, an Israeli El Al jet, in 1968. Other early attacks attributed to the PLO include a hijacking and destruction of three jet airplanes at the same time in 1970. Taken over by *Al-Fatah* commandos, the three jets were flown to a desert location where, the passengers removed, all three were blown up by high explosives in a scene relayed by satellites to millions of television viewers throughout the world. The next PLO coup was destined to be much bloodier. In the same year, a Swissair jet was blown up in mid-air, resulting in the deaths of all forty-seven aboard the doomed plane.

From the early 1970s, the PLO and the Popular Front for the Liberation of Palestine (PFLP) of Dr. George Habash were helped out by the alliance of terror groups that grew like mushrooms throughout Europe and Asia. (All during the terror war, it seems the PFLP was more interested in disputing Arafat's claim to supremacy in the Palestinian movement than in mounting a

---

*Although outside the scope of the present work, it is interesting to note that the Soviet Union became the de facto enemy of Israel, especially since the United States and the Soviet Union were the two great powers that backed the UN resolution giving statehood to Israel in 1948.

united front against Israel.) Most bloody—and successful—of the European terrorists who shared "solidarity" with the PLO were the German Baader-Meinhof Gang, named after its founders, Andreas Baader and Ulrike Meinhof, and its offshoot, the Red Army Faction, which easily combined the anti-Semitism of Hitler's Nazis with their dedication to the Palestinian cause. In Italy, the Brigati Rossi, or the Red Brigade, cut as murderous a swath through their country as the two German factions did both in Germany and abroad.

Between Yassir Arafat and George Habash, the Lebanese doctor seems, with the virtue of hindsight, to have been the better, and more cerebral, of the two leaders. While Arafat opted to wear, and still does, a red and white checked *kafiyeh*, or headdress, and an army uniform, Habash chose to wear everyday civilian clothes. While Arafat thirsted, and still does, for the light of publicity, Habash was more interested in orchestrating the terror network sponsored by the PFLP. It was Habash, as early as 1968, who sought to internationalize the Palestinian movement and bring it in concert with the other revolutionary and terror groups in the world. The year 1968 has gone down in history as one of revolutions in Europe, the year that radicalized the whole post–World War II generation of European youth. Led by charismatic leaders like Daniel Cohn-Bendit and "Red Rudy" Deutschke, many of the students radicalized in 1968 later went on to join or actively support groups like the Baader-Meinhof Gang or the Red Army Faction. Horst Mahler was the father of the Red Army Faction, which would turn out to have a much longer life than most of the 1970s radical groups. In 1984, police in Paris raided a Red Army Faction safe house and made an alarming discovery: The organization had been preparing for a biological warfare attack. U.S. Air Force Lt. Col. Terry N. Mayer wrote about it in *Battlefield of the Future*, published by the U.S. Air Force Air University at Maxwell Air Force Base. Mayer wrote, "As [the police] conducted their search, they found documents that revealed a strong working knowledge of lethal biological agents. As the police continued the search to the bathroom, they came across a bathtub containing many flasks filled with what turned out to be Clostridium Botulinum, the microorganism that produced botulism, one of the most lethal biological substances known to man."[5] The Red Army Faction thus has the dubious distinction of perhaps being the first modern terrorist group to consider using biological warfare. But it would not be the last.

During the same period, although not energized by dreams of Marxist revolution, the same radicalization swept through Northern Ireland. Inspired by the nonviolent movement for African-American liberation in the United States led by the Rev. Dr. Martin Luther King Jr., an Irish Civil Rights movement grew up to campaign for equal rights of the Irish Catholics, who were discriminated against by the ruling Irish Protestants, in concert with the government in London. The six counties of Northern Ireland were considered part of the United Kingdom. When peaceful civil rights marches were brutally broken up by extremist Protestant gangs led by the firebrand Rev. Ian Paisely, some of the civil rights supporters turned toward the Irish Republican Army (IRA), which by this time had become almost a spent force in Irish politics. The IRA had become a Marxist organization, far from what it had been when it had started under Michael Collins in the Anglo-Irish War of 1919–22, which had led to eventual independence for the twenty-six counties of the Irish Republic. By the early 1970s, the more radical wing of the IRA formed the Provisional IRA or the PIRA, and this is the group that waged the long, recent war against the British and their adherents in Northern Ireland.

Using camps in Yemen and in Lebanon, Habash, aided by Wadi Haddad, trained the best and the brightest of this revolutionary generation in the fine arts of terrorism, sabotage, and guerrilla war. From East and West Germany, Japan, Ireland, and throughout the world, would-be terrorists and revolutionaries flocked to the training camps of the PFLP, which would later be augmented by training camps in Quaddafi's Libya. Even such groups as the Basque nationalist group fighting for freedom from Spain, and the leftist Tupamaro National Liberation Front from Uruguay joined the roster of students at the Habash camps. Trainers were supplied by countries allied with the Soviet Union, like Fidel Castro's Cuba and East Germany. In an address at his camp at Baddawi in Lebanon, Habash boasted, with good reason, "we have forged organic links with the revolution of the whole world." At the same time, not to be outdone, the PLO was opening training camps for would-be revolutionaries as well. Included among those trained for terror and guerrilla struggle by the PFLP and the PLO were four members of the militant Black Panther party from the United States.

(A point that should be made here is that Baddawi, the camp Habash used, was technically a refugee camp, not one dedicated for PFLP instruction. From the beginning of the Palestinian-Israeli struggle to the present, the Palestinians have used United Nations–sanctioned refugee camps as both terrorist recruiting and training facilities. Indeed, today instructors from the *Tamzin*, the new PLO paramilitary group, regularly train fighters in the refugee camps in the West Bank of the Jordan River and the Gaza Strip. Although the United Nations has always been quick to decry any actions against the PLO by Israel, that international body has been strangely silent about the PLO using the United Nations' own refugee camps for military purposes.)

The most bizarre of the PLO's and George Habash's kindred organizations was the Japanese Red Army, whose headquarters were in Japan, thousands of miles away from the Israeli-Palestinian strife. Nevertheless, to express their comradeship with the PLO, the Japanese Red Army executed one of the bloodiest strikes in the terror war. In 1972, at Israel's Ben-Gurion airport, commandos of the Red Army were responsible for a grenade and automatic rifle attack that took twenty-six lives and wounded seventy-six others. The end, when it came, for the Japanese Red Army was in keeping with the history of a country where gory last stands become the stuff of legends. The Japanese still honor the memory of the forty-seven *ronin*, or leaderless *samurai* warriors. In the seventeenth century, they avenged the death of their *daimyo*, lord, by killing the lord responsible for his demise. When sentenced to death by the emperor, they carried out the sentences on themselves. Each of them took his life by the ritual belly-cutting of *seppuku*, or *hara-kiri*. Their graves are still honored as national memorials today. With the Japanese Red Army, although their memory is far from revered in Japan, the end was played out with the same sense of high drama, as in a Japanese *No* or *kabuki* play. Finally, later in 1972, the Japanese Army and security agencies surrounded the leadership of the Red Army in a deserted resort hotel in Karuizawa. As Claire Sterling relates the incident in her *Terror Network*, of the thirty hard-liners left, after a ten-day siege, half had sentenced the other half to death for being unfaithful to their movement. According to Sterling, "the fourteen bodies recovered by police had been stripped, bound and gagged, tortured, mutilated, ritually stabbed, strangled, buried alive under floorboards, or left in the snow to die of exposure."[6]

However, the best known terrorist of the time was an admitted Marxist, Carlos Ilich Ramirez Sanchez, "The Jackal."[7] In his youth in 1968, Sanchez had attended Patrice Lumumba University in Moscow, which was the center for all left-wing Third World students whom the Soviet Union felt would do its bidding in the world. Yet, before that, he had already received instruction in terrorism in Cuba at Camp Matanzas, where Latin American terrorists were trained to export Communist world revolution to their countries.

However, Carlos's next stop involved him in the struggle against Israel.

After his time at Patrice Lumumba University, he seems to have gone for advanced training to one of the camps operated by the PLO in Jordan. He is recorded as fighting with the Palestinians when King Hussein launched his Bedouin troops against them in 1970. (Later, according to Sterling, he would attend another graduate course in Moscow around 1974.) However, his commitment to the Palestinian cause seems to have been one he wore easily, as perhaps he did his Communism.

While Carlos worked largely as a coordinator for terrorist activity in Europe with the Palestinian mastermind Wadi Haddad, he also personally led some of the bloodiest terror strikes of the period. While in London, he compiled a hit list of prominent Jews and supporters of Israel to be marked for assassination. One of them was Joseph Edward "Teddy" Sief, owner of the Marks and Spencer clothing corporation and a leading supporter within England of Israel. On December 30, 1973, Sief was shot by a Palestinian terrorist, most likely operating from the list Carlos had prepared.

It was in Paris that the Jackal made his debut on the streets as a gunman. He seems to have been part of an ad hoc terror group called Parisienne Orientale, or "the Eastern Paris Lady." In 1974, he bombed the chic Paris Le Drugstore on the Boulevard St. Germain, with a barrage of hand grenades. Two people were killed and twenty wounded in the detonations. Twice, he tried to savage El Al aircraft at Paris's Orly airport, only to fail in each attempt. The French intelligence organization SDECE put Carlos on their list, as did the other main French intelligence unit, the DST. Then, in June 1975, three agents of the DST, Jean Herranz, Raymond Dous, and Jean Donatini, went to Carlos's apartment at 9, Rue Toullier. In accordance with the Interior Ministry policy, the three agents went for a talk with Carlos, and they went unarmed. The three DST men sat down with Carlos and his aide, Michel Mourkabal. During the talk, Carlos believed that Mourkabal had betrayed his activities to French intelligence. When Herranz asked for his passport, Carlos disappeared and then came back with his 7.62 mm Russian Tokarev pistol. Quickly firing five shots, the Jackal killed Mourkabal, Dous, and Donatini. Herranz was seriously wounded. Then the Jackal made his escape from Paris to sanctuary in Algiers with help from some old Cuban friends.[8]

French intelligence did not overlook this Communist connection, and Michel Poniatowski, the spokesman for the Interior Minister, to whom the intelligence services answered, announced the expulsion of Cuban "diplomats" from France in retaliation. Poniatowski had wanted to implicate the

Soviet Union directly, but France's President Giscard d'Estaing, for fear of sabotaging French relations with the Russians, did not permit it. In Algiers, the Jackal enjoyed the protection of Col. Kasdi Merbah, chief of Algerian intelligence and also the brother of President Boumedienne.[9]

There Carlos planned his next operation. On December 21, 1975, with German terrorists Hans-Joachim Klein and Gabriele Krucher-Tiedemann, and three Lebanese and Palestinians, he raided the meeting of the Organization of Petroleum Exporting Nations (OPEC) ministers in Vienna. In their attack, Carlos and his comrades killed three people, including a Libyan member of the OPEC meeting. After a gun battle with Austrian police who had surrounded the building, Carlos entered into negotiations with the Austrian government of Chancellor Bruno Kreisky. Finally, an agreement was made to fly Carlos and the terrorists, along with OPEC hostages, out of Vienna and to Carlos's base in Algiers. He arrived at Algiers, and with his current female companion, a fellow Venezuelan named Maria Teresa Lara, settled into his accommodations at the Hotel Edwardier. He and his revolutionary cause were also enriched by a $50 million ransom from the OPEC operation.

Some sources, including Robert Nash in his excellent *Terrorism in the 20th Century*, mention that Carlos was working for the PFLP. This seems unlikely, since many of the Arab countries represented at the meeting in effect paid blackmail money so the terrorists would leave them alone. It seems perhaps that Carlos, by now if not from the beginning, was acting increasingly as a free agent, a mercenary terrorist. However, Ovid Demaris, in *Brothers in Blood: The International Terrorist Network*, mentions a theory that was put out by the Israeli Mossad. According to the Mossad, the OPEC operation had been carried out by the government of Algeria, which would mean Carlos was working with the intelligence network of Col. Kasdi Merbah. The Mossad believed that Algeria was angry with the delegates from the Arab League because they had supported the claims of Mauretania and Morocco to the Spanish Sahara, one of the richest phosphate mining areas in the world. As Demaris wrote, "it was Algeria's hope to pressure the oil-rich Arab states to drop their backing of the Moroccan claim to the Sahara and thereby help Algeria to become a phosphate-rich nation."[10]

If the French Interior Ministry had had a "go soft" policy on terror, it ended with the murders of Dous, Donatini, and the wounding of Herranz on the Rue Toullier. In the summer of 1975, the order went out to French intelligence: "Carlos must be liquidated."[11] Such an order would have come from

Interior Minister Poniatowski, but likely only with the approval of President Valeri Giscard d'Estaing himself. It was up to Adm. Comte de Marenches, who had become head of the SDECE and chief of all France's intelligence branches in 1970, to carry out the assignment. The job was given to the Action Branch of the DST, the trained assassins of French intelligence, heirs to the squads that were used to eliminate the threat from the OAS, the Secret Army Organization, at the time of the war in Algiers (1954–62). The OAS was made up of diehard members from the French colonial community in Algeria, the *pied noirs*, as well as servicemen who felt that then President Charles de Gaulle was betraying France when he agreed to Algerian independence in 1962. The OAS began a bloody terror war against France, which included several attempts to kill de Gaulle. De Gaulle had called into being the hit squads to eliminate of the threat from the OAS, a job that had been done efficiently and effectively.

De Marenches reported on the manhunt for Carlos directly to the Elysees Palace, the French White House. "We had the order to kill Carlos," Marenches said. "We pinpointed his whereabouts a number of times, once in Algiers. We went after him there, but we drew a blank."[12] It would take twenty years for French intelligence to catch up to the Jackal. In 1994, the Sudan handed him over to French authorities. On December 24, 1997, Carlos was sentenced to life imprisonment for the murders of Dous, Donatini, and Mourkabal.

Yet, above all, it was the terrorist attack on the 1972 Olympic Games in Munich, Germany, which showed the outright savagery of the terror war. The Olympic Games had been originally organized in ancient Greece as a peacetime activity devoted to athletic prowess and the worship of the gods. In a society wracked by war among the competing city-states, the Olympics were a chance for the people from these city-states to periodically meet on peaceful, neutral ground. When the modern Olympics began in 1896, the message was the same. Except for the two world wars, the Olympics have been held every four years with that purpose in mind. That is, except for the Olympic Games held in Munich in West Germany in 1972. At that time, with the Cold War still waxing hot, Germany was divided into the Western-leaning German Federal Republic and the Communist ally of Soviet Russia, the German Democratic Republic. The capital of West Germany was the great city of Bonn, while the capital of East Germany was East Berlin; Berlin had been divided into eastern and western zones after World War II.

The 1972 Olympics were the first time that the games had been held in Germany since 1936, the heydey of Adolf Hitler's Third Reich. In 1972, Munich was the Queen City of the new Germany which had risen like a phoenix from the ashes of the Nazi past. Munich was anxious to show off its new face to the world since it had been, with Nuremberg, the two cities which had hosted the thundering celebrations of Hitler's Thousand Year Reich.

Moreover, there was another significance for the 1972 games: The state of Israel was sending an athletic team with its trainers to participate. In the early 1970s, Western Germany was going through the delicate process of opening diplomatic relations with Israel after the terrible Holocaust of European Jewry that the Nazis had carried out in World War II. The presence of the Israeli team was seen as an important milestone in Bonn toward trying to build fruitful relations with the Israeli state. Thus, it was to strike both at the new "capitalist" West Germany and at Israel that the terror group Black September chose to attack the Olympic Village that day in 1972. Black September was a Palestinian group named after the Jordanian attack on the PLO in 1970–71 when Yassir Arafat's group tried to stage a coup against King Hussein and was bloodily repulsed by the Bedouins of Jordan's army. The Communist George Habash had made it clear that the Palestinian attempt was directed at nothing less than the ouster of King Hussein, whom he considered the head of a "reactionary" regime.

At the time, the correspondents of the American ABC television network, which broadcast the games, and the world were amazed at the ease with which the Black September terrorists penetrated the Olympic Village. Viewed with hindsight, it was not so difficult at all: They had inside help. Western intelligence sources have since learned that the Black September terrorists had previously been able to infiltrate the village with the help of the athetic team from Communist East Germany. Apparently, the East Germans had given the members of Black September not only Olympic uniforms but also possibly identification papers to help them scout out the Olympic Village to see where the Israelis were staying. The East German team was probably infiltrated with members of the Stasi, the East German security service, who were able to provide material assistance to the Black September terrorists.

Black September was also inadvertently helped by the West German authorities as well. Anxious to avoid any semblance to the 1936 Games, where the goose-stepping storm troopers of the SS were everywhere, the Bonn government had deliberately downplayed the role of security at the games. Any security personnel there were allegedly dressed as athletes them-selves and none of them carried firearms. Furthermore, also in light of their militaristic past, the government of the new Germany had been reluctant to build the sort of counterterror operation unit that Israel had been compelled to develop years before. These German lapses, although committed from the best of intentions, played right into the hands of the terrorists.

Thus it was that on September 5, 1972, eight armed Black September operatives stormed the apartment in the Olympic Village where the Israelis were staying. In the initial attack, two Israeli athletes were killed, including a brave wrestler who tried to fight bare-handed with his armed attackers. One of the most vivid pictures of that day was the photo, beamed to millions of television sets the world over, of a Black September member in a ski mask, peering over the balcony of the Israeli apartment. The Black September gunmen demanded from Israeli Prime Minister Golda Meir the release of 234 Palestinian prisoners held in Israeli jails, as well as two German terror leaders who were in prison in the Federal Republic. They also demanded safe passage out of West Germany to Cairo. The West German authorities, after a seventeen-hour stand-off, agreed to let the terrorists board a Cairo-bound jet at a military air base. The terrorists put nine Israeli team members in a bus as hostages and drove to the air base.

It was here that the West German lack of a trained counterterror force became terribly clear. Agents of the Israeli Mossad had arrived in Germany to help the West Germans handle the situation but the Germans insisted that they carry out their operation their own way at the airport. The German plan was for police snipers on the roofs of airport buildings to ambush the terror-ists as they left the bus and headed for the airplane waiting for them, but things went horribly wrong. As the German snipers opened fire, the Pales-tinian terrorists shot back. In the ensuing debacle, all nine Israeli hostages were killed aboard the bus, five of the Black September terrorists died, as did a German policeman. When he saw that they were trapped, a Palestinian had opened fire in the bus and afterward another Black September terrorist had thrown a hand grenade into it, killing any survivors.

However, almost from the beginning, there was doubt as to whether the Black September group really existed at all. In 1972, Abu Daoud, a high member of the *Al-Fatah*, the paramilitary arm of Arafat's PLO, admitted in an interrogation by Jordanian authorities that Black September was in reality a front organization for *Al-Fatah*. Daoud reportedly told the Jordanians, "there is no such organization called Black September. Fatah announces its own operations under this name so that Fatah will not appear as the direct executor of the operation." Daoud repeated this story in December 1999, in an article written by Patrick Goodenough, the Conservative News Service (CNS) chief correspondent in Jerusalem. Daoud, now a member of Yassir Arafat's governing Palestinian Authority, told the story in his book, *Palestine: From Jerusalem to Munich*.[13]

The rage of the Israelis after the Munich massacre was incredible. Prime Minister Golda Meir (1969–74) appeared before the shocked Israeli Knesset, or Parliament, and vowed to strike at the terrorist organizations, calling such action an obligation to peace. Throughout Europe and the Middle East, the Mossad searched for the leaders of Black September to hunt them down and kill them. In the book *Israel and the Arabs*, authors Ahron Bregman and Jihan El-Tahri wrote of how the Mossad carried their campaign of vengeance into Lebanon. On the night of April 10, 1973, an Israeli commando team landed on the beach at Beirut. Based on superior intelligence, they knew that their targets were staying on Verdan Street. There, the commandos "broke into the flats of three senior PLO officials Kamal Nasser, Yusif Najar, and Kamal Edwan—and killed them all."[14] At least twelve of the plotters paid with their lives over the following years.

For the Israelis, the Munich Massacre came as almost a small Holocaust. The pursuit of the killers continued unabated. Disaster struck at Lilliehammer in Norway when a waiter, mistaken for one of the terrorists, was killed by mistake. Nevertheless, Black September managed to strike in the Sudan in 1973. In April, gunmen from the Black September/*Al-Fatah* group took over the Saudi Arabian embassy in Khartoum, apparently angry because they felt the Saudis did not support the PLO enough. During the takeover, the American ambassador to the Sudan was killed.

The hunt for the Munich terrorists continued long after the death of Golda Meir in 1978. In 1988, the Israelis were closing in on one of the last surviving members of the group implicated in the Olympic Village slaughter. On the dark night of April 15, 1988, the Israelis were ready for a replay of their incursion into Beirut in Lebanon in 1973. Fast Zodiac speed boats, probably from an Israeli Navy Dabur missile boat, came ashore at the beach at Ras Carthage in Libya, not far from the ruins of ancient Carthage. The target was Abu Jihad, who for sixteen years had been at the center of PLO terror plots aimed at the Israeli state. In 1985, he had planned the abortive assassination attempt of then Defense Minister Yitzhak Rabin. Now it would be Abu Jihad's turn. Overhead, apparently, an Israeli version of the U.S. Orion air command plane managed to jam communications between the PLO headquarters and other PLO command posts in Tripoli, where Yassir Arafat was then staying. The Israeli force was composed of naval commandos from the Israeli Navy's Force 13, which is stationed at the Mediterranean port of Atlit in Israel, and members of the Sayeret Matkal, the elite commandos from the army who had played a role in the Entebbe hostage rescue operation in July 1976, which will be discussed shortly. The team was met on the beach by *katsas*, agents of the Mossad, who had prepared the ground for the strike force coming in from the Mediterranean.

The Mossadim led the attackers to the villa occupied by Abu Jihad, who had just returned from a meeting with Yassir Arafat. The bodyguards outside his villa were quickly disposed of, and the hit squad entered the villa. There they found Abu Jihad with his wife. Pushing the wife aside, they turned toward Abu Jihad. The operatives took up the positions that Israelis do when they do not wish their target to survive: one shooter stood to the left of Abu Jihad, one in front of him, and one to his right. According to Samuel M. Katz in *The Night Raiders*, "Abu Jihad was killed in a matter of seconds, destroyed in a flurry of seventy-five bullets. According to several reports, the entire operation was videotaped by one of the Israeli commandos."[15] After the hit, the Israeli commandos went back to the beach and boarded their Zodiacs, while the *katsas* apparently disappeared into the darkness of the Tripoli night. One of the last debts left over from the Munich killings had been paid.

The most dramatic episode of the terror war was the hijacking by German terrorists of an Air France Airbus airplane, which contained many Jewish and Israeli passengers, to Entebbe airport in Uganda in July 1976. The operation was carried out on behalf of the Popular Front for the Liberation of Palestine, as author William Stevenson notes in his exciting *90 Minutes at Entebbe*.[16] Wadi Haddad, Dr. Habash's able assistant, was in direct operational control of the skyjacking. A disturbing part of this was the openly pro-PFLP position taken by the Ugandan dictator Idi Amin Dada, President and Field Marshal for Life in Uganda. Dada's "illustrious" military career had begun as a sergeant in the British colonial King's African Rifles before London granted Uganda its independence in 1962.

As soon as news of the skyjacking reached Israel, Prime Minister Yitzhak Rabin and Defense Minister Shimon Peres began preparations to try to free the captives from the airbus, who were housed in buildings at Entebbe airport, guarded not only by their German and Palestinian kidnappers, but by soldiers of the regular Ugandan army. Time was of the essence, because the kidnappers continued to issue ultimatums that the hostages would be killed if their demands were not met.

As military preparations were discussed in emergency sessions of Rabin's cabinet, the Mossad provided intelligence support for any military action in the offing. Gordon Thomas noted in his recent *Gideon's Spies: The Secret History of the Mossad* that two *katsas* were sent across Lake Nairobi by boat to observe Entebbe, while two other *katsas* actually flew over the airport at Entebbe, twenty-one miles from the Ugandan capital at Kampala, in a rented Cessna aircraft to photograph the field from above. During the actual landing of the commandos, six other Mossadim surrounded the airport with portable radio jamming devices to isolate the PFLP and Ugandan soldiers from radio contact with the outside world. By this time, the shadowy PFLP headquarters command had made a second move, this time to Angola, probably escorted by Cuban guards, as though they sensed a rescue mission might be mounted and did not want to be killed in it.

The climax to the rescue came in Operation Thunderbolt, a heroic gambit mounted by the elite of Israeli special operations troops, the Sayeret Matkal. The group was under the command of Jonathan "Yonni" Netanyahu, who had been born in the United States. The two Sayeret Matkal planes were able to stop in Nairobi, Kenya, for refueling after their long flight from Israel. At Nairobi airport, the planes were guarded by members of the Kenyan Recce (Reconnaissance) Company, which filled the role of special forces operatives in Kenya. When the Sayeret Matkal commandos descended in their transport planes at Entebbe airport, the surprise was complete. So much did they take the kidnappers and their Ugandan protectors by surprise that there were only two Israeli casualties. One was an Israeli woman who had been taken to a hospital in Kampala, the capital of Uganda, for a feared heart attack, and probably was murdered on Amin's orders after the successful rescue. The other fatality was Jonathan Netanyahu, who was shot just as he was about to board his transport plane for the return flight to Israel. The killing of "Yonni" left behind a legacy that the Palestinians were to regret: his brother, Benjamin (Binyamin) Netanyahu, became a formidable proponent of a hard-line against terrorism and later became prime minister of Israel.

In 1970, after the Bedouins of the Jordanian army, the heir of the fabled

Arab Legion, had made the Hashemite Kingdom of Jordan too bloody for the *Al-Fatah* warriors of the PLO, the Palestinans had migrated to Lebanon seeking a new promised land. Here, they found a society already teetering on the brink of collapse. Before World War II, Lebanon and Syria had both been part of the same mandate territory, which France had administered in the name of the League of Nations. During the war, the Syrian and Lebanese territory had been occupied by the pro-Nazi Vichy government in France under Marshal Petain, who collaborated with Nazi Germany after the French surrender in June 1940. Those who wanted to continue the fight against the Germans joined the British in the evacuation at Dunkirk and retreated to England. There, Col. Charles de Gaulle began the Free French movement and began a French government in exile in London. In 1941, Gen. Georges Catroux was appointed commander of the Free French troops in the Levant (the old term for the Middle East), by Charles de Gaulle. In June 1941, with help from England and British-led troops from Palestine, Catroux conquered Syria and Lebanon from troops loyal to the Vichy regime. After the end of the war, both countries received their independence from France, Syria having been evacuated by the French in April 1946, and Lebanon in December. Both countries had been formally admitted into the United Nations on April 12, 1945.

After World War II, power had been shared uneasily in Lebanon by Christians and Muslims. While the French had held the mandate from the League of Nations, they initiated a parliamentary system of government which tilted power toward the Christians. This settlement had continued in force, even though the Muslim population in Lebanon was growing. The internal stresses growing in Lebanon had already led to an American intervention in 1958, ordered by President Dwight D. Eisenhower, to stabilize the tottering government. During the next years, the Christians resisted any real electoral reform that could one day lead to Muslim control over Lebanon, a situation which caused increasing Muslim bitterness at the established order. It was into this volatile political landscape that the PLO entered after their eviction from Jordan.

At the time, the Christians in Lebanon were divided among rival factions led by Pierre Gemayel and Camille Chamoun, who dominated the political landscape. Both led private armies that carried the real power in Lebanon. Those led by Gemayel, the Phalangists, was the stronger of the two. About the only thing the Gemayel and Chamoun clans could agree upon was on maintaining Christian dominance in their country. Even before the 1967 war, there had been Palestinian refugee camps in Lebanon, in places like Nabatiyeh and Shatila, outside Beirut. In 1969, the Lebanese Christians committed a fatal mistake: They agreed to permit the Palestinians in Lebanon to carry firearms. It would prove to be a decision they would regret. In the years after the expulsion of the PLO from Jordan, Lebanon became the new home base for Yassir Arafat's organization, with Arafat living there himself. As Sandra Mackey wrote in *Lebanon: Death of a Nation*, "the Palestinians had built a separate world within Lebanon's own domestic anarchy. Despite repeated Israeli reprisals against Lebanon, armed commandos continued to roam southern Lebanon's roads at will. The [refugee] camps still functioned as autonomous territories that government authorities dared not penetrate."[17]

By 1975, the fissure between Christians and Muslims had been exacerbated so much by the presence of the PLO that Lebanon, once considered the most enlightened country in the Middle East, hovered on the brink of civil war. Beirut itself was divided into two armed camps, Christian East Beirut and the Western Muslim Beirut. Then, on the night of April 13, 1975, during the Easter season for the Maronite sect of Christians that controlled Lebanon, PLO riders in a car opened fire on a crowd outside of a Christian church in the Ein Romaneh suburb of East Beirut, a church where Pierre Gemayel and his family were attending services. Four people were killed in the fusillade from the automobile. Retaliation came swiftly. On the afternoon of the same day, Gemayel Phalangist militiamen fired on a bus returning to the Palestinian refugee camp at Tel Zatar through the streets of Ein Romaneh, killing twenty-seven Palestinian passengers. Civil war had come to Lebanon.

For seven years, the internal destruction of Lebanon continued. During these years, the Israelis became the main suppliers of the Christian militias, hoping that the Phalangists and the other Christian groups could carry on the fight against the PLO for them. At the same time, whenever the PLO could spare the time and the men, they bombarded Israeli settlements across the Lebanese border in northern Israel, the ancient Galilee, with Katyusha rockets. Then, in April 1981, Gen. Ariel "Arik" Sharon became the Israeli Defense Minister. Next to Gen. Moshe Dayan, Sharon had become known as the greatest living Israeli Defense Force (IDF) fighter. He had begun his career as a soldier in the legendary Unit 101, a special commando squad formed in 1952 to fight Arab infiltrators into Israel. From then, Sharon had been in the forefront of thirty years of war against the Arabs. In the 1973 war,

he commanded the Israeli forces that had encircled the Egyptian Th
on the Egyptian side of the Suez Canal. Now, when confronting t
fedayeen (fighters) in Lebanon, Sharon was in his element again.

As with another famous fighting general, the American general George
Patton Sr., Sharon made an excellent warrior but was not perhaps cut out to
be a politician. To Sharon, the presence of the PLO in Lebanon and its
shelling of the *kibbutzim* in north Galilee was a reason to attack the PLO and,
after fighting them since the 1967 war, destroy them once and for all. In January 1982, Sharon paid a secret visit to Beirut to visit Pierre Gemayel who,
after his Phalangists had crushed the Chamoun faction in 1980, was the
strongest Christian warlord in Lebanon. Sharon told Pierre and his son Bashir
of the Israeli intention to invade Lebanon, and if possible drive all the way to
Beirut to crush the PLO. Pierre Gemayel, however, had his own plans. He
met with Hani Hassan, a representative of Yassir Arafat, after Sharon had
returned to Israel. Gemayel told Hassan, "tell Yassir Arafat that if we agree
together on the withdrawal of the Palestinians from Lebanon, and the Palestinian weapons are handed over to me, then I can stop Israel from invading
Lebanon. If Israel then invades, I'm prepared to help the PLO fight them."[18]
Arafat never responded to Gemayel's shocking offer, shocking since Tel Aviv
believed Gemayel an ally.

At 11:00 A.M. Jerusalem time, on June 6, 1982, some 75,000 soldiers from
the IDF invaded Lebanon in "Operation Peace for Galilee," heavily supported
by the Israeli navy and air force. It was the fifteenth anniversary of the Six
Day War. The armored spearhead of the Israeli invasion force moved like a
steamroller through the PLO *Al-Fatah* troops who, while skilled at guerrilla
warfare, were woefully untrained for open battle. Although Prime Minister
Menachem Begin (1977–83) had agreed to an invasion to establish a security
zone in southern Lebanon, Defense Minister Sharon intended from the beginning to push on to Beirut for a final showdown with the PLO and Yassir
Arafat. On the second day of the invasion, in the biggest amphibious operation ever undertaken by Israel, the IDF landed at the mouth of the Alawi River
north of the city of Sidon. PLO resistance in the south of Lebanon virtually
collapsed. Syrian forces, in position in the Bekaa Valley in eastern Lebanon in
support of the *Al-Fatah fedayeen*, were routed.

The rout of the Syrian forces caused alarm bells in Damascus, where the
government feared the attack in Lebanon could be preliminary to the Israelis
keeping their drive going into Syria itself. Heavy Syrian reinforcements poured

into Lebanon, and resistance against the IDF stiffened. Serious fighting took place on June 10 and 11 between Syrian and Israeli tank forces around Joub Jannine and Rachaiya in the Bekaa, perhaps the only serious open battle of the war. While a cease fire took place in the Bekaa Valley on June 11, on the west along the sea coast, the IDF continued its push north of Sidon. By the night of the eleventh, almost all Syrian and PLO forces were in retreat.

At 11:00 A.M. on June 13, precisely one week after the opening of Operation Peace for Galilee, forward paratroop units of the IDF met up with Maronite Christian Phalange militia outside Beirut. Sharon was determined to cut Beirut off completely from any Arab help. For over a week, heavy fighting took place on the outskirts of Beirut, especially along the Beirut highway north to Damascus, which was the route the Syrians were using to send reinforcements into the battle. Another in a series of cease fires took place on June 26, but collapsed almost as quickly as it was agreed upon. By this time, the Israelis had trapped in Beirut some 14,000 Arab troops, among them 12,000 PLO fighters and 2,000 Syrians.

On July 3, the formal Israeli siege of Beirut began. The next day, the Israelis began a blockade of Muslim West Beirut, gradually tightening the noose around the PLO. During the siege and blockade, United States envoy Phillip Habib, himself of Lebanese descent, tried to negotiate a cease fire between the Israelis and the Arabs that would hold. Finally, the IDF decided to force a decision, and launched an offensive across the Green Line that separated Christian and Muslim Beirut into the Muslim sector of the city on August 4, 1982. After two days of fierce fighting that crackled along the Green Line, the PLO agreed to a cease fire negotiated by Habib, which included plans for a PLO evacuation to Syria. In two weeks Sharon and the Israelis agreed to the cease fire plans, and the first PLO evacuation began from Beirut on August 21. For those who saw the evacuation on television, it seemed more like a triumph than a retreat. Along the PLO column, *fedayeen* fired off their AK-47s jubilantly. Some 15,000 PLO fighters left Beirut to destinations throughout the Arab world. Even Jordan accepted those with Jordanian passports. But Egypt accepted none. A multinational force which included U.S. marines entered Beirut to supervise the pull-out of the PLO troops. On August 30, Arafat left Lebanon on the Greek cruise ship *Atlantis*, bound for exile in Tunis, Libya.

With a cease fire appearing to be in effect, the multinational force, the MNF, left Beirut on September 10. A photo shows the Lebanese president-elect Bashir Gemayel, the son of warlord Pierre, reviewing a line of elite Italian Bersaglieri troops, wearing their traditional green cock feathers on their white parade helmets, who were part of the Italian contingent of the MNF. Yet, within a week, Bashir Gemayel had been assassinated. With the death of Gemayel, Beirut and Lebanon descended into anarchy again. In revenge for Gemayel, who had been killed by a bomb planted by a Syrian agent, the Phalangists stormed into the Shatila and Sabra refugee camps on September 16, the day of his state funeral. In a slaughter that lasted from September 16 to 18, somewhere around 700 or 800 Muslims were killed by the Phalangist gunmen. In the meantime, the IDF had launched an offensive that conquered West Beirut. Amin Gemayel, who had succeeded his relative Bashir as president, requested the return of the MNF and the marines, for a second time, landed in Beirut.

In the beginning of September 1982, the IDF's attention was drawn again to the border, where pro-PLO fighters were attacking the villages of northern Israel once more. These fighters belonged to groups whose names, like Hamas and Hizbollah, still appear in the papers today. Supported by Iran's Ayatollah Khomeini, they represented a new dimension in the Arab-Israeli conflict. These were Muslim extremists who fought the Israelis more for the concept of the holy war, the Islamic *jihad* against the *kufr*, "the infidels," than for the political considerations which, up until the present time, are the motivating force for Arafat and his PLO. Hizbollah, in fact, means "the party of God" in Arabic. To help combat these new enemies, the Israelis formed a "Southern Lebanese Army" out of the Maronite Christians who supported Israel against the Muslims. For nearly twenty years, the Israelis would occupy a "security zone" in southern Lebanon, aided by their Maronite allies.

While the IDF began to deploy to face the threat along the northern frontier of Israel, the troops of the MNF deployed in Beirut to try to keep the peace. As time went on, almost inevitably the troops of the MNF found themselves drawn into the conflict. The Muslim militias began to see the MNF as an ally of the Gemayel government and of Israel, and began to turn their fire on the peacekeepers in 1983. The experience of the marines was typical of that of the other contingents. The marines were under rules of engagement which severely handicapped their ability to defend themselves against their attackers. Television reporters interviewed marines pinned down in their positions near the Beirut International Airport, under fire from Muslim snipers nearby. When marine commanders asked for permission to suppress the gunmen, their superiors vetoed the suggestion for fear of embroiling the United States even more in the Lebanese conflict.

By October 1983, some seven marines had been killed in the firing from the Muslim neighborhoods overlooking their exposed position. Then, on Sunday, October 23, 1983, hell came to the marines in "The Root," as they had christened Beirut. An Arab driving a truck headed toward the marine barracks began to speed up as he aimed directly at the barracks building. The sentry outside was helpless: Under the rules of engagement designed to minimize American involvement in the Beirut fighting, his M16A2 assault rifle was unloaded. The driver of the truck waved at the sentry. Seconds later, the building collapsed as the driver rammed into it, laden with explosives. Some 241 Marines were killed and 100 wounded. The truck had been carrying some 6 tons of TNT. Across town, another suicide bomber struck the French headquarters, causing some 150 casualties, the first French losses in Lebanon since the fighting against the Druze in the 1920s. On that Sunday afternoon in Beirut, some fifty-eight French soldiers, including Foreign Legionnaires, who had born the brunt of the fight against the Druze, perished. The suicide attack on the marine barracks was the first strike in a new phase of warfare against the United States: the war of the Islamic extremists, the Islamic *jihad* directed against America. Islam taught that those who died in the holy war were martyrs who would immediately ascend to Paradise. With this belief in his heart, the unknown driver had immolated himself and 241 young American marines.

Back home in the United States, it was late Sunday afternoon when news of the bombing was received. In Somers Point, New Jersey, the southern New Jersey chapter of the "Olden Rams," the alumni of West Chester University in West Chester, Pennsylvania, were having their fall meeting. Many members, like my father, were members of the "greatest generation," which had fought and defeated Nazi Germany and Imperial Japan in World War II. Many of them were reminded of another Sunday and another sneak attack: the Japanese strike at Pearl Harbor on December 7, 1941.

After the initial shock of the marine bombing wore off, President Ronald Reagan and his National Security Council began a vigorous hunt through the CIA and the American intelligence community for those responsible for the attack. Not surprisingly, William Casey, head of the CIA, looked to the Israelis for help; accurate intelligence of the Arab forces arrayed against them was a matter of national survival for them. The Mossad; Aman, which is the Israeli Army intelligence service; and Branch 40, an Israeli intelligence agency devoted to countering terrorism, all joined in the hunt for the bombers. Soon, Israeli agents had found a trail that led through Syria all the way to the Iran of Ayatollah Khomeini, the leader of the *jihad* against the United States. As newspaper reporter Bob Woodward described the intelligence hunt in *Veil: The Secret Wars of the CIA, 1981–1987*, the Israelis found that $50,000 had been paid to a Lebanese man named Hassan Hamiz.[19] The payment had come directly from the Iranian embassy in Damascus, which was the nerve center of the Iranian-led terror network in the Middle East, a fact that is probably still true today. A lieutenant colonel in Syrian intelligence was also implicated in planning the bombings, as well as a leader in the Muslim Shiite community in Lebanon, Sheikh Mohammed Hussein Fadlallah. Sheikh Mohammed was one of the leaders of the Hizbollah.

Director Casey was convinced by the evidence that the Israelis had amassed. However, two senior CIA officers, Charles Cogan, the chief of the Near East Division, and Dick Holm, sounded the voice of caution. Holm said there was no "smoking gun," forgetting that in such operations if the perpetrators have covered their tracks well, there never is a smoking gun. On this occasion, Reagan and Casey followed the counsels of caution, and the perpetrators of the worst attack on Americans in the terror war went unpunished. The American response was confined to a few volleys from the battleship *New Jersey*, which had been newly refitted in the military build-up with which Ronald Reagan had begun his presidency. Under the direction of Secretary of the Navy John Lehman, the battleship, which had a glorious record in World War II and Korea, had been outfitted with a new computer guidance system for its massive main armament of 16-inch naval guns and with a sophisticated secondary arsenal of cruise missiles. When the huge shells hit the suspected terrorist camps, the terrorists complained that the shelling was an act of terrorism! In the case of the *New Jersey*, the voices of caution held sway as well. The senior naval commanders were afraid that the big ship would be a target for suicide attackers in small boats (the same way that the *Cole* was in fact attacked in Aden harbor nearly two decades later). They had forgotten that the purpose of the battleship was to sail "into harm's way," as had been done by the navy in World War II. The battlefield admirals of that conflict, William "Bull" Halsey, Arleigh Burke, Raymond Spruance, and Marc Mitscher, would have been amazed at the attitude of their successors.

Even though the United States knew that the training camps for the Hizbollah were in the Syrian-occupied Bekaa Valley, no retaliatory air raids were carried out. Instead, the Americans left this task to the ever-ready French and the Israelis. The timidity of the American response after the bombing of the marine barracks in "The Root" showed the terrorists that the United States was not a power to fear.

One of the *mujahidin* then fighting the Soviets in Afghanistan, Osama bin Laden, would remember America's capitulation in Lebanon in the years to come. Over the years, he would see the United States withdraw from terrorist attack, rather than lash back with the furious response of the Israelis. He would see the United States withdraw from Somalia in 1993, after dead U.S. Army Rangers had been dragged through the streets of Mogadishu. Bin Laden would begin to picture the United States as a "paper tiger." It was a characterization that Americans would dearly regret in September 2001.

On September 20, 1984, the American embassy in the Christian sector of East Beirut was targeted by a Hizbollah suicide bomber. This time, the guards opened fire, but one of their M-16s jammed. The suicide truck managed to hit the embassy and twenty-four people were killed. Another ninety were among the injured, including the American ambassador to Lebanon, Reginald Bartholemew. Later, William Buckley, the CIA's own station chief in Beirut, was abducted by the terrorists, and subsequently tortured and killed. This time, Casey did not let voices of caution stop him. Photographs from overhead satellites revealed terror training operations again in the Bekaa Valley stronghold of the Hizbollah, including the use of a truck similar to the vehicles that had blown up the marine barracks and the American embassy. Casey decided on the elimination of Sheikh Fadlallah, as a means of striking at the chief of Hizbollah. Because American agents were forbidden to assassinate foreign leaders, Casey delegated the task of removing Fadlallah to the Saudi Arabians. Meeting with the Saudi ambassador to the United States, Prince Bandar, Casey inaugurated a plot to kill Sheikh Fadlallah. The conspiracy involved an Englishman who had been a soldier in the 22nd Special Air Service Regiment (SAS), Great Britain's elite counterterror force. With $3 million, the Englishman enlisted Lebanese intelligence agents in the plot to kill the sheikh. On March 8, 1985, a bomb went off less than fifty yards from the high-rise building in which the sheikh lived. Eighty people were killed, and two hundred were wounded in the blast that followed, but the sheikh emerged unharmed. Finally, the Saudis and Americans offered Fadlallah a bribe of $2 million to cease terror attacks. He accepted it, saying he would use the money for the education and welfare of his followers. There were no more terrorist attacks directed by the sheikh against American targets. Said Prince Bandar, "it was easier to bribe him than to kill him!"[20]

For the United States, the Beirut episode was not the last Middle East tragedy. In October 1985, the Italian cruise ship *Achille Lauro* was hijacked by PLO terrorists; some accounts name the PFLP. As soon as the ship was taken over, news reached the Mediterranean headquarters of the U.S. Sixth Fleet in Italy. According to informed sources, word went out to the navy's SEAL Team Six, its counterterror force. Like the subsequent navy Red Cell team, SEAL Team Six had been trained by Richard Marcinko, the legendary "Rogue Warrior" who had distinguished himself leading navy SEALs in the Vietnam War. Apparently, plans were formulated to make a "dynamic entry" to board the cruise liner. Tactics for such an assault would have called for the SEALs to land on the ship at the stern, hoping to take the terrorists by surprise. The final decision for such an operation would most likely have been made by President Reagan, in consultation with the CINCNAVEUR, the Commander-in-Chief of the United States Naval Forces in Europe. However, the signal was never given for the attack on the *Achille Lauro*.

As a result, the PLO gunmen were effectively in command of the cruise vessel. To prove their hatred of Americans and Jews, the "tangos," the terrorists, shot and killed sixty-nine-year-old Leon Klinghoffer, who was confined to a wheelchair. After Klinghoffer was murdered, the tangos forced other passengers to toss him and his wheelchair into the Mediterranean. Unhindered by American action, the hijackers forced the ship's captain to sail the *Achille Lauro* for Egypt, to become the unwelcome guests of President Hosni Mubarak. During high-level consultations about the hijacking, Mubarak used a regular phone, having found the secure telephone system given him by the American National Security Agency too difficult to master. As a result, American ELINT (electronic intelligence) satellites—most likely—were able to pick up the open conversation on Mubarak's telephone. The National Security Agency (NSA) would have immediately forwarded these vital communications to the president as the highest priority, "Whiskey Number" intercepts. This enabled Reagan and his National Security Council members to have an opportunity to eavesdrop on Mubarak's private communications.

According to the intercepts made public by Woodward in *Veil*, President Mubarak thought that American Secretary of State George Schultz was "crazy" to think that he would hand over his Arab brothers to the United States. Instead, Mubarak planned to send the four PLO tangos to safety in Algiers, where the Algerian government must have agreed to accept them. When the *Achille Lauro* anchored at Port Suez, the four gunmen surrendered to the Egyptian authorities. Then the NSA ELINT intercepts revealed that the tangos would be put on an Egyptian Air Boeing 737, which would take off from the Egyptian air force base at Al-Maza in Cairo. Col. Oliver North conceived of a bold plan, which was approved by President Reagan. In a daring stroke, an aerial interception of the Boeing 737 was planned. On the flight to Algiers, the Boeing 737 was intercepted by four U.S. Navy F-14s from the flight deck of the aircraft carrier the *Saratoga*. The plan was to force the Boeing to fly to a NATO air base in Sicily.

In the most likely scenario, the four F-14s would have approached the Boeing 737, probably with two planes on each side of the jumbo jet. The commander of the flight of jets would have given the pilot of the Boeing orders to follow him to the NATO base in Sicily. Once the Boeing was on the ground, Navy SEALs surrounded the jumbo jet. Then, in an almost comic scene, the Italian government, offended by the Americans using Italian air space for such a maneuver, surrounded the Navy SEALs with armed *Carabinieri*, the paramilitary national Italian police! After a brief standoff, the four tangos were handed over to Italian authorities, where they were tried for their crimes. They were convicted and sentenced to prison. Yussuf Magid Molqi, Leon Klinghoffer's murderer, received the longest prison term, thirty years. However, a fifth tango, Mohammed Zaidan Abbas, actually masterminded the plot and may have joined his four comrades in Egypt. While the four others were arrested in Sicily, Abbas was allowed to escape to Belgrade, where he found sanctuary with the Soviet Terror International. Apparently, the Italian authorities were reluctant to hold Abbas, for fear of incurring the wrath of the PLO and the PFLP.

"Operation Peace for Galilee" began an Israeli involvement in Lebanon that would last for twenty years, until former Prime Minister Ehud Barak (1999–2001) abruptly withdrew all IDF forces from the southern Lebanese security zone in the summer of 2000. Those Maronite Christians who could not escape to Israel were left at the mercy of the extremist Muslims of Hamas and Hizbollah that they had been fighting for years. While Israel was embroiled in its own "Vietnam War" in Lebanon, massive internal unrest broke out in December 1987 among the Arabs living in the West Bank and the Gaza Strip sections of Israel over PLO use of south Lebanon as a base from which to attack Israel. It was a spontaneous uprising, which caught Yassir Arafat and the Palestinian leadership, still in Libya, totally by surprise. Barak, who was then the army deputy chief of staff, said later, "it was clear that this uprising was on a new scale, and that these people were not 'terrorists' but the population itself. . . . We spent the first days concentrating on how to prevent a nightmare of wild shooting [by the Israeli troops] into the crowds, which we thought would cause us terrible damage."[21]

The PLO leadership, in its Tunisian exile, raced to get control of the uprising to harness it for political goals. The overall commander of the PLO for the occupied territories was Abu Jihad. He appointed Abu Ali Shaheen, who had spent fifteen years in Israeli prisons, the Tunis director of the uprising, or the *Intifida* as it would go down in history. After another vicious cycle of Palestinian and Israeli fighting broke out in September 2000, this first rising ought to be referred to as the First *Intifida*. PLO cells were organized in the occupied territories to guide the stone-throwing fighters of the *Intifida*. Soon, however, the terrorists of the PLO had turned the *Intifida* into another terror campaign against the Israelis. On March 7, 1988, scientists traveling on a bus along the desert road toward the Israeli nuclear station at Dimona were attacked by PLO gunmen who killed three of them. This attack hardened the Israelis against the *Intifida*, and was the final straw as far as their position on Abu Jihad was concerned. He was eliminated in Tripoli, Libya, in April 1988, by Mossad agents.

However, the violence in the occupied territories continued, again carried out by the population itself, not by the hitmen of the PLO. Fighting civilians was something that the citizen soldiers of the IDF had not been trained to do, and the day-to-day hostilities were taking a toll on them. Defense Minister Yitzhak Rabin, himself a former general, realized this fact. At the same time, Yassir Arafat realized, after the killing of Abu Jihad, that terrorism was not going to bring about the realization of the Palestinian state he had fought for since the end of the 1967 war. Thus, in November 1988, he appeared before the gathering of the Palestinian National Council in Algiers and formally accepted United Nations resolutions 242 and 338 which not only called on the Israelis to withdraw from the territories occupied after the 1967 War, but also recognized the right of Israel to exist as a sovereign state. This was something that Arafat, until now, had refused to do. What would come to be called "the peace process" now began in the Middle East.

In December 1988, Arafat took a step farther down the road of the peace process. Under urging from U.S. Secretary of State George Schultz, he officially renounced terrorism as an instrument of PLO policy, leading the way to talks between the enemies for the first time. Throughout this "peace process," the United States would play a central role because, after the fall of the Soviet Union in 1989 and the defeat of Saddam Hussein's Iraq in the Gulf War of 1991, the United States remained the only great power with the influence to implement such negotiations. However, since Arafat had backed Hussein in the Gulf War, the United States would not consider him as a delegate to any peace conference, although his control of the PLO from behind the scenes in Tunis remained as firm as before. A preliminary conference took place in Madrid on October 31, 1991, but its members disbanded without much more than a promise to meet again. When the next talks occurred in Oslo, Norway, through much of 1993, the results were far more substantive. In return for PLO recognition of the state of Israel, the Israelis agreed to hand over portions of the West Bank and the Gaza Strip to be ruled by the Palestinians. On September 13, 1993, in front of U.S. President Bill Clinton and the White House, Israeli Prime Minister Yitzhak Rabin and Yassir Arafat formally signed the Oslo agreement. Afterward, Arafat personally took power in the new Palestinian-administered lands as the formal head of the Palestinian Authority.

Throughout the period of the early years of the peace talks, the Middle East enjoyed the unique blessing of cooperation in the overall quest for peace between the United States and the Soviet Union. Under Mikhail Gorbachev, the Soviet Union ceased its support for the international terrorism cartel that had been so much a part of Soviet foreign policy in the days of Leonid Brezhnev and Yuri Andropov. The PLO was made to feel the change in Moscow's policy. As Galia Golan, professor at the Hebrew University in Jerusalem, wrote in *Foreign Affairs* (fall 1987), "in this more moderate stand on [Middle East] borders, the proposed Palestinian State would be limited to the West Bank and the Gaza Strip, as distinct from (and in opposition to) the PLO's pre-1974 demand and general aspiration for a 'democratic secular state' in all of Palestine (replacing the state of Israel)."[22]

Although much more remained to be accomplished, the mechanism of the peace process was in place and has remained so, but final agreement has not yet come. Before President Clinton left office he and Israeli Prime Minister Ehud Barak offered a deal to Yassir Arafat that would have given to the PLO the West Bank and the Gaza Strip, along with East Jerusalem to be the capital of the new

Palestinian state. Arafat refused the agreement, however, because it contained no firm statement on the right of the Palestinian refugees to return to their former homes in Israel. The "peace process" itself was now stalled by a second *Intifida* in the Gaza Strip and the West Bank, which the new government of Israeli Prime Minister Ariel Sharon blames personally on Arafat. Sharon's position is that there can be no further negotiation until the violence ceases. In an interview early in 2001 with the new American president, George W. Bush, Sharon received support for his position. The new secretary of state, Colin Powell, who had been the chairman of the American Joint Chiefs of Staff at the time of the Gulf War, reasserted the traditional American support for the state of Israel.

Yet, even earlier, a new element had injected itself into the ongoing peace process. Hamas and Hizbollah, the extremist Muslim terror groups, always had opposed peace talks with Israel. Indeed, their position remained the traditional Arab belief that Israel had no right to exist. Thus, the Islamic extremists began their own process to destabilize the delicate negotiations between Israel and the PLO. They began to employ suicide bombers, just as they had in 1983 against the U.S. Marine barracks in Beirut. Bombers would appear in Israeli streets and shopping plazas to immolate themselves and whoever was in reach of the explosives that they carried on their bodies. Car bombs would detonate with the same devastating effect. The specter of sudden death or mutilation began to stalk the Israeli population in a way unknown even in the days of guerrilla warfare with the *Al-Fatah* of Yassir Arafat. Most of the bombers were Palestinian nationals, usually in their twenties, who had committed themselves to the extremists. In its introduction, found through a link on the Hizbollah English language homepage on the Web, the group underlines its support for such tactics in a polemic entitled "Hezbollah: Identity and Goals." The group makes clear its orientation: "Hezbollah is an Islamic struggle movement." The statement also underlines the connection between the Shi'ite Muslims who rule in Iran and Hizbollah. The Hizbollah Web page underscores the contribution of Iran to the struggle of the Shi'ites in Lebanon who make up the majority of the Hizbollah movement as "the historic tie between the Shiias in Lebanon and in Iran, which is a doctrinal tie." It also makes a shocking admission of the use of the suicide tactics: "Hezbollah also used one of its own special types of resistance against the Zionist [Israeli] enemy, that is the suicide attacks. These attacks dealt great losses to the enemy on all thinkable levels such as militarily and mentally. The attacks also raised the moral[e] across the whole Islamic nation."

Hizbollah's motive is made clear in this introduction: "Hezbollah's ideological ideals see no legitimacy for the existence of 'Israel.'" Although the Web site was apparently last updated in 2000, this remains the stand of Hizbollah, the main extremist party. A separate link leads a Web surfer to the statements of the secretary general of Hizbollah. As recently as April 24, 2001, at a conference in Tehran, the secretary general made clear that Hizbollah has not changed its stand. He declared at an international Islamic conference on the new *Intifida*, "from the historic victory in Lebanon [the withdrawal of the Israeli Army in summer 2000], to the failure of the [peace] negotiations, and the emergence of the *Intifida*, our [Arabic] nation has now a historic opportunity to wipe out the cancerous Israeli project [the state of Israel] which has been threatening our region for fifty years."

Extremism, tragically, also works both ways. In Israel, Yitzhak Rabin had been under increasing attack from ultraconservative Israelis for abandoning the traditional lands of Israel, Galilee, Samaria, and Judea to the Arabs in his search for a peace agreement. On November 4, 1995, he was assassinated by an Israeli right wing zealot Yigal Amir, after giving a speech on behalf of the peace process.

In the overall process, the declaration of war against Israel, which was virtually what the speech of Hizbollah's secretary general in Tehran stood for, reaffirmed the ancient beliefs of Islamic extremism. It harkened back to the days of the Crusades, and earlier. Because from the beginning of the Islamic movement under the Prophet Mohammed, the doctrine of the *jihad*, the holy war, had taken root.

The Rise of
Militant Islam

Mohammed, who has gone down in history as the Prophet of God, of Allah, was born around 571 C.E. in the tribe of the Quraish in what is now Saudi Arabia. He was born in the town of Mecca, in the Hijaz region along the Red Sea. During his early years, he worked in the flourishing caravan trade that knit together the Middle East of his time. It was during this era that he was exposed to the great monotheistic religions of his region, to Judaism and to Christianity. At that time, the Arabs believed in a multiplicity of deities, and Mecca was one of the main centers for their worship.

It was in about 610 C.E. that Mohammed received the first messages from Allah. The message he began to preach about the one true God was not received well by the people of Mecca. In about 622, Mohammed received an invitation from the town of Yathrib, some 220 miles to the north of Mecca. He moved there, a migration that would later be celebrated by Muslims as his hegira. At Yathrib, later known as Medina, Mohammed gradually became the ruler of a spiritual and temporal movement that would soon leave its mark on world history. It was the religion of Islam, which in Arabic means submission to the word of Allah, God himself. With this new belief of submission animating the Arabian tribes, Mohammed was strong enough within eight years to return to Mecca as a conqueror. He overthrew the worship of the pagan idols in Mecca and established it as the spiritual seat of the new religion of Islam, an honor Mecca holds today. According to Muslim pious tradition, Mohammed died on June 8, 632, and was carried into heaven on the back of the sacred stallion Buraq, at the site of the Dome of the Rock mosque in Jerusalem.

While he was alive, Mohammed wrote down the sayings, or surahs, which he believed were revealed to him by God. Succored by the Angel Gabriel, Mohammed began to write down what he believed came from God in a book known to history as the Quran. Later, he would write the Hadith, his commentaries on the Quran. From the beginning, *The Holy Quran* preached a "holy war," a *jihad*, against infidels or unbelievers. In the ninth surah, the Quran is explicit:

> "Fight against those who believe not in God and the Last Day and do not forbid what God and His Messenger [Mohammed] have forbidden —such men as practice not the religion of truth, being of those who have been given the Book—until they pay tribute out of hand and have been humbled." (9:29)

> "And fight the unbelievers totally even as they fight you totally; and know that God is with the god-fearing." (9:36)

Indeed, Mohammed himself had given his seal to the tradition of the holy war for Islam in his campaign to gain control of Mecca, in which he even vanquished the Quraish, the tribe of his youth.

Yet, the Islamic way of war as revealed in the Quran or the Hadith did not encompass the total destruction of the enemy as viewed by the extremists who follow Osama bin Laden or the Taliban today. Those who brought the concept of total war into the Middle East were neither Christians nor Muslims. The concept of war as involving the extermination of the foe was not introduced into the Arab world until it rode in with the Mongols of Genghiz Khan out of the heart of central Asia in the thirteenth century C.E. Beginning in 1219, Genghiz Khan rampaged through much of what is Iran, Iraq, and Afghanistan with his Mongols. So total was his destruction that irrigation systems that had kept the region watered since the time of Alexander the Great were razed. Much of what was rich farm land became the desert wastes we see in central Asia today. An example of Khan's ruthlessness was the destruction of the Afghan city of Herat, which borders on the great Iranian desert to the west, the Dasht-e Kavir. Herat was singled out because the rulers of the city killed Genghiz's ambassadors. Khan attacked the city and killed all who could be caught. However, some Afghans had hidden in the wreckage, hoping to survive. When the Mongols disappeared, the survivors came out, as Genghiz Khan had known they would. A feigned retreat was very much a part of Mongol tactics. When the Heratis came out of hiding, the Mongols returned and under the Khan's personal orders slew the rest of the people. According to *The Secret History of the Mongols*, it was Tolui, father of Kubilai, Mongke, and Hulagu, who ravished Herat for his father, Genghiz Khan: "He was breaking the city of Cugceren [Herat], returning, being come, pitching [his tent], joining himself unto Cinggis Qahan."[1] Yet even Genghiz Khan would grow in wisdom and learn tolerance for those who lived within his empire. Before his death in 1227, Khan realized that to rule an empire meant to build for the future, not to destroy the past. His Yassa, or code of law, was enlightened for its day. It is ironic that in 2001, Mongolia, his home, would be a republic where the constitution guaranteed freedom of worship. But in Afghanistan under the Taliban government, conversion of an Afghan from Islam was punishable by death.

Just when the Muslim states of the Middle East had begun a fitful recovery after the Mongol devastation, 150 years later they were struck by Tamerlane ("Timur the Lame") who believed himself to be Genghiz Khan's direct descendant. Tamerlane visited the same destruction on central Asia as had his idol. When he destroyed a city, Tamerlane made a wide pillar out of the skulls of those his men had slaughtered. The remains of a fortress built by Tamerlane or his successors stands today in Herat in Afghanistan, a city which has seen renewed violence in the bombing of the country after the attack on America on September 11, 2001. During his reign, Tamerlane controlled much of what is now central Asia, Iraq, Iran, Afghanistan, and Pakistan. A third conqueror, Babur the Tiger (1483–1530), claimed descent from both Genghiz Khan and Tamerlane. In 1504, Babur began the conquest of Afghanistan by toppling the reigning Lodhi Dynasty and making Kabul his capital. In 1522, the city of Kandahar would fall to him. Babur's conquests followed the same bloody template as those of his two ancestors.

For centuries then, the heart of central Asia and Iran were ruled by the descendants of Genghiz Khan. First came the Khans like Hulagu, Kubilai, and Mongke, who could claim direct descent from Genghiz. Kubilai would go on to found the Yuan Dynasty of China. Mongke would assume the position of the Great Khan, while Hulagu founded the Il-Khan Dynasty of Iran. These were followed by the "second generation" of Tamerlane and Babur. In all of them, brutality in war was not only something that happened in the heat of battle, but was a concentrated campaign of terror to overawe future targets of conquest. It seems to be no coincidence that those who put the harshest reading on the conduct of Islamic war are those who come from this region, especially Afghanistan. Ethnically and culturally, they have little in common with the Arabs of the Prophet. Much more so, they are the spiritual heirs not of Mohammed, but of Genghiz Khan.

The very climate of Arabia militated against such destruction as practiced by Genghiz Khan and his successors. While central Asia had been once watered by vast irrigation projects, life in the desert depended on something as fragile as water holes. According to one story, one of his followers ran up to Mohammed, told the Prophet that his mother had died, and wanted to know the best alms he could give for her soul. Said the Prophet, "Water! Dig a well for her, and give water to the thirsty!" A war of extermination as practiced by Genghiz Khan and Tamerlane, and as preached by the Afghan-influenced Arab Osama bin Laden and the Taliban, would have been impossible, if not suicidal, for the Arab followers of Mohammed. As practiced by the Bedouins into the twentieth century, desert war was a series of raids for livestock, booty, or women. Even long-standing tribal feuds were conducted in the same, generally bloodless way—because if you destroyed your enemy's oasis, ruined the water, killed his sheep, and cut down his date palms, you might starve or die of thirst yourself. Those you raided one year you might trade with the next. Indeed, the position of a shaikh in a desert tribe was conditioned by his being able to provide for his people in their harsh environment. Anyone who has seen the movie *Lawrence of Arabia* will remember the scene in which Anthony Quinn, playing the real life shaikh of the Howeitat tribe, Auda abu Tayi, gives a tribal banquet in honor of Lawrence (Peter O'Toole). Auda (Quinn) says, "I am a river of life to my people!"

Given the desert background that Mohammed and his followers shared, a far better—and more historically accurate—view of Islamic war comes from another passage in the Quran:

> "To everyone we have given a law and a way. . . . And if God had pleased, he would have made you all one people. But he hath done otherwise, that He might try you in that which he hath severally given unto you: wherefore press forward in good works. Unto God shall ye return, and He will tell you that concerning which ye disagree." (Surah 5:48)

Modern Islamic scholar Mahmud Shaltut upheld this interpretation of the Quran. Shaltut was Egyptian, and taught at al-Azhar University in Cairo. Gamal Abdel Nasser appointed him the Rector of al-Azhar in 1958, a position he held until his death in 1963. About *jihad*, Shaltut wrote that the verses of the Quran "point out that expelling people from their homes, frightening them when they are safe, and preventing them from living peacefully without fear for their lives or possessions is persecution worse than persecution by means of bloodshed and murder."[2] Both Palestinians and Israelis stand accused of violating Shaltut's definition of an Islamic "just war." By Osama bin Laden's reprehensible attacks on America on September 11, 2001, any claims of his fighting a true *jihad* for Islam are utter hypocrisy.

When Mohammed died in 632 C.E., one of his close followers, Abu Bakr, was chosen as as his successor, the first khalifa (caliph). Within twenty-five years, Muslim armies swept out of Arabia in the whirlwind of victory described by Sir John Bagot Glubb, last British commander of Jordan's Arab Legion, in *The Great Arab Conquests*. By 636 C.E., all of Palestine and Syria, save for Jerusalem, was in Arab hands. At Khadisiya, in modern Iraq, the Persian Empire was destroyed. The Arabs under Tariq invaded Spain in 711, and began a wave of European conquests not stopped until Charles Martel defeated the Muslims at Tours in France in 732 C.E. By the tenth century, Mahmud al-Ghazni was raiding western India, taking the same paths through the Hindu Kush that Alexander had taken 1,300 years before.

Yet, paradoxically, by the time al-Ghazni's buccaneering was taking place, the "high tide" of Islamic conquest had abated. A forceful Arab attempt to take Byzantium (Constantinople) had met terrible defeat in 669. Haroun al-Rashid, caliph in Baghdad, led wars against the remaining Byzantines in the Holy Land, but sent a white elephant as a gift to Charlemagne, the descendant of Charles Martel, who had put a stop to the Muslim conquest of Europe! While the Arab civilization that flourished under the Ummayid (661–750) and Abbasid (730–1258) caliphates gave us the culture that produced Ibn-Khaldun and the philosopher Avicenna, clearly the "crusading spirit" had run out of Islam as the heirs of the Prophet enjoyed the earthly pleasures of the Spanish city of Cordova and Iraq's Baghdad. It was a time for a new *jihad* in Islam, but it was not one to be led by the Arabs.

The next impetus for *jihad* would come instead from central Asia, where hardened warriors of Turkey had been converted by wandering Muslim clerics (*mullahs* and *imams*). Almost every Muslim town in central Asia would soon venerate the tomb of one of these unknown Muslim missionaries; often when a town did not have a tomb, they killed a holy man to create one!* These central Asian horse warriors despised the civilized life of "decadent" Baghdad; instead of the *Arabian Nights*, they thrived on epic stories of brave fighters, like the later *Shah-nama*, which the Turks would tell for centuries, like central Asian versions of King Arthur. In much the same way, they despised the Ummayid and Abbasid caliphates as much as modern militants revile Western-oriented Muslim societies. Ibn-Khaldun felt that the *asabiyya*, the instinctive tribal consciousness that had powered the Arab conquests, had simply run out from the Arabic race. As he had observed earlier in the Arabs' history, "the combination of a tribal solidarity and a religious drive is overwhelming." But by the ninth century, the Abbasid caliphs already had become prisoners of their Turkish guards; between 861 and 871 four caliphs were butchered by those who were supposed to protect them![3] The passage of the caliphs was noted in a quatrain in the famous *Rubaiyat* of the Persian Omar Khayyam (*rubaiyat* is Farsi, Persian, for "quatrain"):

> Think, in this battered Caravanserai,
> Whose portals are alternate Night and Day,
> How Sultan after Sultan with his Pomp
> Abode his destined Hour and went his way.

Historian Ibn-Khaldun (1332–1406) would write of such fierce nomads, "they do not stop at the borders of their horizon. They swarm across distant zones and achieve superiority over faraway nations."[4]

The Seljuq Turks who came from central Asia by the eleventh century were no longer content to guard the disintegrating caliphate: They decided to take it for themselves. In 1040, Togrul Beg, "the Falcon," took Khorasan from the Abbasids. In 1055, the Seljuqs seized Baghdad itself, the seat of the caliphate. With the blessing of the Caliph al-Quaim, Togrul became the power behind the Abbasid throne. In 1071, Alp Arslan, Togrul's nephew, showed this power by defeating the Byzantines at Manzikert, capturing (and releasing for a huge ransom) the Byzantine Basileus, or Emperor, Diogenes Romanus IV. The decrepit Abbasid caliphate would last until the Mongols sacked Baghdad in 1258.

---

*A holy man's tomb provided a town with the most sacred of all Muslim sites, even if the townspeople had "created" their own saint!

It was the growing pressure of the Seljuqs and other Turkish tribes on the Byzantine Empire in Asia Minor that led to Pope Urban II's call for the First Crusade at Clermont, France, in November 1095. The crusaders by late in 1096 and early 1097 had reached Byzantium, which, with the help of the emperor, would be their staging point for their invasion of the Turkish lands. The Turks by now controlled much of Asia Minor and virtually all of the Holy Land. Significantly, when the crusaders besieged the city of Antioch from October 1097 to June 1098, the Turkish *beg* (or city governor) Yaghi Siyan, who ruled the city did not seek help from the indigenous Arab lords, who had already made their peace with the crusaders. Instead, he sought help from a massive Turkish army he summoned from the heart of Iraq. Unfortunately for the Turks, although the crusaders were weakened by malnutrition and disease, the tactics of the Frankish, or Western, mounted knights proved too much, and the Turks were scattered from the field. Although many Turks were now considered *ghulam*, heavy cavalry, armed and wearing mail like the crusaders, there were not enough of them to change the decisive tactical outcome at Antioch, which fell to the battle-weary knights in June.

By this time, the empire of the Seljuqs, consolidated by Malik Shah, was already falling apart. (However, Ridwan, his nephew, still ruled much of northern Syria, including Aleppo.) Jerusalem, the main goal of the First Crusade leaders like Raymond of Toulouse, Bohemond of Taranto, and Godfrey of Bouillon, had in fact been taken by an army of the Fatimid Dynasty of Egypt, rivals of the Abbasids for control of the Islamic world. Significantly, a large portion of the Fatimid army which held Jerusalem as the crusaders approached it from Antioch was composed of Sudanese warriors, ancestors of those who would fight Horatio Herbert Kitchener at Omdurman eight centuries later. In the last, great battle of the First Crusade, it would be *mujahidin* from the periphery of *Dar al-Islam*, this time from the Egyptian and Sudanese south, who would carry the green banners of the Prophet.

After the crusaders took Jerusalem in July 1099 from the Fatimid army, a second wave of reinforcements, also led by Raymond, was massacred by the aroused Turks of Asia Minor. The French Orientalist Renee Grousset, in his *Epic of the Crusades*, notes that of 150,000 reinforcements, only a few managed to escape slaughter or capture. Raymond was among the fortunate, fleeing back to Byzantium. However, in spite of repeated Turkish efforts to oust the crusaders from their new kingdoms in the Holy Land, good relations were kept with the indigenous Arab *amirs* and people of the eastern Mediterranean coast. As Grousset writes, the Christians and coastal Arabs, more civilized than the Turks, found much in common, including their belief in chivalry and their tradition of religious asceticism.[5] Fulcher of Chartres, the chronicler of the First Crusade, wrote that "now we who were westerners have become easterners. He who was Italian or French has in this land become a Galilean or a Palestinian."[6] It was in this atmosphere that the Knights Templar must have grown close to the Muslims, with disastrous consequences later on.

When a resurgence of the Muslim religious war spirit arose, it once again came from the remaining Seljuqs, who seemed to hold themselves aloof from the "decadent" Arab Muslims of the Holy Land. In 1129, Zengi became the Seljuq *beg* of Aleppo; in Grousset's description, "the holy war, to which he devoted himself body and soul . . . became the whole meaning of his existence."[7] In December 1444, Zengi took the strategically important crusader stronghold, the county of Edessa. The fall of Edessa prompted the Second Crusade to the Holy Land, composed of French and Germans, under Louis VII of France in 1148. The Second Crusade proved a failure, not least because of friction between the original crusaders and the newcomers. Louis departed Syria for France at Easter 1149. Except for border warfare, the status quo ante bellum reigned between the crusader states and the Muslims of the Holy Land.

It is a misconception that the era of the Crusades represented a period of perpetual war between Christian and Muslim. The period of the Crusades lasted roughly from the First Crusade in 1096 to the 1270 Eighth Crusade of King Louis IX of France to Tunis in North Africa. Yet during much of that time Christians and Muslims lived in peace and relative mutual tolerance. Cordial relationships sprang up between the two faiths in the Holy Land, and on the western rim of the Crusades in Spain. In fact, the great Spanish hero El Cid, Rodrigo de Vivar, fought for Muslim princes as often as he did for those of Christian Spain. The great medieval tradition of the troubadours and their poetry in southern France was sparked by the intercourse between the two peoples. The rich cultural relationship between the two worlds at this time sowed the seeds for the great flowering of European culture in the Renaissance.

Twenty years later, after the Second Crusade ended in 1150, however, the death knell would sound for the crusader kingdoms. And the one who tolled the bell was a central Asian Kurd, the great Saladin. Saladin was the nephew of Shirkuh, chief commander of Nur-ed-din, the son of Zengi, who had succeeded in unifying the Muslim principalities of Aleppo and Damascus. Yet, not content with this coup against the crusaders, the strongest state being the kingdom of Jerusalem under Baldwin III and then Amalric I, Nur-ed-din was determined to extend his power to Egypt. There, the Fatimid Dynasty was moribund and ready to fall into his hands. On November 1, 1168, Amalric had landed in Bilbeis, anxious to add Egypt to his kingdom. However, Shirkuh, also a Kurd, bested the king of Jerusalem. He had the Fatimid vizier, whose loyalty to the Muslims was in doubt, beheaded, and took the position himself. Shirkuh vigorously prosecuted the war against Amalric and, when he died in March 1169, Saladin became vizier in his place. The young warrior forced Amalric to evacuate Egypt in December and, at a young age, became de facto ruler of Egypt. At Nur-ed-din's orders, he brought the Fatimid caliphate to an end.

The 1168 campaign against the Franks, as the Muslims called the crusaders, began Saladin's twenty-year personal *jihad* against the crusader states, especially the principal Kingdom of Jerusalem. Throughout his *jihad*, Saladin was dismayed by the lack of assistance rendered by the local Arabs; at one time he said that the crusaders had kept their religious spirit, and the Muslims had lost theirs! Twice, Saladin invaded the Holy Land, at the county of Tripoli, aiming at Beirut, in 1182, and in 1183 in Galilee, using his Egyptian army, many of which again came from the Sudan. Both times he was thwarted by the leper king of Jerusalem, Baldwin IV. However, the climax came in 1187, after the death of the determined Baldwin. Upon forcing the hapless crusaders into the wilderness of Galilee, Saladin surprised them on July 4 at the hill known as the Horn of Hattin. Weakened by the heat of the summer sun, they were destroyed by Saladin's army.

The climax of Saladin's *jihad* came with his triumphant entry into Jerusalem in September 1187. The fall of Jerusalem galvanized the West to respond with the Third Crusade, when Richard the Lionheart of England, Philip Augustus of France, and Emperor Frederick Barbarossa of the Holy Roman Empire took the cross and led their armies toward the beleaguered Holy Land. In June 1190, Frederick died of a heart attack on the way to Palestine, while crossing a river in Asia Minor. It was not until April 1191 that Philip arrived in the Holy Land; Richard did not come until June! When Richard arrived, he clearly became the fighting heart of the crusaders. His victories at Acre and Jaffa threw Saladin into despair. Saladin's chronicler Beha ed-Din wrote that at Jaffa "so brave were the Franks that our troops, discouraged, contented themselves with keeping them in sight, but at long range." The Frankish chronicler Ambroise dubbed him "Richard the Great."

Yet Richard, deserted by Philip, lacked the manpower to challenge Saladin in a final battle for Jerusalem. In September 1192, Richard and Saladin agreed to a compromise which gave to the crusaders the coastal strip, but the interior—including Jerusalem—remained in Saladin's hands.

However, at the same time Saladin was expressing the spirit of the *jihad* on the battlefield, another movement was alive within Islam that, when allied to the *jihad*, gave birth to the militant Islamic terrorism with which we are faced today. This was the rise of the secret society of the Assassins. The roots of the Assassins stretched back to the eleventh century, the time of the Seljuqs, in the Ismaili sect of the Shi'a (shi'ite) branch of Islam, which was at war with the dominant Sunni branch, as is still the case today. In Iraq, Saddam Hussein, a Sunni, still wishes to destroy the Shi'as of southern Iraq, who revolted against him during the aftermath of the Gulf War in 1991. Iran is the only Muslim country today in which the Shi'as predominate. The rivalry between the two dates almost from the foundation years of Islam itself. The Shi'as began as the followers of the fourth caliph after the Prophet, Ali, who was murdered in 661. To the Shi'as, Ali was the last authoritative heir of the Prophet, and ever since they have been religiously opposed to the dominant Sunnis, who were followers of the one who took power after Ali was killed—Muawiyya, who founded the Ummayid Dynasty. Even today, mothers in the Shi'a sect cut the faces of their sons with knives on the anniversary of Ali's death, the Feast of Ashura, to commemorate the shedding of his blood, and grown men slash themselves with knives. Some will hit upon their wounds to make them keep bleeding, and dance until they faint from loss of blood.

The Shi'ites were hounded by the Sunnis as a direct threat to their rule in the Muslim caliphate in Umayyid times. However, the Shi'ites reached a position of eminence in 909, when they were strong enough to found the Fatimid Dynasty in Egypt, so called because the sect claimed descent from Mohammed's daughter, Fatima, the wife of the slain Ali. It was the Fatimid Dynasty that controlled Jerusalem at the time it was attacked by the knights of the First Crusade in 1099, and which Saladin later served in Egypt. The leaders of the Shi'ites were known as imams, not caliphs, and the Ismailis were the followers of Ismail, the seventh Imam after the murdered Ali. It was the Ismaili sect of the Shi'ites that gave birth to the secret society of the Assassins.

The father of the Assassins, Hasan-i Sabah, was born around the middle of the eleventh century in the Shi'ite religious stronghold of Qum in what is now Iran, the city which would later be the center of power for the Ayatollah

Khomeini, who ruled as an imam in Iran from 1979 to his death in 1989. Hasan-i Sabah from the beginning felt it was his calling to wage war against the Sunni Muslim leaders, wherever he could find them. It was for this reason he called into being the cult of the Assassins, the world's first true Muslim terrorists.[8] From the days of Hasan-i Sabah, the leader of the Assassins would always be known as the "Old Man of the Mountain," because of his castle on Mount Alamut, the "lair of the eagle."

From their earliest days, the Assassins were a secret society, bound together by a code of silence which the American Mafia might envy. The original term was *Hashishin*, referring to the belief that these killers were drugged with hashish, a derivative of marijuana, in the preparation for their missions. The Assassins referred to their fellow members as *rafiq*, a term that can be translated as "comrade" or "brother." Throughout the crusading period, the Ismaili Assassins, following the lead of Hasan-i Sabah, became a powerful "third force" in the Middle East, feared by both the Christians and the orthodox Muslims. At first, the Seljuqs became the target of the Assassins' daggers. In 1113, they killed the Seljuq Emir of Mosul, Mawdud, in Damascus. In the time of the Third Crusade, under their leader Sinan, the Assassins twice tried to kill Saladin, who wreaked terrible vengeance on the towns where Ismailis lived. They succeeded, however, in killing Conrad of Monferrat, the candidate for Christian king of Jerusalem. Confident in their power to strike terror into the hearts of their foes, the Assassins cleverly played off each side against the other.

The justification for the terrorism of the Assassins, so foreign to the notions of Islamic chivalry as practiced by Saladin and his paladins, lay, as Bernard Lewis wrote in his 1967 study of the Assassins in the Shi'ite principle of *Taqiyya*. In ordinary Shi'ite belief, *Taqiyya* denoted a religious dispensation which the Shi'ites could invoke to conceal their beliefs from the hostile Sunni majority. According to a Shi'ite encyclopedia available on-line from Stanford University, edited by Ali Abbas, Quranic justifiation from Surah 16 is offered as explanation for this duplicity: "any one, who accepting the faith in Allah, utters disbelief [in Islam], except under compulsion, his heart remaining firm in faith—but such as open their breast to unbelief—on them is Wrath from Allah, and theirs will be a dreadful chastisement."[9] Even today, the falling away from belief in Islam and the adoption of another creed, the religious crime of apostasy, is considered a cause for death among devout Muslims.

However, there was a darker side to *Taqiyya*, whose legacy has been lived out by Islamic terrorists for the past thirty years. *Taqiyya* could also, as Lewis wrote, "be cited as an answer to the self-destroying militancy that had led so many [Shi'ites] to their deaths in utterly hopeless rebellions" against the Sunni hegemony. Under leaders like the Old Man of the Mountain and Osama bin Laden, *Taqiyya* can be perverted into an Islamic version of "the end justifies the means," where the act—including acts of egregious terror—can be justified if the leader of the group believes such action will defend or further the cause of Islam. it is this *interpretation* of the doctrine of *Taqiyya* which gives theological validity to the actions of the so-called suicide bombers who have been such a terrible feature of modern Islamic terrorism, and which establishes the Assassins as the first true militant Muslim terrorist movement. It was the Shi'ite belief in *Taqiyya* which laid the theological foundation for the terror attacks on the United States in September 2001. In all ways, Osama bin Laden is the spiritual descendant of Hasan-i Sabah and Sinan.

In the middle of the Crusades, Emperor Frederick of the Holy Roman Empire demonstrated in his career the toleration that could extend from the Christian world to Islam. Emperor Frederick was indeed a unique man, dubbed the *stupor mundi*, the wonder of the world, for his grasp of the arts and sciences. Notably, he was a man of letters as devoted to Arab as to Christian learning. Frederick realized that Egypt, with the rise of Saladin, had become the southern focus of the power of Islam. Around 1225, Frederick became allies with Saladin's nephew, al-Qamil, the sultan of Egypt. Between 1226 and 1227, al-Qamil's ambassador, the emir Fakr ad-Din, paid two visits to Frederick's palace in Sicily. Frederick himself sent an ambassador to Cairo, recognizing Egypt as the real seat of Muslim power in the Middle East. The friendship between al-Qamil and Frederick eventually led to a monumental achievement in the history of the Crusades: the return to the Christians of the kingdom of Jerusalem by treaty with Frederick for a truce in February 1229. As Arab historian Ibn Wasil recalled, "it was finally agreed that he should have Jerusalem on condition that he did not attempt to rebuild the walls" of the holy city.[10]

However, the agreement of 1229 did not last, since Turks from modern-day Iraq, fleeing the Mongol hordes behind them, took Jerusalem again. However, Damascus and Egypt remained strong under another of Saladin's nephews, as-Sali Ayub (the dynasty Saladin founded is known as the Ayubbid Dynasty). In 1248, Louis IX of France took the cross with much of the

French nobility and followed in the path of Frederick II: He sailed for Egypt in the Seventh Crusade. This crusade had special spiritual dynamism because the keys to Jerusalem itself were now housed in Cairo. On June 4, 1249, after a stopover at the Christian kingdom of Cyprus, Louis's fleet anchored off the Nile River delta at Damietta. Jean de Joinville, the historian with the king, recorded the first sight of Ayub's army as "a host fair to look upon, for the sultan's arms are of gold, and when the sun struck upon them, they were resplendent."[11] In spite of valiant fighting, the crusading army was overwhelmed by the Mamluks, the slave soldiers of the Ayubbids, under their commander, Baibars (1233–1277). King Louis was taken prisoner by Baibars's troops and, taking advantage of his strength, Baibars had Sultan Turanshah, the last of the house of Saladin, put to death. Baibars nevertheless freed King Louis upon payment of an exorbitant ransom, and signed a treaty with him that gave possession of the Holy Land back to the crusaders. Louis IX sailed from the Holy Land back to France in April 1254.

While accounts of the Crusades have always centered on the struggle in the Holy Land, it cannot be overlooked that at the same time the Christian kingdoms of Spain, such as Aragon, Navarre, Leon, and Castille, fought for centuries to drive the Muslims from the Iberian Peninsula. Many times during these wars, as happened in the Holy Land, alliances became blurred, and Christians and Muslims would find themselves on the same side, as in the case of the celebrated Spanish hero, El Cid, Rodrigo Diaz de Vivar. (It shows the cultural interrelationships between Muslim and Christian that Rodrigo's title "El Cid" is derived from Arabic *sayyid*, or "lord," which also bears relationship to the Muslim North African title of *caid*, or "chief.") However, for much of his career El Cid fought for Alfonso VI of Castille. The years of the First Crusade in Palestine (1096–99) correspond to the greatest years of triumph of Spain's national hero. El Cid conquered the city of Murviedro in June 1098, as Richard Fletcher notes in *The Quest for El Cid*. The great city of Valencia also came under El Cid's rule during this period, while he was nominally allied with Alfonso.

By the time of El Cid, the Reconquista, or "reconquest" of Spain from the Muslims, or Moors, was well under way, with Alfonso in the Christian vanguard. However, just as the Moorish, or *taifa*, kingdoms in Al-Andalus, as the Moors called Spain, were reeling from the Christian offensive, help came to them from North Africa, from where Tariq had first begun the Muslim offensive against Spain. This time, the threat to the Christian kingdoms came from the Almoravid Dynasty under Yusuf, who ruled his empire from Marrakech, in Morrocco. Once again, troops from the southern frontier of *Dar al-Islam* posed a potent threat to Christianity in Spain, when Yusuf invaded with 50,000 warriors. Included among these warriors of the *jihad* were both Tuaregs and Berbers, whose descendants would later fight for their faith in Morocco in the 1920s under Abd el Krim—again against the Spanish. Unfortunately, Yusuf landed near El Cid's city of Valencia, where Rodrigo dealt the Almoravids a stinging defeat. From then on, the Christian forces were able to keep up the fight against this new Muslim enemy from the south. Coincidentally, El Cid, after a final victory, died in July 1099, the month Jerusalem fell to the men of the First Crusade.

For a century, the warfare continued fiercely between the Almoravids and the Christian kingdoms. Then, the Almoravids were vanquished by another wave of holy warriors from North Africa, the militant Almohad sect. The Almohads proved even a more serious threat to the Christian kingdoms than the Almoravids before them. Their army had enlisted Muslims from the entire region of North Africa and as far south as western Africa. Finally, a call for a Spanish crusade was made in 1212 to defeat the Almohads, a crusade in which the often feuding Christian kings united in common cause under the leadership of Alfonso VIII of Castille. On July 16, at Las Navas de Tolosa, the Christian army scored a decisive victory over the Almohad forces under their king, Mohammed I. Although the war between the Christians and Muslims in Spain would continue for two centuries, the Christian victory at Las Navas de Tolosa marked the turning of the tide. Yet it would not be until 1492, nearly a century after the Christian defeat at Nicopolis, and almost fifty years after Constantinople fell to the Ottoman Mehmed II, that the Reconquista would be completed, when Ferdinand and Isabella captured the last Moorish citadel in Spain, the *taifa* kingdom of Grenada, ruled by Boabdil. Once again, the history of the Reconquista of Spain points out that it was always from the militant frontiers of *Dar al-Islam* that the real source of Muslim strength for the holy *jihad* was found.

The preeminence of the periphery of *Dar al-Islam* as its military heart was sealed by the rise of the ruler Baibars, first of the Mamluk sultans. Significantly, most of these slave soldiers were Turks from central Asia, like the Seljuqs two centuries before. Baibars had himself been bought as a slave in the market at Damascus for 800 dinars; his new owner got his money back when he discovered Baibars had a cataract in one eye. Baibars proved once and for all the hegemony of the frontier in Islam in September 1260, at Ayn Jalut outside Jerusalem, when his army defeated the Mongols under Kit Boga, commander of Hulagu, stopping the unbeatable ride of triumph they had enjoyed since the days of Genghiz Khan, who had died in 1227. When Baibars had the captured Kit Boga before him, as Harold Lamb wrote in his *March of the Barbarians*, "the mamluks cut off his head and fastened it to a pole."[12] The nobility of Europe, significantly, had been devastated by the Mongol horde in several bloody battles. The Mongols under Hulagu had also smashed the surviving Seljuq sultanate of Rum in Asia Minor, giving the Byzantine Empire much-needed breathing space. In 1256, Hulagu Khan had defeated the Ismaili Assassins and killed the last Grand Master of the Order, Rukn al-Din.

The final upsurge of militant Islam from the heart of Turkish central Asia was the rise of the Ottoman Turks, whose name derived from one of the founders of their tribe, Othman, who became their leader in 1281. Under Othman, or Osman, and his son Orhan, who succeeded him in 1326, the tribe of Ottomans experienced a meteoric rise to power. The Byzantine emperor John Cantacuzenus actually enlisted Orhan's help in a Byzantine civil war; in 1344, Cantacuzenus even married his daughter Theodora to Orhan. When Cantacuzenus fell in 1355, Orhan sent an Ottoman army under his son Suleiman a year later to invade Europe across the Dardanelles. Gradually, Byzantium became a shrinking Christian isle in a Turkish sea. On June 15, 1389, at Kosovo, the kingdom of Serbia, led by King Lazar, a former Turk vassal, was destroyed on this "Field of Blackbirds" (as "Kosovo" is translated from the Serbo-Croat language) by the army of Ottoman sultan Murad. Although a Turkish noble killed Murad in his tent that night, the victory was complete. Murad's son continued the consolidation of Ottoman power in the Balkans. Then, in 1396, the Ottoman sultan Bayezit's plans to conquer Byzantium were frustrated by the last major crusade against the Ottomans, led by King Sigismund of Hungary and joined by knights from all over the Christian West. The crusade was crushed by the Turks and Bayezit at Nicopolis the same year.

Ironically, Bayezit's plans to take Byzantium were frustrated by Tamerlane, the last of the great central Asian Turks, who demanded that Bayezit return to the emperor all the Byzantine lands he had seized. Tamerlane claimed descent from Genghiz Khan himself. When Tamerlane and Bayezit met in battle at Ankara in 1402, Tamerlane's horde crushed the Ottomans and took Bayezit and his second son, Musa, captive. According to Steven

Runciman in *The Fall of Constantinople*, Bayezit and his son were treated kindly by Tamerlane, but Bayezit apparently killed himself in 1403. Two years later, at the age of seventy-two, Tamerlane died in his capital at Samarkand, while contemplating following Genghiz Khan's footsteps by conquering China. Tamerlane's whirlwind appearance from central Asia only postponed the fate of Constaninople. In 1453, the city fell to Sultan Mehmet II after a bitter siege. The last Basileus, or emperor, Constantine XI Paleologus, died while defending his city.

Throughout the years of the Ottoman conquests, the Arabs, those who first waged *jihad* in the cause of Islam, were largely relegated to the role of auxiliaries to the disciplined Turkish forces. However, in this capacity the Arabs, especially the Bedouin tribes, would have performed invaluable service as light cavalry in the Turkish army, employing the same "hit and run" tactics that they later used under Prince Faisal and Lawrence of Arabia against the Turks in World War I.

With the consolidation of Ottoman influence in the Balkans in the fourteenth and fifteenth centuries, a third frontier was added to Islam: the Balkans. It was in the roots of this Ottomanization of the Balkans that the struggle in the former Yugoslavia was born, for some Balkan Christians, as in Albania and Bosnia, embraced Islam—to the everlasting hatred of those who remained faithful to Orthodox Christianity, like the Serbs. It was in the Balkans that the Ottomans introduced one of the most brutal of ways to keep the Christian population subdued: the forceful enlistment of young Christian men into the *yeni cheris*, the feared Janissaries, the elite of the sultan's army. Dragged away from their families in a human tax called the *devshirme*, these young boys were raised to be fanatical warriors in the cause of Islam. It would be these Janissaries who would lead the final assault on the last major citadel of Christianity in the Balkans: Constantinople itself.

The Ottoman incursion into the Balkans was the origin, as mentioned above, of the genocidal warfare that has wracked the former Yugoslavia up through the 1990s. This is true not only for the Albanians, Serbs, and Bosnian Muslims, but extends farther up the peninsula to what is now Croatia and Romania. In the years of the Ottoman Empire in Europe, this latter region marked the battle-torn northern march, or frontier, of Ottoman power in the

Balkans, where it was in almost continual warfare with the Christian states which it bordered, such as Hungary and the Holy Roman Empire. John Hunyadi, Prince of Transylvania and Regent of Hungary, a crusader against the Turks, unfortunately died in 1456, three years after the fall of Constantinople. One of his allies was Vlad Dracula, prince of Wallachia, later de facto ruler of Transylvania as well, who would gain infamy as the progenitor of Dracula the vampire. By all accounts, although cruel, even by the standards of his time, Vlad Dracula was a fearless warrior against the Turks in these Balkan wars, even becoming a member of one of the most select of the crusading knightly orders, the Order of the Dragon of the Holy Roman Empire. In 1461, acting as an ally to Hunyadi's son, King Matthias Corvinus of Hungary, Dracula would conduct a spectacular crusade at the behest of Pope Pius II. (Significantly, Dracula was spurred to action by the Turkish demands that young Wallachians be conscripted into the Janissaries, according to Raymond T. McNally and Radu Florescu in *Dracula, Prince of Many Faces*.) Dracula, at least historically, would die in an ambush by the Turks in 1476.

Along the *Grenze*, or military frontier, which the Christian powers, Hungary and the Holy Roman Empire, erected against the Turkish onslaught, all warfare was carried on with the ferocity shown by Prince Dracula, known as Vlad the Impaler because he emulated the Turkish practice of impaling prisoners on wooden stakes. Foremost among the *Grenze* troops were the Croats, many of whom were refugees from Turkish attack. Serbs fled also to the Austrian frontier, where they offered their military services as well against their Turkish oppressors. The Serbs settled along the military frontier, called in Serbo-Croat the Krajina. During the war between Croatia and the Bosnian Serbs in 1992, the Serbs from what was then the province of Krajina were expelled by the Croats in one of the largest ethnic cleansings of this third Balkan war. At that time some 150,00 to 200,000 Serbs were expelled by the Krajina Croats.

By the same token, the Ottomans employed as their frontier troops the newly converted Muslims of Bosnia, which had fallen to the Turks in 1463. These "Bosniaks," as they were known to German-speakers, equalled or excelled the Christian *grenztruppen* in sheer barbarity. In the 1550s, one of the Janissaries taken from the Christians of Bosnia, Mehmet Sokollu (Sokolovic), would become Grand Vizier of the Ottoman Empire. As John A. Donia and John V. A. Fine Jr. write in *Bosnia and Hercegovina: A Tradition Betrayed*, those who provided the Muslim military forces for the frontier, as distinct from the Janissaries, "were descended from members of the Ottoman military class who received their lands in exchange for military service," much like the lords of Christian Europe in the Middle Ages. Ironically, Sokollu, who served the Ottomans well, would be murdered by a Muslim dervish (similar to a monk or friar) from Bosnia in 1579.[13]

Indeed, it seemed like the Muslim conquest of the Balkans would continue. In 1526, the king of Hungary and his chivalry were slaughtered by the Turks at the Battle of Mohacs by the great Suleiman. It would not be until the victory of Polish King John Sobieski outside Vienna in 1683 that the tide of Ottoman conquest would really begin to recede. Nevertheless, the heritage of the savage warfare between Christian and Muslim in the Balkans is the root of the ethnic and religious hate which still threatens renewed war in that tortured region today.

While the Ottoman rule was writ large in the Middle East, unusual religious toleration existed under the sultans. Under the system known as the Millet, the different religious groups were organized together under the empire into their own communities. Hans E. Tutch described the workings of the Millet: "the Jews and the different Christian denominations, as well as the heterodox Muslim communities, were preserved as separate entities, and their spiritual leaders were responsible to the ruler for administration, the collection of taxes, the personal relations, and the good behavior of members of their group."[14] While the wars of religion tore apart western Europe, and the Christian European witch craze caused the deaths of unknown thousands, people of different creeds lived and worked together. In a very real way, the Ottoman Empire represented a version of a tolerant society that the West would not recognize until the Enlightenment of the eighteenth century, and which today is endangered in the countries of the Arab world.

The system of the Millet went beyond the organization of the empire and embraced the culture of the Ottoman world as well. The dates listed in the *Almanach de l'usage de Levant* were given in Muslim, Jewish, Old Style Christian for the Syrian and Greek Orthodox, New Style Christian for Catholics and Protestants, and Rumi for some government departments. The religious holidays were given for Muslims, Christians, and Jews. To show the universality of the almanac, the text was written in Ladino, the language of Sephardic Jews; and also in Greek, Armenian, French, and Bulgarian; as well as in Hebrew letters. "The different means of telling the time of day," Philip Mansel wrote, "from sunset for Muslims and Jews, from midnight for Christians, were also recorded in the almanach."[15]

One group, however, was always treated with mistrust in the empire: The mystical orders of the dervishes aroused concern in the Sunni Islam that has been felt by the charismatic movement in the Roman Catholic Church since the 1960s. Mysticism is something at which traditional, organized religion has always looked askance, and the whirling dances and vigorous chanting of the dervishes set them quite a distance apart from mainstream Islam. At a state level, the Sufis alarmed the empire because they were kin to the Shi'ism that was the form of Islam practiced in the rival Muslim empire of Persia. However, the Sultan Bayezid II became a Sufi himself. Sufism shared many of the practices of Shi'ite Islam. The dervish, or darwish, Order of the Howling Dervishes, or Rufai, practiced the same cutting with knives and sharp objects as the Shi'ites did on the Feast of Ashura.[16]

4

Islam and Arab Nationalism

As the centuries passed, the power of the Ottoman Empire ebbed under the continuing blows of the Christian powers, namely the Holy Roman Empire and tsarist Russia, as well as succumbing increasingly to internal decay and corruption. Even the Janissaries would eventually revolt and in 1826 be abolished as a military corps entirely. Militarily, this "countercrusade" was most vigorously prosecuted by the Holy Roman Empire, of which Hungary became a de facto part when Maximilian II became king of Hungary as well as Holy Roman emperor (1564–76). Throughout this long battle, again, the Ottomans were helped by the Balkan Christians who converted to Islam. Damad Ibrahim, a Bosnian, became commander of the elite Janissary corps, the Janissary Aga, in April 1580.[1] Following Prince Eugene's victory at Zenta, all except a small part of Hungary was cleared of Turks at the Treaty of Karlowitz (1699).

The reconquest of land from the Turks would be the main theme of eastern European history throughout the eighteenth and nineteenth centuries. With Russian help, the Serbs gained freedom in the first years of the nineteenth century. In 1826, Greece would regain its independence from the Turks. In 1877, Bulgaria, with Russian aid, gained freedom from the Ottomans. In 1878, Bosnia became a protectorate of Austria-Hungary, as the Holy Roman Empire was then known, while Great Britain took control of Cyprus, the first stepping stone to its occupation of Egypt. The agreement forged at the Congress of Berlin in 1878 virtually saved the Ottomans from total Russian conquest. Bernard Lewis wrote in his book *The Middle East*, "only the intervention of Western, chiefly British, diplomacy was able to save Turkey from total disaster, and the treaty of Berlin in 1878 again set limits to Russian expansion at Ottoman expense."[2]

By the time of the Napoleonic Wars (1796–1815), individual pashas, or Turkish governors, were able to declare almost autonomous principalities, like Ali Pasha, at Janina in the Balkans, and Pasvanoglu at Vidin. The classic example was Mohammed Ali, a former Mamluk born in Albania, who was able to carve out his own empire in Egypt, the Sudan, and parts of the Holy Land, while paying lip service to the sultan and Sublime Porte (the main Ottoman governing authority) far away in Constantinople. It was on account of his son's expedition to the Sudan that Egypt established its claim to its southern neighbor.

It was no surprise that by the 1870s, Ottoman Turkey was known as the "Sick Man of Europe." The Congress of Berlin in 1878 made the disintegration of the Ottoman Empire a diplomatic fact. Serbia, Bulgaria, and Montenegro were given their freedom while, as stated previously, Bosnia (including Hercegovina) was given to Austria-Hungary to administer, and Cyprus to England.

The weakness of the Ottoman Empire naturally had tempted the European powers to seize parts of the imperial domains, most noticeably those on the periphery. France had invaded Algeria, already only nominally under the sultan, in 1831. Here, under Abd el-Kader, the French provoked an uprising, basically religious in nature, which took years of fighting and much French treasure and lives to suppress. (It also gave birth to the French Foreign Legion, so that foreigners, instead of native Frenchmen, would suffer the casualties of French empire-building.) Abd el-Kader's uprising required a major military effort to subdue. It made the career of Thomas Robert Bugeaud. As Charles Mercer wrote in his history of the French Foreign Legion, *Legion of Strangers*, "[Bugeaud] was named Marshal of France in 1843 and rewarded with the title of Duke of Isly after he defeated Abd el-Kader at Isly a year later."[3] As with Abd el-Kader in Algeria, the growth of European imperialism later on in the century provoked a Muslim reaction. Significantly, unlike Abd el-Kader, this response was more political than religious, more anticolonial uprisings than *jihads*.

The primary example is the case of Egypt referred to earlier. France had held a prominent position in Egypt since the building of the Suez Canal in

1867; with the obvious implications of a shorter route to her imperium in India, Great Britain naturally followed suit. The ruler, Khedive Tewfik, was widely seen as a pawn of the Anglo-French financial interests. In February 1881, a nationalist army revolt was led by Arabi Pasha, leader of the Nationalist party, much as, seventy years later, a military coup ousted King Farouk. The khedive, however, remained in power, but became controlled by Arabi. Arabi became minister of war in January 1882 (he actually was appointed pasha in March), and soon assumed virtual dictatorial powers. Following a massacre of Europeans in June, the British landed troops and, at Tel-el-Kebir on September 13, Arabi was defeated. On September 15, Gen. Sir Garnet Wolseley, the British commander, reached Cairo. "Tewfik was restored [to power], Arabi exiled, and the British government was now, although this was not realized, committed to a very long occupation."[4] Thus England's long involvement in Egypt and the Sudan began.

It cannot be stated too plainly that movements like Arabi's were political in nature; they were early examples of anticolonial uprisings and were not religious in nature. Indeed, increasingly, these nationalist movements were led by Western-oriented parliamentarians, intent on their homelands being freed from European dominance. Ironically, this up and coming political elite was often educated in foreign-run mission schools, rather than the orthodox schools run by the Westernized states, schools which naturally had a vested interest in maintaining the status quo of the Western-influenced regimes. As George Antonius remarks in *The Arab Awakening*, "in course of time a generation grew up who felt more at home in French, English, or Russian than in their mother Arabic."[5] In fact, Antonius traces the birth of the modern Arab nationalist movement to students at the Protestant Syrian College in Beirut in 1875. Paradoxically, this nationalism also enforced a cultural isolation from the type of native fundamentalism that would give rise to the Mahdi in the Sudan. Such a schism still exists in the Muslim world today, since the elites of Middle Eastern countries still look to the West for culture and enlightenment.

Nowhere was this new political influence felt more strongly than in the "Sick Man of Europe," the Ottoman Empire. Ruled by the despotic Sultan Abdul Hamid, the Turkish empire's impotence in international affairs led to widespread disillusionment with the sultanate itself. Although Abdul Hamid attempted an Islamic revival to reunite the people with the sultanate, it was a case of too little, too late. In July 1908, a military revolt by the secular and politically liberal Committee of Union and Progress, backed by the revolutionary Young Turks group, broke out in Constantinople. Although the sultanate continued nominally under Abdul's brother, Sultan Mehmed V, it was clear that the committee and the Young Turks were in actual power now in the Ottoman Empire. While Talaat Bey was the chairman of the committee, Enver Pasha was in charge of military affairs. For the Arab population of the empire, the Young Turks' revolt held out hope of having a say in their own self-government, if not complete independence.

However, it soon became apparent to the Arab population that the new rule of the Young Turks, and the constitution that Abdul Hamid had been forced to grant, did not mean freedom for them: The Young Turks intended to keep them subjects of the empire. With hopes of Arab participation in the empire, let alone liberty, dashed, Arab secret societies were formed that worked underground to bring about the ousting of the Turks from the Middle East. One of those involved in this secret movement was Prince Faisal, who was held hostage by the Turks to assure the loyalty of his father, Sharif Hussein, who was keeper of the Holy Places of Mecca, and semi-autonomous ruler of the Hejaz, the northwest region of today's Saudi Arabia. Before his appointment by Abdul Hamid, Hussein himself had been a hostage to the sultan for sixteen years.

Sharif Hussein and his second son, Abdullah, who had been a member of the Ottoman Parliament in Constantinople, were becoming anxious to assert their political independence from the Turks. When Faisal was returned to the Hejaz, their plans became more feasible, since his life was no longer at stake. Hussein and Abdullah had tentatively sought help from Egypt in February 1914, where Gen. Horatio Herbert Kitchener was now the British Agent, the power behind the khedive's throne. However, since Turkey and England were still at peace, Kitchener advised the Arabs that the British could not help. However, when World War I broke out in August 1914, Turkey became an ally of England's enemy Germany in October. (Turkey had had a close relationship with Imperial Germany for years, and it had been with German assistance that the Turkish army had been modernized.) Now, the British could openly support the burgeoning Arab nationalist movement in the Hejaz. Indeed, with the threat that Turkish forces posed to the Suez Canal, such cooperation was a strategic necessity.

The sharif, however, struck first. In 1916 he declared open war against the Turks, and on June 9 liberated the Mecca from the Turkish garrison. While the sultan had actually proclaimed a *jihad* against England in his role as caliph, it did not deter the Arabs from fighting for their freedom. It was then that the British sent an advisory body from the Arab Bureau in Cairo, one of whose members was T. E. Lawrence, later the fabled Lawrence of Arabia. With Faisal in command of the armies of the Arab revolt, Lawrence came into his own as a leader of the Bedouin guerrilla forces of the sharif. Although pilloried by detractors like Lawrence's fiercest critic Richard Aldington, Lawrence carried on a highly effective guerrilla struggle, supported by Faisal, which tied down large numbers of Turkish forces and caused grave disruption in their rear with constant hit-and-run raiding on the vital Hejaz Railway. In this, the Bedouin irregulars were in their natural element. Not the least of Lawrence's achievements was the taking of the strategic Red Sea port of Aqaba on July 6, 1917. Antonius writes that "there were more Turkish troops fighting the Arabs in the Ma'an area and the Hejaz than there were in Palestine to resist the British northward advance."[6] After British commander Gen. Edmund Allenby's defeat of the Turkish Fourth Army, the ferocious pursuit by Faisal, Lawrence and the tribesmen turned the Turkish retreat into a rout in September 1918 and destroyed any chance of the Turks reforming as a cohesive fighting force. Commenting on how fast his troops could move, Lawrence would write, "The Arab war was simple and individual. Every enrolled man served in the line of battle, and was self-contained. We had no lines of communication or labour troops."[7] B. H. Liddell-Hart wrote in *Colonel Lawrence: The Man behind the Legend* that "what the absence of these [Turkish] numbers meant to the success of Allenby's stroke it is easy to see. Nor did the Arab operation end when it had opened the way. For in the issue, it was the Arabs, almost entirely, who wiped out the Fourth Army, the still intact force that might have barred the way to final victory."[8]

It cannot be overemphasized that the purpose of the Arab revolt was political in nature—to gain an independent Arab state. It was not a religious movement, not a militant *jihad*. Throughout the campaign, as Antonius wrote, "efforts were made to win the population over to the Arab side . . . in the name of King Husain and Arab freedom."[9] Neither the sharif, Faisal, nor Abdullah contemplated a fundamentalist state on the order of Iran under Ayatollah Ruhollah Khomeini or what would become Talibani Afghanistan. This was the reason that Lawrence tried to beat Allenby's regulars in the rush to Damascus, so that the Arabs could claim the city as the capital of their Arab state. In fact, Lawrence and the Arabs won the race: The sharif's banner was raised in Damascus on October 1. (At that time, Syria and Lebanon were considered part of Greater Syria, as the Syrians still claim today. Lawrence and Faisal contemplated an Arab nation that would encompass all of Palestine and this Greater Syria.) However, unknown to the Arabs, and possibly to Lawrence himself, England and France had decided in the 1916 Sykes-Picot Agreement to divide the Holy Land between them, with England receiving Palestine and France Greater Syria.

Lawrence, true to his beliefs, continued to fight with Faisal for an Arab state at the Paris Peace Conference following the war. An Arab Congress in Damascus actually chose Faisal to be King of Syria and Abdullah King of Iraq in 1920. However, at the San Remo Conference in Italy, Britain and France reaffirmed the division of the spoils as set forth in the Sykes-Picot compact, to which Britain added the suzerainty of Iraq. France moved to oust Faisal from Syria. Soon, the tribes in Syria and Iraq revolted against their wartime allies and it seemed a new Arab revolt, this time against France and England, was beginning.

Against this volatile background, Great Britain convened a conference in Cairo in March 1921 in a frantic attempt at Middle East damage control. Chairing the conference as colonial secretary was Winston Churchill, but influential as well were Lawrence and another distinguished British Arabist, Gertrude Bell. As Lawrence commented about Churchill in his *Seven Pillars of Wisdom*, "Mr. Winston Churchill was entrusted by our harassed Cabinet with the settlement of the Middle East."[10] While the Cairo Conference was not the *deus ex machina* the Colonial Office hoped it would be, it did help bring some order out of the chaotic region, especially since the Balfour Declaration had also promised the Jews a "homeland" in Palestine as well![11] The settlement provided in its essentials for Abdullah to become ruler of Transjordan, the eastern part of Palestine, under British tutelage, and for Faisal to become king of Iraq. Lawrence remained faithful to his Arab friends to the end. The French mandate for Greater Syria was, however, confirmed.

Conspicuously absent from the ranks of the Arab revolt was Abd al-Aziz Ibn Saud, the emir of Nejd, who controlled much of the central part of the Arabian peninsula. Although he professed support vocally for the uprising in the beginning, his attitude could best be termed "armed neutrality," since numbers of Turkish forces were forced to watch him in the Nejd as well as the Arabs in the Yemen. In 1915, however, in a letter Lawrence wrote to

British administrator D. G. Hogarth, the pro-Turkish "Ibn Rashid has been heavily defeated by Ibn Saud" in a battle.[12] This seems to have been Ibn Saud's only active contribution to the revolt—he certainly sent no forces north to help Lawrence or Faisal. The reason is clear: Ibn Saud, like Hussein, wished to become leader of a united Arabian kingdom. To accomplish this, he had made a bargain with the Wahabi Brotherhood, the Ikwhan, a radical fundamentalist movement that had arisen in the wastes of eighteenth-century Arabia. It had been founded by a Muslim judge named Mohammad ibn Abd al-Wahab (1703–92). In the time of Mohammad Ali of Egypt, the Wahabis had overrun most of Arabia and posed a threat for a time to Mohammad Ali himself. In 1818, Mohammad Ali smashed the Wahabi threat and drove them back to the Nejd in Arabia, where they remained a potent force into Ibn Saud's time, allies of his family.

Chaos reigned in Arabia at the time of the Cairo Conference (1921), and Ibn Saud saw fit to make his move.[13] After the war, the Sharif Hussein had become redundant in the British postwar vision of the Middle East: His wartime contributions were conveniently forgotten. According to Antonius, the British felt he was becoming an obstacle to their plans for a Jewish homeland in Palestine, and his demands for clarification of British wartime promises to the Arabs soon began to be ridiculed. Ibn Saud watched carefully the waning of British support for Hussein and struck in 1924. The excuse was Hussein's claim to be caliph in March after Turkey gave up the caliphate, although as guardian of the Holy Places of Mecca and Medina he had a good case to claim the title of caliph. But his claim not only irritated the British but served to isolate him in the Muslim world at the time he most needed support. In the summer of 1924, Ibn Saud unleashed the Wahabi Ikwhan. In August they attacked the town of Taif, the childhood home of the Prophet Mohammed, from whom the sharif claimed descent, where they massacred 500 with the approval of Ibn Saud, who felt such an act of terror would weaken the resolve of the supporters of Hussein. He was right. Meanwhile, St. John Philby, the British agent with Ibn Saud, kept informing London that Hussein did not stand a chance and was not worth helping.[14] The British government followed his advice.

Hussein abdicated in favor of his eldest son, Ali, but Ibn Saud was not appeased. On October 13, he occupied Mecca and Hussein fled to Aqaba. For a year, Ali kept up a futile resistance, but, finally, in December 1925, Ali and the sharifian forces surrendered to Ibn Saud. Ibn Saud was now the undisputed ruler of Arabia, incorporating the Hejaz into his kingdom, which the British government confirmed in the Treaty of Jedda in 1927. However, even before this, Ibn Saud realized the inherent difficulties of trying to harness militant Islam to serve the interests of Arabian Realpolitik. Not content with conquering the sharifian forces, the Wahabis began heavy raiding into southern Iraq, where England had recognized Faisal as king. The British used their military strength, including a unique combination of Rolls Royce armored cars and the Royal Air Force, to drive the Wahabis south into Arabia, which now can safely be called Saudi Arabia. The northern frontier between Saudi Arabia and Iraq was settled in the Muhammara Agreement in 1922, which was signed by Ibn Saud and Great Britain.

However, like the genie in the lamp in the *Arabian Nights*, once Ibn Saud began to depend on the Wahabis as his army, they proved harder to control than he had expected. He was forced to accommodate his new state to their puritanical fundamentalism, because they could always become a threat to him. Indeed, in 1929, with British support, Ibn Saud was forced to put down an Ikwhan uprising. Nevertheless, in 1934, they proved their ability again by overrunning Yemen after a boundary dispute, but Ibn Saud did not incorporate Yemen into his new kingdom. Even today, the House of Saud must take into consideration the wishes of the Wahabis, who still are a strong force for Islamic fundamentalism in the kingdom. It was to placate them that no religions emblems or signs were worn by the United States troops defending Saudi Arabia from Saddam Hussein's Iraq in 1990–91, and the "religious right" of Wahabism is the most vocal foe of having "infidel" troops stationed in the kingdom even today. In Saudi Arabia, the *sharia*, the body of Islamic law, "is the only law of the land."[15]

It was the positioning of American troops on the soil of Saudi Arabia at the time of the Gulf War that appears to have led to Osama bin Laden's hatred of the United States. He was apparently in the Saudi kingdom at the time of the Gulf War. His father's firm was one of the largest construction companies in Saudi Arabia at that time. With close ties to the royal family, it is likely that the bin Laden company would have been given construction contracts to work on the elaborate American bases which were built in the kingdom during this period, like the huge Prince Sultan base. It is possible that Osama bin Laden may have worked for his father's company, and actually taken part in the construction of American base facilities. In this way, he would have had firsthand daily intercourse with Americans. It would be one more irony if bin Laden had learned his hatred of American ways by working on the bases the United States was establishing to help the Saudis defend themselves from Saddam Hussein. After the war, bin Laden's increasingly strident criticism of the Saudis' relationship with the Americans led to his eventual exile from the kingdom.

It should be noted that at this time, and perhaps even into the modern period, there is a perfectly valid reason why the Wahabis have never posed a threat to Transjordan, today the Hashemite Kingdom of Jordan. This is true for one main reason. The Bedouin tribes, or Bedawi, have always been fanatic in their loyalty to the Hashemite family, seen as direct descendants of the Prophet, and just as fanatic in their hatred of the Wahabi Brethren, an animosity kept in check by the will of the Hashemite kings. Visiting the Beni Sakhr tribe of Bedouins in Jordan in the 1920s, American adventurer William B. Seabrook wrote in his *Adventures in Arabia* that "good-natured humor is the strongest prophylaxis against fanaticism. Not only were these Bedouin always ready to make jokes against overpious adherents of their own faith, but they seem to have no special antagonism toward the Nazara [Christians]. The harsh Fundamentalism of the Wahabi Meccan group further south was totally foreign to them."[16] Mansour, a wealthy black slave, most likely of Sudanese origin, had been awarded riches and lands for helping the Beni Sakhr tribe when the Wahabis under Ibn Saud had ridden against Transjordan at the end of World War I. Shaikh Mitkhal of the Beni Sakhr was a life-long friend of Amir, later King, Abdullah of Transjordan. According to Seabrook, the Bedawi, or Bedouin, were "hereditary enemies of Ibn Saud and the Wahabi." While Ibn Saud had sat on the fence during the war, the Beni Sakhr, with other large tribes like the Rouallah and Howeitat, along with smaller tribes like the El Khour of Sheik Haditha, had formed a great part of the sharifian array which Lawrence and Prince Faisal had led against the Turks. One reason that Ibn Saud had attacked Sharif Hussein after the war was that the British, not deeming the sharif worthy of support anymore, had stopped paying Ibn Saud 60,000 British pounds a year as a subsidy for not attacking the sharif, as Robert Lacey wrote in *The Kingdom: Arabia and the House of Saud*.[17]

Ironically, the place where the Ottoman call to *jihad* was most readily answered was on the North-West Frontier of British India. Operating in Afghanistan, the German agent, Dr. Wilhelm Wassmuss, Germany's equivalent to Lawrence of Arabia, was instrumental in instigating war between the king of Afghanistan and the British in 1919 to prevent Indian army reinforcements from reaching the fighting in the Middle East. (In the beginning of World War I, the fighting in Iraq, then Mesopatamia, had been run by the Indian army.) The Pathan tribes joyfully joined this Third Afghan War, and actually succeeded in occupying Peshawar, the most important city in British India's North-West Frontier Province. After the war, the British, using air power and ground reinforcements, were successful in pushing back the tribesmen and giving the Afghans a proper thrashing to preserve the territorial integrity of the North-West Frontier from further Afghan incursions.

Indeed, the 1920s and 1930s, unsuspected by the European colonial powers of the time, really represent the birth of modern Islamic militancy, inspired by the European colonialism that seemed to strike at the very heart of the traditional Muslim world. The Third Afghan War can really be called the historic beginning. It was around this time that the Muslim Brotherhood, in Arabic the Ikwhan al-Muslimin, founded by Hassan al Banna, arose in British-occupied Egypt. During the same period, Abd el-Krim (1882?–1963) began his revolt against both the Spanish and French in what was then Spanish and French Morocco. It took from 1921 to 1926 and massive numbers of troops to quell Abd el-Krim's religious-inspired uprising, called the Riff War, after the high Riff Mountains which were his base of operations. During this same time period, religious-motivated revolts swept Libya, which Italy had conquered from the Ottomans in 1911, and Somalia, a British protectorate. Between 1900 and into the 1920s, Mohammed Abdille Hassan, styled the "Mad *Mullah*" by the British, kept Somaliland aflame with his guerrilla warfare, in spite of the efforts of British, Egyptian, and Italian troops to subdue him. In Libya, the Italians had aroused the ire of the Senussis, a fundamentalist group similar to the Wahabis of Saudi Arabia, but having roots in the mystical Sufi tradition. Throughout World War I, supplied by the Turks and their German allies, the Senussis kept up a guerrilla war against the Italians, who joined the Allies in 1915. On November 7, 1915, the Senussi leader Said Ahmed also declared a *jihad* against Italians and the Allies. The Senussis also raided into Egypt and the Sudan. Although the end of World War I brought an end to Turkish and German assistance, militant Islam in Libya was still very much alive. In the 1930s, a Senussi *mullah* named Omar Mukhtar led an uprising against the government of Mussolini. Frustrating continued Italian attempts to subdue him, Mukhtar was finally defeated and killed by Marshal Graziani, who would later begin World War II in North Africa with his invasion of Egypt from Libya in 1940. The

Senussis were ultimately successful in their *jihad* in Libya, for King Idris, the monarch who was recognized by the victorious Western Allies in the years after the war, belonged to this religious sect.

Once again, the revival of militant Islam had been on the periphery of the Holy Land, rather than within it, ironically, on the outskirts of what today is considered to be the home of the Islamic fundamentalists like Hamas and the Islamic *Jihad*. Just as in the time of the Crusades, the religious uprisings, the Wahabis, Senussis, Abd-el Krim, came from the southern and eastern frontiers of the Muslim world. Then, as now, this fact was not appreciated. The colonial powers saw them as mere revolts to be put down in the colonies, no different from any others. In the United States, they were virtually unknown. While Lowell Thomas made T. E. Lawrence a household word with the publication of his *With Lawrence in Arabia*, few Americans read Vincent Sheehan, the only American journalist of note to cover the Riff Wars. It was an unlearned lesson that would have dire consequences for the United States, which was now just beginning to show interest in the Arab world because of its plentiful oil reserves. The British had taken the lead in the exploitation of the seemingly inexhaustible oil supplies of the Middle East from the beginning of the twentieth century, using in part the great skills of one of the great secret agents of history, Sydney Reilly, "The Ace of Spies." However, by middle of World War II, taking advantage of its great financial resources, the United States, through negotiations with King Ibn Saud's government in Saudi Arabia, supplanted the British as the main Western agent in the oil business in the Middle East. The first big American company was ARAMCO, short for the Arabian-American Oil Company. Standard Oil of California was the first American company in the ARAMCO consortium in 1933, followed by Texaco in 1936.[18]

Indeed, there was, after the colonial settlement of the Cairo Conference in 1921, no real violence of any seriousness in the Holy Land, or more specifically Palestine, then a British Mandate, until the 1930s. This new unrest was no real religious uprising, instead it was stress caused by an upsurge in Jewish immigration in the wake of the coming to power in Germany in 1933 of Adolf Hitler and the anti-Semitic Nazi party. The Arab Grand Mufti of Jerusalem, *Hajj* Muhammed Amin al Husseini, instigated the Arab riots of 1936–38, a major public disturbance for the British authorities, but it was more of a political than a religious struggle, since the Mufti aroused the Arabs with cries that the Jews would dispossess them of their ancestral lands.

At this time, George Antonius, a Greek Orthodox Palestinian, was writing his great work on Arab nationalism, *The Arab Awakening*. While absolutely against any idea of a future Jewish state placed among the Arabs by the British, he sadly reflected on the violence that was contorting the people he loved: "Violence defeats its own ends; and such immediate gains as it may score are invariably discounted by the harm which is inseparable from it. Nothing but harm can come from the terror raging in Palestine."[19] It is so sad that over sixty years later the situation is still the same.

With the coming of World War II in Europe in 1939, and in 1941 for the United States, the oil reserves of the Middle East, especially those of Saudi Arabia, became of paramount importance to the Allied cause, especially since Adolf Hitler had cast his eyes on the same treasure. One of the first American, rather than British, oil concessions was given to Standard Oil Company of California in 1933, for which the company paid in gold 50,000 British pounds sterling. To show the importance of Saudi oil to the Allied cause, President Franklin D. Roosevelt personally met Ibn Saud on an American warship during an Allied conference. As a sign of American commitment to keep Saudi Arabia on the Allied side, and to keep Ibn Saud from lapsing into the neutrality he followed in World War I, President Roosevelt authorized the extension of wartime lend-lease funding to King Ibn Saud in February 1943. With the king the guardian of the Holy Places of Mecca and Medina, and with his kingdom occupying a virtual land bridge between Egypt and the rest of the Middle East—not to mention his oil reserves—it was deemed absolutely necessary to keep Saudi Arabia on the side of the Allies.

During the war, the political views of the Arabs were of intense concern to the British, who were largely in charge of the defense of the Middle East. In Egypt, many nationalists openly favored an Axis victory, because they felt the Axis Powers would free them from British control. (They conveniently forgot the record of Mussolini's new "Roman" imperialism in nearby Libya in the 1930s.) Indeed, when Field Marshal Erwin Rommel came close to invading Egypt in 1941–42, many in the Egyptian army, including young officers like Gamal Abdel Nasser and Anwar Sadat, hoped for Rommel to reach the Suez Canal. Because of such disloyalty, the Egyptian army played a very small role, if any, in the North African campaign against the Afrika Korps. In February 1942, at the height of the campaign, King Farouk was about to appoint an anti-Allied prime minister. Determined to prevent such a threat in the British rear, the British ambassador surrounded Farouk's palace with tanks and forced him to accept the pro-Allied Nahas Pasha, of the Wafd party, as Egypt's prime minister.

Again, it must be stated that the Arab nationalism now, like the anticolonialism of Arabi Pasha in 1882, was motivated by political concerns: There was none of the militant fundamentalism found among the Senussis or Wahabis. This was brought all too clearly into focus by the coup of the pro-Nazi Rashid Ali in Iraq in 1941. Drawing on support from the Vichy French in nearby Syria, Rashid Ali intended to make Iraq a German outpost in the desert. With Rommel already a threat from North Africa, the British moved quickly to thwart Rashid Ali's plans. In 1941, Brig. Joseph Kingstone led an expedition, named "Kingcol" after himself, in a dash for Baghdad to restore the pro-British regime that had been established by the now dead Faisal. On May 31, 1941, the Rashid Ali forces capitulated and the British entered Baghdad. Somerset de Chair, whose book *The Golden Carpet* is the only eyewitness account of the thirty-day campaign, met with the Iraqi emissaries to negotiate the truce that ended hostilities.[20]

At the same time in 1942, the Vichy occupation of Syria posed another distinct threat to the British rear; German fighters from Syrian bases had attacked Kingcol on its march through the desert to Baghdad. In fact, the Grand Mufti of Jerusalem sought from Adolf Hitler asylum in Berlin for the duration of the war on the grounds of British charges that he fomented sedition among the Arab population. Prior to the rout of the Rashid Ali forces in Iraq, the Mufti had been in Baghdad as the religious advisor to the pro-Nazi government. From Berlin, he would broadcast his anti-British diatribes to his Muslim disciples over Radio Deutschlandsender.

Ironically, of all the Western authorities to have felt the powerful union of Muslim forces on the north and east, it was only Heinrich Himmler's SS that seemed to really grasp it. Axis agents were actually parachuted down near Jericho to foment Arab dissension, and German Luftwaffe air wings were well accepted by the Arabs and Vichy French in Syria.

From 1941 on, with the appearance of Rommel and his Afrika Korps in February of that year, the prospect of a British defeat in the Middle East seemed quite real. This was doubly so with the possibility that the German troops fighting in the Russian Caucasus might sweep through neutral Turkey and try to unite in the Middle East with Rommel coming east from Libya. To help combat this dual German threat, and the lack of cooperation, even subversion, from the Arabs, the British had to call on the Yishuv, the Jewish community in Palestine, for military aid. When the call for enlistment had gone out, the Arab response had been, according to Allon's *Shield of David: The Story of Israel's Armed Forces*, "snail-like," while the Jews, knowing what would befall them if the Germans won, had responded with alacrity. Allon notes that "130,000 [Jews] registered for military service within a few weeks of the outbreak of the war."[21]

The Jews were a ready pool of military service for the British. The service of the Jewish Legion, of which David Ben-Gurion, first prime minister of an independent Israel, had been a member, had proven its worth to the British in World War I. By 1918, the Jewish Legion formed one-fifth of Gen. Edmund Allenby's Imperial Forces. During the intervening years, the ruling committee of the Yishuv had established the Haganah, a force to defend Israeli settlements in Palestine from Arab raids, which intensified in the 1920s and 1930s. The Haganah could trace its descent from the settlement *Hashomer*, or Watchmen, in the beginning of the century. In the Arab riots in Palestine, Orde Wingate had organized his Special Night Squads to combat Arab terrorism and attacks on the vital oil pipelines. The majority of the Special Night Squads had been quietly recruited from the ranks of the Haganah; thus a precedent existed for using Jewish troops under British military command. The growing likelihood of the Axis victory caused the Yishuv committee to realize that something more was needed than the essentially defensive Haganah. The elite of the Haganah was organized in May 1941 into the Palmach, or "striking companies," which could be used for offensive operations, by one of the members of the old Jewish Legion, Yitzach Sadeh. Among the members of the Palmach were future Israeli army commanders Yigael Allon and Moshe Dayan. It was from among the officers and men of the Palmach that much of the later Israeli Defense Force was later recruited.

Among the first uses of the Palmach strike companies was in the conquest of Vichy Syria. Here, the Palmach was heavily employed alongside British troops in the campaign. It was in the fighting in Syria that Moshe Dayan acquired his signature eyepatch. One day, while scouting out Vichy positions using binoculars, a Vichy sniper managed to aim a shot which went through one of Dayan's binocular lenses, destroying one of his eyes. Jewish forces fought with the British not only in Palestine, but in Europe as well, where the Jewish Brigade fought gallantly in Italy. German-speaking Jews served in Occupied Europe as spies for the British, just as Jews had performed intelligence services for Allenby in World War I in Palestine behind the Turkish lines.

The Zenith of Arab Nationalism

After World War II, thousands of Jewish refugees from Nazi persecution in Europe wished to flock to the "Jewish homeland" in Palestine, as evoked in Leon Uris's novel *Exodus*. Most of these people had been imprisoned in the concentration camps that Adolf Hitler and the Nazis had spread like a virus throughout much of central and eastern Europe. When the camps were liberated by the American, British, and French armies advancing from the west, and the Russian Red Army attacking from the east, many of the former prisoners had been thrown on their own resources. Facing anti-Semitism in many of the countries where the camps were—for example in Poland where Auschwitz was located—many of the survivors were forced to struggle to stay alive. Other Jews had escaped from the urban ghettoes before the round-ups for the camps had begun and had joined the partisans who were fighting with the Red Army against the German invaders. In the fall of 1944, Josef Stalin, the leader of the Soviet Union, disbanded the Jewish partisan groups because he became concerned that they were fighting more for their own cause than for that of Russia. Some of the Jews formed their own private armies to continue the fight. Not wanting to remain in Russia or Poland, where a history of virulent anti-Semitism had predated the 1941 arrival of the Germans by centuries, after the war many of these Jewish partisans made their way to Italy. There, the partisans sought out the Jewish Brigade of the British army, which was fighting the Germans there. When the war ended, the partisans and many soldiers from the Jewish Brigade wanted to join the exodus to Palestine. However, London was anxious not to alienate the Arabs in Palestine by permitting trained Jewish soldiers to emigrate. Many of these former fighters found themselves in British detention camps in Cyprus. Morris Beckman wrote in *The Jewish Brigade*, the story of the Jews who fought with the British army in Italy, "this time the guards' uniforms were not grey or black, khaki. The detainees switched their hatred to their new jailers, and it was not surprising that, when they eventually reached Palestine, many joined extremist groups. The [most militant of the Zionist groups, the] Irgun Zvai Leumi and the Stern Gang had no shortage of willing recruits."[1]

From Cyprus, many of the Jews eventually made the trip to Palestine, often illegally. The original ship *Exodus* had carried illegal Jewish immigrants from Cyprus to Palestine. In his novel, Leon Uris writes of the arrival of two of his characters, Kitty Fremont and Ari ben Canaan, in Palestine: "Ari and Kitty arrived at the *kibbutz* of Beth Alonim—the House of the Oaks—at the foot of Mount Tabor, shortly before dawn. It was the *kibbutz* which gave birth to the Palmach during the war."[2] The influx of the survivors of the Holocaust in Europe resulted in renewed Arab unrest against Jewish immigration, which the British thus tried to contain. The unrest was again fomented by the Grand Mufti of Jerusalem, whom the British had unwisely permitted to return to the Holy Land after his exile in Berlin during the war. While a guest of Hitler, the Mufti had blessed Muslim troops, including Waffen SS formations, which served with the Germans, including Bosnian Muslims, whom he exhorted to fight for their true faith and the German Fatherland, an unlikely combination, but the same one the Germans had used with the Muslims in World War I. The Bosnian Muslim Handschar SS Division committed great brutalities against the largely Serb Resistance under Marshall Tito, and thus helped sow the dragon's teeth for the Bosnian and Kosovo blood baths of the 1990s.

The proclamation of the state of Israel on May 15, 1948, when the British mandate in Palestine lapsed, ignited the first Arab-Israeli War.[3] This day symbolically marked the birth of modern Arab political nationalism, for a Jewish state had come into political existence on what the Arabs considered their own land. Once again, as in the 1936 riots, the Grand Mufti fomented anti-Jewish feeling and formed a private army to fight on the Arab side which behaved so brutally that the other, more professional, Arab armies like that of Egypt and Jordan's Arab Legion grew to despise it. One of the commanders of the Mufti's Arab irregulars was Fawzi el-Kutub, who had actually received SS commando training in Nazi Germany during the Mufti's exile in

Berlin. El-Kutub was responsible for one of the worst Arab atrocities of the 1948, the bombing at Ben Yehuda Street, "the street of the Jews," in the Jewish quarter of Jerusalem, which resulted in fifty-seven dead and eighty-eight wounded. During the war, the Jewish extremists of the Irgun* would perpetrate a similar massacre at the Arab village of Dir Yassin in April 1948. A few days after Dir Yassin, Arab extremists would retaliate by killing ninety members of a Jewish medical convoy that was headed for Jerusalem. Even in 1946, before the war began, the Irgun, in a scene dramatized in *Exodus*, blew up the King David Hotel, the British headquarters in Jerusalem. Along with the British who were killed were eighty civilians, many of whom were Jews. The war continued until 1949, when the United Nations negotiated armistices between Egypt and the new state of Israel in February, Lebanon in March, Jordan in April, and Syria in July. Radical Arab nationalists felt that Arab pride had been scalded by the Jewish victory, when the Israeli Defense Force was able to frustrate the might of all the Arab states. It was this Arab sense of disgrace that fostered the political Pan-Arabism that influenced actions during much of the next decades. Another legacy of the Israeli war of independence was the horrid legitimization of terror as a means of achieving political and ideological ends.

The political repercussions of defeat in the Arab nations was immense and terrible. Mahmoud Nakrashy Pasha, who had tried to keep Egypt out of the war, was shot by the Muslim Brotherhood in December 1948, as Larry Collins and Dominique Lapierre write in their classic account of the 1948 War, *O Jerusalem!* Killed too was Lebanon's Diplomat Riad Sohl. King Abdullah I of Jordan, the surviving son of the Sharif Hussein and now king of Jordan, was murdered while going to attend Friday prayers at Jerusalem's Mosque of Omar in 1951. This act was in direct revenge by the Grand Mufti for King Abdullah deposing him from his position after the end of World War II. In an eerie way, Abdullah had foreseen his own death. Shortly before he was shot outside the mosque, he had said that the best way to die was to be shot quickly "by a nobody." That was exactly how he met his death. Abdullah had been warned not to go to Jerusalem because of the climate of hatred that had been stirred up against him by the forces of the Grand Mufti, and to worship that Friday in a mosque in his capital city of Amman. But he had been

---

*The Irgun was the source of the Luchmei Herut Israel, or "Freedom Fighters of Israel," when its founder Avraham Stern broke off from the Irgun to found his own group. The "Stern Gang" was the name given by the British to the Luchmei.

determined to go worship at the mosque on the Temple Mount of Jerusalem, partly because the tomb of his father, Sharif Hussein, was nearby. Some of the extremist governments against Israel were later accused of putting a bounty on the head of Abdullah for "betraying" the Arab cause by seeking peace with the new state of Israel. Abdullah had told Elias Sasson, son of Moshe Sasson of the Israeli Foreign Ministry, "it is in the supreme interest of the Arab nation to make peace with you."[4]

In July 1952, King Farouk of Egypt was toppled from power by the Free Officers Movement led by Gen. Mohammed Naguib, although Gamal Abdel Nasser later supplanted Naguib as ruler in 1954. Anwar Sadat was also part of the movement. Nasser had been involved in the Egyptian attack against Israel from the south through the Sinai Desert. The Egyptians had met fierce resistance from the *kibbutzim* guards, the defenders of the Israeli settlements in the Negev Desert, the southern boundary of Israel. They had been turned back by the bravery of the guards and the actions of a special group of Israeli soldiers, the "Negev Rats," who had been specially trained in desert war. They took their name from the Desert Rats, the Australians who had defended Tobruk in Libya against Rommel in World War II.

Once again, the extremism of the (now former) Grand Mufti showed in all its homicidal rage. He inflamed Arab indignation at the Israeli victory into hatred of the Arab rulers who had led them into the war (which, of course, they had entered largely at his instigation). The power of the Mufti's influence was felt as far east as Pakistan, where the premier, Liaquat Ali Khan, was killed by Muslim terrorists in October 1951 for refusing to go to war with India.

For nearly the next thirty years, the Arab-Israeli wars and conflicts convulsed the Middle East: in 1956, in 1967, and again in 1973. Beginning especially after the Arab loss in 1967, Arab terrorist or guerrilla attacks on Israel began on a scale not seen in the region since the Palestine Arab riots of 1936–38. Chief among the groups, composed of Palestinian Arabs who were dispossessed by Israeli soldiers, was the Palestine Liberation Organization, led by Yassir Arafat, whose military arm was the *fedayeen*, a Muslim term for "soldiers of the faith." Although there were other resistance groups like the Popular Front for the Liberation of Palestine, led by Dr. George Habash, and ad hoc groups like that led by Abu Nidal, it is Arafat's PLO that has had the greatest impact upon the political history of the Middle East. Writing of the importance of the PLO to terrorist movements, Jillian Becker said, "with

PLO help, terrorist groups became sufficiently well-equipped and trained to constitute a real threat to African and Latin American states, and to disturb most of the liberal democracies."[5]

Abu Nidal, however, had always been the "wild card" among Palestinian terrorists. He had been one of the first recruits to join Arafat's *Al-Fatah* in Kuwait, where Arafat had gone in 1957 to work as a petroleum engineer.[6] However, a split developed between them and in 1974, following Abu Nidal's defection to Iraq, Arafat's PLO sentenced him to death. Nidal spread his terror activities globally, including contacts in South America. However, he continued his civil war with the PLO and in 1983 he was behind the killing in Portugal of Issam Sartaoui, who had been Arafat's contact with Israelis who wished a peace settlement with the Palestinians. Although rumors spread that the Egyptians had arrested him in 1998, Cairo denied that Abu Nidal was in Egyptian custody, according to an Internet notice posted in October 2001 by the European Institute for Research on Mediterranean and Euro-Arab Cooperation.

The defeatism of the Arabs in the wake of their conflicts with Israel was assuaged by the early successes of the Arab armies, especially those of Egypt, in the War of 1973. This reawakening of Arab pride, and the Israeli realization that an accommodation had to be made now with the growing Arab strength, led to what could be called the zenith of modern Arab nationalism. In 1977, under the tutelage of U.S. President Jimmy Carter, President Anwar Sadat of Egypt signed the Camp David Accords with Israeli Prime Minister Menachem Begin, who had led the radical Irgun Zvai Leumi in the 1948 War (against both the Arabs *and* the Haganah of David Ben-Gurion). The Camp David settlement provided for the return to Egypt of Sinai Desert land which Israeli troops had seized as a defense buffer against Egyptian commando attacks in the Six Day War in 1967. Moreover, the accords provided for the first peace treaty between a modern Arab nation, Egypt, and the state of Israel. It was a moment of great pride for both Sadat and Begin, for Sadat had gained a historic return of Arab land, an act of great symbolic importance, and Begin had received the first political recognition of the state of Israel from an Arab country. Tragically, although President Sadat stood that day as the most prominent of Arab leaders, the Camp David Accords would prove to be his own death warrant in years to come.

Throughout this entire period of Pan-Arabism, of the rebirth of Arab nationalism, the struggle with Israel was fought on political lines. The Arab statesmen, from Nasser to Sadat and Arafat, had their battle with the state of Israel: It was a political struggle, not a religious one couched in the moral terms of the Islamic *jihad.* During years of Palestinian terror attacks on Israel, apparently not one synagogue has been bombed, although many other targets have been destroyed, from buses to airplanes. When the United Nations passed its notorious Resolution 272, it condemned the political philosophy of Zionism, which stood at the heart of the creation of the state of Israel, not the Jewish religion. Among all the Palestinians I have interviewed in the United States, this same distinction is made: Their animus is directed against the "Zionist" state, not the religion of its people. (Yassir Arafat, in fact, is married to a Christian.)

Within the Arab world, as the sporadic conflict with Israel continued, the leaders of these secular states were concerned with, as the saying then went, bringing their countries "into the twentieth century." Realizing the relative backwardness of their nations, leaders like the charismatic Nasser of Egypt embarked upon a rapid program of modernization. It was for this reason that Nasser undertook the building in the 1960s of the Aswan High Dam on the Nile River, which marked the introduction of a Russian presence into the country to help complete it. The Aswan High Dam was completed in 1970, the year of Nasser's death. Nasser intended the dam to regulate the flooding of the Nile River and thus make more reliable the flow of water to the Egyptian farmers below it. In 1958, Nasser became president of the short-lived United Arab Republic, which, as mentioned, briefly united Egypt with Syria. The republic comprised a Northern Region (Syria) with a Southern Region in Egypt. With the addition of what was then called North Yemen in 1961, Nasser seemed to be approaching his dream of a truly united Arab state, able to stand with any others in the world after World War II. However, a military coup in Syria caused that country to secede in 1961, and North Yemen soon followed.

However, the grandiose visions of Nasser, as symbolized in the Aswan High Dam at home and the United Arab Republic abroad, marked him as the most respected and powerful Arab or Muslim leader of his generation. Edmond Taylor wrote in 1956 that Nasser "has become the perfect, irreproachable, untouchable champion of Arabism against the world."[7] Nasser's career mirrored the rise of Arab nationalism in the twentieth century. He had been arrested by the British authorities in Egypt in 1935 for his revolutionary activities against the Egyptian government, when Egypt was a virtual British colony with a British Proconsul backed by nationalist British troops. It was Nasser who in 1942 founded the Free Officers Society in the Egyptian army. The nationalism in the Egyptian army made the force so unreliable that the British did not call on the Egyptians to fight even when Field Marshal Erwin Rommel's Afrika Korps threatened to conquer the country in 1942. Indeed, Nasser and another Free Officers Society member, and a future president of Egypt, Anwar Sadat, were imprisoned by the British for their pro-German sympathies. In July 1952, after the Israeli defeat of Egypt in the 1948 war, Nasser led the military coup that toppled then Egyptian King Farouk from power. Although Gen. Mohammed Naguib became the nominal chief of state, Nasser remained the real power. After an attempt on his life in 1954, Nasser arrested Naguib and became chief of state in name as well as in fact.

Naguib, Nasser, and the rest of the members of the Free Officers Society represented a new phenomenon in the Arab world. In Egypt, Syria, and Jordan, the officer corps represented one of the best-educated blocs of people in the population. This rise of the "modernizing military elite" was a new development throughout the Third World. Even King Hussein II of Jordan was a graduate of the British Royal Military Academy at Sandhurst, as was his son Abdullah II, who succeeded him. However, while the military academy education provided Arab officers with a technical expertise well-suited for the modernization of their countries, few of them came away with any understanding of the democratic system that supported the Western countries where many of them had studied. Consequently, the Arab world, as with Latin America, saw the rise of the *caudillos*, military officers who ruled their nations dictatorially in most cases like the *shoguns* had governed Japan in their Bakufu, or "military tent government."

A schism appeared in the nationalist movement that, later on, would lead to a wide rift in *Dar al-Islam* which would pit those who supported nationalism against those who clung to traditional society. Writing of the beginning of modern Arab nationalism in the era before World War I, George E. Kirk noted, "the nationalist movement, however, was still confined to a very small group of army officers and upper class intellectuals, and touched the masses hardly at all."[8] Throughout the golden age of Arab nationalism, the governments were unable to match the promise of their rhetoric with real life concerns. The benefits of modernization did not filter down to the villagers, peasants, and urban underclass, who were left largely in the poverty in which they had lived in the Ottoman times. The isolation of these groups worked against modernization in two critical ways. First, since the phaoronic era in Egypt, the lower class were the ones who clung the most to traditional society. Second, any hope of wedding them to the nationalist movement evaporated when this underclass saw that they were still left out of the mainstream of progress. The resulting alienation of these groups from modernizing Arab political nationalism made them a natural recruiting ground in the future for charismatic figures like Ayatollah Khomeini to muster for a return to the traditional mores and society of the past, when a chimeric Islamic utopia had existed, with all in the *Ummah*, the community of Islam united under the strict tenets of the *sharia*. And as with many such utopian movements in twentieth-century Europe like Nazism and Communism, the path would become one of violence and ferocity.

Moreover, the fact that the military controlled the countries meant that any changes in power were instituted by armed means. The Arab nations were convulsed by a series of military coups which created an atmosphere of profound instability throughout the region. In Syria alone, there were four military coups between 1949 and 1952. The history of neighboring Iraq is the history of one military seizure of power after another. It was in 1979 that Saddam Hussein came to power in Iraq, succeeding the previous military dictator, Gen. Ahmed Hassan al-Bakr. As early as 1959, at the age of twenty-two, Saddam had taken part in a coup attempt against the Iraqi strong man, General Abdul Karim Kassem. Both were wounded in the attempt and Hussein fled to Nasser's Egypt. In July 1958, Kassem had come to power in a bloody soldiers' coup that ended with the last king of Iraq, Faisal II, executed in the al-Rihab Palace in Baghdad. The king's body was later put on public display, hung by the feet. Faisal II was the grandson of the first king of Iraq, Faisal I, who had fought with Lawrence of Arabia in World War I against the Ottoman Turks. The uprising against Faisal II had the support of Nasser, since the Hashemite kingdoms of Iraq and Jordan were opposed to his dominance of the Arab world.

While the Arabs were revolting against the Turks in World War I, within the reeling empire a frantic attempt at modernization was afoot. In 1908, the Young Turk party came to power in Istanbul. The Young Turks desperately tried to modernize the Turkish army as a way to keep the empire's position as a great power. Accepting German aid, the Young Turks allowed the first German military mission to arrive in Istanbul in 1913. The Young Turks would continue the relationship with Imperial Germany and would join Germany in the First World War. When the army went to war, German officers served as advisers at every level. One of the leading German advisers was Gen. Liman von Sanders, who took the honorific Turkish title of pasha, or "high officer." When the British and French invaded European Turkey, one of the Turkish commanders who earned a reputation in the fighting at Gallipoli was Mustafa Kemal. Kemal was born in Thessalonica in 1881, and Turks were celebrating the 120th anniversary of his birth in the year Osama bin Laden's suicide bombers struck the World Trade Center. After the war, Sultan Mohammed VI, hoping to rid his throne of such a popular leader, sent Kemal to Eastern Anatolia.

In spite of the sultan, Kemal would continue to grow in influence. In 1919, Kemal formed the Turkish Nationalist party and his own army. When Greece, Turkey's eternal enemy, attempted to take control of part of Anatolia, Kemal led the forces of resistance in a fierce campaign from 1921–22. (Later in the 1920s, he would sign a treaty of peace with Premier Leftherios Venizelos of Greece. Capitalizing on his popularity, Kemal advanced on Istanbul.) In 1922, bowing to the inevitable, Mohammed VI went into exile in Italy. At the Treaty of Lausanne in 1923, Kemal won recognition of Turkey as an independent nation. One year later, he was elected president of the Turkish Republic, a position he would hold until his death in 1938. While president, with the unanimous backing of the army, Kemal began a whirlwind series of reforms to make Turkey a strong modern power, able to hold its own against the European powers that had tried to carve up Turkey at the end of World War I.

Believing Islam to be a barrier to reform, Kemal abolished the caliphate in 1924, and with the caliphate, the history of the dynasty of Othman drew to a close.

By destroying the power of the caliphate, Kemal opened the door to Turkey being able to modernize in a way untrammeled by ecclesiastical opposition. He thus was following the path that Western European countries had taken in the past. When the French Revolution began the forced modernization of France in 1789, the power of the Roman Catholic Church was broken in national affairs. During the Ottoman Empire, the supreme power of the sultan had inaugurated modernization despite opposition from the Muslim clerics. In 1869, the Ottoman school system had been reorganized, and was headed toward secularization. The state took power from the mosque. In the same year, the first girls' school was opened. A modern university was inaugurated in 1870. When it opened, the minister of education declared, "it is therefore necessary for all classes of the empire to adapt themselves to the requirements of the time and to enter upon the road of progress in all branches of the sciences and the arts."9 Kemal continued vigorously in the campaign for modernization. Without clerical resistance, he was able to abolish the influence of the Islamic religious code of the *sharia*, and established a Western system of justice. To help Turkish education, he introduced a new Roman-based alphabet, and even traveled through the country with blackboard and chalk to spread its knowledge among the Turkish people.

Kemal made religious faith a matter of conscience in his secular state and extended tolerance of Christians and Jews beyond that under the sultans. Economically, he urged sweeping reforms in transportation, industry, and agriculture. His Civil Code of 1926 guaranteed complete legal equality for Turkish women, giving them equal rights in inheritance, child custody, and divorce. Before his death, some eighteen women had been elected to the parliament. Education was open to all, and at state expense. Unlike fundamentalist Muslim nations, education was coeducational, opening up avenues for advancement to women as well as men. In 1922, Kemal had said, "we shall emphasize putting our women's secondary and higher education on an equal footing with men."10 To emphasize the commitment to modernization, he introduced Western clothing for men and women, banning the fez hat for men and the all-covering *chador* for the women. In 1934, the Turkish parliament awarded him the title of Ataturk, "Father of the Turks." When he died in November 1938, the League of Nations, which had invited Turkey to join in 1932, mourned him as a "genius international peacemaker." Kemal Ataturk set Turkey on a course of modernization that has continued to this day. The Turkish army, seeing him as its father, has intervened in recent years when extremist Muslims attempted to reintroduce the *sharia* and religious rule in modern Turkey.

The Pahlavi Dynasty, the last dynasty to rule Iran, also came to power through military means. Reza Khan had begun his military career in Iran as a mercenary; he had ridden with a band of Russian Cossacks when Russia controlled the north of Iran and Great Britain the south. Reza Khan emerged supreme in Iran in when he was crowned Reza Shah Pahlavi in April 1926. "Pahlavi," in the Farsi language of Iran, means "the heroic." The new shah embarked on a program of Westernization for Iran, much as his role model, Kemal Attaturk, had done in Turkey. Reza sought to drastically improve the economy of Iran, the name he chose to replace the ancient *Persia*, which he felt symbolized the backwardness of the country he now ruled. The Trans-Iranian Railroad was completed. In 1935, the first Western-style university was established in Tehran. The new shah organized the establishment of state-owned factories for consumer goods to be produced for the population. Under Justice Minister Ali Akhbar Davar, a Westernized code of law was introduced between 1927 and 1932.[11]

Part of Reza Shah's policy was to thwart the power of the traditional Muslim clergy, something that had also been part of Ataturk's program in Turkey. Pahlavi gained government control over the religious seminaries, or *madrassas*, and even saw to governmental licensing of the *mullahs*, the Islamic clerics who graduated from the religious schools. Mosques were even razed to make room for streets. The students at the schools, where the curriculum revolved around the study of the Quran, including the expectation that all students would memorize it word by word, were known as the *tale-bahs*, "the students." It is from this term that the words "Talib" and "Taliban" would emerge at a later point in Middle Eastern history. Any voices of dissent among the *madrassas* or the *mullahs* were harshly put down by Cossack tactics, ruthlessly overriding any opposition. Significantly, Reza Shah also moved in the direction of women's rights, removing the requirement to wear the traditional veil in 1936. He ordered the wearing of Western clothes for both sexes, eliminating the Islamic *chador* for Iranian women. More significantly, he ordered for the first time the total civil emancipation of the women and opened the secular schools to them. Before this, the religious hierarchy had controlled all education in Persia/Iran and women had been banned from attending school.

Reza Khan's tough rule preempted the rise of any Islamic political opposition to his reforms. In 1936, the year that the veil was abolished, his troops broke up a religious meeting to protest his reforms in the city of Mashdad, resulting in the killing of dozens and injury to many more. Reza Khan's overthrow, however, came from other sources. During the beginning of World War II, he alarmed both England and the Soviet Union with his pro-Nazi foreign policy, something shared with Rashid Ali in neighboring Iraq, who had seized power from Faisal II. Faisal II had only been three years old when his father King Ghazi I had been killed in a car accident in 1939. The regent appointed to rule in Faisal's name in Iraq was the little king's uncle Amir Abd al-Ilah. The Prime Minister was Nuri as-Said. In April 1941, the pro-German

Rashid Ali took power in Baghdad, forcing the regent and the prime minister to flee. It would take troops from the British forces then facing Rommel's Afrika Korps in North Africa to overthrow Rashid Ali and restore the regent and Nuri as-Said. When Reza Khan thus began to show pro-Nazi sympathies in Iran, England and the Soviets forced him from power, also in 1941. The first Pahlavi shah abdicated and went into exile in South Africa, where he died three years later. His twenty-two-year-old son, Mohammed Reza, succeeded him on Iran's Peacock Throne.*

It was in 1956 that Gamal Abdel Nasser of Egypt scored his greatest personal triumph: the seizure of the Suez Canal. The Suez Canal had been built in 1869, during the reign of the Khedive Ismail, who became the prototype of the modernizers to come in the Middle East. (The title *khedive* was of Persian origin and meant "ruler" or "sovereign." Ismail did not call himself "king" because Egypt was still technically part of the Ottoman Empire.) The khedive even set up a semirepresentative Chamber of Deputies in Cairo, probably the first even remotely democratic institution in the Arab world. He embarked on a massive program of administrative reform, which involved most aspects of Egyptian life, including education, agriculture, and the legal system. To modernize the Egyptian army, he turned to the U.S. Army for officers to retrain it in modern warfare. By doing so, Ismail become one of the few foreign rulers who realized that, after the American Civil War, the United States had one of the most advanced armies of the period. An American officer, Charles Stone, became the chief of staff of the Egyptian army.

The reforms Ismail inaugurated, however, ran up a tremendous debt, which reached some 90 to 100 million British pounds by the 1870s.[12] In 1875, in order to offset this indebtedness, the khedive sold his shares in the Suez Canal to the British through the negotiations of Prime Minister Benjamin Disraeli. The British purchase of the Suez Canal marked the beginning of the growth of British power in Egypt. When, in response to growing popular sentiment about great power interference in Egypt, Ismail defied England and France, their pressure on the Ottoman Empire forced the Sultan Abdul Hamid II to remove Ismail as the khedive. Ismail retired to Naples and exile while his son Tewfik succeeded him in Cairo. Yet the populist current

---

*Originally built for Mughal emperor Shah Jahan in the early seventeenth century, the Peacock Throne was among the most splendid thrones ever crafted. The golden chair was stolen from India by the Persians in 1739, but was lost sometime thereafter. It (and its reproductions) remained the symbol of Persian (or Iranian) monarchy, much as the term "the White House" represents the American presidency.

continued to run, and its spokesman would be the minister of war in Tewfik's administration, Major-General, previously Colonel, Arabi Pasha. In many wars, the rise of Arabi, the son of a village shaikh, to prominence mirrored the later rise of Nasser and the rest of the Free Officers Movement. He used the army as his path to influence in Tewfik's Egypt. When Arabi's power increased in Egypt, Tewfik removed him as minister of war. Arabi responded by having some shaikhs issue a *fatwa*, or religious ruling, that Tewfik was attacking both Egyptian sovereignty and Islam by continuing his father's policy of Westernization. The shaikh in fact lacked theological status to issue his degree, as only religious leaders can issue *authentic fatwas*! In Arabi's revolt, we see perhaps the first signs of an Islamic reaction to the modernization of a Muslim country. In 1882, the British invasion and conquest of the country had led to Egypt falling under the control of the British Empire.

On July 26, 1956, Nasser ordered the nationalization of the Suez Canal. His decision prompted a violent response from Great Britain; from France, which had an interest in the canal since its building by the Frenchman Ferdinand de Lesseps; and from Israel. Together, they invaded Egypt in the fall of 1956 and seized the canal. The threat of intervention by Soviet Premier Nikita Khrushchev caused American President Dwight D. Eisenhower to put pressure on the three countries to withdraw their armies. The resulting international uproar caused British Prime Minister Anthony Eden to resign from office. The image of Nasser standing up to the former imperial powers in Egypt and to the West in general made him a hero of epic proportions in the Arab world. Nasser dared to reach even further. He wrote of a union of all the Muslims of the world, "when I consider these hundreds of millions united by a single creed, I emerge with a sense of the tremendous possibilities which we might realize through the cooperation of all these Muslims."[13] There had been no Muslim or Arab leader of Nasser's stature since Saladin during the Third Crusade (1189–92).

Yet Nasser's thoughts were directed toward the modernization of the Arab world, not toward any real religious return to the roots of Islam. He was a classic example of the military modernizers who emerged at the same time in the underdeveloped Third World, anxious to drag their countries by any means into the modern world. Within Egypt, the building of the Aswan High Dam was only symbolic of the modernization Nasser envisaged for his homeland. He pushed through a campaign of what has been called Arab socialism in his efforts to make Egypt a rival of any country in the world.

Along with the changes in Egypt came an infusion of Western culture, since the West was—and still remains in 2002—the model for any country bent on modernization. Cairo became as Beirut once was, the most cosmopolitan city in the Arab world. Along with Western ideas came a liberalization of views on women. During more Islamic times, women had been restricted from taking part in Egyptian life and lived in semi-isolation in the condition known as *purdah*, the separation of Muslim women into their own closed society. This all dramatically changed as Egypt entered the modern world. Over the years, the women in Cairo began to abandon the *chador*, the whole-body covering of Islam, in favor of Western attire. It is no surprise that perhaps the first Arab feminist was an Egyptian woman, Dr. Doriah Shafaq, since Egyptian women, beginning with the French building of the Suez Canal, were the first to be exposed to Western ideas.[14]

At the same time, the country's educational institutions were open to Western ideas, a process that began during the British rule in the country. A new generation arose educated in the Western model, and receptive to new suggestions about Egypt and what should be the future of the country. The university graduates, the most forward-thinking people in the country, began to be faced with chronic underemployment as Egypt could not cope with the flood of educated people in her economy. This problem had begun during the period when England was the de facto ruler of the land of the pharaohs. In 1937, as Daniel Lerner wrote in *The Passing of Traditional Society*, "jobless Baccalaureates [university graduates] were estimated at 7,500 and unemployed graduates of Higher Schools at 3,500."[15] The restlessness of this educated class with nowhere to go would be a continual cause of instability in Egypt for years to come. Indeed, throughout the Arab world, it would be in many cases that the new traditionalist movement found its leaders among this disillusioned group in society.

Nasser's campaign to make Egypt the equal of any other power in the region, notably Israel, ignited a struggle for the spiritual soul of the country. Although Egypt was perhaps the first Arab country to be so affected, as with so much else in the modern history of the Middle East, the experience of Egypt, the intellectual capital of the Arab world, served as paradigm for the rest of the region. To paraphrase what the French say about Paris, when Egypt sneezes, the rest of the Middle East catches cold. As Nasser pushed Egypt into the present, he unwittingly set off a backlash among those who feared that traditional Islamic values and culture would be washed away by the tidal wave of modernity. In 1958, Lerner wrote, "the traditional founts of sacred symbolism are being overtaken by the new disseminators of secular knowledge."[16] Those who felt this way began to champion a return to traditional Islam—sometimes an idealized version of Islam that never really existed. Ironically, many of these were graduates of Egypt's modern universities who found "themselves torn by the imposed need to define Egypt's course in terms acceptable to traditional Islam."[17]

Throughout the Arab world, the same scenario was played out. The combination of harsh repression of political dissent as well as the ushering in of Western ways led to the growth of resentment against both the culture of the Western world and the repressive Arab regimes. The lack of any democratic outlet for public protest led many into the arms of the Islamic extremists who not only wanted to banish Western culture from *Dar al-Islam* but also the governments that seemed to be fostering it. It was the beginning of a cultural and political clash whose aftershocks are felt even today.

The clash between Islam and nationalism was a problem that colored the thought of one of the great voices of Arab nationalism, the Syrian Christian Orthodox Michel Aflaq. He had met Salah al-Din Bitar, a politician, and in 1940 had helped found the Movement for Arab Renaissance, or the Ba'ath movement, to build a modern—and secular—Syrian state. During a stormy career, he served in 1949 as minister for education in Syria, and in 1954 he became the secretary-general of the Ba'aths when the party merged with the Arab Socialist party. In 1968, Aflaq moved to Iraq when the Ba'ath party took power there. In 1970, he left Baghdad when he felt that Iraq was not giving enough support to the Palestinians, with whose struggle he identified. When he returned to Baghdad in 1974, he led the National Command of the party, and would live there until his death in 1989. Throughout his career, Aflaq kept to his vision of a secular Arab nationalism that would not be colored by religious creed: "There is no fear that nationalism will clash with religion, for, like religion, it flows from the heart and issues from the will of God; they walk arm in arm, supporting each other, especially when religion represents the genius of the nationality and is in harmony with nature."[18] It is one of the coincidences of this saga that Aflaq, the spokesman for a secular Arab nationalism, died in 1989, the same year as the Ayatollah Khomeini, the symbol of the extremist Islamic movement, which had at its heart the rejection of modern nationalism in the Arab world.

The Rebirth of Militant Islam

A militant Islamic reaction thus began within the new Arab states as a traditionalist backlash to the modernization of the Arab world after World War II. One of the hidden casualties of this new radicalism within *Dar al-Islam* is the Christian population of the Muslim states. From the Greek and Armenian Christians of Turkey to the Copts of Egypt, the Christians of the Middle East have religious roots that predate the Muslim conquest. The Acts of the Apostles in the New Testament refers to how the Christian community of Antioch, now in Syria, became the real center of Christianity after the schism with the Jews of Jerusalem over the need for circumcision as a sign of entry into the community. The Christians decided that circumcision was not needed to mark one as one of God's chosen people, while the Jews of Jerusalem adhered to the idea that it was. As William Dalrymple as observed in his book *From the Holy Mountain: A Journey among the Christians of the Middle East*, even though many of the Christians are racially Arab, like the Palestinian Christian wife of Yassir Arafat, the radical Muslims are on the offensive against them. In Turkey, old churches were being converted into mosques, and, goaded by the growing Muslim radicalism, there is a fear among Christian people of the type of pogroms that struck the Suriani and Armenian Christians in Turkey during the First World War. In the village of Tur Abdin, an old priest told Dalrymple, "all our people are leaving. One by one our monasteries and our Christian communities are emptying."[1]

The reaction against the native Christians was no more grim than within Egypt. In 1992, writes Dalrymple, the Islamist guerrillas of the Gema'at' al-Islamiyya, the terrorist group destabilizing Egypt today, slaughtered fourteen Copts in Asyut because they refused to pay into the Islamist protection racket, an act of terrorism more closely associated with American gangster Al Capone than with Islam.[2] In 1994, also in Asyut, two Coptic monks and two lay people were killed at the old Coptic church of Deir ul-Muharraq. When Dalrymple was in Egypt, the Church of St. Michael and the Virgin in the Cairene suburb of Ein Shams was attacked by Islamic *irhebi*, terrorists, who cried out "*Islamaya Islamaya, la Mesihaya wa la Yahoudaya*" ("Islam, Islam, no Christians, no Jews"), and "Kill the Christians! Kill the Christians!"[3] The police, in keeping with President Mubarak's policy of protecting the Christians, sent two trucks of officers to drive away the rioters. Nevertheless, the riots were symptomatic of the new persecution of Christians in the Middle East by the radical Muslims, a persecution which is causing some of the region's best hope for a modernized future, the educated Christian class, whether Arab or not, to seek religious freedom largely in the United States, like the Pilgrims did three hundred years ago. The loss to Middle Eastern progress of this Christian "brain drain" cannot be assessed as yet, but it will be great. It should be noted that the largest group of Christians in the area, according to my Lebanese sources, live in Lebanon, where most of them adhere to the Maronite Rite of the Roman Catholic Church; many of the Lebanese, according to my sources, claim descent from the Phoenicians of ancient times, predating by millennia the arrival of the Arabs into the coastal plain. Many of the names associated with Arab nationalism, both for good and ill, have been Christians, from George Antonius, author of the landmark book *The Arab Awakening*, to the Palestinian terrorist George Habash. It is a unique commentary on the intolerance of today's radicals that Habash, one of the *betes noires* the "worst fears" of the West and of Israel in the 1970s, might be rejected by the militants of today because of his religion! Indeed, if he were an Afghan Muslim who converted to Christianity, Habash would very likely be executed.

Considering the ferocity of modern Islamic radicalism in Egypt, it is not surprising that Egypt was its birthplace, with the Muslim Brotherhood in 1928. The founder of the Muslim Brotherhood, *al-Ikhwan al Muslimun*, was school teacher Hassan al-Banna. The Egyptian Sayyid Qutb, who studied in the United States, was an outstanding spokesman of the new fundamentalism, and critic of the secularism of Arab leaders like Nasser. Consequently, Nasser would imprison him, and in 1968 execute him. Earlier, al-Banna had preceded Qutb to the grave. During World War II era, al-Banna had tried to form an alliance with the Free Officers, but they rebuffed him because they were following a secular agenda for Egypt. When the Brotherhood's activities were seen to threaten the Egyptian government after the war, Prime Minister Mahmud Nurashi banned the organization. The prime minister was later assassinated, as mentioned above, by a member of the Brotherhood. In retaliation, al-Banna was killed, most likely by government agents, on February 12, 1949.

Qutb drew on the thinking of Indian Muslim Maulana Maudoodi, according to Emmanuel Sivan in *Radical Islam: Medieval Theology and Modern Politics*. Qutb developed a philosophy that those Arab states that pursued a modern pragmatic policy were as much enemies of Islam as were the traditional foes outside the Muslim world. Writing in his book *Signposts on the Road*, Qutb stated his declaration of war against modern Arab Pan-Arabism: "[A Muslim's] *jihad* is solely geared to protect the religion of Allah and His Sha'ria and to save the Abode of Islam [*Dar al-Islam*] and no other territory. . . . Any land that combats the Faith, hampers Muslims from practicing their religion, or does not apply the Sha'ria, becomes ipso facto part of the Abode of War [*Dar al-Harb*]."[4]

Qutb went so far as to divide societies into those of the Order of Islam, which followed traditional Islamic teaching, and those of the Order of Jahiliya, meaning those that were ignorant, decadent, and corrupt. In the Order of Jahiliya, he placed all the modernist Arab regimes, including his own. Indeed, in his writings like the *Shubuhat Hawl al-Islam*, published in Cairo in 1954, Qutb used the term for "crusader," *salibi*, and the word *al-salibiyah*, "the land of the crusaders," to describe the Western world of his own day. The writings of the lesser-known Abd Allah Inan point out the same identification of the modern West with the Crusaders of the Middle Ages. An English language translation of his main work, *Decisive Moments in the History of Islam*, was published in Lahore, Pakistan, in 1949. In the revised editions of the original Arabic edition of his work, which first appeared in Cairo in 1934, Inan's introduction grew ever more strident against the *salibi* West. Wrote Inan, "the basic idea of this book [is] the perpetual struggle between East and West, Islam and Christianity. The reader will see how the Crusading idea has remained for centuries the axis of this struggle, and how it has blazed the more vigorously whenever a new Islamic outburst of power or revival has appeared."[5] It is in these writings that one can see the ideological grounds for the modern Islamic *jihad*, or holy war, against the United States and the West.

Another critical Islamic thinker was Abu al-Ala Mawdudi, who lived in what is now Pakistan. He is probably the same writer referred to by Emmanuel Sivan as Maulana Maudoudi and by Khalid Bin Sayeed in *Western Dominance and Politcal Islam* as "Sayyid Abul Ala Maudoudi." In a lecture given at the University of Maryland on March 28, 2000, Professor of Government and Politics at George Mason University Dr. Adeed Dawisha discussed how Mawdudi and Qutb's growing ideology formed the background for the Islamic backlash toward the West and the Arab governments that had embraced Western institutions. Mawdudi especially loathed nationalism, secularism, and democracy as "imported institutions" which had no place, and no legitimacy, in the Islamic community, the *umma islamiyya*. Mawdudi felt that these three concepts were thoroughly corrupt and the cause of much of the evil of mankind, according to Dawisha. Furthermore, Mawdudi saw such manmade concepts as totally out of context in an Islamic society whose sole source of law would be the divinely inspired *sharia*. The idea that people should make laws, which of course is at the heart of democracy, he considered to be absolute apostasy. Without manmade laws, there could be no guarantee of human dignity or human rights, the cornerstone of the Western political tradition which both Qutb and Mawdudi totally rejected. Here lay the root of the theological tyranny that the Ayatollah Khomeini would one day inspire in Iran and the Taliban's leader Mullah Mohammed Omar would institute in Afghanistan. Without any acknowledged charter of rights, the citizens of a country would be totally subject to the interpretation of the *sharia* by the theocrats who ruled their country. And since theocrats were considered to be the only ones qualified to rule on such matters, there was no recourse to their dictates.

In short, the new fundamentalist philosophers were now leveling the same charges at the current generation of pragmatist Muslim political leaders that their ancestors had made against the Crusaders and the Mongols! These ideologues of extremism found ready support in organizations like the Brotherhood. As Thomas W. Lippman pointed out, "the organization's appeal—austere, puritannical, culturally untainted by the West, dedicated—provides useful coloration for any revolutionary network in the Muslim world, where politics often take on a religious guise."[6]

Mention must be again made here of the terminology I have been employing. It is helpful to be reminded that by "Islamic fundamentalism," I do not mean those devout Muslims who follow dutifully the commands of their faith, adhering closely to the Islamic way of life as propagated in the Quran, the sayings of the Prophet, and the decisions over the years of Muslim ecclesiastical authorities according to the *sharia*. Here I mean by "Islamic fundamentalism" the intolerant and dictatorial view of groups like the Taliban in Afghanistan who believe in a harsh rule imposed by a state theocratic dictatorship that follows the most severe interpretation of the Quran and the *sharia*, a dire religious view which was never contemplated by Mohammed, and which had no place in the glory days of the caliphate itself. Human rights groups like Amnesty International and Human Rights Watch have censored "fundamentalist" regimes like the Taliban for their harshness, especially toward Muslim women, who were denied even basic education by the *mullahs* of Kabul.

The ideological extremism of the new "fundamentalists" in Islam can easily be understood in Western terms—it is no philosophical enigma. One only has to look back at the French Revolution of 1789 to see a historic antecedent for what has been going on in the Sudan under Turabi and Iran under Khomeini and his followers. Indeed, Turabi and Khomeini represent the St. Just and the Marat of the French Revolution. Once they had deposed Louis XVI in France, much as Khomeini deposed the shah in Iran some 190 years later, the French revolutionaries tried to build a republic of morality, the rule of virtue, in France. However, when a republic is built on morality, those who cannot live up to its tenets are not just criminals, but heretics who must be destroyed. As Albert Camus wrote in *The Rebel* about the French revolutionary Republic of Virtue, "every form of disobedience to law therefore comes, not from an imperfection in the law, which is presumed to be impossible, but from a lack of virtue in the refractory citizen."[7] Camus goes on to say that in such a case, "morality, when it is formal, devours," because since "absolute virtue is impossible . . . the republic of forgiveness leads, with implacable logic, to the republic of the guillotine."[8] This is the lesson that the Iranians learned under Ayatollah Khomeini, and the Sudan is learning today under Turabi. Let us hope that the current president of Iran, the Ayatollah Khameni, represents the beginning of Iran's Thermidorian Reaction (which took place in France after the execution—by guillotine—of the arch state-terrorist Robespierre), when cooler heads can prevail than during the revolutionary heyday of Khomeini's Republican Guards.

Naturally, the new secularist Muslim governments considered such thinkers a real danger to their states and secular leaders, like Nasser in Egypt, reacted harshly against them. When the Free Officers Movement took power in 1952 and overthrew King Farouk, "the three political parties which could have challenged the power of the officers—the Wafd, the Communists, and the Moslem Brethren—were legally abolished, their leaders prosecuted and imprisoned."[9] Throughout the 1960s and 1970s, the secularist governments kept close watch on the Brotherhood and its many offshoots, vigorously cracking down on signs of unrest. There were grounds for such vigilance. In Egypt in 1974, the Islamic Liberation Group attempted an attack on the Technical Military Academy in Cairo. In Syria, the Muslim Brotherhood engaged in large-scale rioting against the Ba'ath party government in 1964 and 1967.

However, it would take more than ten years for the Islamic militancy of the Brotherhood and its spiritual children to become a force to be reckoned with in the Muslim world. And this would occur, once again, on one of the frontiers of *Dar al-Islam*: Afghanistan. On April 27, 1978, Nur Mohammed Taraki, chief of the Marxist Peoples' Democratic party (PDP), took power in Kabul. Christian fundamentalist Rev. Carl McIntyre of New Jersey was the only eyewitness to provide an account of the army tanks in the streets of the capital city the night of the coup on short wave radio. The coup was the end result of years of infiltration of the Afghan armed forces by the Communists, backed by their powerful neighbor, the Soviet Union. In December 1978, Taraki's regime signed a Treaty of Peace and Friendship with the USSR, a pact that would have dire consequences for Afghanistan before the year's end. However, disunion within the ranks of the PDP apparently caused the mysterious death of President Taraki on October 6, 1979. The Soviets were still not content with Hafizullah Amin, who took the place of the deceased Taraki. All along they had favored the more pro-Moscow Babrak Karmal of the Parcham Wing of the PDP.

As 1979 wore on, it became evident that President Amin was losing the fight against the growing fundamentalist movement that resented both the Communist regime in Kabul and the increasing presence of the "infidel" Soviets. Amin had to appeal for Soviet help to fight the insurgents. It became increasingly clear to the Soviet ground commander Marshal Ivan Pavlovsky, that Amin could not control the situation. Therefore, a process began whereby growing numbers of Soviet troops, most of central Asian stock, entered Afghanistan in a creeping takeover. The process culminated on December 27, 1979, when Soviet *spetsnaz* special forces attacked Amin in the Darulaman Palace and killed him and his family. In Amin's place, the

Soviets put Babrak Karmal, who was brought from Moscow to lead the new Parcham government.

To the Soviets, and to the Communist Karmal, the occupation of Afghanistan was just another exercise of the Brezhnev Doctrine, under which Soviet and Warsaw Bloc forces had invaded Czechoslovakia in 1968. The Brezhnev Doctrine held that when events in a Soviet "satellite" went contrary to the foreign policy of the USSR, Soviet and allied forces had a need to intervene. The Soviet Union felt threatened by the liberalism of Alexander Dubcek in Prague in 1968, and the inability of Amin to quell the growing militant Islamic revolt in Afghanistan, which Moscow feared might spread to Soviet central Asia, which was largely Muslim. Hence, in both incidents, the Soviet Union intervened militarily to protect its interests—coincidentally, the elite 104th Guards Airborne Division led both attacks. (Today, the 104th is part of the Byelorussian Army.)

However, unlike the surrender of Dubcek's regime, which had no lasting effects (after "rehabilitation" Dubcek served as an administrator in the Czech Forestry Department), the coup in Kabul only served to inflame the growing Muslim backlash against the Communist infidels in the Darulaman Palace. The fighters in what was rapidly becoming a true *jihad* called themselves the *mujahidin*, or "soldiers of the faith." While the administration of U.S. President Jimmy Carter saw the Soviet invasion of Afghanistan as simply another Soviet expansion of the Cold War, President Ronald Reagan saw it in more metaphysical terms. As a lifelong anti-Communist, Reagan saw the Soviet invasion as another attack of the "evil empire." Indeed, of all Western leaders he was the closest in mindset to the *mujahidin* in Afghanistan: For him, too, the war against aggression by the Soviet "evil empire" was a holy war. Consequently, upon his inauguration as president in January 1981, Regan began an intensive program of covert aid to the *mujahidin*, using the CIA as one of the prime means, but also relying heavily on the support of the Pakistan of pro-Western leader President Mohammed Zia al-Haq. Pakistani intelligence provided invaluable support to the CIA because of its intimate knowledge of the country and the people, which in the southern part of Afghanistan were Pathan. In a sense, the Pathan tribes, now Pakistani citizens, were involved in their third *jihad* in ninety years: the North-West Frontier Rising in 1898, the Third Afghan War of 1919, and now the Soviet invasion of Afghanistan, which can be called the Fourth Afghan War. Supply caravans would leave Pakistan for Afghanistan and deliver their supplies to the *mujahidin* "in country." Although begun by President Carter as the covert CIA Operation Cyclone, aid to the resistance reached new highs during the Reagan administration. It was the authorization of President Reagan to supply the resistance with advanced weapons like the Stinger ground-to-air missiles which helped neutralize the air superiority the Soviets and their Parcham Afghan allies enjoyed. The Afghan Resistance movements also had their headquarters in Pakistani cities like Lahore and Quetta, as would the supporters of the Taliban and al-Qaeda in 2001.

Although the Afghan resistance would remain fragmented, during the course of the decade of war, thousands of Muslims throughout the Islamic world flocked to join the Afghan *jihad*. It had the galvanizing effect on a generation of Muslims similar to the effect that the Spanish Civil War had had sixty years earlier on American and European liberals and leftists. These "Arab Afghans" became imbued with the spirit of *jihad* as Muslims had not been since the days of the Crusades. One of these fighters in what the Russians called the *Afghansti voina,* the Afghan war, was a young Saudi Arabian named Osama bin Laden. At first, bin Laden would be dismissed as "the Bedouin," but the Afghan fighters would later respect him for the combat uses to which he would put the Saudi engineering education he had received at Abdul Aziz University.

Another Afghan alumnus was Ramzi Ahmed Yousef, convicted in September 1996 in the 1993 World Trade Center bombing in New York City. Yousef would be arrested in Pakistan, one of the main training grounds for the Arab Afghans during the war, as would be Mir Aimal Kansi, who had shot to death two CIA officials outside of the agency's headquarters in 1993. In retrospect, Yousef seemed to provide a sinister link between the bombing of the World Trade Center in 1993 and the devastating assault on September 11, 2001. During the investigation into the 1993 incident, the FBI had discovered that Yousef had talked about flying a plane into a building. His confederate Abdul Hakim Murad had taken flying lessons. It is possible that the fanatic dreams of Murad and Yousef may have in fact been the rough draft of the conspiracy that resulted in the attacks of September 11, 2001.

The spirit of the *jihad* also affected the Muslim troops who had first been sent into Afghanistan by the Soviet Union, like the Uzbeks and Tajiks. Increasingly, they were relegated to garrison duties in the cities like Kabul and Herat, while the search-and-destroy operations conducted by the Soviets on behalf of their Parcham allies were entrusted to the European Russian soldiers, who would be immune to the cry of the *mullahs*. For the European Russians, such an experience was a disaster in morale, as they were committed to fighting a war that virtually made the entire population of the country their enemies.

In 1989, Soviet Premier Gorbachev began the Soviet withdrawal from the Afghan quagmire, with the morale of his troops terribly low. (However, well-placed sources have informed me that full Soviet withdrawal was never made; that Soviet elite troops simply changed into the uniforms of the Communist regime still in power in Kabul. Other sources have told me that the Tajik and Uzbek warlords still holding out against the Taliban in northern Afghanistan were actually former Soviet central Asian soldiers who simply stopped wearing any uniforms at all!) However, by the spring of 2001, their rear guard fight against the Taliban militants seemed largely to be doomed. When in 2001 the Taliban fundamentalist regime in Kabul announced their policy of destroying Afghanistan's ancient Buddhist statues at Bamiyan as a part of a campaign against "idolatry" in Afghanistan, the Taliban fighters controlled some 90 percent of the country. Nevertheless, an interesting figure in this new "great game" was the Uzbek warlord Abdul Rashid Dostam, from Afghanistan's Jawzjan province. In an article, "Taliban Turnaround: The Rise and Fall of Afghanistan's Islamic Militia," in the February 1999 *Soldier of Fortune* magazine, interesting photos were published, although uninterpreted by the author Jake Bordner. In one photo, Dostam's troops are pictured fully armed and wearing uniforms, including battle helmets, hardly the romantic picture of the bearded and turbaned *mujahidin* of the 1980s! Dostam's troops are marching as professional soldiers in perfect, Russian-style formation. In fact, they all appear to be carrying Russian AK-74s, and carrying them in characteristic Russian style. This photo, and another accompanying it, argue, I feel, for the theory of a continued, if covert, Russian presence in northern Afghanistan in the armies of "Afghan" warlords like Abdul Dostam.) In 1992, with the inability of Moscow to continue to support its client state in Afghanistan, Kabul fell to the Afghan resistance, which immediately began to fight among itself over a division of the spoils. However, whatever the fate of Kabul, a new type of Muslim warrior had been created: the Arab Afghan. Formed in the crucible of the Afghan war, these fundamentalist fighters were determined to continue the holy war against all infidels in the *Dar-al-Harb*—including their former American allies, who only late in the game realized the potential threat of these militant Islamic soldiers. By 1990, with the postwar situation becoming apparent in Afghanistan, some people in the public sector were already voicing concern about an extremist Islamic regime taking power in Kabul. In pre-Taliban Afghanistan, the main concern was for Gulbuddin Hekmatyar and his Hizb-i-Islami. Hekmatyar had already gained a reputation for a fierceness beyond that of the rest of the *mujahidin*. Prime Minister of Pakistan Benazir Bhutto (1988–90; 1993–96), who had succeeded Zia ul-Haq, warned the American ambassador that the United States was creating a "Frankenstein monster" in Afghanistan. At the same time, Russian leader Mikhail Gorbachev, for his part, wished to prop up Najibullah, the Soviet proxy in Kabul, as a way of preventing the extremists from gaining power in Afghanistan after the Soviet retreat. Graham E. Fuller, former vice chairman of the National Intelligence Council and in 1990 a senior political scientist at the Rand Corporation think tank, wrote in the spring 1990 issue of *Foreign Policy*, "the last thing Moscow needs is an ideologically hostile regime in Kabul bent on revenge against the Soviet Union—especially on the heels of such a powerful, symbolic event to Soviet Muslims as a *mujahidin* Islamic victory over the Red Army. . . . Almost any political settlement in Afghanistan would suffice for Gorbachev, unless it brought to power radical Islamic fundamentalists—something the United States does not want either."[10] Moreover, the war in Afghanistan against the hated Shurawi, the Russians, made possible what had always seemed impossible, the strategic unification of both militant Sunni and Shi'ite Muslim groups in the face of the common Soviet enemy. This development would have dire consequences for the future growth of fundamentalist terrorism, including its impact on the United States.

During the time of the radicalization of the Arab Afghans in the war, militant Islam experienced a spiritual revival with the 1979 fall of the shah, Reza Shah Pahlavi, in Iran, who had been the American ally in the battle against the Russians in neighboring Afghanistan. Although speculative, it would not have been beyond the reach of the Soviet KGB to have played a role in destabilizing the shah, since he was America's main ally in the early days of the Afghan War. Additionally, Iran and the Soviet Union had had a defense pact since the 1920s, which could have given any Iranian communists grounds to covertly invoke the Brezhnev Doctrine to gain Soviet support for removing the shah. Prior to the fall of the Peacock Throne, the Iranian Tudeh party had probably been the strongest communist party in Asia outside the Soviet Union. Thus, in 1979, the shah was toppled from his throne by the fundamentalist Ayatollah Ruhollah Khomeini, *ayatollah* meaning a *mullah* who had attained a high degree of sacred wisdom. Immediately, Islamic fervor became the hallmark of the new regime in Tehran as the Islamic Guards seized the U.S. embassy, America having been cast by the militant Iranian *ayatollahs* as the new "Great Satan," the symbol of all that was corrupt and decadent about the West. To them, the shah had been merely a corrupt and willing puppet of the American Satan.

It is interesting that the Soviet Union took great pains never to antagonize Iran, largely, one assumes, because of the fear that Tehran could ignite the religious fervor of the Muslim multitudes in Soviet central Asia. Significantly, when the Ayatollah Khomeini issued his *fatwa* of death against author Salman Rushdie for allegedly blaspheming the Prophet Mohammed in his *Satanic Verses*, no Russian literary organization voice was raised to join the chorus of denunciation. In June 1989, after Khomeini's death, Gorbachev personally welcomed to Moscow the representative of the government in Tehran, the Ayatollah Hashemi Rafsanjani. Gorbachev said on the occasion, "we are receiving a representative of the state which is our old neighbor and which embarked on the path of revolutionary renewal. . . . We heard that your visit is the realization of the will of the late Imam [Khomeini]."[11] And, one may add, the Soviet embassy had not been seized in 1979.

While Khomeini was establishing his theocracy on the remnants of the Pahlavi monarchy, war broke out between Iran and Iraq in the fall of 1980. Ostensibly over control of the Shatt al Arab waterway, it was really a contest to see which country would be the great power in the region: Iraq or Iran. About this time, Saddam Hussein was strengthening his hold over the Ba'ath party, which controlled Iraq. What started as a traditional struggle between two countries for supremacy developed into a struggle between two ideologies. Hussein saw himself as the successor to Nasser as the strong man of the Arab world; he was the epitome of the modern Arab *shoguns*. Hussein embraced the modernization of the Arab world and the riches which came to him with his power. A Muslim friend told me rumors of the opulence of Hussein's palaces: They supposedly had golden banisters inside. Hussein also was rumored to have some $3 to 4 billion (U.S.) in Swiss bank accounts for a retirement fund if he were ever overthrown.

The downfall of the shah was not the sole goal of Ayatollah Khomeini. As Robin Wright notes in her *Sacred Rage: The Wrath of Militant Islam*, "the second phase of the Islamic crusade [was] the use of Arab cadre, recruited or imported from surrounding countries, to spread the revolution" begun with the overthrow of the decadent and corrupt shah.[12] Muslim militants, whether Shi'ite or Sunni, were all welcomed by the new "Council for the Islamic Revolution," which was headed by the ayatollah's heir apparent, the Ayatollah Hussein Ali Montazeri. In November 1979, the same month the American embassy in Tehran was seized, Iranian President Ali Khameni boasted, "We have aided the [Islamic] liberation movements in the best possible way."[13] Islamic Iran would now be the source of funds and training camps for any Muslims anxious to carry out the permanent holy war preached by the Ayatollah Khomeini and his disciples.

With the war against Iraq, Khomeini saw an opportunity to export his puritanic version of Islam while humbling Iran's national rival, Iraq. To do so, he drew on a third, cultural factor—the belief in total war that was the heritage of central Asia, brought into the region by Genghiz Khan. The boundary line between Iraq and Iran was more than just a "line in the sand" drawn by the former British colonial masters, it marked the cultural fault line between the Arab world and the world of central Asia, with Iranians and Turkish tribes farther to the east and the Mongols to the northeast around the Altai Mountains. The clash between Saddam and Khomeini underscored yet again the often forgotten truth that while all who profess Islam are Muslims not all Muslims are Arabs.

In the beginning of the war, Iran suffered from the chaos in its army caused by the fall of the shah. To offset this tactical deficit, Khomeini crafted a strategy that was as cynical as it was brilliant. Religious fanaticism had always been a hallmark of Shi'ite Islam as practiced in Iran. In 680 C.E., Hussein, the grandson of Mohammed the Prophet, was killed in battle at Qarbala in Iraq, defending his legitimacy as the successor to Mohammed against the Umayyid caliph. His followers, the Shi'ites, commemorate his death each year in the Feast of Ashura, when men cut themselves with knives in memory of his bloody death. The Shi'ite sect derives its name from the Arabic word meaning "party." Thus the Shi'ites, or Shi'ias as they have also been referred to, consider themselves to be "the party" of Ali. The Shi'ite interpretation of Islam was used by Khomeini in his establishment of a Muslim theocracy in the hitherto secular society of Iran. An explanation of this theocratic tendency can be found in this quote from *Shi'a*, written by Allamah Sayyid Husayn Tabatabai and translated by Sayyid Husayn Nasr:*

---

*Tabatabai's work is a book available on the Internet only.

Shi'ism believes that the Divine Law of Islam (Shari'ah), whose substance is found in the Book of God [*The Holy Quran*] and in the tradition (Sunnah) of the Prophet, will remain valid until the Day of Judgement and can never, nor will ever, be altered. A government which is really Islamic cannot under any pretext refuse completely to carry out the Sha'riah's injunctions. The only duty of an Islamic government is to make decisions by consultation within the limits set by the Sha'riah and in accordance with the demands of the moment.[14]

Ingeniously, Khomeini married this tradition of Shi'ite zealotry to the central Asian tradition of total warfare. The result were the *basiji*, who played a major role in the Iranian Fateh offensive against the Iraqis in March and April 1982. According to Robin Wright, who saw them in action, they were young boys, only nine to sixteen years old, who led the Iranian attacks by running through the Iraqi mine fields to clear the way for the Iranian regular army and Republican Guards! As Wright reported in *Sacred Rage*, "wearing white headbands to signify the embracing of death, and shouting '*Shahid! Shahid!* (Martyr! Martyr!),' they literally blew their way into heaven." The number of these youths was never disclosed but, as Wright noted, "a walk through the residential suburbs of Iranian cities provided a clue. Window after window, block after block, displayed black-bordered photographs of teenage or pre-teen youths."[15]

The recourse to suicide squads in the Fateh offensive was perhaps the first time that this tactic had been seen in the Middle East since the Turkish and Mongol tribes had been united in Genghiz Khan's horde. When Khan launched his attack in battle, the *Mangudai*, or "God-belonging," were the first to be thrown against the enemy.[16] It was this "suicide squad" which opened the battles Khan fought in the Kharesmian Empire, which controlled Iran and Iraq during his march of conquest around 1219. There had been fanatical charges when the Janissaries of Mehmet II had hurled themselves against the high walls of Constantinople in 1453, but these were born of military necessity to take the city after a long siege. The Janissaries were no more self-consciously seeking death than the "forlorn hope" squadrons which the British Duke of Wellington had sent against the gates of Badajoz and San Sebastian when he fought the French armies in Spain during the Napoleonic Wars, or for that matter the charges of Napoleon's own heavy cavalry cuirassiers against the infantry squares of Wellington's army at

Waterloo in 1815. On the other hand, the *Mangudai* of Genghiz Khan and the *basiji* of Khomeini actively sought death and paradise in battle, unlike the Janissaries, who fought for victory and glory. For the first time in the 750 years since the *Mangudai* had fought on Iranian soil, Khomeini had introduced suicide warriors into the Middle East. The region, and the world, would never be the same again.

Khomeini later included older men in the ranks of the *basiji*, only these were to be used to export his personal *jihad* into the rest of the Muslim world. An issue of *Jeune Afrique* magazine in 1984 carried a photo of bearded young Iranian men sitting in a class, wearing a red bandanna painted with Quranic scriptures around their heads and photos of their ayatollah on their breasts. By the hollow look in their eyes as they peered at the camera, it seemed that they had already made their "covenant with death." Young men from all over the Muslim world, animated by the Khomeini revolution in Iran and the war against the Soviet Union in Afghanistan, went to join the Iranian *basiji*. Once trained and indoctrinated, they were ready to return to their native countries and spread the ideology of suicidal warfare.

It was not long before the radicalized Arabs were able to spread the doctrine of their new holy war throughout the world, both in the land of Islam and the land of war. On October 6, 1982, while watching a parade commemorating the 1973 Arab-Israeli War, President Anwar Sadat of Egypt was assassinated by Egyptian army militants in revenge for his signing in 1977 the Camp David Accords with Israel. The leader of the hit squad was Lt. Khalid Amid Shawki Islambouli. He and his fellow conspirators belonged to the Al Jihad Organization, whose spiritual leader was Shaikh Omar Abdul Rahman, a blind cleric who taught at Asyut University in Egypt. In 1978, using his religious powers, the shaikh had issued a *fatwa*, religious decree, branding Sadat an infidel and deserving of death for abandoning Islam by making peace with the Zionist enemy. (Such a crime, apostasy, is one of the few offenses, Muslim religious leaders have told me, that is a capital offense within Islam.) Ten years later, the shaikh's son would be leading militant Muslims, Arab Afghans, against the government of the new Republic of Tajikistan.

Hosni Mubarak, Sadat's successor, kept up the peace efforts with Israel and also firmly repressed the militant movement in Islam. Islambouli and all his accomplices were executed for their plot to kill President Sadat. In 1982, the militants attempted to kill Mubarak, which only intensified his campaign against them. In the 1980s, the Muslim Brotherhood, with which Mubarak had tried to reach an agreement, began increasingly to support radical groups like the Al Jihad organization. According to the (Paris) *International Herald Tribune* (June 27–28, 1987), militant groups could call on some 70,000 to 100,000 adherents in Egypt alone.

Indeed, the battle between the militants and Mubarak's government continues unabated today. By late 1998, some 45,000 or more had been killed in what amounts to a civil war between the government and the militants. On June 26, 1995, the Islamic terrorists struck at President Mubarak himself. While visiting Ethiopia, Mubarak was ambushed in the capital, Addis Ababa. Although Mubarak escaped injury, two Ethiopian policemen and two terrorists were killed in the attack. The severity of the fighting was brought home to us in the West when some forty tourists at the historic site of Luxor were massacred in 1997 by the militants, who have declared that foreign tourists are now considered open targets of opportunity by the Muslim Brotherhood and its radical allies. Again, the militants see themselves fighting for a purified Muslim state against a corrupt and decadent Westernized regime in Cairo. The spirit of Sayyid Qutb is alive and well in Egypt thirty years after his death.

Up until 2002, the only country in the historic Holy Land to be affected by such militancy has been Syria, which even in the days of the Crusader states could be said to have constituted a warlike northern front of Islam against the crusaders. It was in Greater Syria, at Antioch, rather than in Palestine, that the Seljuqs had contested the passage of the First Crusade. Even throughout the crusader period, strong Seljuq states like the Sultanate of Rum in Greater Syria and Asia Minor fought the knights of the Cross. Modern militancy in Syria was, however, a direct importation from Egypt, in the fighting south. Its Muslim Brotherhood was established in Syria in the 1930s by religious students returning from Egypt. In 1944, the chief of the group in Damascus was Mustafa al Sibai, a graduate from Al Azhar University in Cairo. During his sojurn in Egypt Sibai was also a friend of Hassan al-Banna, who had founded the Brotherhood in Egypt in 1928. Also, when Nasser banned the Muslim Brotherhood in Egypt in 1954, many of its brethren found sanctuary in Syria.

When the Ba'ath party seized power in Damascus in 1963, the Brotherhood was banned, as was any group that stood in the way of the Ba'athist program of secularist Arabic socialism. Maxime Rodinson wrote in *Israel and the Arabs*, "thus in the spring of 1963, the Eastern Arab world was dominated by two regimes, both avowedly socialist in spirit and both pan-Arab nationalist: the Ba'ath in Iraq and Syria, and Nasserism in Egypt."[17] From the beginning, the Brotherhood found itself on a collision course with the Ba'athists, who still rule Syria. Throughout the Ba'ath period, the Brotherhood continued to fight a struggle, often violent, against the Ba'ath party and its secular and modernizing program for Syria. In June 1979, the paramilitary Brotherhood raided the Aleppo Artillery School, and succeeded in killing eighty-three cadets in the surprise attack. Infuriated by the Aleppo slaughter, Syrian Presiden Hafez Assad (1931–2000) was anxious for a day of reckoning. In early February 1982, the Brotherhood, now united with other militants in the Islamic Front, ambushed elements of the Syrian 3rd Armored Division near the city of Hama, which they then seized. Assad decided it was time to settle accounts with the Brotherhood once and for all. With 12,000 soldiers, the Syrian army fought the Brotherhood for possession of the city. When the two-week struggle ended, some 5,000 to 10,000 people had been killed, including 1,000 troops. However, with his ruthless use of force, Assad crushed the Islamic Front as a danger to his rule and that of the Ba'ath party. It may be interesting to note that a stronghold of the Assassins was a castle outside Hama. It may be possible that descendants of the order have continued to live in the region ever since its "destruction" and that, in common with the secret societies that are so much a part of militant Islam, it played a role in the rebellion against Assad and the Ba'athist regime. Masyaf, in the southern Syrian coastal mountains, was a center of the Nizaris or Assassins, during the Crusading period as well, and even today a Nizari community occupies the town. Thus, the involvement of the ancient Order of Assassins in modern Islamic militancy, as well as more modern evolutions like the Muslim Brotherhood, cannot be dismissed. Indeed, the imagery of the Order of Assassins continues today. Osama bin Laden, concealed in the rugged vastness of Afghanistan and sending his suicidal killers out to carry on his personal *jihad*, is as close as we shall get to a modern version of Hasan-i Sabah, "the Old Man of the Mountains."

Meanwhile, the militant movement had spread like a new *jihad* throughout the lands of the Mahgreb, "the land of the sunset," in North Africa, in Islam's robust African southern frontier. Fundamentalists in these countries, which had once supplied the manpower for the Muslim invasions of Spain, now turned on their own secularist governments. In Algeria, the FLN, the National Liberation Front, which had ruled the country since winning independence from Gaullist France in 1962, was opposed by the Islamic Salvation Front (FIS), which, as in so many other cases, perceived the FLN as too pro-Western, especially pro-French, and against the establishment of a truly Islamic state based on the severe application of the Muslim *sharia*. The enforcement of the *sharia* as the law of the land is the touchstone of all the modern militant movements. When the FIS was on the verge of winning control of the country through national elections, the westernized Algerian army seized power in January 1992. As Mark Huband wrote in *Warriors of the Prophet: The Struggle for Islam*, "a five-man collective leadership was appointed as the public front of the military regime, under the name of the High Committee of the State."[18] The chief of the committee was Gen. Mohammed Boudiaf, a hero of the war against the French, one of the nine "chiefs" who founded the FLN. On June 29, 1992, the terrorists of the FIS killed Boudiaf while he was giving a speech. In 1994, Gen. Liamine Zeroual became chief of state. (In the two years before Zeroual took power, Algerian leadership had been in a deadly state of flux.)

Seeing itself denied victory in the election, the FIS began a savage guerrilla warfare against the Algerian government. Here again, a militant uprising was aided by the Arab Afghans. According to Huband's informant, Karim Omar, a Syrian who had fought in Afghanistan, "between 1988 and 1992, around a thousand Algerians returned home from Afghanistan, even before the crisis started."[19] Among these were Jaafar al-Afghani and Tayeb al-Afghani. These former *mujahidin* would become the strike troops, the modern *ghazis*, of the FIS in the war that had started. The military arm of the FIS would be known as the Armed Islamic Group (GIA). Other Islamic militant groups sprang up to battle the government in Algiers.

The roots of the modern militant movement in Algeria, however, precede the return of the Algerian Afghans. It should be noted that President Houari Boumedienne, the general who took power in a 1965 coup, unwittingly began the modern Islamic movement when, as was happening in Saudi Arabia at the same time, he gave shelter to thousands of teachers who were refugees from the persecution of the Muslim Brotherhood then occurring in Egypt. Boumedienne's successor, President Chadli Benjedid, is blamed by the Algerian secularists and francophiles for encouraging the rise of the FIS. Miller notes that "British historian Hugh Roberts argues that Chadli, in effect, colluded with the FIS to authorize and encourage the then fledgling Islamic political party. Chadli viewed the FIS as less a threat than the 'Boumediennists,' the radical socialists and other opponents within his own ruling FLN."[20] When Chadli recognized the FIS as a legitimate party in 1989, both President Mubarak of Egypt and Colonel Quaddafi of Libya were shocked and alarmed. Even today, Egypt and Libya support the Algerian government against the FIS.

If Chadli conspired with the FIS as many observers say, his calculated political move backfired severely. On June 29, 1992, as mentioned above, the terrorists of the FIS killed Boudiaf as he was giving a speech. However, some believe that Boudiaf was actually killed by members of the FLN or the army who feared he would expose their corruption to the public. (Ironically, the Algerian government in fact has had to seek help from France, whose rule it had thrown off some thirty years earlier!) The insensate civil war continues in Algeria, with some 85,000 dead and counting in 2002. Nobody even seems to know who is doing all the killing, the government or the rebels. The words of Albert Camus, the great French author of *The Plague* who lived and died in Algeria, seem prophetic. What he wrote about the plague applies now to the violence in his beloved Algeria: "[It is] like the slow, deliberate progress of some monstrous thing crushing out all upon its path."[21]

The Islamic militants in Algeria, angry at the help the government was receiving from France, would carry their campaign of terror into France itself in 1995. Even before Saddam Hussein's invasion of Kuwait, in 1990, former French Prime Minister Michel Debre had told the Israeli newspaper *Ha'aretz* on June 27, 1990, that "[militant] Islam is today the number one enemy of Europe, and primarily that of France." Debre warned that "the hypothesis that the entire Maghreb will serve as a theater for a Jihad has become a credible hypothesis. The Islamic movement constitutes a danger for France." Led by Khaled Kelkal, the Islamic militants descended on France in the summer. As Jay Robert Nash writes in *Terrorism in the Twentieth Century*, on July 25, 1995, the terrorists placed a bomb aboard a car of the Paris metro. It exploded at the Latin Quarter stop, "killing seven persons and wounding dozens more."[22] On August 16, 1990, however, an unexploded bomb aboard the Lyon to Paris train revealed Kelkal's fingerprints, identifying him to French security authorities. After Kelkal escaped a French counterterrorist force attack outside Lyon on September 28, the French succeeded in killing him two days later.

Throughout the Muslim world, the new *jihad* carries on. It even rages on the northern front of *Dar al-Islam*. In Bosnia, during the recent war, Arab Afghans came by the hundreds to fight with their Muslim brothers against the Serbs. The Bosnian 3rd Corps was almost totally composed of these *mujahidin*. Indeed, concern about the new Muslim presence in the Balkans was even expressed by Croat president Franjo Tudjman. In an interview with the Paris *Le Figaro* on January 18, 1993, Tudjman said that the Muslims "want to continue the war at all costs in the form of a holy Islamic war." In the current condition, Tudjman added, Croatia felt "threatened by Muslim aspirations to create an Islamic state" in Bosnia. (This was, of course, at the time that Croatia was allied with the Bosnian Muslims against the Serbs, and Tudjman had no feelings of hostility to color his judgment against his Muslim allies.) Then, as if to give credence to the Croatian president's remarks, ten days later, speaking to F. Relea of *El Pais* on January 27, Sefer Halilovic, commander-in-chief of the Bosnian army, threatened, "if Europe does not change its attitude [toward Bosnia], we will take steps and unleash terror on its territories. Many European capitals will be ablaze."

There seems to be anecdotal evidence to support the contention that Iran is working toward establishing an Islamic beachhead in the Balkans. Hamid Mowlana wrote in the Tehran-based English-language newspaper *Kayhan International* (August 23, 1992), about what appeared to be Tehran's official view on the opportunities offered militant Islam by the fighting in the Balkans: "Islamic countries as a bloc have a unique and historic opportunity to produce the desired political changes in the global system. . . . Such opportunities are unlikely to repeat themselves in history." Therefore, "the Bosnia-Hercegovina tragedy and others likely to happen in the near future should act as wake-up calls for leaders in the Islamic countries and the big Islamic *Ummah* [community of the faithful] to come to their senses and accomplish their historical responsibility." The "others likely to happen" must include the on-going crisis in Indonesia, the increasing Muslim terrorism in India, especially in the province of Baluchistan, and the festering Moro insurrection in the Republic of the Philippines.

There already exists documentary evidence (although not often in American newspapers) to support this theory. The Arabic newspaper *Al-Wafd* of Cairo reported as early as December 4, 1991, that a forward command apparatus had already been established in neighboring Bulgaria as early as the fall of 1991 for Islamic support of the struggle of the Bosnian Muslims against the Serbs. M. Yared chronicled in *Jeune Afrique* from spring to fall of 1992 how the Armed Islamic Movement (AIM) was moving in to help the Muslims defend Sarajevo. Their commander was Mahmud Abd-al-Aziz, a veteran "holy warrior" who had already fought in the cause of the new *jihad* in Afghanistan, among the Pakistani-backed militants in Kashmir; in the Philippines; and also had done work for Turabi and the Muslim fundamentalist regime in Khartoum, Sudan, a city that is now one of the headquarters of the new militant Islamic network. Yared reinforces my fear that the forces that buttressed the Bosnian Muslims represented a cross-section of holy warriors from throughout *Dar al-Islam*. But the most pertinent concern is the continued presence in Bosnia of members of Tehran's elite military Pasdaran forces, which are also now in the Sudan. The *Philadelphia Inquirer* later confirmed that elements of the United Nations forces had found evidence of these Iranian forces during military "sweeps" undertaken in Bosnia territory.

Ever since the beginning of the fighting with Serbia in 1999, Islamic militants have been battling the largely Muslim Kosovo Liberation Army (KLA) in the Serb province of Kosovo. These Muslims have received much help from neighboring Albania, historically the only Balkan country where Islam has been the predominant religion. The Muslims in Kosovo consider themselves to be ethnic Albanians. In Kosovo, then-President Slobodan Milosevic of Serbia had been pursuing his bloody pogrom of "ethnic cleansing." While the Serbian forces were successful on all fronts when Milosevic's campaign began, the KLA had grown into a formidable foe for the Serbian forces, well-trained and even wearing uniforms. A peace conference was planned for Paris, where NATO hoped to force Milosevic to give a large degree of autonomy to Kosovo province for this pogrom. If any success results from the peace talks, it will entail the placement "in country" of some 20,000 NATO troops, including from 4,000 to 5,000 American soldiers. (In January 2002, Milosevic is finally facing trial for war crimes at an international tribunal in the Netherlands.)

It is my opinion that the change in the KLA from a ragged guerrilla force some three years ago into the formidable army it is today is due to the influence of the same Arab Afghans who helped turn the Bosnian Muslims some years ago into a potent military force. Moreover, the KLA has been implicated in drug-running, much like the *mujahidin* in Afghanistan, which is one reason they had an increasingly "lower profile" in the plans of the administration of President Bill Clinton and in the news media. By the spring of 2001, it had become painfully clear that the KLA had originated among Muslim clans whose main object was to extend their control of the narcotics traffic in the Balkans. Their Islamic extremism was only one product that they wished to export from their safe home in the UN-created haven of Kosovo. Of the two, heroin was by far the more profitable.[23]

With Albania already involved in the drug trade, the KLA has a ready pipeline to funnel its drugs through Europe to Amsterdam, the main port for the opium trade in Western Europe, and on to the United States. Of course, a large number of the Kosovar refugees arriving in the United States are supporters of the KLA already, and thus constitute potential terrorists and drug criminals in the United States.

It would be a supreme irony if we repeated in the Balkans the tragedy of Afghanistan where, by training the Afghans to combat the Soviet "evil empire," we in fact created the legions of Arab Afghans who have brought the bloody Islamic *jihad* to our own shores. Furthermore, former Secretary of State Madeleine Albright's efforts to bring about a three-year interim period while the ethnic Kosovar Albanians enjoy increased autonomy may very well lead to an independent Muslim Kosovo, closely allied to Muslim Albania and Bosnia. The compact that Albright envisioned actually was agreed to by the Kosovar Albanians on March 15, 1999. The Serb government would also eventually agree to the compact, but with considerable reluctance. The NATO intervention in the Kosovo crisis could result in the creation of a Balkan Islamic enclave, embracing an independent Kosovo, Albania, and Bosnia, which could become the focal point for a major outbreak of Islamic terrorism in Europe, which would find ready recruits among the discontented Turkish guest workers now in almost every European country, as well as among the Kosovar refugees who have been made homeless by the NATO bombing or expelled by Milosevic's security forces using the bombing as an excuse for more "ethnic cleansing." As part of the Clinton administration's prolix policy on Kosovo, Kosovar refugees were to be sent to the United States. On May 5, 1999, the first arrived. Although this is undoubtedly being done as a humanitarian gesture, it cannot be overlooked that some of the refugees will be supporters of the KLA—and thus potential Islamic terrorists here in the United States.

In March 2001, the fighting had been spread by allies of the KLA into the neighboring state of Macedonia. Macedonian Islamic guerrillas began a concerted campaign against the Macedonian government, which had not supported Serbia in the 1999 war against NATO. Much as in South Vietnam where the Viet Cong used "neutral" Cambodia as a sanctuary from pursuing American and South Vietnamese troops in the early years of the Vietnam War, the fighters in Macedonia hid in the border territory of Kosovo after their hit-and-run raids in Macedonia. NATO troops would bolster their position in this frontier region in February and March 2001 in an attempt to deny this sanctuary to the Islamic fighters, but the warfare increased in Macedonia. Finally, not wanting to see NATO troops embroiled in another Balkan country, the NATO command in Kosovo agreed in the last week of March 2001 to Macedonian troops and paramilitary police launching an all-out offensive against the Muslim guerrillas in their country, backed by heavy artillery fire.

Politically, the influence of these new militants is being felt elsewhere as well. In Pakistan, Nawaz Sharif was elected prime minister on a fundamentalist platform, which goes far to explain Pakistan's whole-hearted support of the Taliban in neighboring Afghanistan. However, the traditionally conservative Pakistani military deposed Sharif in 1999. In his place, Gen. Pervez Musharraf, a foe of the extremist "jehadis," *jihadists*, in his country, became the president of Pakistan. In Turkey, a pro-militant president, Necmettin Erbakin (1996–97), was elected, giving rise to fears that the pro-Western army, a bastion of modernism since the days of Kemal Ataturk, would take power in a coup to prevent fundamentalism from becoming the law in secular Turkey. The return to power by the army of the secularist Prime Minister Bulent Ecevit and President Suleiman Demirel seems to have put these fears to rest, at least for now. Nevertheless, women are increasingly seen in full Muslim garb in the streets of Istanbul, especially among recent migrants from the countryside. However, one cannot ignore the resurgence of Pan-Turkish feeling, dormant since the time of Kemal Ataturk. Previous Istanbul governments have spoken with determination of spreading Turkish influence throughout the old realm of the Ottoman Empire. The Turks have made great efforts to cultivate the new independent republics of Uzbekistan, Kyrgyzstan, Turkmenistan, Kazakhstan, and Tajikistan in their old central Asian homeland. They have also made a bid to increase their efforts in the growing Muslim community in the Balkans, the old northern provinces of the Ottoman Empire. The 1998 decision of the Turkish navy to use ports in the Turkish-controlled eastern part of Cyprus, in spite of fervent Greek diplomatic protests, may be seen in this light.

Therefore, it might not be too speculative to envision a growing Iranian-Turkish rivalry over which country will exert influence on the Muslim territory now expanding in the Balkans, with the prospect of an independent Muslim Kosovo serving as a bridge between Muslim Bosnia and Albania. It should be remembered that in central Asia, Muslim Iran under shahs like Abbas the Great were perennially at war with the Ottoman Empire over control of the region, a rivalry neither Istanbul nor Tehran has ever forgotten.

There are already indications that Turkey and Iran are battling diplomatically over influence in the Muslim republics of central Asia today. The importance of the potential oil boom in central Asia figures high in this rivalry, even more than the fact that Turkey has seen itself as a bastion against the Islamic extremism promulgated from Tehran in Iran. From the very beginning of the Young Turks revolt against the sultan in 1908, the reformist movement in Turkey has been directed toward modernizing and westernizing the country in order to help Turkey stand tall among the world's great powers. The need for thorough reform in Turkey was only shown more clearly by the defeat of Turkey in the Balkan Wars of 1912 to 1913 and her defeat by the Allies when she fatally decided to support Germany in World War I.

The Turkish revolution was given great impetus by Mustafa Kemal. While pursuing his modernization within Turkey, he kept Turkey from becoming involved with the fundamentalist *Basmach* Movement in central Asia, that had developed to thwart the penetration of the atheistic new Russian Bolshevik regime into the traditionally Muslim lands of central Asia.[24] Wilfred Cantwell Smith wrote of the essentially secular Turkish reform in *Islam in Modern History*, "the Turks gave the whole matter a distinctive and indeed crucial twist, by making the fundamental shift of its being [a] Turkish rather than a Muslim society whose cause they are serving, as it has seemed to some Muslims as well as to some Western observers. Their revolution is accordingly seen as on a nationalistic rather than a religious basis."[25]

Today, there are two possible routes for the massive pipeline being planned to carry the oil from its source around the Caspian Sea to its ultimate destination on the Mediterranean. A northern route would benefit Russia, the southern one Turkey and the United States, Turkey's ally in NATO. In March 2001, Iran allied itself with Russia in favor of the more northern route, creating increased tension between Tehran and Turkey.

❋ ❋ ❋

From the early 1970s, there has been in place an Islamic terrorist infrastructure in the United States, although none of its actions would compare with the destruction of the World Trade Center in 2001. The seed bed of Islamic militancy were chapters of the Muslim Students Association, whose father was the Iranian revolutionary Mustafa Chamran Savehi, who had been a student at the University of California at Berkeley. As Amir Terreri would write in his *Holy Terror*, students from the American Muslim Student Association would travel to Lebanon in the 1970s, when that country was embroiled in the PLO-inspired civil war, receive combat instruction and probably some active service there, and then return to the United States to form clandestine cells. These cells were "sleepers," in the intelligence sense of the word, waiting the word of command to attack the "Great Satan" at home. All of these groups, whether Islamic *Jihad*, Hizbollah, or the Muslim Students Association in the United States, had all been radicalized by the Khomeini brand of militant Islam.

However, not to be undone, the other exponent of militant Islam, Muammar Quaddafi, exploiting his greater financial influence, from Libyan oil reserves, soon established himself as a leading shaper of the radical Islamic movement growing within the United States. In June 1982 and April 1983, Quaddafi held two international terrorist conclaves in Tripoli, both of which attracted members from a wide spectrum of radical American groups, including the Native American Indian Movement and the Nation of Islam.[26] A major conduit of Libyan funds in this period in support of future terrorist activities was the Manara Travel Agency, which had been established in Washington, D.C., as early as 1980 by Libyan agent Mussa Hawamdah.[27] The Gulf of Sidra incident in March 1986, in which planes from the United States Mediterranean fleet shot down Libyan fighters over the disputed gulf, and American bombers struck targets in Libya, only sharpened Quaddafi's support of Islamic extremists within our country. Prior to this, as our intelligence agencies know, Colonel Quaddafi established "suicide squads" within the United States, similar to those terrorist groups like Islamic *Jihad* and Hizbollah have utilized against American and Israeli targets in the Middle East with numbing regularity. It was such a suicide truck bomber who demolished the U.S. Marine Corps barracks in Beirut, Lebanon, in October 1993. According to a Voice of Lebanon radio broadcast on August 31, 1985, a direct link was made when Lt. Col. Abdallah Hijazi, one of Quaddafi's lieutenants, met with Hasan Hashim, head of the Lebanon-based Amal Organization's chief executive to receive instruction on the development of the Lebanese-based suicide forces. The ominous thing is that Hashim was a resident of the United States. Quaddafi's plans, far from eliciting opposition from Tehran, only found praise from the Iranians, who were at this time using suicide battalions in attacks against well-entrenched Iraqi troops. On January 7, 1986, the Tehran International Service, a short wave broadcast, announced that "the Libyan people's committees have voiced their readiness to strike serious blows against the United States—even through the kamikaze groups they have set up in the avenues of Washington." On February 6, 1986, the international short wave broadcast of Radio Monte Carlo carried news of the meeting of the Pan-Arab Command for Leading the Revolutionary Forces in the Arab Homeland in Tripoli. There, speaking for a bloc of Palestinian forces, the terrorist Ahmad Jibril, part of the Popular Front for the Liberation of Palestine–General Command, announced that "the United States has declared war on the Arabs. Therefore, the Palestinian revolution believes that the war has started [against America] and that it is no longer responsible for what may happen." In 1968, Jibril had split from the Popular Front for the Liberation of Palestine, headed by Dr. George Habash, according to the U.S. State Department's 1997 Internet report on global terrorism. The reason given was that Ahmad Jibril had found Habash's group "too political," and wanted to devote himself to full-scale terrorism instead of any communist ideological discussion, which Habash liked to do.

However, it soon became apparent that perhaps the most serious threat to the security of the United States might come not from terrorists from the Muslim world, but from discontented American citizens here at home: namely, Louis Farakhan's Nation of Islam. As early as 1984, two years before Quaddafi was inflamed by the Gulf of Sidra incident, Farakhan had already paid a private visit to the Libyan mystical leader. June 22, 1984, an article in *Information Digest* detailed just how involved the Nation of Islam had already become with Libyan-sponsored state terrorism. After the 1983 meeting, Libyan funds apparently began to reach the coffers of the Nation of Islam. As a result of the infusion of the Libyan money, a vicious Chicago street gang with aspirations toward Islam, Al-Rukn, was recruited by Farakhan to add strength to the shock troops of his organization, the Fruit of Islam. Leaders of Al-Rukn would later follow in Farakhan's footsteps with their own pilgrimage to Libya. It would not be long before Al-Rukn became the first authentic militant Islamic terror group in the United States, according to the Chicago police. The *Washington Times* and the *Chicago Sun Times* reported in October 1986 that five members of Al-Rukn planned to carry out strikes in the United States on behalf of Libya. Although four were apprehended, the fifth managed to escape arrest.

Just how prominent Farakhan became in Libyan circles was demonstrated by his role at the Second International Conference of the International

Center for Combating Imperialism, Zionism, Racism, Reaction, and Fascism, which was held in Tripoli in March 1986. At the conference, Farakhan was given the honor, as reported by the Tripoli Radio Service broadcast of March 17, of introducing a keynote address by Colonel Quaddafi. In his own talk to the assembly, Farakhan minced no words in speaking of his solidarity with those assembled at the convocation. He said in his address the that Nation of Islam did not "recognize the right of [President] Reagan legally, morally, and also according to God-given law" to govern the United States. Furthermore, Farakhan stated that the Palestinians convened at the meeting "are not terrorists because they are struggling to undermine imperialism and racism. . . . The pledges of [these] real freedom-fighters are the only ones that will bring about victory over imperialism and neo-colonialism." Indeed, by August 19, 1992, the *Washington Times* reported that Louis Farakhan's Nation of Islam, now split off from the main Black Muslim group founded by Elijah Muhammed, was a major recipient of Libyan funds. In 1997, Farakhan made another trip to Libya to visit his patron Quaddafi. On the same excursion, he also stopped at the other African nexus of Islamic terrorism, Khartoum in the Sudan. In these visits, as well as on his return to the United States, Farakhan expressed his support for the struggle of militant Islam against imperialism and racism. Such continued trips to terrorist headquarters made Farakhan the most vocal spokesperson in the United States for militant Islam before the events of September 11, 2001.

Furthermore, Farakhan and his supporters made an effort to target support among the African-American prison population to recruit them for the Nation of Islam. However, Farakhan and his militant Islamic supporters also made a major recruitment drive among disgruntled African-American Vietnam War veterans, the "Bloods." T. Washington, writing in the *Washington Post Magazine* (December 16, 1992), broke the story that many of these "Bloods" had been converted to Shi'ite Islam and had fought as "African-American Afghans" among the *mujahidin* in the Afghan War. More ominous still, Tehran had infiltrated some of them back into the United States to be prepared to carry out terror operations in this country.

The American bombing of Tripoli in March 1986, in which members of Quaddafi's family were slain, had signaled the massive build-up in the Libyan terrorist network in the United States. Libya was helped by all the major Palestinian terror groups, such as Hizbollah and Islamic *Jihad*, and Iran as well, just as in the past. At the same time, as the guerrilla wars in El

Salvador and Nicaragua continued, these same groups, with the help of Cuba, also infiltrated Latin American guerrilla groups to use them as a stepping stone for proposed attacks within the United States itself, according to Yossef Bodansky in his *Target America: Terrorism in the US Today*. Indicative of the growth of the Palestinian terror network in the Americas, Bodansky states, was the increasing involvement of the Abu Nidal Organization with the Sendero Luminoso Marxist guerrillas in Peru, including the vital contribution of experienced Palestinian commandos to train the Sendero Luminoso, so that its members were transferred from machete-wielding banditos into a modern terrorist force.[28] Although it took place after Bodansky's book was published in 1993, the terrorist takeover of the Japanese embassy in Lima in December 1996 by members of the Tupac Amaru Revolutionary Movement (MRTA) showed a professionalization of Peruvian terrorists unheard of a decade before. It seems likely, therefore, that a Palestinian presence among the Marxist groups in Peru may have continued, and could still possibly be in place. Libyan influence has been documented as well in the growing guerrilla movement in Colombia, where Marxist terror groups have been so strong that the current Colombian administration has been compelled to enter into open negotiations with them in a country where the violence has claimed perhaps 30,000 lives over the past 30 years.

One of the backers of the underground army known as M-19 was Fidel Castro. With Castro's secret police closely integrated with the then-Soviet KGB, Cuba became a type of terrorist clearinghouse for the Americas for aid coming from the Soviet Union. It was for this reason (that Castro would, as Fidel had promised, use Cuba as base for fomenting Communist revolutions throughout the Americas) that the Reagan administration invaded Grenada in 1983 and carried out the contra movement against the Marxist Sandinista regime in Nicaragua. President Reagan was a firm believer in the idea of Moscow as the nexus of international terrorism, as was his secretary of state Alexander Haig, and the then Director of Central Intelligence, William Casey. Cuba was put on the American list of those states sponsoring terrorism because of Castro's support of the M-19 movement, which had carried out an attack on the Colombian Palace of Justice in Bogota in November 1985.

When the U.S. Department of State released its 1999 report on international terrorism, Cuba still was at the head of the list, in the "Overview of State-Sponsored Terrorism," which is available through the State Department's home page on the Internet. Cuba was listed as providing continued support for the Marxist guerrillas who are threatening to turn Colombia into another Vietnam for the United States. Two of these groups are the FARC, which in English is the Revolutionary Armed Forces of Colombia, and the ELN, the (Colombian) National Liberation Army. But Castro seems to be liberalizing his position on sponsoring such terror groups, in view of hopes of warming relations with the United States. The return of the Cuban child Elian Gonzalez from his relatives' home in Miami back to the custody of his father in Cuba in 2000 was widely seen as a gesture on the part of the Clinton administration toward trying to normalize the relations of the United States with Cuba. Young Elian had been found clinging to an inner tube by a fisherman off the coast of Florida, after his mother had drowned trying to get herself and Elian to sanctuary in the United States. In 1999, Fidel Castro also hosted meetings between representatives of the Colombian government and spokesmen for the ELN in Havana.

Back in the 1980s, preparations increased for an Islamic terrorist strike within the United States, with Tehran and Syria gradually overtaking Libya as the main support of the nascent militant movement in the United States. Indicative of the growing activism were Islamic conferences held by student groups in the United States in the summer of 1987 in Plainfield, Illinois; Houston, Texas; and Oklahoma City, Oklahoma, later to be the site of the largest terrorist bombing yet seen in the United States. Former Prime Minister of Israel Benjamin Netanyahu mentions in his book *Fighting Terrorism* a conclave in 1989 in Kansas City that featured the participation of representatives from the Islamic militants in Egypt, the Jordanian Muslim Liberation party, the Algerian FIS, the Al-Nahdha, and Hamas! The participants at the Oklahoma City rally were urged "to adhere to their faith in words and deeds because it is the only true way to salvation." Hasan-i Sabah, the founder of the Assassins, would have nodded his head in heartfelt agreement. The *Bulletin* of the Islamic Center in Washington, D.C., in August 1987 had issued what could only be called a clarion call for an Islamic *jihad* in the United States. The bulletin declared that the United States was a *kufr*, or "infidel" country, and that for Muslims "to put an end to the existence of the illegitimate Zionist state [Israel], Muslims have to cancel all the puppet regimes in their own countries," including within the United States. "*Jihad* is the only way to restore the honor of the Muslim peoples and bring about a Muslim revolution. . . . All Muslims should move and take up arms to shake the earth under the feet of the *Kufr* [infidels]."[29] By the middle 1980s there were some 60,000 Muslim students in the United States, according to columnists Jack Anderson and Dale Van Atta, in the *Washington Post* (January 17, 1986). Thirty thousand of these were from Iran, many of them adherents of Khomeini's form of militant Shi'ism. Among the Muslim students were one hundred who had received terrorist training abroad, and had infiltrated the United States by way of Mexico. *US News & World Report* noted on March 9, 1989, that Tehran could count on 1,000 Muslim students in the United States who would be ready to carry out or support terror activities in this country, a number which Hamas or Hizbollah would be proud to claim on the West Bank. As with militant Muslims everywhere, the radicals in the United States were emboldened by the defeat of the Soviets in Afghanistan. Abdullah Azzam, one of the most virulent apostles of the new *jihad* in this country, exulted in Oklahoma City that "after Afghanistan, nothing is impossible for us anymore. . . . What matters is the willpower that springs from our religious belief."

It is possible that Abdullah Azzam may be connected to Azzam Publications, which characterizes itself as the voice of the *mujahidin* on the Internet. Since the attacks on the World Trade Center and the Pentagon on September 11, Internet contact with Azzam Publications has been blocked, apparently by U.S. intelligence. Although this would ordinarily raise some concern about First Amendment rights of communication, apparently the federal government fears that the e-mail link with Azzam Publications may be used as an electronic portal for communication with the terrorists. Elsewhere in this book, I have commented on the concern of American intelligence that Osama bin Laden's comrades in the United States have been using sophisticated communications to keep in touch with al-Qaeda. The September 11 hijackers were known to have used computers. Another concern is that bin Laden's confederates were using stenography, a cryptologic practice which enables the sender to enclose a hidden message inside another one, a concealed message which only the recipient is able to decode.

In July 1987, an agreement was negotiated between Iranian agents in Afghanistan and Gulbuddin Hekmatyar, described by my confidential sources as the most opportunistic of the Afghan warlords then fighting the Marxist government in Kabul and its Soviet allies. (Hekmatyar was also arguably the most ruthless as well: Two journalists disappeared, and were later found murdered, after they disagreed with him at the end of an interview.) Hekmatyar agreed with the Iranians that, as Yossef Bodansky explains, "Tehran would increase its help to his Hizb-i-Islami group, and in return Iranians would be infiltrated into the West, especially the United States and Canada, using documents [fake passports, etc.] provided by the Hizb-i-Islami."[30] Bodansky stated that "in the late 1980s, Iran was the undisputed leader of international terrorism in the United States and Canada. Its Islamist terrorist infrastructure was by far the most comprehensive and capable in the world."[31]

By the late 1980s, Iran, with the help of Hizbollah, which was largely controlled by Tehran, was ready to launch some tentative terror strikes within the continental United States. As a way to more closely coordinate its terror operations planned for the United States, Tehran established a command and control structure operating on our very borders. Two senior level Iranian terrorists were appointed to the Iranian embassies in Canada and Cuba—Sayyid Ali Mussavi was posted to Ottawa while Muhammed Sadri was dispatched to Havana. To aid it in its American plans, Tehran was able to call on the services of one of the world's most dedicated terror groups, the Japanese Red Army (JRA), which had a long history of helping Hizbollah in terror attacks in the Middle East. As chronicled by W. R. Farrell in his definitive study of the JRA, *Blood and Rage*, Red Army terrorist Yu Kikumura was arrested on the New Jersey Turnpike with explosives in his car on April 12, 1988.[32] His goal had been to set off three bombs in Manhattan to mark the second anniversary of the American bombing mission to Tripoli. On March 11, 1989, near the third anniversary of the bombing of Tripoli, the *New York Times* announced that the day before a pipe bomb had gone off under the van of Mrs. Sharon Lee Rogers, in San Diego, California; Mrs. Rogers was the wife of the captain of the USS *Vincennes*, the American warship that in July 1988 had by error brought down with a ground-to-air missile the Iranian Airways Airbus off the coast of Iran. Fortunately, Mrs. Rogers was unhurt. In 1992, however, the Iranian terrorists in the United States did not miss. On March 26, according to the *New York Times*, in Franklin Lakes, New Jersey, an Iranian hit squad succeeded in killing Mrs. Parivash Rafizadeh outside her home. Her crime was that her husband and brother had served in the SAVAK, the shah's secret police.

While Tehran was active against those *emigres* from the shah's rule, other Islamic terrorist groups (most with Iranian or Libyan support) were organizing in the United States. Confidential sources in the FBI have indicated that Hamas, Islamic *Jihad*, and the father of all militant groups, the Muslim Brotherhood, established radical cells in the American Islamic community, especially among student groups. At the time of the Gulf War, Hamas spokesman Rashid al-Ganushi proclaimed "today the fight against America is a priority for Islam and Muslims." So important was the struggle against America becoming to Islamic militants of all persuasions that Mohammed Qutb, brother of the Egyptian radical Sayyid Qutb, was a participant at a meeting of the Islamic Society of North America, which was held August 31 to September 1, 1990. In December 1991, the Islamic *Jihad* and the Muslim Brotherhood cosponsored a convention in Phoenix, Arizona, attended by leaders of militant terrorist organizations, according to Bodansky. The Arabic newspaper *Al-Wafd* on December 4, 1991, carried an article in which the leaders of these groups urged their American supporters to await the order to attack. The rise in Islamic militancy benefitted the movement in two ways: Not only was the Muslim radical element being prepared for attacks within the United States, but it was also sending more financial help to the terrorist groups active there, according to a confidential Israeli source. On January 31, 1993, the Israeli government announced the detention within Israel of two Arab-Americans with Hamas ties, Mohammed Abdel-Hamid Salah and Mohammed Joma Hilmi Jarad. Both had arrived in Israel to help rebuild the Hamas infrastructure which had been shredded by Israeli security sweeps in December 1992.

However, Tehran was not to be outdone by the other militant Islamic groups, proving again that the main strength of *jihad* still lay on Islam's frontiers. The day after the murder of Mrs. Rafizadeh in New Jersey, Tehran sponsored a massive Al-Quds [Jerusalem] Day on March 27 all over the United States and Canada. Sponsored by the Muslim Student Association, major rallies were held in Washington, D.C.; St. Louis, Missouri; Ann Arbor and Dearborn, Michigan; and Montreal and Toronto in Canada, two of the cities with the largest Muslim populations in North America. From then on, Tehran became the main center for Islamic terrorism in the United States, reducing the Turabi's Sudan to the role of a surrogate.

By 1992, Tehran had gone well beyond the public rallies and congresses that had marked its first decade of militant activism with the United States. The ayatollahs in Tehran were readying their network for a major offensive in the United States. The terrorist apparatus was tightly controlled in Tehran by a group of Iran's most dedicated exponents of the Khomeini *jihad*: Hashemi-Rafsanjani, who had met with Gorbachev; Ali Fallayihan; Ali Akbar Mohtasheni; and Mushin Reza'i. High in their councils was Sayyid Hassan Nasrullah, chief of the Tehran-based Hizbollah, which most likely took over direct operational command of the terrorist bases established in Canada and in Cuba. Mohtasheni had spoken for the command structure of this "Terrorist International" when he stated on Radio Tehran on August 7, 1989, that "throughout the world there are many Hizbollah cells . . . established by the Imam's [Khomeini's] holy breath, and they carry the banner of death to the superpower [the United States] and global arrogance." Moreover, he said that Khomeini always had "an attacking-offensive attitude toward the U.S."

When the blow finally came, it would be, according to a Muslim newspaper, orchestrated by the man responsible for the assassination of President Anwar Sadat in 1982, Shaikh Omar Abdul Rahman. The Paris-based newspaper *Al Watan al-Arabi* stated that the shaikh had been specially ordered by Tehran and Khartoum to carry out offensive operations within the United States. The forces of militant Islam thus made their dramatic debut in the United States on February 26, 1993, when terrorists set off a bomb under the World Trade Center in New York City. A van carrying a 1,200 bomb into a parking garage was detonated, killing six and wounding 1,000. Although the religious shaikh may have issued the *fatwa* for the bombing operation, the ultimate orders, according to M. Juffe in the *New York Post* (March 5, 1993) came from Tehran. Arrested in Egypt in April 1989 for his part in the Sadat killing, Rahman was placed under house arrest and later allowed to leave the country. The shaikh had then been living in Khartoum, which since the 1970s and the 1986 overthrow of President Jaafar Numeiry had become a hotbed for Islamic militants throughout the Muslim world. Rahman had become an important supporter of the Turabi regime in the Sudan, and would become an important player in Turabi's game plan to export militant Islam. Turabi's role in the growing world of Islamic fundamentalism cannot be discounted, even if he lacks the financial influence of Tehran, because his religious influence is steadily growing, much like Ayatollah Khomeini's some twenty years before. Rory Nugent gave a very perceptive analysis of Turabi in an article written for *Spin* magazine in May 1995, called "The March of the Green Flag," which of course is the banner of Islam. Wrote Nugent, "today, by all accounts, [Turabi] is the leading intellectual of fundamentalist Islam, arguably among the ten most powerful men in the world. Many believe Turabi to be the enabler of the entire fundamentalist cause, animator of millions who seek a new world order based on the Koran. His books, pamphlets, audiocassettes, and videos are snapped up around the globe" by Islamic militants everywhere. However, in 2001, as part of growing concern over world opinion, Turabi's influence was severely restricted.

The fact that the Sudanese handed over the terrorist Carlos Ilich Sanchez, "The Jackal," to the French in August 1994 from his asylum in Khartoum may point very much toward the increasing Islamic character of the terror movement. While Carlos was an effective gun for hire during the epoch of Palestinian terrorism in the 1970s, "an international fighter who served liberation movements," as his old ally George Habash called him at the time of his capture, his political opportunism and lack of real political conviction would not endear him to doctrinaire Muslim radicals. Therefore, Sudan's President Hassan Omar al-Bashir (with tacit agreement of Turabi, no doubt) agreed to hand Carlos over to the French in return for the repatriation of two terrorists to Tehran, Sudan's partner in terror; French intelligence cooperation; and (no doubt) large French bribes. The French had desperately wanted the Jackal since he had killed two agents of the French DST, the Direction de la Surveillance du Territoire, the French counterterror police, in Paris in 1974.

From the Sudan, Shaikh Rahman had also mounted a campaign to undermine the government of Hosni Mubarak in Egypt. He cleverly followed the strategy that Khomeini had followed when he was in exile in France before his triumphant return to Iran: Rahman recorded and sent to his disciples in Egypt tapes that called for them to rally and throw out President Mubarak. The Egyptian government took this threat seriously, especially as the shaikh continued his attacks on Mubarak even after he moved to the United States.

Significantly, the first major bombing of a United States installation overseas had been the terrorist bombing of the American embassy in Khartoum on March 2, 1973, when U.S. Ambassador Cleo A. Noel Jr. and two other embassy officials were slain by Palestinian gunmen. The Muslim militancy that the Mahdi had created in the deserts of the Sudan was reborn. Ironically, Shaikh Rahman was on the State Department "watch list," a list of suspected terrorists, at the same embassy in Khartoum. Despite this, the shaikh was granted a visa to enter the United States, where he set up a mosque in Brooklyn in New York City in 1990; he apparently ministered to his flock in Jersey City, New Jersey, too, in the Masjid al-Salam Mosque. Several of those who were later indicted with him in the World Trade Center conspiracy had been worshippers at his mosque, including Ibrahim Elgabrowny and Mohammed Salameh. As stated before, one of those convicted, Ramzi

Ahmed Yousef, was an Arab Afghan who was apprehended in Pakistan, where Rahman had established a fall-back headquarters. Tragically, and unforeseen at the time, the training that the United States Operation Cyclone had given to the *mujahidin* in their effort to repel the Soviets in Afghanistan had come full circle to bring Islamic terror home to the United States. Like Jason in the Greek myth, we had sown the dragon's teeth that turned into soldiers—only to see these soldiers turn against us.

In any discussion of domestic terror, the topic of the tragic flight of TWA 800 which exploded over Long Island on July 17, 1996, inevitably arises. The final verdict from the U.S. National Transportation Safety Board (NTSB), supported by the FBI, was that the crash of the jumbo jet was caused by a fire or explosion in the mid-section of the plane. However, the final NTSB report admits that the cause of this tragedy, which claimed some 230 lives (212 passengers and 18 crew), will never be definitively known. The belief that an onboard failure caused the crash was voiced early in the investigation, but was later challenged by the FBI SAC (Special Agent in Charge) James Kallstrom, from the New York office. As soon as I received news of the disaster, I faxed Mr. Kallstrom and offered him my help, since aviation intelligence is a specialty of mine (I have published in this field).

My fax, sent two days after the crash on July 17 and based in my own confidential background, may have been one of the first mentions of the possibility that a Stinger ground-to-air missile, launched from a small boat offshore, *might* have been used to bring down the Boeing 747. I know from experienced men in the air force that the missile can be positioned and then launched within minutes, and that the launch tube can then be crushed with one foot and, in the case of a marine launching, be quickly thrown overboard. As is well known, the theory that a missile downed Flight 800 was possibly substantiated at the time by an air traffic controller at JFK International Airport in New York, who noted on his radar the large "blip" of Flight 800, as well as a smaller "blip" heading for the jet. The smaller "blip" merged with Flight 800 before the plane disintegrated in the midair explosion. Three crewmen on an Air National Guard C-130, from the 106th New York Air National Guard Unit, also saw a small streak of light arc up to intercept the airplane before it exploded. Also from the 106th, helicopter pilot Major Meyer said in a press conference on July 18 that he "saw something that looked to me like a shooting star. Now you don't see a shooting star when the sun is up. It was still bright. It was probably just at the moment of sunset, and the sky was very bright. . . . I saw what appeared to be the sort of course and trajectory that you see when a shooting star enters the atmosphere. Almost immediately thereafter, I saw, in rapid succession, a small explosion and then a large explosion."[33]

The famous photograph by Linda Kabot, of East Moriches, Long Island, taken while she was at a party the same night, shows what seems to be a similar streak of light headed toward the plane; charting the trajectory of the streak implies that it could conceivably have been a missile fired from fairly close by, either from land or on board a vessel. Mrs. Kabot was at a Republican fundraising dinner at an outdoor restaurant overlooking Shinnecock Bay, with clear line of sight for her photography seaward to where the disaster took place. There would have been no lights over Long Island Sound to distort what she had photographed.

While the possibility that a Stinger missile may have brought down Flight 800 is only a theory, and is presented as such, some anecdotal evidence may point in that direction. While American sources have said that the Stinger is not capable of destroying a plane at Flight 800's given altitude of 13,000 feet (although the Stinger's true altitude capability is top secret), two Russian missiles, the SA-7 "Grail" and SA-14 "Gremlin" are known to be able to reach such an altitude easily, according to defense publications like *Jane's*.

Another possible culprit in the missile scenario is the Chinese clone of the Stinger, the Red Parakeet. What makes the Red Parakeet an interesting suspect is that in May 1996, some months before the TWA 800 disaster, a cargo of 2,000 of the Chinese type-56 version of the Russian AK-47 assault rifle had been seized by U.S. Customs and Bureau of Alcohol, Tobacco, and Firearms officers as they were being smuggled into the country by Norinco, the China Northern Industrial Corporation. The Norinco official named in the federal indictment was Richard Chen. Such companies are believed by the CIA to be affiliated with the Peoples' Liberation Army. In the story carried by CNN on May 23, 1996, U.S. Attorney for Northern California Michael Yamaguchi said of the seized weaponry, "this is an incredible arsenal." The undercover sting operation which resulted in the seizure of the firearms was called "Operation Dragon Fire," and had been carried out for sixteen months prior to the seizure of the guns aboard the Chinese merchant ship *Empress Phoenix*. A resident of California, Hammond Ku, according to affidavits filed in federal court, served as the middleman in the arms deal. AK-47s figured in the infamous Bank America bank robbery in Los Angeles in the beginning of 1997, as well as in other bank robberies and gang ambushes, as reported by the Los Angeles Police Department. It is possible that these AK-47s were from Norinco, since the federal affidavit filed by customs Agent Michael King stated that a "Kevin Wong . . . stores automatic weapons at his house for Hammond Ku." And these weapons appear to be separate from those seized on the *Empress Phoenix*. Moreover, Ku told an undercover operative that the AK-47s would be ideal for gang members—"gang bangers," according to the affidavit. Yet Hammond Ku was willing to offer the undercover agents more than lethal assault rifles! Ku supplied an undercover agent (who was only identified in King's affidavit as UC-1—Undercover Agent-1) with a copy of the catalogue from the Chinese-related firm of Polytech USA. The catalogue included, according to the affidavit, "various Chinese weapons and munitions for sale, including surface-to-air missiles [likely to have been Red Parakeets], tanks, anti-personnel mines, aircraft and other munitions." This same charge was reiterated in federal court by Wayne Yamashita of the Customs Department.

Article 96 of the indictment affidavit is particularly damning and deserves quoting at some length. According to Article 96, "Ku also offered the UCs [undercover agents] 'Red Parakeet' missiles, which Ku character-ized as being like the US Stinger (surface to air) [missile]. Ku said they were very expensive (in the thousands [of dollars]), but that it was very effective. Ku said they could take out a 747." While it must be emphasized that no information has been forthcoming from any American intelligence source that any Red Parakeet missiles ever did reach American shores, it *is known* from these sources that the Chinese shipping company known as COSCO, which owned the *Empress Phoenix*, regularly plies the Pacific to the Panama Canal, which from the middle-1990s has been heavily subsidized by the Peo-ples Republic of China. Thus, while admittedly speculation, *it cannot be ruled out* that Red Parakeet missiles may have been off-loaded at the Canal Zone and been smuggled north to terrorists within the United States—*and that one of them may have brought down TWA Flight 800 in July 1996.*[34]

Along with Mr. Kallstrom's support of the missile hypothesis to some degree in public statements, there was also a very suggestive piece of foreign information. The London *Times* noted in a story on August 25, 1996, that

"US officials are investigating reports that Islamic terrorists have smuggled Stinger ground-to-air missiles into the United States from Pakistan. Senior Iranian sources close to the fundamentalist regime in Tehran claimed this weekend that the TWA flight 800 was shot . . . by one of these shoulder-fired Stingers of the type used by Islamic guerrillas during the Afghanistan war. The sources said the missiles arrived in America seven months ago after being shipped from Karachi via Rotterdam and on to the Canadian port of Halifax." The *Times* identified the terrorists as belonging to the *Gama'at al-Islamiya*, the Egyptian group led by Shaikh Omar Abdul Rahman.

In June 1996 Hizbollah delegates from over thirty nations including the United States, Canada, Italy, France, Germany, and Britain attended a terrorist meeting. A three-man triumvirate which would coordinate the new terror attacks was chosen: Imad Mughaniyah of the Lebanese Hizbollah, "Party of God," Special Operations Command; Ahmed Salah Salim, a member of the Egyptian *Jihad*, with probable links to Shaikh Rahman; and Osama bin Laden. Bin Laden was, according to the article, assigned to blow up the Dharan, Saudi Arabia, target, while Imad Mughaniyah was charged with downing TWA Flight 800. At the time of the *Policy* review article Osama bin Laden was just another aspiring terrorist on an already crowded stage. At the time of the downing of Flight 800, the use of a hand-held missile to bring down the passenger jet seemed highly unlikely. However, how many Americans would have dreamed in July 1996 that a little over five years later, four jet planes could be hijacked by the followers of bin Laden and three of them crash into the World Trade Center and the Pentagon?

While the United States was reeling from the aftershocks of the 1993 World Trade Center bombing, the former Soviet Union, now the Congress of Independent States (CIS), was encountering the new *jihad* in the Republic of Chechnya. After the Chechens in the Causcasus declared their independence from the CIS, President Boris Yeltsin made an uncoordinated attempt to reconquer the "lost province." The Russian military effort was bloody and mishandled from the beginning. The Chechen capital of Grozny was brutally shelled with no real military purpose. However, the Russian invasion ignited the spark of *jihad* in the hearts of the Muslim Chechens. For them, the struggle against Russia was now not merely a fight for independence, but a holy war. It was in Chechnya, and neighboring Daghestan, that the *mullah* Shamyl had defied the armies of Tsar Nicholas II for nearly two decades in the nineteenth century. Dzhokar Dudayev, one of the leaders of the Chechen resistance, acknowledged in an interview with the *Los Angeles Times* (August 4, 1996) that some Chechens had been sent to Afghanistan for training to fight the Russians. (These may have been the same camps Osama bin Laden was funding.) This does not take into account the numbers of Arab Afghans who later came to swell the ranks of the Chechen fighters.

The Russians had reason to fear the Chechen *jihad*, for the warfare in Chechnya was concurrent with the drive for power in Afghanistan of the Taliban, a puritanical Muslim movement covertly supported by Pakistan in her drive to gain influence in Afghanistan. The Talibani militants had a direct and very adverse impact upon the Muslim republics that were once part of Soviet central Asia. Around 1992, a militant revolt had broken out in Tajikistan, supported by the Taliban, against the secularist, pro-Russian regime. Shaikh Omar Abdul Rahman's son took part in this fighting. The concern became so great that in 1993, the Russian Defense Minister Viktor Barrannikov warned that Russia reserved the right to intervene militarily again in Afghanistan if the Taliban continued its support of the Tajik insurgents. The Russians had been supplying the anti-Taliban forces in northern Afghanistan from secret Tajik bases, beginning around 1996.

Meanwhile, the Taliban had continued its battle for control of Afghanistan. The northern warlords, ethnic Uzbeks, and Tajiks held on to their corner of Afghanistan. However, Kabul and most of the major cities were in the hands of the Taliban, which enforced its extreme form of Muslim militancy upon those Afghans who fell under its power. However, the question remained open what the Russians would do if the Taliban successfully defeated the northerners. Following upon Barrannikov's warning about Russian intervention if the Taliban were to claim victory, it was a real possibility that Russia, rather than see a *jihad* sweep through central Asia (such as happened with the *basmachi* movement after World War I), would definitely intervene in Afghanistan militarily again, in spite of the consequences of any such attack on Russian relations with the United States. Of course, any chance of pre-emptive Russian move against the Taliban was coopted pre-remptorily by the American attack on Afghanistan in October 2001, in revenge for the attack of Osama bin Laden's al-Qaeda terrorists on September 11, 2001. Rather than moving to make central Asia a Russian outpost again, Soviet Premier Vladimir Putin was forced to surrender any great power initiatives once the Americans launched their air offensive on Kabul on October 7, 2001.

In December 2001, when the United States was vigorously prosecuting its war against al-Qaeda and its Afghan Taliban allies, an incident in India threatened to add another war front to southern Asia. On December 13, Islamic militants in India with ties to those in Kashmir staged a dramatic suicide raid on the Indian Parliament building in New Delhi, India's capital city. The raid of the five gunmen brought back memories of the suicide attacks on the World Trade Center and the Pentagon a brief two months earlier. CNN reported on December 15 that six Indian security officers and a gardener had been killed in a thirty-minute frenzy of gunfire. All five attackers were slain. Although the Pakistani government of President Gen. Pervez Musharraf denied any Pakistani complicity in the raid, the Indian Defense Ministry blamed extremists in the Pakistani intelligence service for backing the Kashmiri militants—as they had supported al-Qaeda and the Taliban. While negotiations continued between the two nuclear powers of the Indian subcontinent in the middle of January 2002, the threat of war remained palpable in the cold air over the contested Kashmir border between India and Pakistan.

In 1999, on the eastern border of central Asia, the Peoples' Republic of China was facing its own Muslim insurrection in the strategic province of Xinjiang, the home of China's nuclear facilities. Ethnic Muslim Uighurs began to battle the influx of Han, or ethnic Chinese, into Xinjiang, which they saw as a threat to their traditional way of life. An attempted coup took place in Urumchi, the capital of Xinjiang, in 1992. Increasingly, the Uighurs have shown a willingness to take their struggle into the Chinese heartland.

Ever since the fall of Sudanese President Numeiri in 1985, that country has been rocked by a civil war between the Muslim government in Khartoum and southern forces that are mostly Christian or native animists. The conflict actually began in 1981 when the southern Sudan Peoples' Liberation Army (SPLA), whose leader now is John Garang, first took up arms against growing Islamic policies fostered by the central government. Although Gen. Omar Hassan al-Bashir is president, the real power is held by Hassan al-Turabi, former chief of the Muslim Brotherhood in the Sudan who now heads his own National Islamic Front (NIF). Heavily politicized in the Sudan, the doctrine of *jihad* is still used by the Khartoum regime to justify its war in the south. Al-Turabi told author Mark Huband, "[there is *jihad*] in the south [of Sudan], because this is a nation. That's why it is used."[35] The degree to which *jihad* has been subverted to serve the territorial temporal aims in the Sudan is shown by the way that al-Turabi, who was the deputy prime minister of President Sayyid Sadiq al-Mahdi, direct descendant of the first Mahdi, supported General Bashir in the 1989 overthrow of the Mahdi's blood heir. Indeed, during the Bashir period, 1989 until today, the Sudan has become host to many fundamentalist Islamic groups, as did Muammar Quaddafi's Libya in the 1970s and early 1980s. These groups have received training and funds to spread the Sudanese version of *jihad* throughout much of central and eastern Africa, including Eritrea and probably Somalia. It is no mistake that zealots like Osama bin Laden and Omar Abdul Rahman have found pleasant shelter under the shadow of the walls of the Mahdi's tomb. Among the services Turabi performed for the Islamic cause, he was instrumental in obtaining Sudanese passports for Shaikh Omar Abdul Rahman and the then virtually unknown Saudi radical, Osama bin Laden.

The civil war in southern Sudan has seen a return of the slave trade as well as the government in Khartoum turning to raids to capture Sudanese southern blacks to sell to buyers in the Arab Middle East, where Sudanese and Somali slaves have always been prized for their loyalty and intelligence.* Children kidnapped from the south, Judith Miller reports in her *God Has Ninety-Nine Names: Reporting from a Militant Middle East*, can be ransomed from the Islamic schools where they are held captive in the north. "In the Sudan," she writes, "in the summer of 1994, they could be ransomed [for] 372–465 US dollars at the official exchange rate, half that sum on the black market, the real rate of exchange."[36]

A new factor in the Sudanese war has been the introduction of Iraqi troops on the side of the Khartoum regime. First reported in fall 1998 in *Soldier of Fortune*, increasingly these Iraqi reinforcements are taking the brunt against the forces of John Garang and other southern rebels, much like Cuban mercenaries on the side of the Communist government in Angola fought the UNITA army of Jonas Savimbi. (The province of Equatoria, as Miller writes, where Garang has his redoubt, had never been totally subdued by the Khalifa Abdullahi during the Mahdist Era [1885–98], the blacks there being unwilling to submit to Islam again and its slavery.) This will become a growing factor now in the wake of the 1991 Gulf War. With Saddam Hussein's continued defiance, it can be anticipated by his bellicose statements

---

*In the Arab revolt, while T. E. Lawrence drew his guards from the Agheyl tribe, Faisal's was formed from black Sudanese. Even in the Anglo-Egyptian army, Sudanese troops were prized. At Omdurman in 1898, Sudanese serving under Hector MacDonald saved the day for the commanding general, Horatio Herbert Kitchener, in the face of a surprise attack by the *Ansar*.

that he will increasingly strive to take the place of Quaddafi as "leader" of the Arab world against the "aggressive" United States. Such a policy will virtually assure the sending of more Iraqi troops, including Republican Guard units, to join the war in the Sudan. According to a *Jane's* magazine disclosure after Operation Desert Storm, Saddam Hussein managed to spirit a part of his biochemical weapons apparatus to the Sudan, which goes far to explain the presence of Iraqi troops there. Another article in the newsletter *Jane's Pointer* for March 1998 affirmed that the Khartoum regime was going on with "chemical and bacteriological" weapons development; however, this particular facility was not one of those targeted by cruise missiles, following Iraqi practice, it was located in a residential area of Khartoum.

An important development in Saddam Hussein's effort to portray himself as the champion of the Arabs came on January 5, 1998. In a major address, he called on all Arabs to overthrow those governments that were lackeys of the West and were not pursuing the goals of a united Islam. Such an attempt by him to garb himself in the mantle of a *jihad* could be a clear and present sign of serious trouble for the United States in the entire region. In January 1998, some 700 pro-Hamas demonstrators turned out in the streets of Hebron on Israel's West Bank to answer Saddam's call for a united Muslim front against the United States and the Western powers. Such a call was added to his new policy of challenging American and British planes in the northern and southern no-fly zones in Iraq. This same policy on the part of Saddam in challenging American and British overflights would lead to another air campaign against Iraq in 2001, shortly before the September 11 attacks on America.

In addition, according to "Targeting Sudan," by Al J. Venter in *Soldier of Fortune* magazine (December 1998), Khartoum has leased its two main Red Sea ports of Port Sudan and Suakin, strategic sites since the time of the Mahdi's war, to Iran for twenty-five years. Moreover, according to Venter, Cairo was concerned because thousands of the Pasdaran, the Iranian Revolutionary Guards, were apparently stationed in the Sudan. Once again, we see the eastern and southern frontiers of *Dar al-Islam* united against the enemies of the faith, as they were in the days of Saladin.

Furthermore, Venter claims that in October 1997 Turabi hosted a meeting in Khartoum of the militant Islamic Council which included representatives from Afghanistan, Iran, Algeria, the Egyptian Muslim Brotherhood, and even members of fundamentalist groups from Ethiopia and Eritrea. Indeed, it seems like Khartoum has become an Islamic version of the Stalinist Comintern of the

1930s in which representatives of all the world's Communist parties met together to plan a joint strategy against the "capitalist" enemies. (Part of the rationale for the bombing of bin Laden's headquarters in Afghanistan seems to have been the hope of killing Islamic terrorist leaders who were thought to be attending a conference at his compound at that time.) Following a cease-fire agreement in 2000, a peace agreement negotiated by Egypt and Libya was signed between Garang and the government in Khartoum. At the time of the peace accord with Khartoum, Garang had been the leader of the SPLA for two decades. While the peace accord broke down, a new one was put into effect in January 2002 for a six-month cease-fire.

It would be interesting for a moment to consider how the new Islamic Terrorist International is receiving the money for its worldwide operations. Although Claire Sterling speculated in her book *The Terror Network* that the Soviet Union played the role of the "golden goose" for international terrorism, those days are now long past. It is my opinion that the main source of the funds for militant Islam comes from the global trade in illicit drugs. I have already mentioned how the *mujahidin* in Afghanistan paid for its long war by the selling opium (*Papaver somniferum*) cultivated in that country and shipped with the rest of the opium from the "Golden Crescent"* to the ready markets in the West. However, it seems that the role of the Islamic terrorists in the drug trade is much greater than I had anticipated. Abbas Samaya of MENA revealed on December 13, 1992, that some 1,200 Arab-Afghans in Pakistan were involved in smuggling narcotics into the United States and the West. An exposé of the opium traffic from the not-so-puritanical Taliban-controlled areas of Afghanistan appeared in the September 1997 issue of *The Middle East* magazine. Peter Willems reported that "according to the United Nations Drug Control Programme (UNDCP), 40 per cent of all opium on the international drug market—approximately 2,300 metric tons of raw opium—is produced in Afghanistan. The Middle East country now rivals Burma (Myanmar) as the world's leading producer. . . . The UNDCP estimates that 96 per cent of the raw opium produced in Afghanistan comes from Taliban-held areas." The opium trade is extremely profitable to the Afghans, even to the farmers who cultivate the poppy. Willems says that "even though refined heroin commands 50 times more than the price paid the farmer, once it

---

*"Golden Crescent" refers to the opium-producing countries of Turkey, Afghanistan, Iran, and Pakistan in western Asia. Eastern Asia's opium-producing countries, including Myanmar (Burma) and Thailand, are known as the Golden Triangle.

reaches London, Paris, or San Francisco, the poppy farmers of Afghanistan pulled in an estimated $85 million last year [in 1996] alone."

In Afghanistan, the opium problem drew the attention of Radio Free Europe/Radio Liberty on June 26, 2000, the International Day Against Drug Abuse and Illicit Trafficking, the day chosen to draw worldwide attention to the drug trade. Charles Recknagel and Azam Gorgin, in an on-line article titled "Afghanistan: Iran and Other Neighbors Face Growing Drug Problems," note that Afghanistan "produces three more times the opium base than all the other areas of the world combined. The opium base is refined [in Afghanistan] into crude opium and heroin and smuggled through Iran, Pakistan, and Central Asia to markets in the Arab Gulf States and Europe." In a special report on January 1, 2001, Radio Australia quoted a report on Afghan drug trafficking from the UNDCP. The article stated that UNDCP believes that "Afghanistan under the fundamentalist [Taliban] Islamic militia has become the world's largest producer of opium, the raw ingredient of heroin." However, neither the UNDCP or Radio Free Europe/Radio Liberty reported exact figures on the tonnage of the annual Afghan opium crop in their reports.

This opium smuggling was probably the source of the $100 million that Turabi received from Tehran, and which later most likely helped pay for the 1993 World Trade Center disaster. Although the Drug Enforcement Agency (DEA) and Interpol have always listed Turkey and Burma among the top opium producing countries in the world, the opium cultivation in Iran itself seems to have largely been overlooked. As a matter of fact, the opium grown in Iran is of a very superior kind: It has a morphine content of 12 to 13 percent as compared to 7 to 8 percent for the Chinese kind which, as "China White," has been hailed as a worldwide benchmark for its purity. Indeed, in *Hitler's Plot to Kill the Big Three*, about the German attempt to kill Roosevelt, Stalin, and Churchill at the Tehran Conference in 1943, author Laslo Havas estimated that 20 percent "of Iran's total population made a living by growing *Papaver somniferum*."[37] The opium grown in Afghanistan and other Middle Eastern countries, including Iran, by the early 1990s had been redirected from the Golden Triangle route to travel instead to Karachi and Quetta in Pakistan for shipment from there to markets in Europe and the United States.[38]

Islamic militants have turned to illegal drugs as a new kind of "chemical warfare" against the United States. Speaking in *Soldier of Fortune* magazine in May 1988, "Q," a spokesman for Hizbollah, declared, "we are making these drugs for the Devil; the Devil is Americans, Jews, et al. We cannot kill them with guns so we will kill them with drugs." "Q's" statement points to a related prospect of the alliance with Islamic terrorists like the Abu Nidal group with the terrorists of Latin America. Increasingly in recent years, guerrilla groups like the Colombian Fuerzas Armadas de Columbia (FARC), "the Armed Forces of Colombia," have been appropriating the lucrative drug traffic into the United States as a way of funding their war against their governments. Increasingly, the "*narcotrafficantes*," the drug smugglers of the 1970s have been displaced by the "*narcoterroristas*," the terrorists dealing in narcotics in the late 1980s and the 1990s. Emblematic of the unholy union between the Latin *narcoterroristas* and the Islamic militants is the story of the Lebanese drug runner Emilio Checa Kuri, who was affiliated with a Syrian-sponsored terror group. Arrested in Mexico in 1988, while on bail he and his son escaped on Lebanese diplomatic passports and found asylum in Libya. The new alliance between the Colombian drug cartels and Islamic terrorists in the Middle East has fostered a new crop for the Levant as well: Using their understanding with the Colombians, the terrorists in the Middle East are now cultivating cocaine in their homeland to add to the profit coming from their traditional trade in opium. The importance of drug money to the *narcoterroristas* was stated by none other than Colombian President Ernesto Samper in 1997, "the terrorist group FARC has financed its activities with $600 million from the Colombian drug dealers." The international trade in drugs for weapons has given the Colombian guerrillas some unlikely allies—and the United States some new worries. Glenn E. Schweitzer writes in his *Super-Terrorism* how the Russian Mafia has supplied the Colombian terrorists (here the term is used interchangeably with guerrillas) with weapons of war. Schwietzer writes how "Russian vessels have off-loaded AK-47 assault rifles and rocket-propelled grenades in Turbo, Columbia, in exchange for drugs. . . . There have also been reports of alliances among Russian criminals and the Sicilian Mafia, with the mix of arms and drugs central to their joint activities."[39]

Today, there also exists the possibility that we will begin to eat the bitter fruit that was planted with the Panama Canal Treaty during the Carter administration. The Stars and Stripes were lowered forever as we surrendered our last holdings in the Canal Zone to the unstable Panamanian government, already ridden with drug trade corruption, on December 31, 1999. The most immediate casualty of our capitulation was the jungle warfare school that has been operated there by the U.S. Army, where the Spanish-speaking 7th Special Forces taught counterguerrilla warfare to two generations of Latin American soldiers to prepare them to fight the Marxist guerrillas active in their home countries; our army as well has been deprived of this excellent jungle war training facility. Great Britain's 22nd SAS Regiment also participated in the training at the School of the Americas, where the students benefitted from the SAS operations in Borneo against Indonesia, when President Achmed Sukarno had tried to seize the entire island for his country. Confidential sources indicate the SAS, along with the American Delta Force, most likely provided assistance to the Peruvian commandos during their well-known attack on the Japanese Embassy in Lima when it was taken from the terrorist group MRTA in December 1996.

Another danger directly ties the drug trafficking of the Latin Americans with the Chinese once more. COSCO, the Chinese Overseas Shipping Company, is owned, much like Norinco, by the Peoples' Liberation Army. Already, COSCO has leased port facilities at the eastern and the western entrances to the Panama Canal. This development is fraught with danger for the United States for two reasons. The first, strategic, reason, is that in the event of future hostilities with the People's Repubic of China (PRC) over Taiwan, it can be counted on that COSCO will destroy these facilities, thus denying the use of the canal to America in the time of a national emergency. Second, the port facilities make it easy for COSCO to carry out the same drugs-for-weapons deals with Latin American terrorists that Norinco used with the Los Angeles gangs. A new development in the evolution of this traffic is that some of the West Coast gangs in the United States are now Asian, especially Vietnamese and Chinese. An earlier sting operation on the West Coast in 1989–90, Operation Leatherneck, involved the abortive effort of the Vietnamese and Chinese governments to smuggle a treasure trove of Vietnam War surplus weapons from southeast Asia to the gangs on the West Coast. Some of the leaders of these gangs are former militant members of the Maoist Red Guards, who would certainly be dedicated to spreading terrorism within the United States in the event of a crisis with the PRC. Some of these new gangs probably have links with the Chinese triads (criminal organizations) that now operate in most major American and Canadian cities, such as the Golden Dragon, 14K, and On Leong triad. However, in 1999, the Peoples' Republic did not face the serious threat from her restive Muslim minority that it does today, and there had been no attack on America to alert the world's nations to the critical danger posed by international terror. In the aftermath of September 11, previous speculation seems irrelevant.

Terrorist and resistance groups like the FARC already show a high degree of technological sophistication. An increasing number of these groups have short-wave stations to broadcast their messages; some of these stations can be heard in the United States depending on the time of day and atmospheric conditions via the short wave band. FARC, for example, broadcasts "La Voz de la Resistencia," the Voice of the Resistance, on the short wave band on 6240 kHz (kilohertz) at 11:00 A.M. and 10:00 P.M., GMT (Greenwich Mean Time). "The Voice of the Sudan" run by the anti-Khartoum National Democratic Alliance is heard 4:00 to 6:00 A.M. GMT and again at 4:00 to 6:00 P.M. GMT daily (8000, 9025, 10000, and 12000 or 12008 kHz). The "Voice of the Sudan" is based at 16 Camaret Court, Lorne Gardens, in London; transmissions are in Arabic. The "Voice of the Sudan Alliance Forces," also known as the "Voice of the Popular Armed Uprising," can be heard in Arabic from 4:00 to 5:00 A.M. and P.M. at 7000 kHz.

No attempt to document the financing of the Islamic terrorists can be complete without some words about the Bank of Credit and Commerce International (BCCI), which the CIA's Richard Gates would later label "the Bank of Crooks and Criminals International." Although full coverage of this interesting financial institution is not possible here, brief comment must be made because of the unique "window" the bank provided the FBI and CIA into the world of the financing of terror's black operations. If intelligence is, as the CIA's James Jesus Angleton remarked, a "wilderness of mirrors," then the BCCI was a looking glass extraordinaire! Bank of Credit and Commerce International was apparently founded in 1972 by the Pakistani entrepreneur Agha Hasan Abedi. Throughout its history, the BCCI would keep the Middle Eastern connection, like a thread running throughout one of the magical carpets in the *Arabian Nights*. The last chief shareholders of the bank, after its operations were shut down amid an avalanche of widespread fraud, was Shaikh Said ibn Sultan al-Nayahan, ruler of Abu Dhabi and president of the United Arab Emirates (UAE), who in 1991 was supposed to pay off some of BCCI's outstanding debt. Abu Dhabi's officials estimated the debt pay-outs might reach $12 billion.[40]

From the late 1970s on, the BCCI seems to have become involved in the world of drug trafficking, from the time of the Afghan War when Islamabad and Karachi would become major entrepôts for heroin destined for the West and the United States. Stories from many sources persist of the involvement of the Pakistani intelligence service in this illegal narcotics activity. An unnamed arms dealer told reporter Jonathan Beaty in a September 1991 *Time* magazine article, "you can't draw a line separating the bank's black operatives and Pakistan's intelligence services. And in Karachi [the] bankers are surprisingly patriotic." Pakistan's Finance Minister Sartaj Asis admitted that the BCCI's Karachi office did handle funds from the heroin trade, which was generated by *mujahidin* groups in Afghanistan, under the aegis of the Pakistani intelligence, which grew opium to help finance their struggle with the Russians.

Showing the growing congruence of drug trade with terrorism at this time, Abu Nidal, under the pseudonym of Shakir Farhan, had an account in the London affiliate of the BCCI. At the same time, the Medellin Cartel of Colombia utilized the bank's Latin American offices as a depository for its cocaine profits. Indeed, the "shadow" accounts that turned up in the audits of the BCCI may have been used to help fund the Abu Nidal group's terror operations in the Western Hemisphere.

At the same time, the CIA and Saudi Arabia may have used the BCCI to help funnel money to the Afghan *mujahidin* in their fight against the Russians. Tom Morganthau, writing in *Newsweek* in August 1991, alleges that the CIA sent $2 billion through the bank to finance the *mujahidin*'s war effort against the Russians. These allegations may indeed be true, and in the world of realpolitik of the time the CIA may have been forced to utilize the good offices of the BCCI. At the time of the Afghan War, the Reagan administration, like the Carter presidency previous to it, was justly concerned that if Afghanistan could be completely subdued by the Soviets, then Pakistan would soon follow, and Russia would have its long desired ports near the Persian Gulf. Furthermore, with the treaties that India had made with the Soviet Union, and the one Iran had with the Soviets since the 1920s, it would be obvious that both Iran and India would have cast their lots in with the victors and the Persian Gulf would become a Soviet sea. The entire region's oil supply would have been the Soviets'. At the time, many Americans were opposed to our intervention in Afghanistan and more public funding might have been quashed. Therefore, the Reagan administration and the CIA really would have had no choice other than to use the BCCI as a "back channel" to fund the *mujahidin*—if Afghanistan were to be prevented from falling to the Soviet Union. The funding of the struggle against the Soviets in Afghanistan, it is interesting to note that Shaikh Kamal Adham, chief of Saudi intelligence, was also a figure in the BCCI story. A shareholder in BCCI, Adham is also identified as "among key contacts in the Middle East for US intelligence."[41]

Furthermore, the CIA's involvement with the BCCI gave the agency a unique "inside" perspective from which to chart and observe the transfers of funds that were the financial lifeblood of international terrorism. An unnamed American intelligence source told Morganthau "the opportunity to collect intelligence far outweighed [the risk of] any dealings with unsavory characters. When you're pursuing scoundrels, you can't be a boy scout." Intelligence gathering, after all, was the CIA's main mission when it was chartered by the National Security Act of 1947. (It may be mentioned parenthetically that Abu Nidal's terror operations seem to have closed down once funding from BCCI accounts was no longer accessible. If the CIA was instrumental in disclosing covertly the information that made possible the downfall of the BCCI, after we no longer needed it to help finance the Afghan War, then it presented an excellent view of how to orchestrate an intelligence operation.)

However, during the week of March 15, 1999, a new and dangerous development occurred in the ongoing story of the alliance between the *narcoterroristas* and the radical Muslims. Apparently, the alliance of the *narcoterroristas* and the Islamic militants had spread to the United States, following the well-worn paths of the drug trade from Mexico and South America. On March 16, the FBI announced that a raid in Los Angeles had uncovered an operation which, according to CBS Radio News, had provided bogus passports and other needed papers (such as immigration "green cards" and welfare cards, it can be assumed) to hundreds of people with direct links to the "Muhahideen al-Khalq," the Iranian terrorist student group that had seized the American embassy in Tehran in 1978.

7

The United States and Jihad

T he beginnings of Muslim antipathy toward the United States of course stretch back to May 1948, when the United States became the main supporter of the state of Israel. (It never seemed to bother Muslim logic that the other great power to help create the state of Israel was the Soviet Union, which was the Arabs' main backer in the subsequent Arab-Israeli wars.) On the eve of the Six Day War in 1967, Egypt's President Gamal Abdel Nasser made the Arabs' feelings clear. He stated that "we are confronting Israel and the West as well—the West, which created Israel and despised us Arabs, and which ignored us before and after 1948."

During the years since 1948, the United States has born the brunt of Arab hostility for its support of the state of Israel, an anti-American ideology crystallized in the Ayatollah Khomeini damning the United States as the "Great Satan." Yet, consistently, through Democratic and Republican administrations—a political cohesion rarely seen in political history—the American people have continued to support the forces of political freedom in the Middle East, whether it has been by preserving Israel from the threat of annihilation in the Middle East wars of 1848, 1967, and 1973, or of sending in U.S. Marines to support peace efforts in Lebanon in 1958 and 1982. On January 20, 1961, President John F. Kennedy enunciated in his Inaugural Address the philosophy of his generation: "Let every nation know, whether it wishes us well or ill, that we shall pay any price, bear any burden, meet any hardship, support any friend, oppose any foe to assure the survival and the success of liberty." This has been the cornerstone of American foreign policy in the Middle East, regardless of its myriad foreign and domestic detractors, up to—and beyond—the attack on America in September 2001.

Typical of Arab hatred, is Libya's Col. Muammar Quaddafi, whom American intelligence has determined to be an opportunistic purveyor of terror. However, it may be we have truly underestimated Quaddafi's real devotion to Islam and *jihad*. Indeed, Iraq's Saddam Hussein appears to have transferred his chemical and biological warfare supplies through Libya to their final destination in the Sudan. The colonel's *Green Book* seems to be a sincere effort at reconciling Islam to the demands and realities of the modern world, not some pop propaganda like *The Thoughts of Chairman Mao*. Moreover, his frequent retreats into the desert may actually be what he claims them to be—religious journeys of meditation—and not public relations gambits aimed at the common people of Tripoli. A key point in this is that the white Arabic attire, especially the unique way he wraps his head, is identical to the garb worn by earlier Senussi mystics in Libya—perhaps Colonel Quaddafi is a genuine, modern one. However much the Lockerbie attack and the World Trade Center bombing of 1993 have influenced our thinking, it is necessary to look ahead at what may be the future of an Islamic *jihad* targeted against the United States.

The first obvious question to be answered is why the East African embassies were targeted in the first place, instead of high-profile targets like embassies in Beirut (bombed in 1983) or even our military barracks in Riyadh, Saudi Arabia? One answer is their very remoteness from the perceived epicenter of the "Middle East problem"—Saudi Arabia, Israel, Lebanon, and Syria. When the U.S. ambassador to Kenya, in an unusual moment of precognition, asked for money to improve the defenses of the embassy against terrorist attack, the State Department refused the request for the additional funds. I believe the response would have been much different if the ambassador had called from Beirut or Amman in Jordan! The African embassies were easier targets.

Another answer is the lack of realization of the important part Africa has played in the history of Islam, similar to the lack of perception of the vitality of central Asia to *Dar al-Islam*. This dates back, of course, to the great era of the Arab conquests. From the conquest of Egypt (642 C.E.), the Arab armies had their eyes on Sudan and the rest of sub-Saharan and equatorial Africa. The Fatimids are believed to have been the first to consolidate Muslim power in the Sudan. At the same time that conquering Muslim armies were following the Blue and White Niles south, Arabs at sea were colonizing the entire east coast of Africa, as far as what would today be Tanzania, whose capital, Dar-es-Salaam, means "the place of peace" in Arabic. For eight centuries before Vasco da Gama's fleet of Portuguese caravels put into the harbor of Calicut in southwest India, sea-going Arab *dhows* dominated the trade of the Indian Ocean.

The ultimate paradox of the Muslim experience in East Africa is that, while intertribal slavery had existed from the time of ancient Zimbabwe, it was the entrepreneurial Arabs who made the slave trade one of the world's first great industries. Thousands, if not millions, of Africans were captured by Arab slavers to feed the bazaars of the Ottoman Empire and the Middle East. In 1898, a place called Tsavo gained notoriety when John Patterson, a British officer of the royal engineers, killed two man-eating lions at Tsavo Junction while trying to lay a bridge there for the British East African Railway. Patterson wrote about his stunning feat in his book, *The Man-Eaters of Tsavo*. In the native dialect, *Tsavo* means "the place of slaughter," because so many blacks were killed by the slavers here when it was felt they were not strong enough to make the trip to Mombasa and Zanzibar, the major slave ports on the coast. Indeed, Zanzibar, the wealthiest Arab emirate on the east coast, made its wealth over this trade in "black ivory," slaves. Thus it is one of the enduring ironies of African history that so many black Africans have embraced the faith whose devotees made slaves of so many of them. It was to attack the slave trade that the British conquered Zanzibar. Nevertheless, it is true that thousands of black Africans became converted to Islam, and became willing adherents to their new creed, the name of which after all, means submission to the will of Allah.

Thus, when Osama bin Laden chose to attack in Kenya and Tanzania, he not only benefitted from embassies in a part of the world least prepared for terror strikes, but also from the support of indigenous African Muslims, like Mohammed Saddiq Odeh, who were as devoutly servants of the *jihad* as was bin Laden himself. The East African coast was also the home to Kenyans who had fought in Afghanistan, thus introducing a new type of Islamic warrior into the modern *jihad*, the African Afghan. It is significant that, about two days before President Clinton visited the politically charged Middle East in December 1998, with stops in both Israel and in the Palestinian Authority (including Gaza), forty embassies in Africa, not the Middle East, were closed for fear of terror attacks in the wake of any action taken against Iraq. While embassies in Africa were shut down for fear of terrorism, President Clinton safely appeared before the Palestinian Assembly, next to Yassir Arafat, to the tumultuous applause of some of the worst "anti-American" terrorists of the past thirty years!

Although one hates to be a Cassandra, it appears there will be more of the same. The Muslim ire will remain while we support the state of Israel and maintain troops of "unbelievers" on the soil of Saudi Arabia. However, the future of this policy may be in doubt. Prince Sultan, the member of the Saudi royal family who was honorary commander-in-chief of the Allied forces in the Gulf War, wrote an article calling for the possible removal of all American forces from his country. According to a press release from the Saudi press agency dated May 3, 1999, on a state visit to Iran, Prince Sultan spoke of the possiblity of forming a pan-Islamic Defense Force: "Prince Sultan said this was a good idea, and one to be discussed by the various Islamic oranizations. He added that it would be a positive development if Muslims, who constitute one-third of the world's population, could develop a non-agressive force to serve the cause of security in the Muslim world." After the September 11 attack on America, there was no further mention of Prince Sultan's plan. Although shocking to the American defense community, the prince's comments made perfect sense: He was playing realpolitik, Saudi style. With the unstable health of the current King Fahd, and the malleable order of succession to the throne, Prince Sultan may be positioning himself to be the next king (or the power behind the throne) by playing the "Ibn Saud" card: by allying himself with the country's militant Wahabi sect. Ever since the 1929–30 Wahabi rebellion, Ibn Saud's dynasty has taken great pains not to alienate the explosive power of Saudi Arabia's "religious right." Indeed, fear of antagonizing this potent force is what is behind the notable reluctance of the Saudi government to move forward with the investigation of the 1996 bombing of our barracks there, at Dharan. With the bombing of the barracks as a grim reminder, we can never relax our security in Saudi Arabia again. The alliance Ibn Saud began with the Wahabi Ikwhan brings to mind the old Appalachian saying, "if you dance with the devil, you don't change the devil—the devil changes you!" The wrath of the United States in the aftermath of the 2001 attacks on Washington and New York City may have caused His Highness to reconsider any overt plan against American troops in Saudi Arabia, especially since it would look as though he were supporting Osama bin Laden.

On May 4, 2000, a serious piece of news appeared in the newspapers, but was not given the front page coverage it merited. The wire services reported that Prince Sultan was involved in serious negotiations with Iran to form a mutual defense agreement with that country, and even went to Tehran to discuss the terms of the treaty. This development posed a very grave threat to the entire American position in the Middle East. If Prince Sultan's negotiations reached fruition a defensive pact would be forged between Saudi Arabia, our hitherto best ally, and our worst enemy in the entire Middle Eastern region, Iran, the sponsor of state-directed terrorism against the United States. Such a pact is a matter of grave concern even if the moderate Ayatollah Khameni remains in power in Tehran—if militants overthrow him, it could be a catastrophe. This movement of Prince Sultan to embrace Islamic militancy is shocking indeed. Depending on how far he intends to go to position himself as the friend of the militants in Saudi Arabia, it may even end in a Saudi request for us to vacate our bases in Saudi Arabia, thus virtually destroying our current geostrategic position in the entire Middle East. Since the initial overtures, however, nothing more has been heard of the prince's diplomatic initiative. Apparently, in the collegial decision-making that goes on within the royal House of Saud, the family decided that the kingdom still needed to rely on the United States to provide a protective shield for their dynasty. It is well known that bin Laden would like to remove the House of Saud even more than he would care to evict the Americans from his Saudi homeland.

In 1979, the Saudi royal house received an unwanted reminder of the continued power of the Ikhwan in the most sensational terror attack ever seen in a Muslim nation. During the early morning hours of November 20, the Grand Mosque in Mecca was invaded by a force of armed Ikhwan under the leadership of Juhaiman Ibn Mohammed Utaibi, a former Saudi National Guardsman. Wilhelm Dietl notes in his 1984 book *Holy War* that during Utaibi's youth the Ikhwan had been revitalized by the preaching of the charismatic Shaikh Abdul Asis Ibn Bas, who was blind like Shaikh Omar Abdul Rahman. Supported by fundamentalists from countries as diverse as Egypt and Kuwait, Utaibi was determined to take over the Grand Mosque on this date because it marked the beginning of the Muslim New Year. Utaibi proclaimed his friend Mohammed Ibn Abdullah al-Qahtani the new Mahdi, the Expected One of Allah. The Ikhwan rebellion soon spread to the cities of Taif and Riyadh, where a bomb was exploded at the king's palace.

Unable to defeat the Ikhwan, and faced with the same fate as the shah of

Iran, King Khalid was forced to call on outside help from the French to bring the Ikhwan uprising to an end. On November 23, a four-man force from the French anti-terrorist group, Groupement d'Intervention de la Gendarmerie Nationale (GIGN), comprising a Captain Barril and three non-commissioned officers, was brought to Mecca to help in the siege of the Grand Mosque. After suffering severe losses, the Saudi security forces under the direction of the French defeated the last of the Ikhwan on the afternoon of December 4. Some 117 of the 500 or more Ikhwan were killed before the rest surrendered; among those killed was the new Mahdi, al-Qahtani. Sixty-three of the rebels, most likely including Juhaiman, were beheaded on the orders of the king on January 9, 1980. It was not until nearly the end of January that rioting in the Shi'ia community, inspired by the preaching of Ayatollah Khomeini and the seizure of the mosque in Mecca, was finally put down.

More ominous still is that there was a secretive purge of the Saudi armed forces, in which the commander of the army himself was fired. According to Dietl in *The Holy War*, "the Saudi armed forces were thoroughly purged. Six high officers, including the commander of the army and police, lost their posts. Just how far the purge of lower-ranking officers went is difficult to ascertain."[1] This points to the possibility that the fundamentalist uprising was more far-reaching than was supposed in the West, and extended within the armed forces themselves. The memory of the 1979 crisis, when for a few days King Khalid seemed to be on the verge of following the shah on the road into exile, is still strong in the Saudi royal house, and virtually guarantees that no member of the royal family would ever challenge the militants in the kingdom if a confrontation can be avoided by any means necessary. Herein perhaps lies the reason that the Saudis have been so notably noncompliant in helping to find the bombers of the Al-Khobar Towers at Dharan in 1996; either members of the royal family and the security services are afraid of the power of the Ikhwan, or they are in fact members, or at least supporters, of the grim Wahabi Brotherhood.

The possibility of continued terrorism on the African continent, especially in East Africa and the Mahgreb (the countries of northwest Africa), where there is a Muslim majority, remains an enduring threat for the future. Perhaps the most pro-Western country in the Mahgreb is Morocco. At the height of Palestinian terrorism against Israel and the West, His Royal Highness King Hassan II permitted American movie director John Huston to film *The Man Who Would Be King* in his country. He even permitted a troupe of female folk dancers to perform for the American camera, surely an enlightened act in any Muslim country! Indeed, the Moroccans I know are the most cosmopolitan of the Arabs and Muslims I have met, reflecting their country's historic position as a gateway between Europe and the Arab lands. However, the possibility of the fanaticism in neighboring Algeria bleeding over into Morrocco cannot be ignored, especially among the Berber tribes who once followed Abd el-Krim. The Muslim Brotherhood even has a branch in this far outpost of Islam, although it has up until now been relatively benign, having adherents mainly in the academic circles. Wilhelm Dietl observed that one of its leaders, Shaikh Abdessalem Yassine, was inspector of education in Morocco, and would have been in a good position to proselytize radical Islamicist ideology in the country's educational system. Although pacific up until now, the infrastructure of the Muslim Brotherhood could quickly be activated for terrorist activities. Three of the Ikhwan commandos who took part in the 1979 attack at the Grand Mosque in Mecca, it should be noted, were Moroccans. Additionally, the ancestors of today's Moroccans are the warriors who several times carried bloody *jihad* across the Straits of Gibraltar into Spain.

Before his tragic death in 2000, King Hussein of Jordan had used his considerable influence to bring about the signing of the Wye River Agreement on October 23, 1998, by the Palestinians and the Israelis. The agreement bound Israel to hand over a further 13 percent of the West Bank of the Jordan to the Palestinians. This would have brought the territory on the West Bank under the control of Yassir Arafat's Palestinian Authority to 40 percent. In return, Arafat promised to curtail the activities of terrorists attacking Israel from Palestinian soil. The Wye River Agreement was one of the casualties of the renewed fighting between Israel and the Palestinians when the Second *Intifida*, or uprising, against the Israelis began on September 28, 2000, after Israel Prime Minister Ariel Sharon, whom Arabs regard as their mortal enemy, visited the al-Aqsa mosque complex in Jerusalem.

A week prior to his death, King Hussein shocked the Jordanian population and the entire Middle East by removing his brother Prince Hassan as heir apparent, after Hassan had held that position for some thirty-four years. In Hassan's place, Hussein appointed his own son, Prince Abdullah. Abdullah lacks the diplomatic experience of Hassan, however, Abdullah has made the military his career. After attending the British Royal Military Academy at Sandhurst, where his father the king had been a cadet, Abdullah served as a tank officer with the British army in Europe. More importantly for Jordan, he is credited with bringing the Jordanian army to a new level of combat readiness and has presided over the improvement of the army's mainly Bedouin Royal Special Forces, which are also charged with protection of the king and his family. Considering the country's large Palestinian populace, the fact that Abdullah's wife is a Palestinian may help keep that group from becoming a threat to the stability of the kingdom, as they were in 1970.

Islamic militancy has had a long history in the Hashemite Kingdom of Jordan. According to Judith Miller in *God Has Ninety-Nine Names: Reporting from a Militant Middle East*, some accounts date the arrival of the Muslim Brotherhood in Jordan to 1934. But, most likely the Brotherhood came to the kingdom with the founding of a chapter in Amman in 1945. At the time, then Emir Abdullah told the Brotherhood that they would be tolerated if they avoided politics and just "stuck to the mosque and prayer." Throughout the early years of the kingdom, in the reign of Abdullah II, after he became king, and through much of Hussein's reign, the Brotherhood stood by the throne. Even in 1970, when King Hussein pushed out the PLO, the Jordanian Brotherhood supported him; Palestinians were notably few among the ranks of the Brotherhood. (However, some of the Palestinian brethren did open up a training camp in 1969, but too late to have any effect in the "Black September" battles.) Nevertheless, the king's concern with the Brotherhood, although not viewing it really as a threat to his throne, mounted. In the 1980s, for example, membership was up to some 3,000 adherents, according to Jordanian intelligence estimates. Even worse, the Brotherhood began to recruit among the Jordanian army, the backbone of Hashemite rule since the 1918 foundation of the state.

However, in 1986, economic problems led to civil unrest, which prompted Hussein to carry out a democratization of the Hashemite system. Press restrictions were liberalized, and a new parliament was elected in 1989, the first since 1967, the year of the Six Day War with Israel, which Nasser of Egypt had duped Hussein into entering by lying that the Israeli Air Force had already been destroyed! To Hussein's chagrin, the Brotherhood and other militant groups won a considerable percentage of the seats in the new parliament. Unlike the Brotherhood, other Islamic parties had been openly hostile to the Hashemite rule. Among these was the Hizb-al-Tahrir, the Liberation party, which had been founded by Shaikh Taqi al-Din al-Nabhani, a Palestinian firebrand who had once belonged to the Jordanian Brotherhood.

Before the Gulf War began in 1990, Hussein reversed his earlier policy of attacking the Palestinian militants. Indeed, Judith Miller recalls that George Habash of the PFLP and Nayef Hawarmeh, of the Democratic Front for the Liberation of Palestine, were enthusiastically welcomed by the king, even though he had forcefully evicted both of them in 1970. During the conflict, King Hussein, to Washington's intense displeasure, embraced the cause of Saddam Hussein (although he never committed any Jordanian forces to help the Iraqis across the desert frontier). Sensing the growth of Pan-Arabic and Islamic feeling as the people started to view Saddam as a new Saladin, fighting the infidel in the Gulf, Hussein made Mudar Badran, an Islamic sympathizer, his prime minister, and Abdel-Latif Arabiyat speaker of the parliament. Arabiyat was a member of the Brotherhood. The Islamist "War Cabinet," however, soon began to foist Islamic decrees on the secularist Jordanian society, a move which caused widespread resistance. When moderate Muslim and Christian opposition grew toward the War Cabinet (by this time the war was over and Saddam had been defeated), King Hussein listened to the popular voice and happily disbanded it. Hussein completed the symbolic destruction of the power of the Islamists by signing his historic peace treaty with Israel in 1995.

Indeed, a potent reason for Hussein having appointed Abdullah to follow him is that the late monarch remembered the "Black September" attempt in 1970 by Yassir Arafat and the Palestinians to seize power in Jordan, and the power shown by the militants in the 1989 elections. There had been many attempts on King Hussein's life, quite a few of which were the work of Palestinians who never have forgotten the slaughter of the PLO in 1970, especially in the decisive battle of Jesreh. (One cannot forget either that the young Hussein was with his grandfather, King Abdullah, when Palestinians shot and killed Abdullah on his way to prayer at the Al-Aqsa mosque; the young prince barely escaped wounding or death himself. A bullet fired at the young prince only missed killing him because it bounced off a bar of medals he was wearing at the time—his grandfather had insisted he accompany him to the Al-Aqsa mosque in military uniform, which King Abdullah rarely wore, even when reviewing his Arab Legion, the predecessor of the modern Jordanian army.) Throughout Hussein's reign, most of the critics in Jordan were among the largely Palestinian-born, educated elite. Realizing the hostility of the Palestinians, it must have occurred to Hussein that in the event of his death Arafat and the PLO could be tempted to seize power in Jordan once more. Therefore, it was imperative that Crown Prince Abdullah, with the fierce loyalty of the Bedouin and the mainly Bedouin armed forces, succeed him on the throne of the Hashemite Kingdom.

While King Hussein was on the throne, he moved to create a more tolerant atmosphere in Jordan among Christians, Jews, and Muslims. In 1996, while the Mullah Omar was creating a theocratic Islamic dictatorship in Afghanistan, Hussein was working on the Royal Institute for Inter-Faith Studies in his capital city of Amman. As Roland Dallas wrote in his biography of the king, "no institute for the study of Christianity existed in the Muslim world until the Royal Institute was founded."[2] Its director, the historian Kamal Salibi, was also proud of the fact that the members of the institute carried on a fruitful discussion with its counterparts in Israel. This was in complete variance with bin Laden's often voiced hatred of "Crusaders and Jews."

❀ ❀ ❀

During 1999, Islamic terrorism spread to the Republic of South Africa. A Muslim fundamentalist group in Cape Town, styling itself the People Against Gangsterism and Drugs (PAGAD), had begun a war against alleged criminals and drug sellers in the poorer neighborhoods of the city. However, the PAGAD has become dangerously politicized. According to the U.S. State Department's "Patterns of Global Terrorism 2000," listed on the Internet, PAGAD "by early 1998 . . . had become antigovernment and anti-Western." Now, declaring itself a supporter of Islamic fundamentalism (PAGAD was founded by a militant group known as Quibla), it has launched an all-out attack against moderate Muslims in the city, targeting their clerics for attack as well as bombing their mosques. Indeed, an explosion on January 1, 1999, took place on the city's waterfront, not far from the Planet Hollywood club, the site of the third terrorist bombing experienced in Africa in August 1998. Two were killed and twenty injured in the Planet Hollywood atrocity. A police captain was ambushed and killed in Cape Town on January 14 by three gunmen thought to be from PAGAD. (Anecdotal evidence indicates that PAGAD provided the bombers who carried out bin Laden's wishes in Cape Town.) The situation became so serious that former president Nelson Mandela's government dispatched troops to the affected areas of Cape Town to try to restore law and order, as assaults on moderate Muslims continued to mount. Then Deputy President Thabo Mbeki personally visited the area as a testimony to the government's intentions to restore order to the restive city. (Mbeki succeeded Nelson Mandela as president on June 16, 1999.) Speaking for the moderate Muslims in the city, Imam Rachid Omar told *Philadelphia Inquirer* reporter Andrew Maykooth (January 24, 1999), "we gave the deputy president a moral mandate. We said to him in no uncertain terms that the government should do whatever it requires to bring peace and stability to our region."

It seems more than coincidental that within a week of the renewed bombings attributed to PAGAD, Executive Outcomes (EO), the highly successful modern mercenary company, was closed down abruptly in South Africa. Executive Outcomes has had a very close relationship with the Mandela government. As David Shearer writes, "the company was established in 1989 by Eeben Barlow and is staffed almost exclusively by veterans from the former South African Defense Force. Executive Outcomes has enjoyed a notable combat record, being responsible for the severe battering of Jonas Savimbi's UNITA, when hired by the Angolan government in May 1993. It also savaged the Revolutionary United Front (RUF) terrorists when it went to work in Sierra Leone in 1995."[3]

It seems apparent that EO was formed clandestinely with the approval of Nelson Mandela, who became president of South Africa at about the same time Barlow founded EO. The very troops who would have posed a potential threat to the establishment of Mandela's government were the members of the South African Defense Force, which had fought against Mandela's African National Congress (ANC) guerrillas for nearly thirty years. This is especially true when one considers that the Defense Force had already absorbed former members of the Rhodesian army, including the celebrated antiterrorist Selous Scouts, named for the British hunter and explorer Frederick Courtenay Selous, who was killed while fighting the Germans in East Africa during World War I. The South African special forces even conducted high-profile and devastating raids into neighboring black African countries which provided bases for the ANC's guerrilla army.

Indeed, it seems that Executive Outcomes was really Mandela's version of the French Foreign Legion. Executive Outcomes was founded to channel the energies of veterans of the Defense Force who might pose a danger to Mandela's administration by using them in highly profitable mercenary operations in a very volatile Africa.

With the continuance of wars and skirmishes in Africa, it at first seems mysterious that Executive Outcomes would close down its operations, especially when it was one of South Africa's main sources of dearly needed hard currency. However, the rise of violent Islamic militancy with the PAGAD campaign may have changed the equation for the Mandela government. Already having to commit troops to what was fast becoming an Islamic insurrection, it might have seemed more important for the South African government to cause Executive Outcomes to go out of business—in case its well-trained troops might be needed to keep order within South Africa itself!

Somalia is best known to Americans for the tragic debacle in 1993 which resulted in the deaths of the U.S. Army Rangers in the capital of Mogadishu. On October 3, 1993, a force of the U.S. Army 75th Rangers regiment and the elite Delta Force were sent to arrest the Somali warlord Mohammed Fara Aidid, but the strength of Aidid's militia was seriously underestimated. By the time our forces were finally rescued on October 4 by a relief force from the United Nations contingent they were serving with, some eighteen Americans had been killed. Although viewed at the time as a battle between competing factions, it now seems that militant Islamists were also involved in the fighting (most Somalis are Muslim). Indeed, there are rumors that Osama bin Laden was in Mogadishu during the United Nations' failed peace-keeping operation. Bin Laden himself boasted of being involved in the shooting down of the helicopter bearing the Rangers to their target in the squalid town.

The presence of Islamic militancy cannot be taken out of the Somali equation, even today. In the past, in the 1970s and early 1980s, Somalia was a hotbed of Muslim and Palestinian militancy under the rule of Mohammed Siad Barre, and could become a bastion of the *jihad* again, especially with the influence of bin Laden. Barre was a de facto ally of the Soviet Union and received bountiful military supplies from the Soviets, including the use of some 6,000 Soviet military advisors. (In return for which, the Soviet navy received the right to use the old British colonial port of Berbera on the Red Sea and a Soviet military presence was established in the country, to the chagrin of the United States.) During the capture of the French Airbus Flight 139 that precipitated the July 1976 Israeli rescue attempt at Entebbe, the terror advance team was stationed in Somalia and later moved to Uganda when the plane landed at Entebbe. As if to make up for the Entebbe failure a year before, in October 1977, a German Lufthansa airliner was seized by the

Palestinian PFLP and flown to Mogadishu airport. On October 17, in a classic raid, the plane was taken back and the hostages saved by the (then) West German anti-terrorist force, the GSG-9, under its commander, later Brig. Gen. Ulrich Wegener. (The GSG-9, the Grenzchutzgruppe-9, is part of the German Border Police, or then the Bundesgrenzchutz.)

In December 1976, as Alvin Z. Rubinstein wrote in *Moscow's Third World Strategy*, the Ethiopian government, the Derg, which had overthrown pro-American Emperor Haile Selassie in 1974, also had signed an arms agreement with the USSR, and proclaimed itself a "Marxist-Leninist" state. Mengitsu Haile Mariam later emerged as the strongman in the Derg. In March and April 1977, Soviet President Nikolai Podgorny and Cuban Premier Fidel Castro, whose army provided the Soviets with mercenary proxies in Africa, both tried to broker a peace between feuding Somalia and Ethiopia, but to no avail. With the military arsenal the Soviets had supplied, Barre then launched a clandestine attack on the Ogaden Province of neighboring Ethiopia (which was ethnically Somali), with the Western Somali Liberation Front, and then launched the open ruinous invasion in July 1977 of the Ogaden. The Soviets, never ones to miss an opportunity, then switched all their support to the Marxist Ethiopian government of Mengitsu Haile Mariam. According to the May 14, 1977 (London) *Economist*, one Soviet diplomat pointedly told a Somali in Mogadishu at this time, "if Socialism wins in Ethiopia we will have 30 million friends there plus the ports of Assab and Massawa. You Somalis are only 3 million." It was then that Barre abrogated his treaty with the Soviets, turning to the United States for help instead. From then on, both the Soviet Union and Ethiopia waged a covert campaign aimed at bringing about Barre's downfall. However, Barre turned again toward Moscow in 1988. He subsequently lost power in 1991 in a coup led by Mohammed Aidid. The Somali downfall into clan warfare and anarchy soon followed, including the tragic intervention of U.S. troops.

❁ ❁ ❁

As stated previously, the Balkans, the traditional northern frontier of Islam since Ottoman times, will continue to remain a fecund area for the growth of Islamic terrorism throughout Europe. Once the U.N. forces leave the former Yugoslavia, it is a real possibility that the militant cells which the Iranians have established in Bosnia will awake, like espionage "sleeper" agents, to begin acts of sabotage and terror against the Western and American infidels. This is especially true if a future independent state is made for the Muslims of Kosovo Province, in spite of the fact that the Serbs claim Kosovo as the birth place of their nation, and thus it joins the ranks of Muslim Albania and Bosnia. Indeed, with the pivotal position of the Balkans in Europe, these terrorists, stiffened by a backbone of Arab Afghans, could really unleash a campaign of terrorism unseen in Europe since the days of the Red Brigade and the Baader-Meinhof Gang in the 1970s.

It is a certainty that American embassies and other installations will remain targets of opportunity for Islamic terrorists throughout the world because of our steadfast support of Israel and, again, our continued military presence in the Persian Gulf. Given the recent bellicose actions of Saddam Hussein, this presence in the Gulf seems to be becoming a permanent fixture of American strategy abroad, as indeed might be said of the continued positioning of U.S. forces in the Balkans. In the Middle East, terror groups like Hamas and Hizbollah, who do not recognize Yassir Arafat's Palestinian Authority, will continue to remain the greatest potential danger to both Americans and Israelis. It should be noted, however, that Arafat, in his declared quest for peace, never expressed any grief or sympathy after the bombings of the American embassies in East Africa. Furthermore, Arafat's announced goal of proclaiming a Palestinian state in May 1999 carried with it the possibility of heightened tension with Israel, if not the renewal of outright war. Fortunately, cooler heads prevailed and Arafat in the interests of peace refrained from issuing such a volatile declaration. When the international criminals of al-Qaeda struck at the United States on September 2001, Arafat issued an apparently severe message of condolence to the American people. Moreover, the *Philadelphia Inquirer* and the *New York Times* reported how his security forces physically intimidated photographers trying to film any pro–bin Laden demonstrations among the Palestinians.

Central Asia will remain a hotbed of Islamic militancy, even after the defeat of al-Qaeda and the Taliban in December 2001. While organized resistance had collapsed by Christmas of 2001, guerrilla attacks by former al-Qaeda and Taliban supporters against the new American installations like those at Kandahar airfield quickly began. As long as Osama bin Laden and Mullah Omar remain alive and free, they will remain as symbols for their former followers to rally around. The threat will increase if the UN peace-keeping force and American troops withdraw sometime in 2002 and leave behind the fragile government of new Afghan President Hamid Karzai. Additionally, the fundamentalist ayatollahs in Iran still control important government ministries like those of defense and internal security, and continue to exert influence there. The efforts of Iranian president Mohammed Khatami to moderate the extremist heritage of the Ayatollah Khomeini continue to be frustrated. For example, on January 6, 1998, the Islamic Intelligence Agency of the Tehran government arrested some of its own agents in the murders of five liberal Iranians who backed Khatami's proposed reforms in their country.

In the crisis in September 2001, the Iranian response reflected more the internal situation than the foreign one. While Ayatollah Khatami, the embattled liberalizing president, expressed sincere regret at the tragedies in New York and Washington, he also warned the United States not to violate Iranian air space in the event of any military operations in Afghanistan. Most noteworthy is the fact that when the attack took place, the Iranian government did not vigorously condemn it. Moreover, there was nowhere near the violent eruption in the streets in Tehran or Qum as there was in Quetta or Peshawar in Afghanistan. Such a mixed policy reflected the political reality in Tehran that while Khatami was reelected president by an overwhelming majority, the Interior Ministry and the army are still in the hands of ayatollahs who are devoted followers of Khomeini.

Nevertheless, the potential for a still alive and free bin Laden to foment trouble in the central Asian region cannot be underestimated. This is especially true in countries like India, bordering Pakistan, which has a sizable Muslim population growing increasingly restive under the fundamentalist Hindu government, formed by the same party that killed Mahatma Gandhi for trying to seek peace with the Muslims after Indian independence in 1947. Indeed, there already is an incipient Muslim terrorist campaign within India, which began when a Muslim shot to death a Hindu policeman in November 1997. On February 14, 1998, Muslim terrorists set off thirteen bombs in Coimbatore, India, when the fundamentalist Hindu leader, Lal Krishna Advani, was scheduled to speak in the city. With the long-standing animosity between Hindus and Muslims in India, which goes back to the founding of the country and the partition of the British Indian Empire into Muslim Pakistan and Hindu India, the country's Muslim element is fertile ground for a full-scale Islamic insurgency. At the same time, one must remember the militant Islamic resistance in Kashmir, which certainly is in a position to influence its coreligionists in the rest of India. The poor Muslims in India and Bangladesh, formerly East Pakistan, could provide a full reservoir of fighters for bin Laden's brand of *jihad*, much like the refugees in the Palestinian camps provided the first fighters for Yassir Arafat's *Al-Fatah*. With nothing to lose, they have nothing to fear, especially if paradise is promised them as the reward for dying for their faith.

The outbreak of violence in December 2001 along the Kashmir frontier zone between India and Pakistan only shows the incessant volatility of this region. Caught in a time warp like the Protestants and Catholics in Northern Ireland, the feud between these two nations only underscores the dangers of nuclear proliferation in an unstable section of the globe. The recent low-level warfare in the disputed zone was given shocking global immediacy when Kashmiri terrorists, whom Indian security authorities said were linked to Muslim militants, launched a surprise attack on India's Parliament House in New Delhi on December 13, 2001. Blaming the Pakistani government in Islamabad, Indian troops moved up to the Line of Control dividing the disputed Kashmir, as Pakistani soldiers advanced on their side of the frontier. As January 2002 moved on, the danger of war between the two nations remained high. On January 24, *The Times of India* reported that the Indian Prime Minister Atal Bihari Vajpayee had declared that "we do not want war, we do not desire war. But if it happens we will have to face it with courage and win."

Current economic and political turbulence has opened the door to the rise of Islamic fundamentalism in Indonesia. In July 2001, President Megawati Sukarnoputri became the leader of the nation with the world's largest Muslim population. She faced serious economic problems left her by the ineffective regime of presidents Abdurraman Wahid (1999–2001) and Bacharuddin Habibie (1997–99). Furthermore, the worsening economic climate opened the door to the rise of Islamic fundamentalism. The rage of much of the populace has been directed against the overseas Chinese community, which control much of the economic life of the archipelago. However, with the large Muslim population growth, economic discontent could provide a fertile breeding ground for Islamic militancy as well. It should be remembered that Indonesia has had a huge Muslim population since Muslim traders started to visit islands like Sumatra and Java in the tenth century. As is often the case, it would not be hard for Islamic agitators to turn this unrest into hostility against the United States, since we play such an important role in the World Bank and International Monetary Fund, which are trying to restore the crippled Indonesian economic infrastructure. As part of their plans to aid national economics in peril, the World Bank and the International Monetary Fund often place conditions upon their help. These might form a rallying point for Islamic extremists against both financial institutions and the United States, as their senior member nation.

What proved of assistance to former President Abdurrahman Wahid was an alliance that Mohammed Suharto cultivated during his administration with the Israeli Mossad. The Israeli triumph in the 1967 Six Day War coincided with the consolidation of General Suharto's power after his overthrow of Achmed Sukarno and the purge of the Indonesian Communist party beginning in 1965. Impressed with the Israelis' prowess in the war, Suharto clandestinely invited the Mossad into Indonesia, since he could not, as a leader of a predominantly Muslim country, be seen to openly embrace Israel. The Mossad, under a commercial "cover," opened a large office in the capital city of Jakarta, and continued to provide Suharto with intelligence expertise. I assume that President Megawati will keep up the relationship, especially since she is now facing an Islamic radical upsurge. Indeed, with the growing Islamic movement in neighboring Malaysia as well, this entire region of southeast Asia could be threatened by a major Islamic challenge in the future, a fact that calls for increased CIA observation in the years to come. It is significant that it was in Malaysia that the FBI filmed a meeting between the suicide bombers who blew up the USS *Cole* and one of the members of the September 11 conspiracy.

Another future Pacific trouble spot could be the Republic of the Philippines, which has to my knowledge received nowhere near enough attention as a possible site of anti-American terror. Although largely Catholic, the Philippines has a large population of Muslims on the island of Mindanao and other islands in its proximity. The Moros, as these Muslims are called, have been warriors who have ranked with the Hadendowah of the Sudan and the Pathans of India's North-West Frontier as among the hardiest and most zealous of Islamic fighters. The Moros were converted to Islam by missionaries and traders who began to arrive in the island archipelago around 1210 C.E. The term *Moro* was applied to them by the Spanish, who began their settlement of the Philippines in 1565, with the founding of Manila. *Moro* is simply the Spanish term for "Moor" or "Muslim." Those we think of today as the Moros live in largely the Sulu archipelago and the islands of Mindanao and Palawan. Although belonging to Sunni Islam, the Filipino Moros retain elements of indigenous beliefs surviving from pre-Islamic times, including the belief in benevolent or benign *diwatas*, or spirits. When the United States annexed the Philippines a century ago in the wake of the Spanish-American War of 1898, the Moros fought against it for decades after organized Filipino resistance ended with the surrender of Emilio Aguinaldo. They were by far the most resolute and fiercest combatants confronted by the Americans during the occupation of the archipelago.

Since the Philippines gained their independence after World War II, the Moros have waged a long insurgency against the capital, Manila, to gain their independence from the Philippines. The Moro insurrection reached the gravity of a full-scale war during the presidency of Ferdinand Marcos (1965–86) and continued through the administrations of Corazon Aquino (1986–92) and President (formerly General) Fidel Ramos. In an attempt to bring the uprising to an end, Ramos was compelled to grant the Moros a large degree of autonomy in their internal affairs during peace talks in September 1996 with the main Moro group, the Moro National Liberation Front (MNLF). President Ramos signed the pact with Nur Misaud, the chief of the MNLF. However, there are indications today that one of the Moro groups, the Moro Islamic Liberation Front (MILF), is becoming alienated from the pact and there is a real danger that serious fighting on Mindanao could flare up anew. Unlike Nur Misaud's organization, the MILF is an avowedly Islamist group, whose leader, Salamat Hashim, returned to the Philippines in 1997 after a fifteen-year exile in the Middle East. There Hashim undoubtedly formed alliances with extremist Islamic groups, and he may indeed be Osama bin Laden's representative in the Filipino Republic.

With a dedicated Muslim warrior race like the Moros, it would not be difficult for the bin Laden organization to find recruits for his *jihad* in Mindanao, especially in light of the continuing American presence in the Philippines in spite of the 1992 closings of the Subic Bay and Clark Field military bases. It would not be surprising if Moro delegates join the Islamic "Comintern" which has its headquarters in Khartoum.

In 1996, a peace agreement was reached between the MNLF and the government in Manila. Indeed, the MNLF joined in governing the new Autonomous Region in Muslim Mindanao (ARMM), a regional government aimed at giving Moros a larger voice in their own self-government, according to CNN.com on January 8, 2002. There also exists the possiblity of negotiations with the MILF. However, the extremist splinter Islamist groups, like Abu Sayyaf, still continued their war against the Manila government in February 2002. The Abu Sayyaf group, which has consistently carried on its plan for *jihad*, was reinforced by followers of Nur Misuari, the governor of the ARMM, who is being held by the Manila government on charges of rebellion. Furthermore, in January 2002, splinter groups from the MNLF resumed their armed struggle against the Filipino government of President Gloria Arroyo.

It goes without saying that the greatest concern of the American government is acts of terrorism committed here at home. Prior to the 1990s, terrorism on the domestic front was given little attention, as compared to the resources focused on overseas acts. However, there were certainly precursor events that showed that heightened domestic terror was indeed on the horizon. For example, the American white supremacist group the Covenant, Sword, and Arm of the Lord had a stockpile of chemical weapons seized by the FBI as far back as 1985.[4] Among many other terrorist acts perpetrated over the past twenty-five years by radical groups within the United States, the Symbionese Liberation Army, which gained prominence when heiress Patty Hearst joined its ranks, attempted to gain access to germ warfare information in 1975.

However, it was the 1993 World Trade Center bombing and the 1995 bombing of the Murrah Federal Building in Oklahoma City which set off alarm bells throughout the federal government and the American intelligence community. An abortive attempt to commit further bombings in New York City only a year or so after the World Trade Center attack was thwarted just in time. Thus it is only since the mid-1990s that the federal government has taken serious steps to combat the threat of terror attack in the United States, whether from domestic or international terrorists. In June 1995, President Clinton issued a Presidential Decision Directive causing federal, state, and local law enforcement authorities to marshal their efforts against the threat of terrorists using weapons of mass destruction in the United States. Then, as Ehud Sprinzak writes, "the Anti-Terrorism Act of 1996 enlarged the Federal criminal code to include within its scope a prohibition on any attempts, threats, and conspiracies to acquire or use biological agents, chemical agents or toxins" within the United States.[5]

The legislation mentioned above appeared several years ago, but actual implementation of an antiterrorism program only began in 1998. And considering the actions of Osama bin Laden, such implementation did not come any time too soon. In interviews with *Time* and *Newsweek* (January 11, 1999, editions), Osama bin Laden made his plans to carry *jihad* to the United States, against both our government and citizens. Bin Laden told *Newsweek*, "If the Israelis are killing the small children in Palestine, and the Americans are killing the innocent people in Iraq, and if the majority of the American people support their dissolute president, this means the American people are fighting us and we have the right to target them."[6]

Bin Laden's declaration of war against all Americans, regardless of age or sex, is remarkably similar to what former prime minister of Israel Benjamin Netanyahu wrote in *Terrorism: How the West Can Win*, a book he edited in 1986. Said Netenyahu about the modern terrorist, "it is here where the terrorist parts company with humanity. He declares a total war on the society he attacks. For him everyone is a legitimate target. A baby is fair game; he may, after all, grow up to be a soldier. So is the baby's mother; she gave birth to this future soldier. No one is spared, ordinary citizens and leaders alike [are targets]."[7]

Past experience has shown the Pandora's Box of weaponry available to terrorists committed enough to their cause to risk their lives in the act: Chemical and biological warfare agents like anthrax, bubonic plague, and sarin and other nerve gases, along with a veritable dictionary of explosives stand ready to be used in the terrorist's arsenal of destruction. The Institute for Strategic Studies has noted that one gram of anthrax (*Bacillis anthracis*) can release a trillion spores—with the potential for 100 million lethal doses. Just 50 kilograms of anthrax can produce 95,000 dead and 125,000 victims incapacitated.[8] Nerve gas is also a likely item to be on Osama bin Laden's shopping list. Nerve gases had their origin in German research on organophosphates conducted in the 1930s, when German chemist Gerhard Schrader was looking for an improved insecticide late in 1936. (The notorious defoliant Agent Orange used during the Vietnam War also comes from the organophosphate family of chemical compounds.)

Because of the fact that nerve gas is the most lethal item on Osama bin Laden's terrorist shopping list, perhaps some words about its chemical profile would be in order. As defined by the *McGraw-Hill Dictionary of Chemistry*, an organophosphate is "a soluble fertilizer material made up of organic phosphate esters such as glucose, glycol, or sorbitol; useful for providing phosphorous to deep root structures." An ester is "the compound formed by the elimination of water and the bonding of an alcohol and an organic acid." Some of the pesticides that have been developed using organophosphates are dimefox, malathion, parathion, and one that Dr. Schrader named after him-self, schradan. Tabun was the first nerve gas to be developed while sarin was developed in 1938. Soman (GD), sarin (GB), and tabun (GA) are those known best historically, but now the American VX gas and the Russian VR agent have become the Fourth and Fifth Horsemen of the Apocalypse of nerve gas warfare. VX gas was developed by the United States during the Cold War. Robert L. Sherrow writes in "Better Killing through Chemistry," then "the USSR thickened GD . . . and then followed up with the formulation of VR-55. Concerned with safety as well as possible terrorism developed a new family of binary nerve gases including GB-1 and VX-1."[9] During the long and bloody war between Iran and Iraq, both belligerents had recourse to nerve gas agents. Regarding a question from Rahimullah Yusafzai, who inter-viewed bin Laden for *Time*, about his attempts to obtain nuclear and chem-ical weapons, bin Laden replied, "acquiring weapons for the defense of Mus-lims is a religious duty. If I have indeed acquired these weapons, then I thank God for enabling me to do so. And if I seek to acquire these weapons, I am carrying out a [religious] duty."[10] Even earlier, bin Laden had made at least one attempt to gain possession of his own nuclear weapon. At the February 2001 trial in New York City for the bombers of the American embassies in East Africa in 1998, testimony by Jamal Ahmad al-Fadl sketched out his attempt to get nuclear materials, specifically weapons-grade uranium, for his master as early as late 1993 or early 1994. Al-Fadl represented the new species of al-Qaeda operative, the African Afghan: he was a native of the Sudan, the same country that offered Turabi to the world of Islamic extremism. Turabi had apparently met bin Laden in Afghanistan. It was through Turabi that bin Laden went to the Sudan to begin his business enter-prise there. One of his investments, however, proved to have a short invest-ment life—it was destroyed by American cruise missiles in revenge for the embassy bombings. On August 21, 1998, President Bill Clinton's National Security Advisor Samuel "Sandy" Berger was interviewed by television reporter Jim Lehrer about the Cruise missile attack on the factory in the Sudan. Berger stated to Lehrer that the air strike "destroyed a factory in the Sudan, which was manufacturing a chemical used to make VX nerve gas. . . . We have physical evidence [from United States intelligence sources] that they were making a chemical which is essentially one step removed from VX gas, a precursor chemical necessary to make VX gas, which does not have other significant commercial purposes."

Tabun, sarin, and tabun are the nerve agents from which we have the most to fear, since they do not require huge installations like the Russian Biopreparat institution to produce. A *Time* magazine article published at the time of the Tokyo subway sarin gas attack by the Aum Shinrikyo cult of Shoko Asahara, notes that insofar as tabun and sarin are concerned, "the ingredients for both of these gases are commercially available and can be put together by a chemist without specialized experience."[11] The price for an amount that would inflict heavy casualties over a one-square-mile zone would only be $10,000 to $20,000—pocket change when it comes to the money earned by the drug gangs in the United States, or terrorists with deep pockets like Osama bin Laden.

In the past, when infiltrating radical groups like the Montana Freemen or the Arizona Vipers, the federal government has been able to use a tool against terrorism that has proven valuable since the days of the tsarist Okrana (secret police): paid informants inside the secret society. However, serious doubts should be raised about the use of informants against Islamic militant organizations. The FBI had an informant in the ranks of Shaikh Omar Abdul Rahman's organization, and the CIA allegedly had an informant identified only as C2 in the group which bin Laden calls the International Islamic Front for *Jihad*. However, neither of these informants, both with apparent advance notice of the terror bombings of the World Trade Center in 1993 and the embassies in East Africa in 1998, informed their "handlers" at the FBI or CIA in time to stop the acts of terrorism. It seems to me that these informers deliberately did not inform their handlers in time because they did not intend to: They merely agreed to "inform" on their brethren in order to deceive the federal authorities that they would provide the needed information in time. Instead, totally committed to their cause, they went along with the plans and actively participated in the acts of terrorism, immune to such blandishments as offers of criminal immunity or financial inducements, which have bought many informants like "Crazy Phil" Leonetti in the Mafia. These Muslim militant cells, fired by their faith, may prove immune to federal attempts to successfully penetrate their ranks with informants, making the efforts to abort their terror attacks in this country and abroad even more difficult in the future.

The terror attacks of September 2001 proved again that the lack of HUMINT, "human intelligence" information, is still a grave problem within the intelligence community. Two events militate against an effective HUMINT component, both of which date from the 1970s. In the 1970s, Senator Frank Church of Idaho held a series of senatorial hearings into alleged CIA misconduct in the Select Committee on Government Intelligence Activities. Church himself was a veteran of U.S. Army Intelligence during World War II. Appearing before the Church committee, then CIA Director William Colby revealed what the agency referred to as "the family jewels," information on sensational CIA activities like the botched attempts to kill Fidel Castro. The reaction to the hearings led to a drastic cutback in the activities of the agency in clandestine activities, as well as using foreign "intelligence assets" whose personal records showed them somewhat less benign than village ministers. When Adm. Stansfield Turner took over Colby's job in the Carter administration in February 1977, he embraced sophisticated efforts at SIGINT, signals intelligence, as a way to prevent the pitfalls and pratfalls that had characterized the "family jewels." American intelligence efforts now looked to the skies to gain satellite intelligence, rather than into the gutter to gather information from unsavory human sources. In his 1985 book, *Secrecy and Democracy*, Turner maintained his belief in the values of SIGINT. He wrote that SIGINT "all but eclipses traditional, human methods of collecting intelligence."[12] The result was that over the next twenty-five years, the CIA virtually lost the HUMINT component that had characterized the agency when it had orchestrated the return of Mohammed Reza Shah to the Iranian throne in 1953 after the premiership of Mohammed Mossadeq. While the agency's record did show excesses, it also showed a command of HUMINT, which was especially important in less technologically advanced countries like Iran or Afghanistan. With the public opinion pendulum now swinging in the direction opposite to the 1970s, it appears that in the aftermath of the September 11 attacks the CIA will again be encouraged to gather HUMINT to help in the hunt for Osama bin Laden and his al-Qaeda network. That will undoubtedly be the path down which the agency will march, at least until a future Church committee holds hearings on the activities of the CIA during the hunt for Osama bin Laden and the al-Qaeda terrorists!

It was only in 1998 that the United States, with government agencies like the Federal Emergency Management Agency (FEMA), began to prepare exercises to protect American cities against chemical and biological weapons, the "poor man's atomic bomb." FEMA and other federal agencies coordinated practice runs with local medical and civil defense personnel in cities like Philadelphia and other metropolitan areas to try to prepare for a sneak attack. However, given the high casualties that would come from an organized anthrax attack, for example, it is an ominous possibility that local authorities might be overwhelmed by the casualties and be forced to call on others like the Centers for Disease Control in Atlanta or the army facility in Fort Dietrich, the U.S. Army Medical Research Institute of Infectious Diseases (USAMRIID), to cope with the emergency room overflows. Concerted attacks in several cities at the same time have the potential to overwhelm the entire nation's emergency response and health care systems. However, the chances of launching a successful anthrax attack are far higher than Americans seemed to believe when an anthrax biowarfare assault was launched on the United States in October 2001 after the more conventional terror attacks on Washington, D.C., and New York City on September 11.

The picture as the old millennium drew to a close did not give comfort to those charged with defending the United States against such a terrorist attack. The State Department's Office of the Coordinator for Counterterrorism in April 2000 released its terror round-up for 1999. Once again, the names of the usual suspects appeared in the Middle East. The office's report on international terrorism is essential for many reasons. Always available through a link on the Web with the home page of the State Department, the report gives a comprehensive account of all internationally recognized terror groups in the past year. It also provides linked Web sites for the significant terror incidents that occurred globally during that past year. Such information helps the State Department prepare the travel advisories issued to for Americans who plan to embark on world travel. An advisory may warn American travelers to stay out of an entire country or just a certain part of a country, as when recent State Department advisories have warned Americans to stay out of the Chiapas Province region in Mexico because of the Zapatista Indian insurgency there, led by the mysterious Subcommandante Marcos. These terror advisories can be found on State Department Web pages and are also located in the travel brochures to various countries and regions of the world that are published by the State Department. They can also be found on the Web page "Travel Security," which is linked to the Officer of the Coordinator for Counterrorism Web site. The brochures are readily available by calling or writing the State Department in Washington. Consular and embassy offices of the State Department also keep copies of these travel advisories on hand.

In the Middle East, the hardliners in the security services of Iran, notably the Ministry of Intelligence and Security and the Revolutionary Guard Corps, continually thwarted the efforts of President Khatami to open his door to the United States. Their support of extremist Muslims continued unabated. Hizbollah, Hamas, Islamic *Jihad* and all other groups dedicated to destroying the peace efforts in the Middle East are actively supported by the Iranian security apparatus. Indeed, in an effort to keep in power, President Khatami is being forced into an uncomfortable embrace with the rejectionist groups. In May 1999, on a state visit to Damascus, Khatami met with leaders of the extremist groups dedicated to scuttling the peace talks. The religious supreme leader of Iran, Ayatollah Khameni, the successor to the Ayatollah Khomeini, hosted a rally of the rejectionists in Tehran on November 9, 1999.

Like Tehran, Saddam Hussein's Iraq continued to play host to extremist Islamic groups in 1999. A nation like Iraq or Iran, it should be noted, can be listed as a state that sponsors terrorism even if it is not actively funding terror operations, as Libya did in the past. Countries like Iraq or Iran are listed by the U.S. State Department as sponsoring terrorism if they provide a base for a terror group, what the department calls providing a "safe haven." Ironically, given the penchant in the past for Islamic extremists like the late Grand Mufti of Jerusalem to make alliances with Nazis and neo-Nazis, the first time this term was used by the State Department was in "Operation Safehaven," an investigation to see in what countries diehard leaders from the Third Reich had found a "safe haven" for the treasure that they had stolen during the Second World War. Under the new meaning of the term "safe haven," Iraq is listed because Saddam Hussein still plays host to the Abu Nidal Organization and to the Arab Liberation Front (ALF). Saddam earned Iraq's place on the list as an active terrorist because of the actions of his own security services. In 1998, Radio Free Europe and Radio Liberty, sister organizations sponsored by the U.S. government, began to beam Arabic language broadcasts into Iraq. Enraged by this, Saddam's security services, led by a close relative of the dictator, planned to blow up the headquarters of Radio Free Europe and Radio Liberty in Prague, Czechoslovakia, in 1999. Luckily, the plot was uncovered before the headquarters went up in smoke, and was only reported on their broadcast.

On the other hand, in anticipation of the trial of the Iraqi suspects in the Lockerbie bombing disaster (the 1988 explosion of Pan Am Flight 103 over Lockerbie, Scotland), which would take place in 2000, Muammar Quaddafi of Libya took steps to burnish his country's tarnished image as a past sponsor of terrorism. The colonel banished from Libya the remaining representatives of the Abu Nidal group, who probably joined their comrades in Baghdad. Of course, given the provocative posture of Saddam Hussein in the spring of 2001, it is always possible he could use these terror groups to launch attacks against American or Israeli targets in the future. In the aftermath of the September Days in 2001, it was reported that Quaddafi continued his efforts at seeking—on his own terms—a rapprochement with the United States and the West. In an article in the *Turkish Daily News*, published in Ankara and Istanbul on October 27, 2001, it was reported that Quaddafi offered intelligence information and police help to find bin Laden. The offer was made in a meeting with Charles Josselin, French Minister for Cooperation, which took place in Libya.

One of the most active sponsors of terrorism continued to be the fundamentalist regime in Khartoum, still under Turabi's influence. The U.S. State Department reported that Khartoum is, as mentioned previously, the hub of what has become an "Islamic Terror International." The most honored guests are the representatives of Osama bin Laden's al-Qaeda group. Indeed, it seems more and more likely that it was from headquarters in Khartoum that the 1998 attacks on the American embassies in Tanzania and Kenya took place. On May 15, 1997, Kenneth R. McKune, the State Department's Acting Coordinator for Counterterrorism, testified before the Subcommittee on Africa of the Senate Foreign Relations Committee that "Sudan harbors a number of terrorist groups. They include an 'old line' secular group, the Abu Nidal Organization, but most of them are militant extremist organizations. Among them are: HAMAS, the Lebanese Hizbollah, the Palestinian Islamic Jihad (IJ), and Egypt's Al-Gama'at Al-Islamiyya. The Sudanese government also supports Islamic and non-Islamic opposition groups in Algeria, Uganda, Tunisia, Ethiopia, and Eritrea." The Gama'at is of course the radical Islamic group cited for responsibility in the slaughter of the tourists at Luxor in Egypt several years ago, and for 1995 assassination attempt in Ethiopia against Egypt's President Hosni Mubarak. The United Nations Security Council has demanded that Khartoum hand over three fugitives wanted in connection with the assassination plot but the Sudanese have yet refused to do so.

Syria continued to support the same terror groups, all of which, including Syria, are united by their rejection of any peace plans with the state of Israel, which they are united by a wish to destroy. Damascus also took advantage of the primacy it has had in Lebanon for nearly a decade now, since Damascus brokered the deal which ended the bloody Lebanese civil war. Syria has maintained its military presence in the Bekaa Valley in Lebanon. There, it has let groups like the Popular Front for the Liberation of Palestine–General Command set up training camps for its members, who then move south to carry out terror attacks on Israel's northern border. In 2000, Israel, under the leadership of Ehud Barak, abruptly gave up the territory it had held in southern Lebanon for twenty years to protect the settlements of north Israel. Now, with the Israeli military presence removed from southern Lebanon, there is nothing to prevent these terror groups from attacking directly into Israel itself. Barak's hasty withdrawal in 2000 left the Lebanese in the south who had supported Israel, especially members of the Christian militia that had fought with the Israeli Defense Force, at the mercy of the extremist groups sponsored by Syria, like Hamas, Hizbollah, and the Islamic *Jihad*. Whether Syria's policy toward supporting terrorism will now change since Hafez Assad's son assumed power after his father's death is yet to be known. However, even while Hafez Assad was alive, Damascus told the terror groups to limit their activities to the political realm and cease active terrorism against Israel. The terrorist groups seem to have pretty much ignored this warning though and kept on their war against the Israelis.

This change in the policy of some of the strongest sponsors of terrorism in the past was noted during the appearance of the Director of Central Intelligence, George Tenet, before the Senate Select Committee on Intelligence on February 7, 2001. Said Tenet in his senatorial testimony, "state-sponsored terrorism appears to have declined over the past five years, but transnational groups—with decentralized leadership that makes them harder to identify and disrupt—are emerging." Of course, Osama bin Laden's group is number one on the list for the CIA as the premier "transnational" terror group. As Tenet testified, bin Laden and his "global network of lieutenants and associates remain the most immediate and serious threat. . . . His organization [al-Qaeda] is continuing to place emphasis on developing surrogates to carry out attacks in an effort to avoid detection, blame, and retaliation."

Yet questions were being raised by the CIA whether Osama bin Laden was really the head of al-Qaeda or was perhaps a figurehead. Two of bin Laden's top lieutenants were Egyptians, most likely from the Muslim Brotherhood. Investigators from the FBI would say in October 2001 during the investigation of the September 11 terrorist atrocity that as of 1998 the Muslim Brotherhood had effectively become part of al-Qaeda. Ayman al-Zawahri was charged in connection with the embassy terrorism in 1998, and furthermore is believed to have taken part in the killing of Anwar Sadat. *Time* magazine reported in its October 1, 2001, issue, that al-Zawahri is felt to "have the operational experience to plot something on the scale of the" September 11 attacks on the Pentagon and the World Trade Center. Bin Laden's other chief lieutenant is Mohammed Atef, a former Egyptian policeman. Atef is believed to have been involved in the East African attacks. While Osama bin Laden's actual position on an organizational chart of al-Qaeda may be uncertain, what is clear is that he has become representative of Muslim extremism's reaction to the Western world, and thus is a hero in much of *Dar al-Islam*. That may be the source of his real strength in al-Qaeda, and in that case he is certainly the *primus inter pares*, "the first among equals."

As the first year of the new millennium drew to a close, the United States faced a wide multitude of threats from modern militant Islam. This is especially true with the advent of entrepreneurial terrorists like Osama bin Laden, who can afford to personally fund a terrorist network, and, as in the case of Afghanistan, sometimes even buy countries! The damage to the USS *Cole* was an example of how the militants can reach out literally anywhere in the Arabic world to strike out at America.

The danger is made even more acute by the existence of the wide, creative arsenal of weapons that are available to the modern-day terror operative. This arsenal is well known to the CIA and the FBI's Global Counterterrorism Office; it runs from anthrax available at research institutes to nuclear weapons from the former Soviet Union, where everything except the Kremlin itself seems to be for sale to the highest bidder. And with the growing scandal in Moscow concerning the influence of the Russian Mafiya in the highest echelons of the Russian government, the Kremlin seems to be on the auction block now too. This is of course not mentioning the new Russian government's policy of selling nuclear technology to Iran, the "godfather" of modern Islamic terrorism, in spite of repeated American protests. As Mark Twain once said of his own death, the reports of the death of the Cold War seem to have been premature. Of course, nobody knows who will be the final recipient, the "end user" of the nuclear technology Iran procures from the Russians. Is Iran the source of the nuclear weaponry that bin Laden hinted at in his interviews?

The danger exists too that Russia may make available to Iran, or to whomever has enough hard currency, the new genetic-engineered anthrax and smallpox bacilli that the Russian government's biological warfare apparatus, the world's largest, has continued to develop in spite of any "detente" or "era of good feelings" since the fall of the Berlin Wall. In his book *Biohazard*, Ken Alibek wrote of the vast germ warfare machinery that the Russians had in place at the Biopreparat installation where he worked before his defection to the United States. Alibek, in testimony before the United States Congress and on an October 13, 1998, special on the Public Broadcast System (PBS) titled *Plague War*, made explicit the danger of continued Russian experimentation in biological warfare.

The rise to power of Vladimir Putin, after the historic resignation of Boris Yeltsin on New Year's Eve of 1999, showed the resurgence to power of the Russian security apparatus. Putin's reign marked the first time that an *apparatchik* of the security services has been in power in Russian since Yuri Andropov. Already, Putin has made moves to silence the more outspoken of the Russian media which has flowered since the fall of the Soviet Union. Another hard-liner, Evgenii Primakov, was making his presence felt, and even made a grab for power before Putin took over the reins in the Kremlin. Primakov is a matter for concern. In the intelligence field, he was the *nomenklatura's* expert on Asian affairs, from Russia to the Pacific, a region referred to in recent Russian geostrategic works as "Eurasia," which refers to a belief, shared also by the nationalist Vladimir Zhironovsky, that Russia's destiny, as reported in a recent issue of *Foreign Affairs*, is to be the political leader of the Eurasian landmass against the decadent modernism of the Western world, led by the United States. This *Weltanschaung* would also make feasible, if Primakov and his adherents gain more power, putting Russia in a position— if it chooses—to be the leader of a vast Islamic movement across Eurasia, using as a base of support the Muslims in the central Asian republics of the former Soviet Union. Russia, of course, has still maintained close ties with both the armed forces and intelligence services of these republics. Although we seldom realize it, the East has exerted its lure on many Russians over the centuries, as it did with the British. The Russian conquest of the Caucasus and central Asia had the same appeal for many Russians, like Leo Tolstoy, who served in the Caucasus and wrote about the campaigns against the militant imam Shamyl in works like the short story "The Raid," that India had for Rudyard Kipling, who used that country as the background for his great works like *Kim*, which was about the espionage war fought against tsarist Russia in central Asia.

Indeed, a step toward such a Russian-dominated Eurasia has already been achieved with the reintegration of Belarus, the former Byelorussian SSR, with Russia. On April 12, 1999, the *Wall Street Journal* reported that an application from Slobodan Milosevic's Yugoslavia had already been received in Moscow to join the new federation. Fortunately, at that time, Russia was more interested in ending the fighting in the former Yugoslavia than in rebuilding its old empire.

As was mentioned earlier, Primakov's desire for Russian hegemony in the Eurasian landmass, now carried on by Vladimir Putin, will only increase because of the discovery in the past ten years of massive quantities of oil in the trans–Caspian Sea region, just at the time when the oil reserves of the Persian Gulf area may prove to be finite. David E. Mark, a retired foreign service officer, wrote about this as far back as winter 1996: "Moscow's long-term concerns over the ultimate interrelationship between Azerbaijan and Turkey, and over that between Azerbaijan and the numerous Azeris inside Iran, have lately been supplemented by anxieties over oil. Moscow fears the birth of a world-class petroleum complex in the Caspian Sea region, free of its influence, and is determined to hamper any such independent evolution."[13] In the past Moscow has felt free to intervene militarily in this region, whenever it felt its economic or geostrategic influence was at risk. It did so in the time of Peter the Great, Catherine the Great, and during the reigns of tsars Alexander I, Nicholas I, and Alexander II; to think Russia incapable of such intervention again is to look at the region through rose-colored glasses.

Yet the continued concern with Osama bin Laden and the entire terror network of which he is the symbol has made the United States and the Russians draw closer together than they have been in several years, especially after the attacks on September 11, 2001. The sinking of the Russian nuclear submarine *Kursk* on August 12, 2000, only a year before the terrorists' bombing of the *Cole*, has made the Russians keenly aware of the fragility of their own navy. Although preliminary investigations show that the *Kursk*, the pride of the Russian Northern Fleet's submarine command, was most likely the victim of the explosion of an onboard experimental Shkoal torpedo, the Russian navy ships which fulfill the dream of Peter the Great by sailing through the Persian Gulf can prove just as vulnerable to an Islamic fundamentalist in a bomb-laden Zodiac speed boat!

The November 27, 2000, *Philadelphia Inquirer* carried a story on how the United States and Russia were formulating plans on how to use the United Nations as a way to apply pressure on the militant Taliban government, still harboring bin Laden and al-Qaeda. In the Security Council, the real power in the United Nations, proposals such as imposing an arms embargo on Afghanistan and restricting foreign travel by Taliban emissaries overseas were seen as ways to bring pressure on the Kabul government because of its hosting of the uncrowned king of terror. In early 2001, the Taliban mission to the United Nations was indeed closed as a result of the movement's refusal to surrender bin Laden.

Russian concerns over Afghanistan are fueled by the role that Taliban advisers are carrying on in support of the Islamic fundamentalists who are still fighting the Russian forces in Chechnya, although the breakaway province is again under Russian control. However, into 2001, the *mujahidin* fighting the Russians in Chechnya were still able to mount shocking hit-and-run attacks against the Russian garrison troops in what appears to be an ongoing guerilla war in the province. Another reason Russia is concerned is that the fundamentalism preached by Osama bin Laden and his Taliban disciples could critically affect the plans to tap the massive potential oil reserves located in the former Soviet states of central Asia by taking over the pipelines being built in Afghanistan.

Russian concerns about Chechnya and the central Asian states persist because of fear of continued clandestine support from the rich and radical Sunni Muslim elements in Saudi Arabia and the oil-rich Gulf states. Russian intelligence sources have pointed out a Muslim religious college, or *midrassah*, in the old Tatar city of Kazan, now the capital of Tatarstan. It was the Russian conquest of Kazan, then Moscovy, that finally marked the end of the power of the Mongols and Tatars in Russia around the reign of Ivan the Terrible (1530–84). Here, the Russians fear a fusion, according to Ariel Cohen of the conservative research group Heritage Foundation, of strong Chechen nationalism with the puritanic Wahabi movement that swept Ibn Saud into power in Saudi Arabia decades ago. Once again, Arab veterans of the Afghan War have joined the Chechens in the fighting in Chechnya and neighboring Daghestan under Shamyl Beshayev.

As with other extremist groups, the Muslim movement now has its own Web page on the Internet, hosted by Azzam Publications, which boasts that it is the *jihad* center for the *mujahidin* on the Web. The Web page, and linked pages, are presented in English, the main language of the Internet. The main highlight of the Azzam Web site, access to which was blocked in September 2001, presumably by U.S. security forces, is the continuing war in Chechnya against the Russians. The Azzam site kept a coherent backlog archive of previous articles that could be accessed from the main Web page. A major showing is a two-part article on the campaign against the state of Daghestan. Any doubts about Muslim fundamentalists being involved in the Daghestani operation are cleared up by this article, which boasts about the participation of the Chechen *mujahidin* in that war.

The Azzam Web site is a highly sophisticated series of linked Web sites (all hosted by Azzam Publications) which gives a penetrating look at the mind of the fundamentalist warriors who threaten the United States today. The Web pages represent a sometimes eerie, sometimes ominous look at a way of thinking totally at odds with the Western outlook today, or for that matter that of the moderate Muslim countries like Turkey, Egypt, and Jordan. So dedicated is Azzam to the *jihad* that it has available the text of almost every religious decree or *fatwa* ever listed regarding the *jihad*. It details, with copious quotes from the Quran, the necessity of all Muslims to support *jihad* under all circumstances. (It should be noted that, as with the Christian Bible, quotations from the Quran can be taken out of context to support any theological or ideological point of view.)

A link to the Azzam home page even provided a detailed list of those who have died as martyrs to the *jihad*, beginning with the 2000 fighting in Afghanistan and going down the list to such countries as the Philippines and Bosnia. This again showed the truly international aspect of Islamic extremism today. On this page, if you clicked on each country, a capsule biography of each of the martyrs could be brought up on the computer screen, listed by the country in which they died. Afghanistan, with about thirteen, led the list. Another page features countries considered to be main areas of the *jihad*; the most recently added was Uzbekistan. The Web pages for other countries like Afghanistan were still under construction in March 2001. On the Afghan Web site, a request for assistance in building the Web page was given, along with an e-mail address where responses could be directed.

In a Western world that is now seriously prosecuting the Serbian war criminals from the war in the former Yugoslavia, another link on the Azzam Publications Web page shows in stark detail the different viewpoint of the *mujahidin* of today. The link described under what circumstances it is permissible to execute prisoners of war in a *jihad*, a concept anathema to Western legal thought about war since the St. Petersburg Conference in Russia in 1868 and the first Hague Conference, held in the Netherlands in

1899, tried to bring some humanity to the rules of law regarding warfare in the nineteenth century.

The Azzam Web pages reflect the high level of education of some of the leaders of today's extremist Muslims. The artistic presentation and design of the home page and the linked pages are truly impressive. One page requests donations to fund publications of the Azzam company, while another link features e-mail letters of support for Azzam and its *jihad* network. Again showing the truly global link of Islamic terrorism, the Azzam Web pages are available in translation into almost ten foreign languages, not including Arabic.

After months of Internet silence, during which the Azzam web page was blocked, Azzam suddenly reappeared on the Web. On November 20, 2001, Azzam Publications posted a farewell message which defended Osama bin Laden and the Taliban from the charges of committing the terror attacks of September 11, 2001. Azzam accepted their words "as Muslims" that they had no complicity in the attack on America.

❀   ❀   ❀

The attack on the *Cole* raises a new concern about the growing strategic sophistication of the bin Laden organization, the focus of today's *mujahidin*, as the new millennium opens. The bombings in East Africa, in Kenya and Tanzania, were classic terror bombings against high-profile American targets, just like the assault on the American barracks in Saudi Arabia before that. However, the kamikaze attack on the *Cole* reflects a new realization on the part of al-Qaeda of the Achilles' heel of the American deployment into the Arab world: the American fleet. A warship, especially anchored in an unsafe harbor, is literally a sitting duck for any fundamentalist willing to exchange his life for a blow at the Stars and Stripes. Even if the U.S. Navy upgrades its security precautions on board ship, such as letting sentries carry loaded weapons, there is nothing to prevent a terrorist who can swim from strapping on a scuba tank and planting a bomb on the bottom of a destroyer or aircraft carrier. Although major ships like the carriers *Eisenhower* and *Kennedy* have always seemed relatively safe against the terrorist threat, the intense power of the C-4 explosive used against the *Cole* makes them appear more vulnerable to a terror bombing attempt.

An important factor to be observed in the struggle with terrorism is the growing federal contact with the two nations that stand on the periphery of the Muslim world and are equally at risk from terrorist attack as the United States: Russia and the Peoples' Republic of China. It was a noteworthy and promising example of cooperation when former FBI Director Louis Freeh traveled in 1999 to Moscow to discuss joint action with the Russian government against the Russian Mafiya, and for the United States to supply the Moscow police with American "power cars" to aid in the pursuit of criminals. This of course was enhanced by Russian-American cooperation at the United Nations Security Council against the Taliban regime in Afghanistan.

Aiding Russia with counterterror expertise also bolsters the Muslim central Asian republics, like Tajikistan, which are now on the front line against Taliban-inspired terrorism. These central Asian members of the Confederation of Independent States (CIS) all have military defense treaties with Russia, according to Radio Free Europe publications, and they are now reintegrating their intelligence services with the modern incarnation of the KGB.

With the 2000 agreement between the Peoples' Republic of China (PRC) and Taiwan to settle future differences peacefully between them, the way now is open to inaugurate counterterrorist cooperation with the PRC, since, as was mentioned previously, the Uighur terrorists which are becoming a national security threat in the Peoples' Republic were probably trained in the same Afghan camps as the bombers who destroyed the embassies in East Africa. The United States can help supply the Peoples' Liberation Army and the Chinese security service with counterterrorist training and support against the Uighur separatists which they may not have at the present time. (When Kang Sheng set up the Chinese secret police in the days of Mao Zedong, it was intended for the detection of subversive elements at home and espionage abroad, not counterterrorism.) An added bonus would be if any Uighurs could be recruited to work for the Chinese against the Uighur terrorists as infiltrators. They would also help us, through shared information, to gain insight into the entire central Asian Islamic terrorist network.[14] The PRC and United States intelligence agencies are currently cooperating in Yunnan Province to try to monitor the flow of opium out of Asia's Golden Triangle—similar operations were conducted to observe Soviet nuclear operations from Xinxiang in the 1980s.

Yet, in the middle of such promising developments, a nagging thought occurs that things could get much worse. In 1999, "Apo" Ocalan was captured in Kenya. Ocalan, a Muslim, was the head of one of the fiercest of the terror groups still operating in the 1990s, the PKK (the Kurdistan Workers

Party). The PKK was a group dedicated to carving out an independent state for the Kurdish population in Turkey, Syria, Iraq, and Iran. Over the years, the Kurds had been used as a cat's paw by one country against another. For several years before his overthrow in 1979 by the Ayatollah Khomeini, Reza Shah Pahlavi, the ruler of Iran, had supported a Kurdish insurrection against the government of Iraq, but when peace was made with Iraq, he sacrificed the Kurds to Iraqi vengeance.

Under the command of Ocalan, the Marxist PKK took no chances in allying itself with other nations, and pursued a bloody war with Turkey, which had been fighting the Kurds sporadically for decades. After traveling around Europe, including a suspicious stay in Russia, Ocalan ended up in Greece. Following his Grecian sojourn, Apo traveled to Kenya. The question must be asked, with so many countries having full-scale Islamic terror networks that would eagerly welcome Ocalan (certainly Libya would), why did he choose to go to Kenya?

Although it is *speculation*, I believe he traveled there to link up with the terror network of Osama bin Laden, which has apparently made Nairobi its East African headquarters. After all, Nairobi is where the U.S. embassy was bombed. If bin Laden and Ocalan had succeeded in joining forces, one could anticipate a terror campaign of epic proportions, since the entire PKK movement would gladly follow Ocalan anywhere. This would open up Europe to a massive terrorist outbreak, given the large number of Kurdish guest workers in European countries. (The ferocious Kurdish rioting at Greek and Israeli embassies in Europe in February 1999, when it was thought Greece had handed Ocalan over to Turkey with the help of Israel, gives an indication of the loyalty the terrorist commands.) Ironically, the ease of traveling among European countries now offered by the formation of the European Union most likely will only increase the possibility of such transnational terror on the Continent. The transparency of European state frontiers was proved all too easily when the conspirators of September 2001 were able to use the entire continent, from Prague in the Czech Republic to London in the United Kingdom, as a vast criminal staging area.

Moreover, it seems that the Greeks had every intention of letting Ocalan remain under their protection in Nairobi, allowing him to live in the ambassador's residence, which again raises the question of Greek complicity in aiding terrorists, as the CIA believed happened unofficially in the 1970s. It was not until FBI agents, in Nairobi to hunt the perpetrators of the August embassy bombing, became aware that Ocalan was in the Greek embassy compound that Athens put pressure on him to move out. On February 13, 1999, he left the embassy grounds, to be apprehended by the Turkish commandos, who drugged him and hustled him to prison in Turkey. Even today, based on open sources, it seems unclear if the Greeks handed Ocalan over to the Turks officially or if someone in the embassy privately tipped off the Turks to Ocalan's departure so they could be waiting in ambush. Unfortunately, the Turks' capture of Ocalan did not at first diminish the PKK's ardor for combat. After his apprehension, Ocalan's followers announced their determination to continue the fight in his behalf, and for a time, their attacks continued unabated.

Late in March 1999, the first PKK suicide bombing took place in Istanbul. This was a bad sign. As doctrinaire Marxists, such self-immolation was never a part of PKK tactics previously. Suicide bombings were always the hallmark of militant *Shi'a* terrorists, like the one who demolished the U.S. Marine barracks in Beirut in October 1983. The introduction of such tactics might tend to point to an alliance of the PKK with extremist Muslim terrorists, something that would be of dire consequences for Western European countries, and American citizens and installations in Western Europe, given the large number of PKK supporters among the immigrant Turkish population currently living there. However, as of March 2001, the threat of continued violence seemed to have faded with the continued incarceration of Ocalan in a Turkish prison. In 2000, the sentence of death on Abdullah "Apo" Ocalan was indefinitely suspended by Turkish judicial authorities, apparently to forestall what could have been an unprecedented PKK terror campaign that would have followed his death by hanging. It seems that the PKK withered and died without the firebrand leadership of Apo Ocalan. However, a link between PKK members and al-Qaeda may emerge from the investigations currently going on in Europe.

Although the United States and Israel have denied Kurdish charges that the Mossad or CIA assisted Turkey in the capture of Ocalan with intelligence information, it seems obvious that one of the countries did. Nairobi is the "listening post" for all of Africa for both the CIA and the Mossad, and one must remember how the Kenyan government helped in the search for the embassy bombers, and how Kenya tacitly aided the Mossad and Israel in the Entebbe incident in July 1976. The possibility that Ocalan could ally with radical Islam must have always been a concern since, as stated above, the

PKK would be a serious recruit to the ranks of the new *jihad*. It would not be the first time that Marxists had helped the Islamic cause: Remember the Baader-Meinhof gang and Carlos the Jackal.

It must also be remembered that the United States is in debt to the Turkish government, since the Turkish air base at Incirlik is the one from which our air patrols of the northern Iraqi "no fly" zones are operated with open Turkish approval. A quid pro quo in aiding Turkey in capturing its Public Enemy Number One would be the only thing to do. Insofar as Israel is concerned, Turkey is the only country in the Muslim world that can rightly be called a friend of Israel; both countries have had a de facto military alliance now for several years. (This again points out the fact that all Muslims are not Arabs, the Turks being Indo-European Aryans like the Iranians. This racial factor has enabled the Turks to stand aloof from the Arab campaign against Israel in the Muslim world.) Thus, it would only be natural for the Mossad to offer to Turkey its good offices as well in capturing Ocalan.

It is possible that American assistance may have gone further than providing hypothetical intelligence support to Turkey's modern Janissaries, the descendants of the Ottoman warrior elite. Certain characteristics of the entire operational scenario tradecraft exhibited by the Turks point to possible U.S. training, most likely by operatives from Delta Force, from Fort Bragg, North Carolina, or Special Forces detachments familiar with Africa. (One has been stationed at French Djibouti, near Somalia.) The videotaping of the exercise by the soldiers was a characteristic Yankee trait; even more telling were the "thumbs up" and "high fives" hand signals the Turks gave each other in triumph once aboard the aircraft on the way home. Such gestures are peculiarly American, especially the "high fives" (the British Royal Air Force had originated the "thumbs up" during the Battle of Britain in the summer of 1940). In any event, such gestures are hardly part of the dictionary of Muslim world body language. It is even credible that operatives from Delta Force, for example, were present "off-site" in Nairobi to help coordinate the Ocalan snatch operation, as may have been the case in the successful storming of the Japanese embassy in April 1997 by Peruvian President Alberto Fujimori's commandos during the Lima hostage crisis. Such "aid and assistance" would of course have been entirely appropriate (if covert) since Turkey has been the eastern pillar of NATO since the alliance's inception.

The Turkish group that carried out the seizing of Apo, as Ocalan is known to his supporters, were probably drawn from the ranks of the twelve companies of the Ozel Intihar Kommando Bolugu, the Jandara Suicide Commandos. Operation Ocalan is well beyond the brief of anything the Jandara units have attempted before, insofar as it entailed a long-range flight to Nairobi, operations in a foreign city, possible refueling in Nairobi, and then the long flight back to Turkey, where Ocalan is now housed in a high-security Turkish military prison in the Sea of Marmara, next to Istanbul. Since the Turkish plane had to touch down at Nairobi during this exfiltration of Ocalan, the plan likely also involved men of the General Services Unit Recce (Reconnaissance Company) of the Kenya Police. The Kenyan Recce Unit has provided security for El Al jets at the Nairobi airport ever since the Entebbe operation. One of Apo's assistants, Melsa Diniz, had mentioned that "black men" took part in the actual kidnapping, which could refer to selected members of the Recce Company, as well as to the Turks in the "ninja" style black commando outfits they were probably wearing, including black Balaklava face masks for purposes of concealment, as seen in the video of Ocalan taken aboard the plane on its return to Turkey.

Because of the great strategic innovation that Operation Ocalan meant for the Jandara commandos, it is likely that they had assistance from either American or Israeli units in the planning as well as the execution of this daring gambit. Indeed, the entire scenario's *modus operandum* reflects very closely that of Operation Thunderbolt itself, the July 1976 rescue of the Israeli hostages in Uganda. If the Jandaras' mentors spoke Hebrew instead of American English, they were likely members of the Sayaret Matkal (the Israeli Defense Force's General Staff Recon Unit), the 35th Parachute Brigade, or the elite Golani Commandos; members of all three units flew with Yonatan (Jonathan) Netanyahu on that memorable flight to Entebbe in 1976. It should be mentioned here that, of course, not all Kurds support Ocalan and his terrorists.

The most intriguing question of all is what role, if any, did Moscow play in the Ocalan affair? We know that Ocalan was in Moscow for five weeks for his first trip to Russia, and perhaps for two during his second sojourn. Ocalan arrived in Rome in November 1998, but the Italian government ordered him out in January 1999, according to special BBC report on the Internet on February 16, 1999. (He had arrived in Italy from Russia, the BBC noted, on a false passport.) When one considers how quickly Rome expelled this international pariah, five weeks was an extremely long time for Ocalan to have been a guest of the Russian government (insofar as is known, he was neither imprisoned nor confined during his Russian "vacation"). More than a Muslim, Ocalan has always been a committed Marxist; certainly his PKK is a Marxist guerrilla army like the Colombian FARC (the Army Revolutionary Forces of Colombia). One must remember that in the past, in the days of the "evil empire" of the USSR, American intelligence, as well as independent commentators like Claire Sterling, targeted Moscow as the command post for the terrorist activities directed against the Western democracies.

Is it possible that Primakov, then virtually ruling Russia in the absence of the ailing Yeltsin, and an alumnus of the old Soviet intelligence KGB organ, had decided to restore Russia as the center for international terrorism? I know from discussions with members of the intelligence world, Russian spying has continued on the West and the United States, despite the common belief that the "evil empire" fell with the Berlin Wall ten years ago. As recently as February 2001, Robert Hanssen, a veteran since 1985 of the FBI counterintelligence bureau, was arrested for having spied for the Russians into 1999. Russia has also continued the development of its submarine fleet, outfitting it as well with a new generation of torpedoes (while Western and American funds feed her population). As mentioned, it is one of these torpedoes, the Shkoal, which is being attributed as the source of the August 2000 explosion which destroyed the Russian submarine *Kursk*. Based on reports from defectors such as Ken Alibek, a former senior Biopreparat official, the Russians have also continued the maturation of their chemical and biological warfare capability at their Biopreparat combine, creating new and more odious strains of anthrax and smallpox through the miracle of genetic engineering. If these observations are true, then so could be the speculation that Moscow under Primakov had decided to resume the role as headquarters of a new Terror International, which it played in the days of Brezhnev and Andropov (himself a secret service *apparatchik*), and that Ocalan was in Moscow to bring his PKK into the new terrorist grand design. Claire Sterling's view of Moscow as the "godfather" of international terrorism during the Andropov and Brezhnev era has been reinforced in Benjamin Netanyahu's *Fighting Terrorism*: "Brezhnev could benefit from the destabilization of the capitalist societies under the pressure of the terrorist weapon, while being able to keep his hands relatively clean." Michael Ledeen, in Netanyahu's previous book, *Terrorism: How the West Can Win*, wrote of how the Soviet Union trained Palestinian terrorists, gave them "diplomatic status" (a vague term which might entail the issuing of fake passports) and allowed them to move through the Warsaw Bloc countries, where they presumably made alliances with the intelligence services of these nations, as they had with the Russian KGB.[15] There already exists the precedent of the Russian-designed Bulgarian intelligence network employing the Turk Mehmet Ali Agca to try to kill Pope John Paul II in May 1981, in retaliation for the pontiff's support of the Solidarity movement in his native Poland. If Moscow used the Bulgarians and their Turkish connection in 1981, why could she not use Ocalan and his Turkish Kurd association in 1999? If this was Moscow's strategy with Primakov in charge, it remains to be seen what policy President Putin will now follow.

There is also potential evidence of a joint Russian-Greek collaboration, which opens up a new window for terrorist penetration of the West. The Clinton administration suspended arms sales to Greece that were needed for the modernization of the Greek army. According to the *Washington Post* of March 1, 2000, the CIA learned that the Greeks had secretly sent to the Russians sophisticated information about NATO, and in particular, American, aircraft capabilities, in return for Russian help in building Greece's anti-aircraft defenses against her old enemy Turkey.

We should continue to support those Arab and Muslim countries that are already in the grip of the struggle against militant Islam, such as Egypt and Jordan, where King Hussein's Bedouin legions drove the Palestinians out of his country when they tried to seize control in the 1970s. Indeed, the threat of terrorist groups traditionally having a base within Egypt became all too real again with the assault on the *Cole*. The Gama'at al-Islamiya and Islamic *Jihad*, both with many followers in the Land of the Pharaohs, are considered prime suspects in the search for support of the two bombers who immolated themselves in the bombing of the *Cole*.

In Jordan, the death of King Hussein on February 7, 1999, brought Crown Prince Abdullah to Jordan's throne. With Abdullah the next Hashemite king, and the only Arabian dynasty that can claim direct descent from the Prophet Mohammed himself, the United States ought to continue its support of Jordan as strongly as it has in the past. (Let's hope Abdullah will prove to be as pro-Western as his late father.) We should couple our support with increased economic assistance in view of the uneasy condition of the Jordanian economy—the last thing we need is to see Jordan slide into the economic chaos that has already claimed Indonesia and given rise to Islamic terrorism there! In 1999, the year the new king took power, an Islamic extremist plot was uncovered by Jordanian security authorities, a clear indication that Hamas, Hizbollah, the PLO, Islamic *Jihad*, and the other major players in the terrorism game will try to exploit the new monarch's inexperience. However, there is no doubt he will continue to command the support of the critical Bedouins, who comprise almost all of Jordan's armed forces, security apparatus, and special forces. While his father still lived, the then crown prince was chief of the Jordanian special operations forces. During the first part of his reign, Abdullah II has not embraced Israel as did his father, who signed the only peace treaty between an Arab nation and Israel since Anwar Sadat of Egypt. However, Jordanian intelligence did help foil al-Qaeda's terror plot for the holy land for the millenium of 2001.

If Jordan continues to help against terrorism, a main reason may be the *Infitidas* of Yassir Arafat. Although directed exclusively at Israel so far, Jordan cannot forget the Black September uprising when the PLO tried to seize control from King Hussein. With a population at least 50 percent Palestinian origin, Amman knows that a second *Intifida*, like the first, could pose as much a threat to Jordan. Another area of concern, which has not been mentioned in the media or by the diplomats, is that the creation of a Palestinian state, as envisioned by the Oslo and Wye River accords, might strike at the legitimacy of Jordan as well as at Israel. The 1948 United Nations decision which set up the state of Israel also established the kingdom of Transjordan, now Jordan. The United Nations' decision clearly divided the former British mandate into a Jewish state, Israel, and an Arab state, Transjordan. No third state for the Palestinian Arabs was envisaged in 1948. The last peace initiative presented by President Bill Clinton before he left office in January 2001 offered the Palestinians much of the West Bank with East Jerusalem as their capital. Before the 1967 War, however, the West Bank and East Jerusalem were in Jordanian hands. It is possible that the agreement with Yassir Arafat may prove a deadly two-edged sword, striking at both Israel *and* Jordan before all is done.

Another problem looming for the new Hashemite king is the uncertain behavior of Iraq's Saddam Hussein. Previously, Saddam seemed to be standing aloof from the struggle going on in between the Palestinians and the Israelis. However, the Middle East desk of the British Broadcasting Corporation (BBC) in early 2001 reported that Saddam had begun to raise a "Jerusalem army" from indoctrinated university-age students for the liberation of Jerusalem from Israel. Iraqi television has shown film footage of volunteers going off for training in desert camps for their role in the Jerusalem army. Since Jordan is on the land road between Iraq and the Palestinians and Israel, any attempt by Saddam's army would take it across the roads of Jordan. Indeed, through Jordan runs the only real road communication between Iraq and the Palestinian struggle.

Of course, American support of Israel should continue, especially during the period of uncertainty following the inauguration of the hard-line war hero, former parachutist Ariel "Arik" Sharon, as prime minister. Although Sharon intends to carry on the Israeli dialogue with Yassir Arafat at some future time, the news of Saddam's sudden support for the Palestinian *Intifida*, the uprising against Israel, bodes ill for the stability of the entire region. *Jane's Intelligence Review* on the Web has even speculated that, should pressure increase from Sharon, Arafat may move his PLO headquarters to Baghdad. This seems unlikely, though, since abandoning the land already ceded to his Palestinian Authority would make it virtually impossible for him to ever again claim to be the spokesman for the Palestinian cause. Arafat however, according to *Jane's*, has already sent his trusted aide, Farouk Kaddoumi, to test the waters for a Baghdad base of operations. Significantly, Kaddoumi has been an opponent of talks with the Israelis since the time of the 1993 Oslo agreement. The threat of possible military action on behalf of the *Intifida* by Saddam is taken very seriously by the Israeli government. Any attempt at a movement of Iraq's army into Jordan, on its way to support of the Palestinians, would certainly call forth a strong response from the Israeli Defense Force (IDF). Indeed, in the entire Middle East the prospect of a light at the end of the tunnel dimmed in the last months 2000 into 2001 with the bombing of the *Cole* and the renewed violence between the Palestinians and the Israelis.

In light of the failed last-ditch initiative of President Clinton to bring peace to the Middle East, the struggle continues between Israel and Yassir Arafat's Palestinian Authority. In February 2002, a new escalation in the continuing Second *Intifida* arose. Palestinian militants, according to the February 12 *San Francisco Examiner*, launched a new, home-made rocket, the Qassam II, at Israeli targets on the West Bank. With a range of three to five miles, the new generation rocket, also associated with Hamas, brought many Israeli towns and villages within range of a terrorist rocket attack. With continued violence in the Israeli-Palestinian dispute, the only winners can be the fundamentalist militants of the Hizbollah and the Hamas, which celebrated the summer 2000 withdrawal of Israeli troops from southern Lebanon, a move ordered by then Israeli Prime Minister Ehud Barak. Barak's public approval rating, due to his inability to bring an end to the fighting, sank to such a low that, when elections were held in 2001, he lost decisively to Ariel Sharon of the hard-line Likud party.

However, at the time of the war in Afghanistan in October 2001, another major incident brought the Palestinians and the Israelis close to the brink of open warfare. The right wing minister of tourism in Sharon's government, Rehavam Zeevi, was shot to death on October 17 by agents of another Palestinian terror group, the new Popular Front for the Liberation of Palestine. Zeevi, whose extreme nationalist policies were tinged by anti-Palestinian racism, had been murdered as retaliation for the Israeli killing of the Popular Front's leader, Mustafa Zibri on August 27 of the same year. Accused of plotting attacks on Israelis, Zibri had been killed by two rockets from an Israeli helicopter fired at him through the windows of his second floor office on the West Bank as he had sat at his desk talking on the phone. The Israelis had sent tanks in to occupy West Bank villages in spite of vehement denunciations by U.S. Press Secretary Ari Fleischer and Secretary of State Colin Powell. On October 25, the Israelis announced they were considering a withdrawal after they had arrested two suspects in the Zeevi killing.

Although we have perhaps forgotten the war fought against Serbia, American troops are still stationed there, and will be so for the forseeable future. They are in the unenvied position of being between the Albanians of Kosovo Province, for whose protection from Slobodan Milosevic the war was fought, and the Serbians. In the months since the 1999 war, the Serbians have felt that United States and NATO forces have sided with the ethnic Albanians over them, and the danger exists that the Serbs may open guerrilla war against our forces and the NATO contingents. However, a greater danger may lie in the Kosovo Liberation Army (KLA), which NATO has allowed to become the de facto armed force in Kosovo Province. The nearly 500,000 refugees created during the NATO bombing of Kosovo and Yugoslavia only resulted in creating another possible 500,000 terrorists against the United States. The Serbs are particularly enraged that we bombed them, when they were our allies against the Germans in World War II and rescued some 500 downed American flyers from German vengeance. The 90,000-plus Serbian-American community is particularly incensed about the bombing campaign, since many of their sons have served honorably in the American armed forces. For example, during World War I, Serbian immigrants, recently arrived in the United States, enlisted in the American armed forces and saw action fighting the Germans in France. One of them, Angelko Allex Mandusic, was born on July 13, 1887, in Streska, Serbia, not far from the holy mountain of Shar Planina. Coming to America in 1912, and known as "Jake Allex," he won the Medal of Honor for hand-to-hand combat against the Germans in August 1918.[16] The depth of the animosity the bombing of Serbia caused among Serbian-Americans in the United States was revealed by CBS Radio News when it reported on April 3, 1999, that the U.S. Secret Service intercepted a mail bomb in Washington, D.C., that was addressed to the White House. Thus, our foggy policy in the Balkans may already be spawning a new wave of domestic terrorism here in the United States. And the Serbs make excellent terrorists: It was grenades and gunshots from Gavrilo Princip and his Serb nationalists that killed the heir to the Austrian throne, Archduke Franz Ferdinand, in the streets of Sarajevo, Bosnia, on June 1914, an act of terror that precipitated World War I!* Until the Bosnian Muslims destroyed them in the current war, the footsteps of Princip where he stood on the Sarajevo street to kill the archduke and his wife were preserved in a monument by the Serbian people.

On April 14, 1999, the FBI and the armed forces were put on alert against a possible Serb terror campaign in the United States. A fax was received by Serbian Orthodox churches and social clubs in Chicago, Milwaukee, Indianapolis, and Sacramento. The FBI said that "the threat letter requested that all Serbian nationalists living in America take action against the NATO decision in the Serbian-Kosovo conflict by killing as many American soldiers in the United States as necessary to stop the NATO attacks in Serbia." A second fax was sent; both were written in Serbo-Croatian. No source was given for the faxes, so I do not know if the source was within the United States or in Serbia itself. Although the Serbian-American population has been intensely patriotic in the past, such a wholesale bombing of their homeland may cause some to consider themselves Serbian first and American second. Given the warlike nature of the Serbs and their passionate devotion to "holy Serbia," such a threat had to be taken very seriously indeed.

---

*In 1908, the Empire of Austria-Hungary had annexed the former Turkish province of Bosnia-Hercegovina. The neighboring Kingdom of Serbia had wanted the province for itself, and Princip was part of a group of Serbian terrorists, the Black Hand, which was loosely tied to Serbian military intelligence.

In early 2001, the Kosovo crisis ignited again. Members of the KLA embarked on another step toward their dream of building a "Greater Albania," which presumably would be an Islamic fundamentalist state. The KLA sent fighters into the border region with Serbia and also into Macedonia, which remained with Serbia as the historic remnant of the once multinational Yugoslavia. The KLA fighters formed a national liberation army among ethnic Albanians in Macedonia to help in the fight for their Greater Albania. Twenty-five percent of the population of the small nation of Macedonia (total population about 2 million) is Albanian, and this sector has become restive following the success of the KLA in the Serbian province of Kosovo.

The renewal of action of the KLA has included border raids into that part of Serbia on the frontier of Kosovo Province, and has caused serious problems for KFOR, the NATO peace-keeping force that has been stationed in Kosovo since the end of the fighting there in 1999. Increasingly, KFOR troops have become caught in the middle between the Serbian police trying to stop the infiltration of the KLA fighters, and the KLA who are determined to keep up the renewed struggle against the Serbs. Finally, on March 12, KFOR finally allowed elite Serb police units to actively attempt to repel the efforts of the KLA, with positive results.

The situation with the Albanian national liberation force in Macedonia grew more intense with every day. The Albanian guerrillas in Macedonia regularly received training and military supplies from the KLA in Kosovo Province. As of March 2001, the Albanians had already engaged the police and small Macedonian army in fierce firefights in areas bordering Kosovo. Their purpose was to start a movement for a Greater Albania among the ethnic Albanians who reside in Macedonia. The Albanians fighting in Macedonia, when pressed by Macedonian authorities, quickly retreated across the border into Kosovo for sanctuary. Macedonia, its resources already stretched to the limit, has tried to seal the border with Kosovo, but attempts have proven to be useless. Indeed, in January 2002, Macedonia remained a possible flash point for another Balkan war.

The Albanian movement in Macedonia was clearly part of the new *jihad*, as is the KLA in Kosovo. In 2000, Azzam Publications had put up a page on the Internet describing the *jihad* being waged in Macedonia, thus confirming that the guerrillas were *mujahidin*. The population of Albania is almost entirely Muslim. The fighting in Macedonia, which was barely successful in staying out of the Serbian War in spring 1999, again threatened to ignite the rest of the Balkans. Any fighting in Macedonia stands the danger of spreading into Greece, which has not had the best relations with Macedonia since the time of the small nation's birth. Greece deeply resented Macedonia because it has always considered the northern part of Greece to be the true Macedonia, which was the home of Alexander the Great.

The unrest in the Balkans put a new emphasis on the *jihad* struggle with the United States, since the NATO troops contained an American contingent. President George W. Bush has already expressed his determination that the Americans in KFOR not be drawn into new unrest in Macedonia, on top of their peace duties in Kosovo. It was to take the pressure off KFOR that the Serbs were allowed into the buffer zone on the Kosovo border, with the hope that they could stop the cross-border traffic of the KLA and their partisans in Macedonia.

In the frontiers of the Arab world, both Algeria and Turkey are still focal points of Islamic agitation. Some 90,000 people have been killed in an atrocious civil war that has continued between the Islamic extremists and the government in Algiers since the army invalidated an Islamic election victory in the early 1990s. There had been a diminution in the level of violence in Algeria as elections approached (the Islamic Salvation Front [FIS] declared a cease-fire out of exhaustion in the summer of 1997), as the Islamic parties appeared to be making another political bid for power. The moderate Islamist parties Hamas and Ennahda, although they had changed their names, were running candidates in the elections. The strongest moderate Islamic candidate was Shaikh Mahfoud Nannah of Hamas. However, the odds were that one of the FLN's long-standing party cadre, Adbelaziz Bouteflika, Foreign Minister under Houari Boumedienne, would succeed Liamine Zeroual as president. Whether the moderate Islamists felt that this time, unlike in 1992, they received a fair chance at winning seats might determine whether or not the bloody civil war would return in all its suicidal rage, for if the Islamists felt they had been denied their fair share, the only Islamist opposition would again be the militants of the FIS. With the defeat of the Islamic parties in the general elections, the bloody guerilla war continued into 2001.

Meanwhile, in Turkey, the pro-militant Welfare party (RP) had been seen by many, including the army, to have been resurrected in the guise of the FP, the Vazilet (Virtue) party. In 1995, the Welfare party formed a brief coalition government with Tansu Ciller's conservative True Path party (DYP) before the military moved in to end it, fearing the influence of the Welfare party. The current Turkish government is unhappy about the newfound popularity of the

Virtue party. Nuh Mete Yuksel, the prosecutor of the Ankara State Security Court, told *The Middle East Magazine* (March 1999) that "there is evidence that the FP is a continuation of the RP, as the high ranking administrators of both parties are the same." From current predictions, it seems that the Virtue party may win up to 30 percent of the ballots cast, forcing conservative and socialist parties to invite it into a coalition government again.

During the spring of 2001 another incident highlighted the fundamentalist, extremist Muslim movement in Turkey. On April 23, the *Philadelphia Inquirer* reported that gunmen from the Muslim extremists operating in Chechnya had taken hostages when they stormed a hotel in Istanbul demanding the Russians evacuate Chechnya. Twenty gunmen, led by Muhammed Tokcan, a Turkish citizen of Chechen descent, had attacked the hotel. This was not the first time that Tokcan had carried the green banner of the *jihad* in Turkey. In 1996, he had hijacked a Turkish ferry in the Black Sea. Not long before the attack on the hotel, he had been freed under a general amnesty law. Tokcan and his group surrendered peacefully to Turkish authorities, letting go some 120 hostages in the luxury Swiss hotel. Reuters news agency reported on April 30 that Tokcan and his accomplices had appeared in a special Turkish security court, where they were charged with "forming an armed gang to commit crime," "curtailing the freedom of others," and "causing panic by firing in a crowded area."

Chechen hijackers have even carried their crusade as far as Saudi Arabia. In March 2001, a Russian jet from Istanbul was taken to Saudi Arabia to protest what the Chechnyan fighters call Russian atrocities in Chechnya. There were 100 hostages aboard when the plane landed in Medina. When the hijackers threatened to blow up the plane, Saudi special forces, likely trained by the American Green Berets, assaulted the plane at the Medina airport. In the shooting, one of the terrorists, a Russian flight attendant, and a Turkish passenger were killed.

Since the Russians effectively reconquered Chechnya in September 1999, Turkey became a base of operations for the fighters still carrying on the *jihad* there. Some 80 Caucasian groups, from Chechnya and neighboring Daghestan, have their bases in Turkey, where the *jihad* against the Russians enjoys wide support. Russia has criticized the government of Prime Minister Bulent Ecevit of going too easily on the Chechen militants operating on Turkish territory.

The Islamic extremists have continued to make Turkey another military front in the *jihad*. Reuters reported on April 30, 2001, that five gunmen from the Turkish Hizbollah group had ambushed and killed Mehmet Kaya, who had earlier left the terrorist group; Kaya was killed as a perceived traitor to the group. Turkish intelligence holds the Turkish Hizbollah responsible for over 150 killings. Many of these victims were killed in Ankara in the house belonging to the chief of the movement, when Turkish authorities raided the property in 2000. The graves of the victims were found, many of whom had been tortured to death. The Turkish Hizbollah was founded in the eastern Kurdish section of Turkey, when it began action in the same wave of terrorism that highlighted Apo Ocalan's activities.

In the Philippines, as covered in Azzam Publications' Web site, the Islamic *jihad* is still a powerful force, especially the Moro insurrection in Mindanao, which appears to be on the verge of erupting again. It is believed that Moro delegates have already met with fellow Islamic militants at the terrorist Comintern in Khartoum, Sudan. On February 8, 2001, *Jane's Intelligence Review* confirmed that Islamic terrorists struck both in the Phillippines and in Indonesia. The terror bombers struck during the Christmas holiday of 2000, deliberately attacking Christian churches to kill congregations during Christmas services. The attacks took place in Jakarta and seven other cities. Eighteen people were killed and fifty wounded in the Indonesian assaults. On December 30, bombers hit in the city of Manila. Some twenty-two were killed and over one hundred were wounded. Osama bin Laden's al-Qaeda had been in touch with the Muslim militants fighting the Filipino government in Manila, especially the Abu Sayyaf group. As proof of this, Azzam Publications began to list "martyrs" who had been killed in the warfare with the Filipino security forces.

In Indonesia, while the "Defenders of Islam" is the oldest Islamic militant organization in Indonesia, the group to watch is the Laskar *Jihad*, or Army of the Holy War. Its chieftain is thirty-nine-year-old Jaffar Omar Thalib, who is also a veteran of the war in Afghanistan. Interestingly, he is known to have studied in Yemen. While there were no plans as of yet to help the Indonesians, the CIA and perhaps U.S. military advisers as well took part in the overthrow of President Achmed Sukarno, the first postwar leader of Indonesia. He was replaced by Gen. Mohammed Suharto, and lived under house arrest until his death in 1970. If the current President Megawati Sukarnoputri, who took over the presidency in 2000, seemed reluctant to help the United States in the aftermath of September 11, one reason may be she is President Sukarno's daughter.

Also, while we focus on plans for the financial recovery of Indonesia, we should step up all plans to shore up the government of Megawati, either with direct American aid or with assistance from the World Bank or the International Monetary Fund. This is especially critical to our interests because, with all the attention given to the fall of President Suharto and the economic and ethnic, anti-Chinese turmoil that followed, we may have lost sight that an Islamic insurrection already has begun in Indonesia. In 1999, four Indonesian soldiers were charged with committing atrocities in the Islamic uprising on the island of Sumatra, in the Aceh District. Clearly, any assistance, economic or military, that we can render the floundering government of President Megawati cannot come too soon! Indeed, the *Philadelphia Inquirer* reported on January 21, 1999, that "rival Christian and Muslim gangs" rioted for two days, killing at least seventeen "on Ambon Island, 1,450 miles northeast of Jakarta, the capital." The rioting had taken a toll of twenty-four dead and hundreds wounded as of January 1999. Thousands of Indonesian troops were being rushed to the scene to restore order, while foreigners, including Americans, were fleeing the region. Additionally, in February 2001, the Animist Dyaks of Kalimantan Province resumed their grisly head-hunting against immigrants to their island homeland. Hundreds have been ritually beheaded, and thousands of the immigrant Madurese are now refugees. Whether the Dyaks have in fact been encouraged in their revolt by the Islamic fundamentalists trying to take over Indonesia is still an open question, but such a possibility would come as no surprise to anyone who has studied the situation in Indonesia since 1998.

After the September 2001 attacks on the World Trade Center and the Pentagon, President Megawati denounced the terrorists. However, she was reluctant to supply help for fear of antagonizing her own Muslim extremists. In Indonesia, the country with the world's largest Muslim population, there was real concern over reaction to the beginning of the October 7, 2001, American attack on Afghanistan. American diplomatic authorities urged U.S. citizens in Indonesia to remain indoors; many of the dependents of American consular and embassy personnel left the country. The immediate crisis passed without major incident, the *Jakarta Post* reported on October 27, and the new American ambassador, Ralph L. Boyce, was able to present his credentials to President Megawati without incident and assume his post.

Fundamentalist Islamic dominance of Indonesia would undoubtedly have terrible side effects for the United States, apart from the obvious political danger being posed by one of the largest nations in Asia falling to the militants. The strategic Strait of Malacca, which lies between Malaysia and the Indonesian island of Sumatra, has, since the time of the Portuguese, been the gateway for all commerce with east Asia. An Islamic regime in Jakarta could quickly assert control over this vital strait, strangling our commercial dealings with the rest of the area. Were missile batteries to be installed here, only war could reopen this essential maritime artery.

Although Osama bin Laden is believed to remain in Afghanistan, he could attempt to flee through neighboring Pakistan, which joined the international alliance against the Taliban only after some tense introspection. While Islamabad's Ministry of Information has uttered heated denials in a letter to the *Philadelphia Inquirer*, it seems pretty clear that Pakistan is the main backer of the Taliban in Afghanistan, as it is of the militants in Kashmir. The United States could surely urge Pakistan further to increase pressure and hence cause bin Laden to be turned over to Islamabad for extradition to the United States. However, it is unlikely if either Pakistan or the remaining Taliban supporters would wish to provoke the wrath of militant Islam by doing so—at least for now. It was not long ago, however, that the Pakistani intelligence service cooperated with the FBI to bring to justice the Pakistani national, Min Aimal Kansi, who murdered CIA operatives outside CIA headquarters with an AK-47, by a raid on his hideout with the FBI SWAT team and Pakistani agents.

With the centrality of bin Laden to the whole danger of a new *jihad*, more must be said about him here. As mentioned above, the possibility that he will be turned over to us or to any international authority is extremely remote—one can only look at the years of negotiations that were expended trying to bring the Libyan perpetrators of the bombing of Pan Am Flight 103 in 1988 over Lockerbie, Scotland, for a case in point. It was not until 2000 that two Libyans, Abdelbaset Ali Mohmed Al Megrahi and Al Amin Khalifa Fhimah, members of the Libyan Intelligence Service, were put on trial for the bombing. When the verdicts were delivered on January 31, 2001, Al Megrahi was sentenced to life imprisonment, but would be eligible to be considered for parole after twenty years in prison, since the death penalty has been abolished in the United Kingdom.* Fhimah was found not guilty and released.

---

*Although the case was tried in the Netherlands, it was conducted under the rules of Scottish law.

Although the Lockerbie bombing is considered to have been a revenge act against the earlier United States air battles with the Libyan Air Force over the contested Gulf of Sidra, what makes the case relevant to a study of modern Islamic terrorism is that Al Megrahi was at the training camp of Sabha. Sabha was, at least until 1988, a Libyan special forces camp that was a likely site for training of the international terror cartel, including of course the Palestinians. Fhimah's part of the indictment brings to life a unique picture of the Soviet-backed network that hosted the terrorists until the breakdown of the Soviet Union in 1991. For doubters of Claire Sterling's thesis of the "terrorist international," a terror cartel funded and directed from Moscow, Fhimah's itinerary would be disappointing reading. The peripatetic Fhimah had lived previously "at the Libyan Peoples' Bureau [Embassy], East Berlin, German Democratic Republic [and] in Prague, Czechoslovakia," according to the text of the indictment which was delivered by Lord Hardie on behalf of the government of the United Kingdom at the trial at Camp Zeist in the Netherlands.

All the while, the war in the Sudan continues between the Islamic government in Khartoum and the fighters under John Garang in the Christian and animist south. Although largely forgotten in light of the recent fighting in West Africa in Sierra Leone, the troops of John Garang and the other groups in the southern Sudan who are at war with the fundamentalist government sitting in Khartoum have been fighting attempts against them that often seem to verge on genocide. These troops, like the Sudanese Peoples' Liberation Army, have played an important part in stopping the new *jihad* of militant Islam. Garang and his associates are ever more needful of aid since it appears that Khartoum is becoming the southern leg of a militant Islamic axis, reaching from Kabul in Afghanistan, through Tehran and Baghdad, and culminating in the Sudan. While the current president of Iran is seeking to find an overture to the West, it appears that Saddam Hussein, in retaliation against the British and American opposition to the lifting of the UN sanctions on Iraqi exports of petroleum and our air attacks in the no-fly zones, seems determined to make Khartoum a base for spreading Iraqi state-inspired terrorism throughout Africa, as Muammar Quaddafi did from Libya ten years ago. Indeed, diplomatic speculation in 1999 bruited it about that it would not be inconceivable for Hussein to consider a move to the Sudan to avoid more Anglo-American vengeance. This would be especially true if the ban against political assassination imposed during the presidency of Gerald Ford were ever lifted in Washington. With his widespread use of "doubles" in his rare public appearances, which has baffled the CIA (men have undergone plastic surgery to more closely resemble him), such a gambit is even more feasible. (The same search for asylum in the Sudan might be true for Osama bin Laden himself.)

Aid to Garang and the fighters in the southern Sudan would also bolster the governments of Kenya and Tanzania in the face of renewed terrorism such as they faced in August 1998 with the bombings of the U.S. embassies. Indeed, it is time that we begin to realize the importance of this region of East Africa in our war against militant Islam because, like it our not, we are at war—if we did not declare it, Osama bin Laden certainly has. Even in Victorian times, the British realized the centrality of the Sudan and Uganda to control East Africa. They were the gateway to the soft underbelly of the colony of Kenya (then Tanzania and German East Africa). Although sunk in impotence since the regime of the infamous Idi Amin Dada, Uganda has returned to its place of strategic value in East Africa in recent years. Under President Musaveni, Uganda has been a major supporter in the struggle in the Congo against President Laurent Kabila, who began his public career as one of the bloody anticolonialist *simbas* (Swahili for "lions") in the Congo war in the 1960s. Although Kabila was shot in early 2001 by one of his bodyguards, his son has succeeded him in power. The geostrategic importance of Uganda is why Lord Lugard went to such lengths to make it a British protectorate in the Age of Empire, as Thomas Pakenham wrote in his classic *The Scramble for Africa*.

By the same token, further inroads into Kenya and Tanzania by Islamic militants cannot be overlooked, especially given the sizable Islamic population already present there. Kenya has always been a place for political moderation in East Africa, as has Tanzania, despite human rights violations by Kenyan President Daniel arap Moi. It cannot be forgotten that when the Israeli commandos launched their air strike to save the hostages at Entebbe air base in Dada's Uganda in 1976, the Kenyan government silently gave approval to the Israelis to use Kenyan air space to fly over their target at Entebbe. The fact of the Kenyan acquiescence in the recent snatch of Apo Ocalan (the Nairobi government did not even lodge a protest about his kidnapping on Kenyan soil) shows how Kenya merits our support. The danger of a Uganda under a militant Islamic regime can be seen when one considers the fact that Idi Amin Dada strongly identified with the Palestinian cause during his dictatorship, and gave the terrorists the right to use Entebbe field in the first place, fully knowing their plans. The attack on tourists in southern

Uganda in the Bwindi National Park, called the Impenetrable Forest, by guerrillas based in the Congo, on March 2, 1999, only shows how vulnerable
Uganda is to terrorist attack. Several tourists, including Americans, were
killed in a national wildlife preserve. If Uganda falls to militant Islam, as has
the government in Khartoum, the *jihad* could easily spread over most of central and eastern Africa. So again, all possible support should be given to not
only Tanzania and Kenya, but also to Uganda, to prevent a Khartoum-style
coup in any of these nations.

If the Islamic uprising already convulsing Algeria should spread to
Tunisia and Morrocco, all of the Mahgreb could fall to the *jihad*, as it did in
the days of the original Arab conquests. Countries to the south of Algeria's
Atlas Mountains, such as Mali, Mauretania, Niger, and Chad, largely forgotten by us since the days of the Cold War, should also take on renewed
importance, given their Muslim populations of warrior tribes like the famous
Tuaregs, who in the Almohad period had been the strike forces in the Almohads' attempt to reinforce the Moors in the Spain of El Cid. Given French
support of Algeria, it is likely that the French already have military missions
in these countries to help fend off any Islamic insurrections in these desert
nations. When Libya threatened Chad in the 1980s, the French were quick to
send potent support to the Chadian government to resist any attempts by the
Libyan-backed opposition to seize power. (At the time, Colonel Quaddafi
still coveted the rich minerals of the Aouzou Strip territory.) France can be
counted on to act again against any militant Islamic menace, given the warm
relations that the French retain with the former African member states of the
French community. (Although the French government announced plans to
scale down its troop commitment in Africa by 40 percent, to about 5,000 in
the year 2000, any real threat to French interests in Africa would be guaranteed to bring about a rapid *volte face* in Paris.) However, if the United States
wants to retain any influence in Saharan Africa, then it is important that we
offer our assistance as well.

Perhaps the newest danger in Africa from extremist Muslims is the rise
of PAGAD in South Africa, mentioned earlier. Its attacks on moderate Muslims has quickly raised it to the status of the most violent of all the world's
militant Islamic groups. Even fundamentalist Hamas or Hizbollah have never
attacked clerics or mosques of congregations that have not agreed with their
warfare against the state of Israel. With former South African president
Nelson Mandela now retired in favor of an unproven successor, it is incum-

bent that the United States continue the "era of good feelings" with the Republic of South Africa that President Bill Clinton inaugurated with his trip to that country in 1998. Elected in June 1999, new president Thabo Mbeki has continued to be a friend of the United States. An Islamic-controlled South Africa would be a disaster to the United States, because such a regime could interdict all commerce past the Cape of Good Hope and into the Indian Ocean and all of Asia beyond.

❀ ❀ ❀

While the administration of George W. Bush is ever more concerned with the gains of the Marxist FARC in Colombia, we should also be concerned with signs of possible increased Islamic terrorism in South America. Experience has shown in the past how Marxist and Islamic terrorists can easily unite against the United States and those countries which support us or oppose Israel. As mentioned previously, there is already a highly sophisticated terrorist infrastructure in place. According to Katherine Ellison in the *Philadelphia Inquirer* (February 12, 1999), the new area of concern centers around where Paraguay meets Uruguay, Argentina, and Brazil. Herein, especially in the town of Chiu in southern Brazil, lives a large Arabic and Muslim population, some 18,000 in number. Although American intelligence has been observing the area for some time, according to Ellison, what focused attention on this region was the capture on January 29 of El Said Hassan Ali Mohammed Mukhlis, who, in the opinion of the American intelligence community, is a trusted courier of Osama bin Laden. It is likely that he is a graduate of one of bin Laden's terrorist camps in Afghanistan, since he has admitted being in that country. The Egyptian Mukharabat, their CIA, suspects him of being involved in the 1997 slaughter of fifty-eight tourists at Luxor, as well as perhaps being involved in the 1995 attempt on the life of President Hosni Mubarak. Mukhlis is also suspected of having served as a courier between Hamas and Hizbollah in the Middle East, and Ellison indicates there is also information that he probably served as a bin Laden intermediary in south Asia, perhaps having been involved in planning some of the terrorist activity in Indonesia. When he was arrested, Mukhlis had with him a Malaysian passport under the name of Ibrahim Mohammada al Thaqaaf. With the overwhelming Muslim population in Malaysia, that country may be second to Indonesia as the site for the next outbreak of *jihad* in the area.

Another intriguing thing about Mukhlis is that he is fluent in Spanish, a language that is rarely, if ever, taught in Middle Eastern countries. It is not, for instance, taught in the elementary or secondary schools in Turkey, Iran, or Jordan; in those countries, English is always the favored foreign language. This gives strength to the argument that Mukhlis was taught Spanish to help him in his terrorist role in South America, which could imply that he intended to make his stay in Chui a long one, helping to make the region a bin Laden outpost and hooking into the terrorist infrastructure already operating in South America.

There also exists another, if rather remote, reason for Mukhlis to arrive in this region of South America in 1993, instead of farther north in Colombia, for example, in the part of northern Latin America where the Abu Nidal organization (ANO) established a presence years ago. The region where Mukhlis lived, the Uruguay, Paraguay, Argentina, southern Brazil area, is also where Nazi refugees like Adolf Eichmann, Martin Bormann, Klaus Barbie, Freddy Schwend, and Josef Mengele found a safe haven after Germany's defeat in World War II. Welcomed by fascist dictators like Juan Peron of Argentina, Hugo Banzer Suarez of Bolivia, and Alfredo Stroessner of Paraguay, along with some like Nazi war criminal Franz Stangl who sought sanctuary in Brazil, they established themselves deeply in the fabric of society, certainly by investing the looted treasure they had brought with them in the local governments. In the 1950s, Bormann is known to have taken sanctuary in the mysterious District X that was rife with Nazis in eastern Paraguay, near the common borders of Paraguay and Bolivia, where Klaus Barbie lived for a time. After Peron was ousted, the Argentine federal police as well as the president's Intelligence Service kept Bormann under close observation, noting particularly his visits with Dr. Josef Mengele. Another prominent Nazi, Luftwaffe fighter ace Hans Ulrich Rudel, author of the wartime memoir *Stuka Pilot*, was a ranking officer in *Der Spinne*, "the Spider's Web," the "old comrades" group of Nazis charged with spiriting their friends out of Europe after the war to escape justice. Rudel had been a friend of Peron's during his first tenure in power, and showed up in Buenos Aires to congratulate him on his return in 1973! Indeed, during the terrible purge of suspected Communists by the Argentine junta before its overthrow, the tortures inflicted on the prisoners are hauntingly similar to those committed by the SS at the Dachau and Auschwitz death camps, and seem to point to former SS men, now refugees in Argentina, who educated the Argentine secret police in the finer art of torture. In 1992, in an Argentine government "white paper," reformist President Carlos Menem of Argentina published a list of some 3,000 Nazis still known to be living in the country, a virtual who's who for Islamic terrorists like Mukhlis to forge alliances with.

The movement of Mukhlis into this region may indeed become the opening move toward an Armageddon in the Americas. We have seen how the Marxists and Islamic militants worked together in the days of Carlos the Jackal and Abu Nidal. A lesser known alliance existed in the past between the Nazis and the Arabs. This devil's bond was a serious threat during World War II. A pro-Nazi government took power in Baghdad early in the war, and threatened to deprive England, hard-pressed by the forces of Nazi Germany, of vital Iraqi oil. During the fighting in North Africa against the famed Desert Fox, German Field Marshal Erwin Rommel, the British were forced to dispatch an expeditionary force 600 miles across the desert to reconquer Iraq. At the same time, the Grand Mufti of Jerusalem had gained a reputation for fomenting the vicious anti-Jewish rioting in Palestine (then united by the British under the League of Nations mandate) from 1936 to 1938. As has been mentioned, when World War II began, the Grand Mufti fled to Berlin, where he was an honored guest of Adolf Hitler. Throughout the war, the Grand Mufti exhorted Muslims to defy the British and side with the Germans. This agitation had great effect in Egypt, where throughout the war the Egyptian army could not be used by the British because it was considered on the point of mutiny. Some officers, notably future Egyptian presidents Gamal Abdel Nasser and Anwar Sadat, were arrested by the British for their openly pro-German sympathies. After the war, Nazis from Germany found as warm a welcome among the Arab countries as they encountered in South America. Former SS officers were instrumental in training the secret police in Syria and in Egypt in the wake of the Arab-Israeli War of 1948. In Egypt, when Nasser was president, German atomic scientists played a vital role in beginning the Egyptian project to be able to use atomic warhead missiles against Israel. This project, a direct threat to Israel's survival, was met by a characteristic Israeli response: Mossad agents were put to work to eliminate the German scientists in Egypt. After several were brutally disposed of, the rest prudently returned to the German Fatherland, dealing Egypt's atomic program a blow from which it has never recovered.[17]

In South America, proof already exists that, despite former Argentine President Carlos Menem's efforts to the contrary, a new alliance might be forming between the neo-Nazis in there and the radical Muslims, something to which Mukhlis would no doubt have strongly contributed. Indeed, there are indications that Menem's government, in spite of its American-style public relations efforts, may be more in sympathy with the neo-Nazis and the militants than first appears. Author George Carpozi Jr. writes that after the terror bombing of the Fraternal Argentine-Israeli Mutual Association, if "the Argentinean government took the slightest interest in getting to the bottom of this heinous massacre and went in pursuit of those responsible for it, there was virtually no indication of it."[18] (It should be noted, however, that President Menem is a political survivalist whose hold on the Argentine presidency was always tenuous and he was afraid to go after the powerful neo-Nazis in the armed forces officer corps too closely for fear of precipitating another military coup.)

Finally, with urging from President Bill Clinton on a goodwill mission to Argentina in 1997, President Menem, promised help by the FBI, began to pursue more vigorously the perpetrators of the Buenos Aires terror bombing. Argentine Judge Juan Jose Galeano conducted an investigation* that pointed to an Iranian connection with the terrorist act through the testimony of one Manoucher Moatamer who described, in a deposition given to the judge in Los Angeles in December 1997, a plot that included the involvement of "intelligence officers" who had "plotted the Buenos Aires bombing." Although his credibility was naturally attacked in Tehran, his veracity was given a boost by his 1994 prediction that the Israeli embassy in London would be bombed—several days before the event actually took place. In early 1998, Argentine prosecutor Jose Barbaccia summed up the official verdict on Moatamer: "What we have found out during these past three years has made him more credible. If his information is authentic, it is important," to say the least. With the reformist President Khatami on the defensive against the fundamentalists in Iran, the possibility of an alliance on our southern border between Marxists, neo-Nazis, bin Laden's movement, and agents from Iraq and Iran is enough to give George J. Tenet, director of the CIA, and Robert S. Mueller, director of the FBI, nightmares.

At the same time, the possibility of better relations with Iran are growing dimmer than in the recent past. When President Khatami took power in 1997, it seemed that the reign of the conservative ayatollahs who had dominated the country since the fall of the shah in 1979 was ending. The new president

---

*In Latin countries, as in France, investigating judges and magistrates do much of the investigative work themselves, unlike the American system of justice.

opened the first window of opportunity to the United States in nearly twenty years. To show his intentions of opening Iran to the West, in spite of the opposition of the militants, Ayatollah Mohammed Khatami paid a state visit to the Vatican, where he had personal interview with Pope John Paul II. Both religious leaders expressed their earnest hopes for a new era of peace and cooperation in the world between Christianity and Islam, the world's "two greatest monotheisms," as they described their faiths in a joint communiqué after their historic meeting.

Now, however, the climate in Iran is very different, with President Khatami fighting a rear guard action against a resurgent militant clergy, whose supporters still dominate the all-important security services in Tehran. Tragically, in 2000 five intellectuals who supported the president's call were killed by hard-liners in the Iranian intelligence service, but already the perpetrators have been caught and hopefully will be brought to justice. Throughout late 2000 and early 2001, there were riots in Tehran between students supporting the president and the hard-liners, with students killed by the security forces. The prospect for a renewal of relations with Iran, and the end of Iranian sponsorship for militant Islamists, seems tragically dim. However, the crisis of the September 11 attacks, and the American move into Afghanistan that followed, means the future of American relations with Iran are anybody's guess.

Domestically, we can become more prepared for the shock of more sophisticated terrorism at home, be it nuclear, chemical, or biological. One of the down sides to the miniaturization of technology that has taken place in the past thirty years is that, as all intelligence agencies know, atomic bombs can now be almost as small as suitcases. The Russian federation has admitted that such portable atomic weapons were developed during the days of the Cold War for the use of such troops as the *Spetsnaz*, who were to have infiltrated behind NATO lines in the beginning of the war to cause widespread havoc in the rear areas, before a main Soviet and Warsaw Bloc assault. (We, of course, simultaneously developed the same type of weaponry for use by our Special Forces.) Unfortunately, the Itar-Tass News Agency reported in 1999 that the Russians admit some of their weapons are now missing. This means that they may already be in the hands of the Russian Mafiya (which some observers believe to be a creation of the old KGB) and ready for sale to the bin Ladens of this world. Such an eventuality means a heightened effort of our CIA and FBI to infiltrate such groups as the Russian Mafiya, in conjunction with foreign intelligence services, to try to stop such weapons from being a tool to bring an atomic *jihad* to New York City or Washington, D.C. In 1993, two incidents alone point out the very real threat of terrorists obtaining a credible nuclear threat. In June and November of that year Russian navy personnel, sailors in June and officers in November, were apprehended with highly enriched uranium (HEU), a key component in the making of a nuclear device, in their possession, apparently intending to peddle it to terrorist groups, according to an Associated Press report.

Additionally, we must continue our internal preparations against chemical and biological weapons assaults against our cities. It was in February 1999 that Johns Hopkins University hosted a federally sponsored conference for American physicians to help them identify the first signs of biological infection among their patients, especially the terrorists' most likely possibility, anthrax. In its incipient phase, an anthrax infection resembles the common cold or the flu; by the time it shows more distinct symptoms, the disease may have progressed beyond the capabilities of medicine. The Associated Press reported at the time that then Health and Human Services Secretary Donna Shalala stated, "we must not be afraid, but we must be aware." However, the budget for that department was only $158 million in 1999 for such a national emergency, and no national stockpile of treatments or vaccines existed. With the terrible lethality of anthrax, such lack of preparation is a national disgrace. I must disagree with Ms. Shalala—there is plenty of reason to be afraid, especially when any chemist with the equipment found in a high school chemistry lab can cook up enough anthrax to kill tens of thousands of people! Obviously, there is a pressing need for the federal government, perhaps using FEMA as a central focal point, to rapidly develop a more credible response to what may be the ultimate terrorist threat within the continental United States: "germ warfare." Tragically, the anthrax attacks in October 2001 proved that, in spite of all the hearings and position papers on the subject, the federal government was still caught by surprise.

In the aftermath of the anthrax attacks, which are covered in detail in chapter 10, perhaps the most massive manhunt in American history was put into effect for the unknown person or persons behind them. Launched by means of contaminated letters, the terror campaign brought the nation's postal service to a near-collapse and the public to the verge of panic. Extensive testing of the anthrax spores (*Bacillus anthracis*) used in the attacks proved that it was from the genetic strain of the bacterium known as Ames anthrax.* Suspicion even pointed at a former member of the American germ warfare establishment, which had been disbanded in 1972. However, as of the middle of February 2002, there had been no substantial breaks in perhaps the most baffling, and terrifying, case in the history of American crime.

Responding to the new American realization of the threat of bioterrorism, the *Philadelphia Inquirer* announced on January 24, 2002, that President George W. Bush would seek a budget for the fiscal year of 2003 that would include "$25 billion for homeland security to fight terrorism." The situation had indeed changed drastically since 1999 when the budget for the Department of Health and Human Services had only been $158 million! Like a national loss of innocence, the American people had learned the reality of being on the front line in the war against terror.

---

*First isolated in 1981 in a cow in Texas, due to its virulence, this form of anthrax has been studied in the army laboratory for biological warfare at Ft. Detrick, Maryland, and distributed to several labs in the United States and abroad to test for an as yet undiscovered vaccine.

8

On the Road
to the Apocalypse?

A t the dawn of the new millennium, the Holy Land has become a new focus for religious fundamentalists, of Islam, Judaism, *and* Christianity. This adds a tremendously volatile element to the seemingly perpetual Palestinian feud with Israel. Jerusalem has taken center stage, as it has so many times in history, because of its sacred image in all three faiths. For the Christians, Jerusalem is the site of the crucifixion and resurrection of Jesus Christ. For Islam, it is the place where Mohammed the Prophet ascended into heaven upon his death. And for the Jews, it is truly their holy city, and the site of the great Temple of Solomon. For centuries, Jews all over the world have uttered the saying, as much a prayer as salutation, "next year, in Jerusalem!"

During this time of preoccupation with the Apocalypse and the end times, Christian fundamentalists over the past several years have continually stressed the importance of the Holy Land, particularly Jerusalem, "the City of Peace." Ironically, it was in Jerusalem that the danger of Christian fundamentalist violence, discussed in the FBI's Project Megiddo, the report on possible terror activity in the millennial year of 2000, came closest to becoming sanguine reality.[1] On the other hand, it would be in the United States that a Muslim millennial danger arose.

An extreme Christian cult, Concerned Christians, had established itself in Denver, Colorado, under Monte Kim Miller. In 1998, Miller and eighty of the Concerned Christians, anticipating the new millennium as the beginning of the end times, moved to Jerusalem. Much like the fundamentalist Ayatollah Khomeini had done twenty years earlier, Miller used audiocassette tapes to spread his message among the true believers. Their purpose was not to join the throng of worshippers who wished to bring in the new millennium with a spirit of hope and prayer for the future. Instead the Concerned Christians intended, according to some sources within Israeli intelligence, to help along the Apocalypse by triggering a blood bath on the Temple Mount. They hoped that by attacking Muslims they would set off the violence that would bring on the End of Days.

The Concerned Christians were watched almost from the first day that they arrived in the Holy Land by Israeli security authorities like the Mossad and the Shin Bet, which is somewhat equivalent to our FBI. It is not known if the more elusive Shabak intelligence service was in on the plan. The Israelis may have been alerted to the arrival of the Concerned Christians by the American intelligence community. The Israelis acted with their usual decisiveness. According to Gershom Gorenberg in *The End of Days*, a strike force of police and the Shin Bet struck at a home occupied by the Concerned Christians in the Jerusalem suburb of Mevasseret Tzion. The members of the cult there were speedily arrested and deported back to Denver. Israeli authorities later said "police and Shin Bet assessments" had come to the conclusion that they, the Concerned Christians, had plans to "carry out violent, extreme actions in the streets of Jerusalem toward the end of 1999 . . . to bring about the Second Coming."[2] Other groups believed to have similar aims were also ejected by the Israelis.

While the Israeli security authorities neutralized any millennium terror plot by the Concerned Christians and other fundamentalists, Osama bin Laden had prepared a millennium strike across the border in Jordan. On January 21, 2000, *Time* magazine told the story of the arrest in Jordan of Khalil Saeed Deek. Deek, who had joint Jordanian-American citizenship, was indicted on possession and manufacture of explosives. He was accused of "affiliation with an outlawed group"—bin Laden's al-Qaeda. In 1993–94, Deek fought with the Taliban in the campaign in which they conquered Afghanistan. When he was arrested in Pehswawar, Pakistan, where he had been living, by Pakistani police, Deek had in his possession a CD with advice on making a bomb. This may have been part of the instruction manual that al-Qaeda has prepared for its agents. Deek was extradited to Jordan on the request of King Abdullah II.

The dragnet in Jordan apprehended some thirteen people, eleven Jordanians, one Iraqi, and an Algerian. Deek admitted in court that from 1997 to 1998 he had actually shared a bank account with Zainul Abideen, also known as Abu Zubaida and the "School Teacher," whom ABC News On-line identified as Osama bin Laden's "chief of operations." Another of those arrested in Jordan was Raed Hijazi, who admitted to the Jordanians that he had been trained in an al-Qaeda camp in Afghanistan. A major link would exist to the most diabolic of all plots, the September 11, 2001, massacres in the United States. ABC News On-line reported on January 29, 2002, that U.S. Customs officials helping out in the investigation in Amman found documents that showed Hijazi had been wired money from Nabil al-Marabh, who was arrested in September 2001 in connection with the bombing of the World Trade Center and the Pentagon on September 11. Both al-Marabh and Hijazi had worked as cab drivers in Boston, thus providing a new link to the city where Flights 11 and 175 had taken off from Logan International Airport prior to their attacks on the World Trade Center. The fiendish plot Deek was arrested on possible complicity with in Jordan involved New Year's Day massacres of Christian pilgrims at the legendary site of Moses' tomb on Mount Nebo and the Church of St. John the Baptist, near where Christ's cousin, John, baptized him in the River Jordan. Deek's plot also involved exploding a bomb at another site; Jordanian authorities seized the bomb-making materials, nitric acid and fertilizer, at a farm outside Amman.

At the same time, al-Qaeda attempted to bomb a U.S. destroyer in the Mediterranean, the USS *The O'Sullivans* (DDG-68).* The attack on *The O'Sullivans* failed because the small boat to be used was found to be unseaworthy when it was loaded with explosives. Nevertheless, the plot was a dress rehearsal for the October 2000 bombing of the USS *Cole* in Aden harbor.

Across the world, Osama bin Laden had made plans to strike within the United States—the first time he attempted to hit American territory. On December 30, 1999, just one day before millions of Americans were waiting to watch Dick Clark ring in the new millennium with the dropping of the traditional brightly lit ball in New York City's Times Square, authorities in the United States uncovered plans by bin Laden to give the United States a more

---

*The O'Sullivans was a missile-firing destroyer in the Arleigh Burke class, like the *Cole*, named for the five O'Sullivan brothers, Albert Leo, Francis Henry, George Thomas, Joseph Eugene, and Madison Abel. In World War II, the brothers had been serving together aboard the light cruiser USS *Juneau*. The *Juneau* was sunk on November 14, 1942, during the Battle for Guadalcanal, and all five brothers perished.

explosive celebration for the year 2000, as reported on the *USA Today* "nation" Web site June 19, 2001.

The FBI and local and state police swooped down in coordinated raids in Washington State, Vermont, Boston, and New York City to arrest at least six men, many of them Algerian, and a Canadian woman in connection with a massive bomb plot to disrupt American celebrations for the first New Year of the third millennium. Before December 30, an Algerian national, Ahmed Ressam, had been arrested at the ferry stop at Port Angeles, Washington, having just arrived from British Columbia. On December 29, according to the *Seattle Times*, United States District Judge John Coughenour signed a material witness warrant for Ressam so that he could be held by the authorities. The city of Seattle had called off its long-anticipated millennium celebration because of the terror threat: Ressam had been arrested at the Port Angeles ferry crossing on December 14 with bomb-making materials in his car. On December 19, the Canadian woman, Lucia Garofalo of Montreal, identified in the *Seattle Times* as being a member of the same terrorist cell of bin Laden's al-Qaeda organization, had been arrested at a border crossing point in Vermont as she tried to enter the United States. The FBI spokeswoman in Boston, Gail Marchinkiewicz, said that all the suspects had been arrested "as part of a concerted sweep to coordinate interviews of individuals who have been identified through the ongoing investigation into Mr. Ressam."

After an investigation of some fifteen months, Ressam was put on trial in Los Angeles for his part in the millennium plot, according to the March 14, 2001, *San Francisco Chronicle*. He was officially tried on the charge of bringing bomb-making equipment into the United States. The case was prosecuted by U.S. Assistant District Attorney Steven Gonzalez. In the court room, according to the *Chronicle*, Gonzalez showed maps which had circled on them three California airports: Los Angeles, Long Beach, and Ontario. Gonzalez also put into evidence against Ressam a guide book which showed a circle drawn around the famous Space Needle in Seattle, which may have been the reason that the city shelved its Year 2000 celebration. Also noted in guidebooks found with Ressam were San Francisco's Transamerica Pyramid and the downtown Los Angeles area.

Meanwhile, in New York City, federal authorities had started to move against other members of the conspiracy, also Algerians. One suspect, Abdel Ghani Meskini, had already pleaded guilty to his complicity in the plot and was mentioned as a possible federal witness in the trial against Ressam in

Los Angeles. Ressam had made his home in Montreal, which might provide the link with Lucia Garofalo. Federal officials in background interviews expressed their certainty that the indicted people were linked to bin Laden's organization, and that some of them may have received advanced training in camps. The whole case provides an excellent example of the way in which Director of Central Intelligence George Tenet described how bin Laden was decentralizing his organization as a way to avoid being tracked down and blamed. Indeed, Tenet mentioned this millennium plot in his testimony in February 2001 before the Senate Select Intelligence Committee.[3]

If Tenet is correct, then another wild card has been played by Osama bin Laden in the terrorism game. Among the Muslim extremist groups operating in the world today, none have amassed the bloody records of the Algerian and Islamic groups. The Egyptian Gama'at al-Islamiyya may be better known than its Algerian counterparts, but is no less savage. Islamic *Jihad* also has its own Egyptian organization. According to the State Department's Global Terrorism report on the Internet for 1997, the main Algerian group is the Armed Islamic Group (GIA). As stated earlier, the GIA was formed after the Algerian army nullified the results of the election in December 1991 when the Islamic Salvation Front (FIS), won the first round of the balloting. Much of the financial support for GIA comes from Algerian expatriates residing in France. The Algerian government has accused Hasan Turabi's Sudan as well as Iran of subsidizing the GIA. Indeed, in 1993, Algeria cut diplomatic relations with Iran. While headlines are made when a few Israeli soldiers or Palestinian civilians are killed in the fighting on the West Bank, the terror groups operating in Algeria and in Egypt have been responsible for civil wars in their countries that have caused an estimated 15,000 casualties in the past ten years (based on Associated Press reports). If Ressam is working for the GIA and al-Qaeda "outsourced" the millennium plot to the GIA, then the terror war bin Laden is waging stands a chance of becoming even more bloody in the future. On April 6, 2001, according to the San Diego *Union-Tribune*, Ressam was convicted on charges of terrorism, which bear a possible 130-year jail sentence, and was scheduled to be sentenced June 28. Earlier on the day he was convicted, a French court in Paris also convicted him of similar charges. The prosecutors in the American trial maintained that he had been trained in Osama bin Laden's camps in Afghanistan and was working as a member of al-Qaeda. The Paris trial, according to Lisa Deutsch writing for the *Union-Tribune*, painted a picture of "a web of Islamic militants with unclear connections who cross paths around the world." Ressam was given a six-year sentence in absentia in Paris, while the ringleader of the group, Fateh Kamel, was sentenced to eight years. The case was truly a victory for the SDECE and all of the French intelligence community.

While the war against terrorism is being fought, the Clinton and now the new Bush administrations have been equally concerned about renewed activity among the great powers of the east: Russia, Iran, China, and Iraq. As we have learned, one of the more recent points of contention has been the Uighur terror attacks in the Peoples' Republic of China, which the Chinese blame partly on Afghan and Iranian help for the terrorists, who have even bombed targets in Beijing. Another is the discovery of potentially vast oil reserves in the region of the Caspian Sea, which seems on the verge of becoming even more important given the finite quality of oil reserves under the sand of Saudi Arabia and the Persian Gulf states. In the struggle to control this possible oil bonanza, Russia and Iran have butted heads like two bull elks at rutting season more than once.

Nevertheless, according to the December 28, 2000, *Washington Post*, Russian and Iranian military officials announced a new agreement between the erstwhile rivals that seriously concerned the American intelligence community and the outgoing Clinton administration. A high-level Russian delegation led by Defense Minister Igor Sergeyev spent three days in Tehran, the first such significant visit since the shah was overthrown in 1979. Only a few weeks earlier, the Putin government in the Kremlin announced that Russia would no longer abide by a 1995 agreement with Washington by which the Russians promised not to send any battlefield weapons to Iran after 1999. Although Washington had threatened economic sanctions against Russia if such a deal went through, both the Russians and Iranians scoffed at such threats. Iranian Rear Admiral Ali Shamkhani boasted that "today marks an historic day in Iran-Russia ties. The two countries have made concrete decisions to expand and deepen all kinds of long-term military, security, and defense relations," according to the *Washington Post* article.

Russian leader Vladimir Putin obviously saw the opening to Iran as a way to also try to gain control of the oil and natural gas bonanza in the Caspian Sea region by doing his best to assure that any pipeline bid Russia makes will be supported by Iran. Also, any such agreement would mean much to a cash-strapped Kremlin, whose only real export commodity was its weapons and nuclear knowledge.

Alas, Washington did not have long to wait to see its worst fears become reality. On March 12, 2001, Iran's reformist president Mohammed Khatami arrived for a four-day visit to the Kremlin, vowing a "new spring" in Iranian relations with Russia. One of the first Russian officials he met with was Putin himself. As feared, one of the first moves that came out of the talks was a decision not to permit the proposed oil pipeline to be dominated by countries friendly to the United States in the region: The pipeline was intended to be run by the Tehran-Moscow axis.

But even more serious, Khatami and Putin reached a compact by which Russia would use its nuclear expertise to help the Iranians build their new nuclear fission reactor at Besher (the old Bushire) in Iran. Although both countries promised that the nuclear fission reactor would be used for peaceful purposes and open to United Nations inspection, these assurances did not assuage American concerns. Any nuclear fission reactor, no matter how peaceful its announced purposes, can be "retrofitted" to produce nuclear weapons–grade uranium and plutoniun, essential ingredients in the manufacture of nuclear bombs. It appeared that the rapprochement between the United States and Russia after the attack on America had its ripple effect on Iran. When Shamkhani returned to Moscow to conclude his arms negotiations, the *New York Times* for October 2 observed that the admiral said that Iran was already supporting the Northern Alliance against the Taliban.

At the same time that Iran and Russia are drawing close, there are disturbing signs of Chinese sales of weapons technology to the Iraq of Saddam Hussein. On March 1, 2001, the *Washington Post* carried the story that the Chinese firm of Huawei Technologies had sold to Iraq quantities of fiberoptic cable to enhance communication between the Iraqi ground-to-air missile installations and the radar command and control sites which are their eyes. It was to destroy these new communications that the British and Americans mounted their latest air offensive against the Iraqi air defense system. Although on its Web page Huawei is billed as a privately owned company, it is virtually impossible for any corporation to exist without at least the approval and backing of the Chinese Peoples' Liberation Army, which operates almost as a state within a state in the Peoples' Republic. It is highly unlikely that any Chinese company would embark on such a sensitive technology transfer as the sale of fiber-optics without at least the blessing of the Peoples' Liberation Army. When one reads Huawei Technologies' Web page, it is plain that it is one of leading developers in fiber-optic technology in

Asia, complete with advanced research into blending together "hybrid trans-mission networks" that can handle any amount of telecommunications traffic. Such a technology system could hardly have been established without the help of the army—and Iraq could hardly have acquired a more sophisti-cated asset for its air defense command.

Atop the agreements reached between Russia and Iran on the one hand, and Iraq and China on the other, comes the question of nuclear missile tech-nology, the greatest threat of all to peace in the Middle East—and the surest way to bring on Armageddon. The American intelligence community is still certain that China has provided covert missile aid to Iran, most likely in ver-sions of the Silkworm and the Parakeet missiles. These missiles, while not intercontinental ballistic missiles such as are included in the American and Russian arsenals, certainly make Iran a stronger regional power if indeed China has given her these weapons. In the event of another Persian Gulf War, these missiles would allow Tehran to deny the gulf to any country it wished to keep out. Furthermore, there is also the danger that Iran may pass these missiles into the hands of the fundamentalist groups it backs against Israel like Hamas or Hizbollah. Iran and Iraq are still on the U.S. State Department list of those countries that follow a policy of state-sponsored terrorism, along with Syria, the Sudan, North Korea, and Cuba, according to the department's 1999 overview, which is available on the Internet from the State Depart-ment's main Web page.

Indeed, as the millennium approached, Iran and Iraq were still major players in the international game of terror. Iraqi secret agents had actually planned to bomb the headquarters of Radio Free Europe and Radio Liberty in Prague, Czechoslovakia, after the twin radio networks had started to beam broadcasts into Iraq in 1998, according to the Prague headquarters. Early in 1999, the Iraqi plot was discovered and thwarted. Prague had emerged as a major Iraqi intelligence center in Europe. It would be in Prague that Mohammed Atta, apparently the chief in the United States of the September 11 plot, met with a representative of Saddam's intelligence service. Saddam Hussein still plays host after all these years to the Abu Nidal organization and the Arab Liberation Front (ALF). In 1999, Libya expelled the Abu Nidal organization from its territory as part of Colonel Quaddafi's attempt at pol-ishing Libya's tattered foreign image in preparation for the trial of the Lockerbie bombers. However, it appears according to the State Department that Libya still hosts the Popular Front for the Liberation of Palestine–General Command (PFLP–GC) of Ahmad Jibril. Apparently, Muammar Quaddafi's old habit of sponsoring terrorist groups is hard to break.

American concern over the spread of missile technology was spurred by the National Intelligence Estimate which was given to the White House by the CIA in August 2000. Details of the results of the study found their way into the news media. The National Intelligence Estimate (NIE) stated the conviction of the CIA that China was still sending missile technology to Iran, North Korea, Libya, and Pakistan. The NIE had carried one of the first confirmations of the transfer of Russian nuclear knowledge to Iran as well.

The danger with such missiles is that they can be loaded with warheads for chemical, biological, or even nuclear warfare. It was the use of similar SCUD missiles by Iraq that threatened the coalition against Saddam Hussein in the Gulf War of 1991. By firing SCUD missiles into the heart of Israel in Tel Aviv, Saddam hoped to bring Israel into the war against it. Saddam gambled that no Arab nation would fight Iraq on the side of Israel, and thus the coalition would fall apart. It took much frantic negotiation on the part of President George Bush Sr. to keep the Israelis from counterattacking Iraq. Israel became so incensed that President Bush was forced to make a personal appeal to then Israeli Prime Minister Yitzhak Shamir to keep the Israelis from attacking Saddam. In a personal phone call recalled in the book *Israel and the Arabs*, Bush begged Shamir to "please stay out of this war."[4] In spite of some forty SCUD missiles landing on Israeli territory, Shamir did not let the president down: Israel stayed out of the Gulf War.

Now, ten years later, Saddam Hussein is still in power, and is even more of a threat to the United States and Israel than ever. American intelligence estimates, as mentioned earlier, have revealed that the Iraqi arsenal, with Chinese help, is now as strong as it was before the 1991 Gulf War. Moreover, with the lack of UN inspection since 1998, Iraq is suspected of having enough weapons-grade material on hand to fashion two nuclear bombs, if in fact she has not done so already. Indeed, Saddam seems to be in as challenging a mood as ever before. The attacks on his air defense system were caused by the fact that the radar system (helped by the new Chinese fiber-optic telecommunications cables) were targeting, or "painting" the American and British jets which were patrolling the no-fly zones established at the time of Saddam's capitulation after the Gulf War. "Painting" a jet fighter means that the pilot can tell from his plane's air defense countermeasure system that the ground-to-air radar has already locked in to his plane, and "acquired" it as a target. In a combat situation, only moments would separate the "acquiring" of a target by the radar and the launching of a ground-to-air missile attached to the radar control. It is no coincidence that a belligerent Saddam Hussein picked the tenth anniversary of his defeat in the Gulf War to display his new aggressiveness.

As recently as August 30, 2001, four American F-16 jets attacked an Iraqi radar station at the oil city of Basra, less than 100 miles from the head of the Persian Gulf, according to the Internet service Milnet.com. The next day, American and British jets pounded anti-aircraft and SAM (surface-to-air) missile sites at Ad Samawah, some 100 miles southwest of Baghdad. The American jets had come from the flight deck of the carrier USS *Enterprise*, and were part of the campaign to reduce the risk to Allied aircraft enforcing the no-fly zones in northern and southern Iraq.

As 2001 unfolded, it appeared that Nigeria was becoming a battleground in the new *jihad* of Islamic extremism, as had Algeria and Egypt before. On February 24, 2000, the *London Daily Telegraph* had reported that some 2,000 people had been killed in religious rioting between Christians and Muslims in the city of Kaduna. The flash point for the rioting was a growing pressure from Islamic militant groups in Nigeria that saw the adoption in many of the northern states in the Nigerian federation (which are heavily Muslim) of the *sharia*, the Islamic religious law. The state of Zamfara was the first to do so. President Olusegun Obasanjo, a Christian, had appealed then for an end to the violence. According to the *Telegraph*, Obasanjo declared, "Islam is a religion of peace and Christianity was established by the prince of peace. . . . Both religions have love in their creed."

In spite of President Obasanjo's eloquent plea for religious toleration, the killings continued. During December 2000, about 300 Nigerians were the victims of religious rioting in the state of Lagos. In July 2001, some 400 people were killed in rioting in the northern Nigerian state of Bauchi. The line was being drawn between the Muslim north and the Christian south. The adoption of *sharia* poses a direct threat to the government of President Obasunjo because, as Ben Omoni noted in Nigeriaworld.com on June 20, 2000, *sharia* "advocates that a non-Muslim should not be made to rule over a Muslim, or even partake in the administration of government." Many Nigerians, as 2001 continued, feared that the country could erupt again in civil war, as it had during the 1960s. Then, some 10,000 to 30,000 members of the predominantly Christian Igbo tribe in the east of Nigeria had been murdered by the Muslims of the Fulani and Hausa tribes. The result was that in 1967 the Christians formed the breakway Republic of Biafra in the east of the country. Some 1 million Biafrans died of starvation before the Nigerian federal government defeated Biafra in 1970. In 2001 the Muslim Fulanis and Hausas were at war against the Christians of the Yoruba tribe. As the year wore on, the future of Nigeria seemed bleak.

Tragically, the new year 2002 did not bring any respite from violence for the people of the strife-wracked African country. The *Philadelphia Inquirer* reported on February 6, 2002, that massive rioting had swept through the capital city of Lagos between Hausas and Yorubas. In three days of ethnic and religious upheaval, at least 95 people had been killed, according to the estimate of Nigerian Red Cross President Emmanuel Ijewere. And, as Associated Press reporter Glenn McKenzie note in the article, there were "more than 150 people hospitalized with gun, machete, and other serious injuries."

In June 2001, justice seemed finally to be coming to those who had bombed the American embassies in Tanzania and in Kenya in 1998. Of the four defendants, three, Mohammed Saddiq Odeh, Khalfan Khamis Mohamed, and Mohammed Rashed Daoud al-Owhali, are foreign nationals, while one, Wadih Hage of Arlington, Texas, is a naturalized American citizen. All four were accused of being operatives in al-Qaeda. The three foreign terrorists were tried for, according to the May 2 *Washington Post*, "direct participation in the embassy bombings, which killed 224 people and wounded nearly 4,600 in the two African capitals." Hage was being tried for setting up the terror cell that directed both bombing attacks, as well as "trying to acquire chemical weapons for bin Laden."

CNN reported on June 6 that al-Owhali, who faced the death penalty, was sentenced to life imprisonment without the possibility of parole. Khalfan Khamis Mohamed also faced the death penalty, but, on October 18, 2001, he also received a sentence of life in prison. The sentence pronounced by U.S. District Court Judge Leonard Sand in New York City had been established by the jury during sentencing hearings in the summer. All four defendants were given life terms. The initial sentencing hearing had been set for September 19, but was postponed because of the attack on the World Trade Center on September 11. It is fortunate for the four defendants that the sentences had been decided upon before, not *after*, September 11.

As the United States and Great Britain were keeping up their patrols of the no-fly zones, something unusual happened in Afghanistan on September 8, 2001. After the last main Russian troop forces had retreated over the Salang Pass in 1989, the Soviets' last ally in Afghanistan, Mohammed Najibullah, had remained in power in Kabul. Although the *mujahidin* groups continued their attack on the man they saw as the infidel puppet of the Soviets, they could not oust his garrisons from the main towns of Afghanistan. Supported by covert Soviet assistance, Najibullah proved immune to *mujahidin* attempts to oust him until the Soviet Union fell and could no longer support him. In April 1992, the opposition forces led by Ahmed Shah Massoud and Rashid Dostum entered Kabul and forced Najibullah to flee to the relative security of the local United Nations compound. However, with the Russians no longer a common foe, the tentative alliances among the various oppostion groups endangered the *mujahidin* alliance. Even before their entry in Kabul, Massoud and Dostum had come to blows with the other main warlord, Golbuddin Hekmatyar. The country soon disintegrated into near chaos, despite efforts of new president Burnahuddin Rabbani to bring order among his fractious countrymen. As the January 1997 Paris *Le Monde Diplomatique* put it, "in the rest of the country, zones of anarchy alternated with provinces at peace, where reconstruction was taking place."*

It was into this power vacuum that the Taliban movement emerged in 1994. The Taliban took its name from the *talibs*, or students at the fundamentalist Islamic schools, the *madrassas*, that had sprung up in the Afghan refugee camps in Pakistan. There had always been *talibs* among the *mujahidin* in the Russian war, since it was the graduates of the *madrassas* who became the Afghan Muslim religious leaders, the *mullahs*. But the Taliban of 1994 was something else. Although its titutlar head was the Mullah Mohammed Omar, the movement was far too well-trained and well-armed to be the Muslim "Childrens' Crusade" which Pakistani sources appeared desirous of making it appear to be. Indeed, it was not long before it appeared that the new Pakistani government of President Benazir Bhutto was attempting to use the Taliban as a proxy to extend Pakistani control over Afghanistan. Ethnically, the Pashtuns (current usage has substituted the name "Pashtun" for the formerly used "Pathan") of the Taliban were brothers to most Pakistanis and the tribes on the old North-West Frontier of British India. According to Dan-

---

*All translations from the French are by the author.

gerfinder.com on the Internet, the Pashtuns "are a group of tribes that make up 40 percent of Afghanistan's populace and 13 percent of Pakistan's." It became clear that the main sponsor of the Taliban was Pakistan's Interservice Intelligence, the ISI. During the war against the Russians, the ISI had served as the main conduit for American CIA support to reach the *mujahidin*.

It was not long before the *talibs*, armed and trained and sometimes led by Pakistan's ISI and army, soon overran their less organized opposition. As *Le Monde Diplomatique* wrote on its Web page, "in the Fall of 1994, Mullah Mohammed Omar Akhunzada, leading the Taliban, arrived in the city of Kandahar, the ancient capital of the kings of Afghanistan, at the age of 31." Within two years, Omar would reach Kabul and take control of the modern capital. On April 3, 1996, a *loya jirga*, or assembly, of 1,000 Muslim clerics pronounced Omar the "Amirul-Mumimeen," the "Supreme Leader of the Muslims." On September 28, 1996, Najibullah and his brother were hanged (after having been tortured) from a construction crane in the Ariana Square outside the presidential palace in Kabul.

Taking power in Kabul, the *talibs* began to enforce a terrible religious tyranny on the people of Afghanistan. They slaughtered any who opposed them, a blood purge in which Osama bin Laden and his Arab Afghans happily joined. The Taliban enforced a theocratic fascism on the country, determined to rule every aspect of peoples' lives in accordance with their fanatically puritanical interpretation of the *sharia*. Public executions were introduced, as was already the case in Saudi Arabia, where murderers are regularly beheaded in "Chop Square" in the capital of Riyadh. Peoples' lives were ruthlessly controlled with a brutality that the Saudi religious police, the Wahabi *matawa*, could never envision.

A ruthless campaign was made to eradicate the pre-Muslim past of Afghanistan. Uncannily, in this the Taliban followed directly in the footsteps of the great Khakhan, Genghiz Khan. Not far from Kabul is Bamiyan. Before World War II, Sir Fitzroy MacLean, who would serve in the SAS, visited Afghanistan, stopping in Bamiyan. He wrote, "here two immense Buddhas are cut in the side of a red sandstone cliff, honeycombed with the cells and passages of a monastery." When Genghiz Khan invaded Afghanistan, he "sacked the city and defaced the great Buddhas."[5] In the summer of 2001, heedless of international outcry, the *talibs* used their artillery to pound into rubble the ancient Buddhist statues at Bamiyan, completing the job of demolition "The Great Khan" had begun nearly 800 years before.

Moreover, it appeared that the Taliban and Osama bin Laden, whom they would embrace, were not satisfied with creating an Islamic state in Afghanistan. Increasingly, as the Taliban allied itself with al-Qaeda, it appeared that the dream was to export their vision of Islam and spread it throughout the Muslim world and even beyond. Osama bin Laden seemed to view himself as a modern incarnation of the medieval Saladin, without any of the latter's generosity or tolerance for other religions. At the height of his triumph in the Third Crusade, when he had compelled King Richard the Lionheart to sign a treaty, Saladin had guaranteed complete freedom of religion to Christians and had placed Christian pilgrims who wished to visit Jerusalem under his personal protection. Such benevolence appears beyond the comprehension of bin Laden. Saladin had indeed taken to heart the beautiful words that open Surah 1 of the Quran: "in the name of God, the Compassionate, the Merciful!"

With the fall of Kabul, the *talibs* had pursued their enemy into the northern part of Afghanistan. By 1998 at the latest, the Taliban was in control of all but about 10 percent of the country in the far north. This was the domain of the Northern Alliance, dominated by the doughty warrior Massoud. During the war against the Russians, Massoud had earned the title of "The Lion of the Panjshir Valley" for the resistance to the invaders of his *Jamiat-I Islami*, or Islamic Society private army of *mujahidin*. Massoud knew both Hekmatyar and Rabbani from his days as a student at the Polytechnic College in Kabul. Now, close to his Russian backers in the former Soviet central Asia, he seemed determined to stand up to the Taliban. A native Tajik, he could also count on support from the Tajik population in central Asia, as well as the Uzbeks, since both groups had been persecuted and killed by the Pashtun *talibs*. The resistance to the Taliban was renamed the United Front of Afghanistan. When the Taliban launched a massive assault against Massoud in late July 1999, he beat it off with heavy *talib* casualties.

Recently, Massoud's fortunes seemed to be on the rise again. Russia and Iran were giving him more aid, fearing a spread of Taliban militancy. Tajikistan, with Russian blessing, had given him a large base camp there. In fact, an Afghan government in exile had already been established in Dushanbe in Tajikistan. On September 8, 2001, however, Massoud gave an interview with two Arab journalists who apparently had come north from Kabul, according to the London *Daily Telegraph* for September 9. They interviewed him in the well-guarded garden in the town of Khwaja Bahauddin. Suddenly, something went terribly wrong. The two "journalists" set off a bomb apparently hidden in their video camera, killing both of them instantly. Massoud suffered severe head injuries in the explosion, according to the *Daily Telegraph*. He was rushed to a Russian army hospital in Tajikistan, but his wounds were too severe. "The Lion of the Panjshir Valley," after twenty years of continous war, was dead, the victim of assassins. On Sunday, September 16, the *Washington Post* confirmed Massoud's death. It was not long before the blame was put on the al-Qaeda group of Osama bin Laden, whose $300 million-plus (U.S.) fortune had virtually made Afghanistan his private country, a country where he was already a hero for his role in the war against the Russians. While bin Laden had been inflicting casualties on the United States through terror attacks such as the bombings of the American embassies in East Africa in the summer of 1998, he had been making a path of even worse bloodshed in Afghanistan. The CIA reported that nearly 3,000 Arabs are in bin Laden's private army, which has fought beside the Taliban, as have Islamic volunteers from Pakistan and Uzbekistan. Bin Laden's Arabs are considered responsible for the massacre of hundreds of innocent villagers in the areas under the control of Massoud's United Front. Two weeks before he was killed, he gave an interview to *Newsweek*'s Antonia Francis, on the Internet at MSNBC.com September 20, 2001. Francis had asked him in the interview, "would you extradite Osama bin Laden?" and Massoud had responded, "we do not support any form of terrorism, including al-Qaeda." Perhaps that answer, repeated by Taliban or al-Qaeda informers in Massoud's own camp, had sealed his fate.

As many Christians and believers in other faiths had feared, it seemed like the coming of the new millennium presaged a battle of apocalyptic magnitude. Throughout the world, terrorist forces, led apparently by al-Qaeda, seemed to be on the offensive. At the same time, Saddam Hussein of Iraq, ten years after his defeat in the 1991 Gulf War, was making belligerent statements again from Baghdad. Adding a more dangerous element to the Middle East situation, American intelligence believed that the Peoples' Republic of China was enhancing Iraq's air-defense capability in an effort to neutralize the American and British surveillance plan flights which policed the no-fly zones in northern and southern Iraq. With the new arrangement between Iraq, the Babylon of biblical times, and China, always considered by the Book of the Apocalypse to be one of the kings of the east, it seemed that the final Battle of Armageddon would indeed take place. Yet, with the connivance of Osama bin Laden and his terrorist followers, the battle would have its beginning in a country not even imagined in the biblical era: the United States of America. The battle would pit Osama bin Laden's ideology of Islamic extremism, with its roots in the darkest days of medieval Islam in the time of Hasan-i-sabah and his Assassins, against the United States, a country which represented for many, including many Muslims living and working there, the best hope for the future of the new millennium.

9

September 11, 2001

During the Crusades, a battle between the Crusaders and the Muslim Saracens was announced with much pomp and circumstance. In the Third Crusade, Richard the Lionheart's heralds would blow their trumpets and parade his great banner of the golden rampant lions. Saladin would begin with the pounding of massive kettle drums, often mounted on a camel, as his bravest *amirs* would carry forward the green flags of the Prophet.

In the new war between extremist Muslims and the West, there is no such medieval panoply and fanfare to announce the opening of a battle. Sometimes people are casualties before they even know that a battle has commenced. It was this way the day that Osama bin Laden decided to bring his brand of Islamic holy war to the homeland of the United States: September 11, 2001.

New York City was doing in September 2001 what New Yorkers usually do in every September: watching their two baseball teams, the Yankees and the Mets, on the final march toward the World Series. The Yankees were slugging onward as they had the previous year, when they had beaten the Mets in the much-touted "Subway Series." On September 1, 2001, Boston's Red Sox had been beaten by "the house that Ruth built" on their home turf in Fenway Park. The final score for the Yankee dynasty: Boston 1, Yankees 2. The Mets were fighting for first place in their league in a vicious three-way combat with the Philadelphia Phillies and the Milwaukee Braves. Perhaps the Mets and Yankees would meet again in a gladiatorial World Series match in the Big Apple.

On the morning of the eleventh, the hijackers moved toward their appointment with death. Some of what happened that infernal morning will forever remain unclear. Some mysteries will remain public mysteries, even if they have been solved, because the solutions will have disappeared into the labyrinthine maze of national security. Although their flight training had been in Florida, the terrorists Mohammed Atta and Marwan al-Shehihi took their trip to Boston's Logan International Airport from Portland, Maine. The only security camera in the small Maine airport captured the two conspirators on film as they passed through the Portland terminal around 6:00 A.M., but it is still unknown what they were doing in that city. This would not be Atta's first experience of terror. *Newsweek* reported on September 24 that he had been suspected in a bombing of an Israeli bus in 1986; the FBI also disclosed that he had been seen around the base of the U.S. Atlantic Fleet in Norfolk, Virginia, in the winter of 2000.[1]

When asked about Atta and al-Shehihi, Portland Police Chief Michael Chitwood admitted their presence in his town was a mystery, "if these guys carried out the attack the way they did, they had a reason to be up here, but who the hell knows what it is?"[2]

It would not be until October 5 that some of the details would be released in Portland's *Press-Herald*. According to the FBI, Atta, who is now considered the tactical mastermind of the plot, and al-Shehihi had checked into Portland's Comfort Inn at 5:45 P.M. on Monday, September 10. Between 8 and 9 o'clock that night, the visited the local Pizza Hut restaurant and made two stops at ATMs for cash. This latter fact might prove of great value later in the investigation. To have used an ATM, Atta had to have access to a bank account, because an ATM can only access cash from a savings or checking account. And that account would have to be either in Atta's name or that of one of his accomplices. At 9:22 P.M., Atta was caught on videotape at the Wal-Mart in Scarborough, Maine. They checked out of their room at the Comfort Inn at 5:33 A.M. the next day for their trip to Portland's airport. On Saturday, September 29, 2001, two weeks after the attacks, the FBI stopped at the local International House of Pancakes restaurant with photos of some twenty men of Middle Eastern descent, but nobody working there admitted to knowing any of them, according to the manager Dee Lamontagne. However, Spruce Whited, head of security at the Portland Public Library, said he was positive that he had seen a man matching Atta's description there as early as April 2000 using the library computers. The FBI has established that all the suspects in the plot used library computers to log on to the Internet for information, since the use of such computers is more difficult to track down in an investigation than would be a personal home computer.

Thus on the morning of September 11, still shrouded in mystery, the pilots of Osama bin Laden's suicide attack force proceeded to the airports where they would hijack the commercial jets. At Boston's Logan International Airport, two planes were ready to take off on the long transcontinental flight to Los Angeles International Airport (LAX). One of these was the American Airlines Flight 11; the other, Flight 175, belonged to United Airlines. More than six months prior to this day, *Newsweek* mentioned in the September 24 issue, Atta may have been spying at Logan Airport. Carefully, without drawing notice, the two hijackers at Logan moved to get their tickets for what proved to be flights to oblivion. Although we shall never know for sure, since all of the hijackers perished in the planes, it appears that their assignments had been made up beforehand. Satam al-Suqami, Waleed al-Shehri, Wail al-Shehri, Mohammed Atta, and Abdulaziz Alomari boarded Flight 11. It is possible that Waleed and Wail may have been brothers or otherwise closely related. At another boarding gateway, Marwan al-Shehihi, Fayez Ahmed, Ahmed al-Ghamdi, and Hamza al-Ghamdi went up the stairs and onto Flight 175 with Mohald al-Shehri. The two al-Ghamdis could have been relatives. Why Marwan al-Shehihi did not board Flight 11 with Atta is a mystery since, as will be seen, they had spent much time in flight training together in Florida waiting for this day. Perhaps Atta was to be the main skyjacker pilot for Flight 11, and his comrade destined for Flight 175. As with so much this terrible September 11, this too must be speculation. Apparently, the black boxes, flight and voice recorders, from both planes have not been recovered from the site wreckage or, if they have, either they were too damaged to reveal anything or that information is being kept secret. The facts, however, are that Flight 175 departed at 7:58 A.M.; Flight 11 soared off the tarmac one minute later at 7:59. In a newspaper scoop by the *Boston Globe* on September 12, the flight manifest for Flight 11 was made public. We know, at least for this ill-fated jet, how the hijackers had positioned themselves. The two brothers, Wail and Waleed al-Shehri, sat beside each other in seats 2A and 2B. Mohammed Atta sat by himself in seat 8D. Alomari had seated himself across the center aisle from Atta in 8G, presumably so that they could quicky move together. Meanwhile, al-Suqami was in seat 10B. Visibility was good for the pilots as their planes took off into the air.

Two minutes later at 8:01 A.M., a third flight on a transcontinental journey took off from Newark, New Jersey's, International Airport. It was American Airlines' Flight 93, and it too had a final destination of LAX. Aboard this plane were Saeed al-Aghamdi, Ahmed al-Haznawi, Ziad Jarrahi, and Ahmed al-Nawi. As Flight 93 would have been ascending to its flying altitude at 8:10 A.M., a fourth flight was moving off the runway for a morning trip to LAX. This plane, American Airlines Flight 77, however, was taking off from Washington-Dulles International Airport. Sitting down with the other passengers were Kaleed al-Midhar, Majed Moqed, brothers Nawaf and Salem al-Hamzi, and Hani Hanjour.

Kaleed, or Khalid, al-Midhar was known to American Intelligence. Indeed, with his track record, one wonders why his entry into the United States, and that of Nawaf al-Hamzi, did not attract more attention. Working with the CIA, authorities in Malaysia had filmed al-Midhar meeting in a hotel in Malaysia's capital, Kuala Lumpur, with a Yemeni named Tawfiq bin Atash. With al-Midhar, Nawaf al-Hamzi had also traveled to Kuala Lumpur. Tawfiq had served as a holy warrior in Afghanistan, most likely with bin Laden's private army. Tawfiq's more belligerent *nomme de guerre* was "Khallad." Terrorists share one trait with entertainment personalities: They want names people will remember. Would people still be talking about "Carlos the Jackal" if he had remained Carlos Ilich Ramirez Sanchez? Would Bernie Schwartz have become a famous movie actor, when "Tony Curtis" did? The meeting between al-Midhar and Atash had taken place in October 1999. Atash and would later achieve infamy by being recognized as one of the planners of the USS *Cole* bombing a year later. A British White Paper that Prime Minister Tony Blair offered to Parliament after the September 11 assault also identified al-Midhar as having played a role in not only the *Cole* raid but also the embassy bombings of 1998!

Whatever happened on board the doomed planes, it is only on Flight 93 that we shall ever really have a good idea. All four flights, based on radar reports from the air controllers on the ground, at first proceeded on their expected courses, flying due east toward California. But then, things began to go wrong. Without any warnings, except from the ill-fated Flight 93, all four planes made radical changes in their flight paths. The ground controllers must have wondered what was going on in the skies. Although the shock of what happened that day will be with us all whenever we recall it, looking back there seems to have been some coordination among the hijackers between boarding the planes and the ultimate destinations only they knew. The course changes did not occur simultaneously, as though the murder squads had a certain timetable in mind. Flight 11, which had taken off at 7:59, soared over Massachusetts and into the skies over northern New York State when it banked sharply to the south at 8:27. Around that time, one voice was heard from the sky. Betty Ong, a flight attendant on board Flight 11 suddenly called her airline supervisor at Logan, the *Washington Post* reported on September 13, stating she had seen three hijackers with knives; at least one passenger had been stabbed. She told her supervisor that the hijackers said they were going to "crash the aircraft in New York City." Flight 93 from Newark flew due east in an almost straight flight path over New Jersey, all of Pennsylvania, and straight on almost to Cleveland, Ohio. Then it, too, banked in a southerly direction around 9:39 A.M. and began to fly east again. The jet from Washington-Dulles International, Flight 77, also flew in a course headed west, over Virginia, high above the Appalachian Mountains, and on through West Virginia and also into the air space above Ohio. Then somewhere in the skies near Ashland, Ohio, not far from the banks of the Ohio River, it made a fateful turn south and then east: Contact with the plane was last made at 8:56 A.M., some forty-six minutes after its departure from Dulles. The first jet that took off from Logan, Flight 175, was off course almost from the start. Rather than flying due west, it almost immediately veered into a southwestern path, straightened out to fly south to Newark and on to somewhere near New Brunswick, New Jersey. There, at 8:59, it turned sharply north.

What happened between the take-offs and when the planes made their fateful turns can be reconstructed in broad terms (again Flight 93 is a separate category). From what information has been gathered and made public as of October 15, 2001, Atta and the other hijackers were armed with box cutters, the kind of instrument with a razor blade used to open cardboard boxes. They had also taken lessons in martial arts in preparation for this day. We can conjecture that at some point after the planes were airborne, the hijackers unbuckled their seat belts; if they had not buckled them when the planes took off they would have aroused suspicion. After they were free from their seat harnesses, the hijackers would probably have gathered together and made a sudden dash for the cockpits where the pilots and crews were seated. Other than for Flight 175, it is not known, and may never be, if the hijackers sat by themselves or in a cluster together. When the initial attack occurred, there would have been a loud commotion on the planes, enough for a crew member in the cockpit, perhaps a navigator, to have opened the door to see what was going on. Somehow, the conspirators managed to overcome any passenger intereference and get into the cockpits. If a struggle took place with other passengers on Flights 11, 175, or 77, we may never know. All this must, it seems, remain speculation. We can be almost certain that the crew on each jet would not have surrendered to the hijackers without a struggle. Thus, the pilot, co-pilot, and other crew members were either killed or otherwise incapacitated. By the time the planes made their momentous turns, the hijackers, all trained in flying the Boeing 757s and 767s, were in full control.

During its unplanned final trip, Flight 175 would unwittingly follow the path of the German dirigible *Hindenburg*, which passed almost directly over the future site of the World Trade Center on its fatal voyage on May 6, 1937. The *Hindenburg* was the pride of Nazi Germany, and the flag ship of the Zeppelin Company, which had made dirigibles to bomb London in World War I. Passing over Manhattan around 3:00 P.M., the *Hindenburg* exploded into flames when it attempted to dock at its mast at the U.S. Navy Air Station at Lakehurst, New Jersey, at about 7:00 P.M. Although attributed officially to natural causes, the cause of the two explosions which destroyed the zeppelin, as the Germans called their air ships, might have been an act of terrorism as well, committed against what German opposition to Hitler considered a symbol of his Reich.

The events that took place after the passenger carriers made their turns are all too vividly etched in our minds like a litany of doom. On Flight 77, veteran CNN correspondent Barbara Olson reached her husband Theodore Olson, the Solicitor General of the United States, via her cell phone. She said the plane had been hijacked. The attackers had knives. They rounded up the passengers and the pilots in the back of the plane. Apparently calling from the back of the plane, she asked, "what do I tell the pilots to do?" At that moment, Barbara was cut off, probably by one of the assassins.

Peter Hanson was a businessman who was on board Flight 175 with his wife and baby. He called his father in Connecticut to say that the plane had been hijacked, and that the hijackers were stabbing flight attendants to get the pilots to open the door of the cockpit. Hanson said, "a stewardess is being stabbed . . . the plane is going down." That was all, his call too was cut off.[3]

At 8:45 A.M., Flight 11 crashed into the north tower of the World Trade Center in New York City, One World Trade Center. Eighteen minutes later at 9:03, Flight 175 smashed into Two World Trade Center (WTC), the south tower. To the south, at 9:45 A.M., Flight 77 tore into the Pentagon in Washington, D.C., between the first and second stories on the western side of the building, tearing a seventy-five-foot hole in the stone structure. Within nanoseconds of hitting the targets at high speed, the jumbo jets virtually disintegrated as their thousands of pounds of high-octane jet fuel caused monumental fireballs encompassing the buildings. Bill Holmberg, who lives in a New York high-rise apartment building near the Twin Towers, would recall that Flight 11 "disappeared into the building" when it hit One World Trade Center.[4] Pillars of smoke climbed upward, darkening the sky as though the sun itself had been eclipsed. For those who saw the horrifying images, it might have seemed as if Armageddon had indeed come.

Of those in the building who were uninjured when the first plane hit the north tower of the WTC, some were so shocked they could not move. Many of these would die. Others, especially those who had been there when terrorists first struck the building in February 1993, fled immediately. Andy Perry grabbed his friend Nathan Shields by the arm and began a dash for life down forty-six flights of steps. On the way down, they passed people horribly burned, for whom there was no hope. Bill Hay was on the 55th floor when Flight 11 tore into the north tower. He was also one of the fortunate ones. He later recalled that the plane "rocked the whole damn building. I mean, we rocked like a rocking chair."[5] Other people were sucked out the holes in the building, and fell like autumn leaves to the street below. To the horror of those watching them, some were on fire all the way down. One man tried to climb down the outside of the tower and amazingly got down two or three floors before he fell to his death.

By this time, alarms were going off all over the city. From the beginning it was clear that a major disaster had struck Lower Manhattan. As workers were still fleeing down the stairs of the north tower, the first firefighters were already climbing up to fight the towering inferno. Some of the firemen, rescue units, and ambulances were outside to see the unbelievable sight of Flight 175 strike the south tower. The same blazing inferno enveloped Two World Trade Center in a wreath of flames. Monty Weschler had arrived on the scene with the Hatzolah Volunteer Ambulance Squad, which had made its way downtown from Brooklyn. Weschler later told reporters that "I saw five people jump out, one by one. You could see the flames behind them. It was red hot."[6] One couple jumped out a window, holding hands, to escape the fire. In a surreal scene, people and office furniture fell down to the ground, blown out by the explosion, as if somebody were hosting a macabre ticker-tape parade. As in the first building hit, communications went dead from the impact, and the fire extinguisher system may have been knocked out as well, yet water cascaded from burst pipes and sprinklers. In any event, a working sprinkler system would not have helped in either tower; water cannot put out a gasoline blaze.

As the people hurried out of the buildings, some did so with controlled emotion, almost knowing that if they gave into their fears they were lost. Others panicked, thus increasing their chance of violent death. Gilbert Richard Ramirez was an employee of Blue Cross/Blue Shield, which had offices on the twentieth floor of the north tower. In the chaos around him, Ramirez tried to keep his head. He tried to reassure coworkers, "Relax, we're going to get out of here. . . . Christ is on our side. We're going to get out of here."[7] There were employees in the Twin Towers who made the mistake of trying to get down the many floors in the elevators—some were able to get out to safety, some did not. In the north tower, One World Trade Center, two men did not succumb to bin Laden's act of intimidation. Michael Benfante and John Cerquiera had worked in the telecommunications firm of Newtork Plus, which had been situated in Suite 8121. Moving down the stairs, they encountered a blonde woman on the sixty-eighth floor, trapped in her wheelchair. Hefting her out of the chair, the two men put her into a special emergency chair in the stairway and carried her down sixty-eight flights of stairs. After an hour of excruciating effort, they brought her out the door and into the safety of an emergency van. Just moments after the three escapees got out, the building collapsed.[8]

As the blazes in the Twin Towers continued uncontrolled, the structural steel supporting the huge complex was itself under attack. A core of steel columns running down the middle of each tower was its spine, supported by a lattice of steel buttressing on the outside, giving the Twin Towers their characteristic look as they dominated the New York skyline. Fighting fires at an elevation of 1,000 feet or more was a terrible challenge for the firefighters inside. Moreover, according to Masoud Sanayei, an instructor at Tufts University, structural steel starts to soften at 800 degrees Fahrenheit. High octane jet fuel burns at a hellish 1,200 to 1,500 degrees Fahrenheit, hotter than any crematorium oven. The steel beams began to soften and expand like melting plastic, causing metal trusses of the floors to push out against the columns and begin to buckle. The trusses began to separate from the walls.

In the south tower, the weight on the damaged floors, 80 to 86, of the floors above them grew too great; some 110,000 tons crushed down on them. At 9:50 A.M., the steel supports of the south tower began to give way under the strain. Before the eyes of thousands of horrified onlookers on the spot, and millions transfixed before their television sets, the south tower began to crumple with a sickening, crunching sound. As one floor gave way, it fell, adding its weight to those below it. Each floor suddenly bore the weight of all the floors above it. Faster and faster, the floors crumbled down. With the smoke and debris like that of a nuclear explosion, the tower collapsed to the ground, shaking the earth with the impact of a 2.0 Richter scale earthquake. At 10:29 A.M., the north tower gave way as well. The *Philadelphia Inquirer* described the sight in terse prose that concealed the horror within it: "The towers collapsed, one and then the other, falling in what seemed like slow motion, kicking up mushroom clouds of smoke."[9]

Those who were able to make it, stumbling down the street, were covered in ash and dirt. They looked like the survivors of the Roman city of Pompeii, after the eruption of Mount Vesuvius buried the city in molten lava and debris in 79 C.E. People accustomed to our age of immediate communication kept trying to contact relatives or friends on their cell phones, not realizing the phones were now useless. All electronic communication had been knocked out by damage from explosions. Suddenly, the modern age had come to a halt. Mass transit was shut down and all vehicle traffic came to an abrupt stop. Refugees from Manhattan had to flee to safety over the Brooklyn Bridge by way of the foot passages on the sides; the main roadway of the bridge was blocked by unmoving autos, SUVs, and trucks. An ironic comment on the entire unbelievable tableau was made by Yoram Landskroner, a visiting Israeli professor living across the street from the WTC: "We came here thinking it would be safe."[10]

Like the Romans fleeing Pompeii, many took to the sea to avoid death. Landskroner, his wife, Dinah, and hundreds of others boarded ferries and tugboats to flee to Jersey City. A de facto evacuation of the tip of Manhattan Island was in full swing. In a bitter dose of irony, hundreds like Landskroner boarded the watercraft from the river bank near the walkway to the Holocaust Museum, devoted to the memory of the millions destroyed in the fiery crematoriums of Adolf Hitler's Thousand Year Reich. Yet, from all the accounts given, and the thousands of feet of coverage shown on television in the hours and days to come, there was no panic, no clambering over the fallen, no crushing them under thousands of stampeding feet. A memorable photograph shows a rescue worker gently carrying a bloodied woman in his arms. A restaurateur at a tony restaurant near the WTC thoughtfully tore up expensive linen tablecloths to give to bleeding refugees as they stumbled by. If bin Laden ever saw the films of that day, he would have been sorely distressed by the amount of panic and terror that his malignant act did *not* cause. If we should ever defeat and kill this venomous man, we may look back and say that the turning of the tide against him took place the very day of his greatest victory. A master terrorist who cannot inspire terror is a toothless tiger indeed.

American national security had taken a disastrous blow in the collapse of the Twin Towers that morning as well. The New York office of the Secret Service was wiped out, some 200 workers lost their lives in their Twin Towers office. Nobody will know how much the investigation after the act of terrorism will be impeded by their loss. Before that day, the main business of the office had been tracking international extortion and confidence games emanating from Nigeria and percolating through the United States like bad African coffee. The Secret Service agents—those in other cities, none were now left in the Big Apple—would look back fondly on those days of innocence.

After the disaster, the *New York Post* reported on October 2 that rescue workers had found fifteen firemen in the stairwell of the north tower, where they had been crushed to death by the avalanche of debris that had fallen on them. Yet nothing they had seen prepared the recovery parties for the baby they found dead sitting in the back seat of a car outside the Twin Towers, after they removed the rubble that had killed him. Some 300 of New York's firemen and over 60 police officers had perished in the disaster. Entire fire department companies had been annihilated, both inside the buildings and among those firemen waiting outside to render them assistance. Ladder Company 7 had been on another fire call that morning, but had been rushed to the World Trade Center when disaster struck. The company was erased when the second tower collapsed, according to a *Newsweek* report on MSNBC.com on September 24. The company had come from their fire station on Manhattan's East 29th Street. After the loss, their names were put on a memorial outside their empty station house: Richard, Princiotta, Cain, Mendez, Foti, and Muldowney. Their names were emblematic of the ethnic mix of the city they died serving. Before September 11, twelve was the largest number of New York firemen to die in any single disaster. Since firefighters are led from the front line, much of the Fire Department's leadership was killed in the collapse of the Twin Towers when the command post on the bottom floor of the towers was inundated by the tons of wreckage. Both William Feehan, the First Deputy Commissioner, and Peter Ganci Jr., the chief of the department, were among those lost. When television reporters were allowed up to the disaster area, forever after to be called Ground Zero, later in the afternoon they found a surreal sight. Large fire engines and police cars had been crushed by the wreckage as though they were toys scattered about by an angry young giant. Some of the vehicles were almost totally covered in ash and soot. As of October 1, some 5,219 were still listed as missing in New York City. There were 344 confirmed dead, of whom 289 had been identified.* On the night of Thursday, October 4, firemen were still hosing down smouldering rubble with water. On October 15, CBS Radio News would report that the debris pile still had within it, according to the New York Fire Department, an incendiary temperature of 3,000 degrees Fahrenheit.

A few people who would otherwise have been at the World Trade Center that day missed the disaster due to luck or grace. Howard Lutnick was the CEO of Cantor Fitzgerald, a financial services corporation in the north tower, One World Trade Center, on the 101st to 105th floors. He had been late getting to the office because he had to take his five-year-old son to his first day at kindergarten. Lutnick just got to the front entrance of One World Trade Center when Flight 11 crashed into the middle of his company. Of the approximately 700 employees who were on the job that day, all perished. The nation saw Lutnick weeping uncontrollably that night on television; his tears were all the more bitter because his brother Gary was among the victims.

New Yorkers were still reeling after the morning shock that afternoon. Plumes of smoke covered Lower Manhattan like a black funeral pall. Then, just when they thought the crisis was over, at 5:20 P.M. Seven World Trade Center also collapsed. Weakened by the huge shower of wreckage that had cascaded from above, the building simply gave way. This catastrophe was shown as it happened to millions of stunned viewers around the country, because the networks were still carrying live footage of what was occurring at the disaster site. The huge World Trade Center complex was in ruins. Several buildings like the Twin Towers and Number Seven collapsed, and of those that remained many were so damaged they would never open their doors again.

---

*By January 2002, as duplicate names were discovered and removed from the lists, casualty figures had been reduced to about 3,100 for the World Trade Center, Pentagon, and western Pnnsylvania crash victims.

In America's darkest hour, two men stand out to exalt the human spirit in its greatest time of trial. John O'Neill had been the FBI's Irish wolfhound on the trail of the bombers of the USS *Cole* in Aden Harbor. He was the FBI's expert on terrorism, and had also investigated the attacks on the American embassies in East Africa in 1998. After September 11, the FBI would reveal that some of the skyjackers had definitely been secretly photographed meeting with men from the *Cole* terror bombing. When he knew that the bureau's agents were in danger, O'Neill had authorized them to carry M-16s to protect themselves. His zeal made an American ambassador to Yemen concerned that he might disrupt diplomatic relations with that country. According to the *Philadelphia Inquirer* (September 20, 2001), when the diplomat had O'Neill recalled to the United States, one of O'Neill's admiring agents said "John has been thrown out of better places than this." Just months before the tragedy, O'Neill had been hired by the World Trade Center to oversee security in the complex. He got out of his office in one of the towers and called his wife on his cell phone to tell her he was all right. Then he went back to help the others still inside. A few moments later the building collapsed, crushing him to death. John O'Neill was buried from St. Nicholas of Tolentine Church in his home town of Atlantic City, New Jersey. Unless I am very much mistaken (and I pray I am), I attended Holy Sprit High School in Absecon, not far outside Atlantic City, with John. John had played intramural sports all four years, and varsity track in his sophomore and junior years. When I read of his death, I looked up his photo in my high school "Spartan" yearbook and cried. He is buried in Holy Cross Cemetery in Mays Landing, not far from where my mother and my grandparents rest. If I go to visit them, I shall stop at his grave and say, "Job well done, Jack."

Father Mychal Judge was an ordained Roman Catholic priest in the Franciscan Order, but he was more than that—he was the chaplain of the New York Fire Department, the FDNY. That ghastly morning found him with the first wave of firemen who answered the alarm after Flight 11 dove into the north tower. The Web page was still up on the Internet that day for the emergency medical services (EMS) banquet on September 27, 1999, two years prior. In March 1996, the EMS had merged with the fire department. The 1999 banquet had been held at Hunter College's Brookdale Health Science Center. Father Mychal was listed as giving the Invocation and the Benediction. Like any other fire chaplain, he was active with the department's Emerald Society Pipe Band, which helped rule the city on each St. Patrick's Day, March 17. (It was somehow fitting that the fire department took control of the EMS on St. Patrick's Day in 1996!) A photo on the Pipe Band Web page shows Father Mychal dwarfed by two of the band's members in their high bearskin caps. Father Mychal was giving the last rites to a dying fireman when he was struck and killed by a piece of falling debris. On Sunday, September 16, the *New York Post* carried a photo covering the entire back page of the newspaper showing the firemen he loved carrying his casket down the steps of the church. The pipes and drums of the FDNY Emerald Society played at his funeral. However, Fireman Durrell "Bronko" Pearsall did not appear with them playing the snare or base drum: He died with the padre. Now, their photos appear on the memorial page of the present and past members of the Pipe Band who perished in the gravest disaster in the history of the FDNY. Father Mychal died as he had lived, serving his flock like the Good Shepherd.

As the ugly morning hours unfolded, it must have seemed to many Americans that the Apocalypse they had feared for the millennium year was now unfolding before their eyes. There are those scholars who said that the new millennium began in 2001, not 2000, anyhow. After all, some said that they had seen the face of Satan emerging from the billowing smoke from the burning World Trade Center. If such things were possible, there was no place on earth on September 11 where the Devil would more likely have been than Lower Manhattan.

On the morning of September 11, Jeremy Glick, Thomas E. Burnett, Todd Beamer, and Mark Bingham—remember well those four names!—had boarded Flight 93 at Newark for the long transcontinental trip to Los Angeles. The four of were young and successful. They represented the cream of the thirty-something generation that had ridden to riches on the wave of the new computer information revolution that was transforming the world economy, as James Watt's steam engine had done over 230 years ago. They probably would not have considered themselves as overly patriotic, and certainly not as heroic. But, as the lesson of the Greatest Generation in World War II taught us, events have the power to make heroes and patriots out of the most ordinary and unassuming of men.[11]

The four of them were sitting in their seats when suddenly, about an hour into the journey, Alnami, Jarrahi, and the other hijackers made their move toward the front of the Boeing 757. We know that Todd Bingham was sitting in seat 4D, using a complementary companion pass from his aunt who was a flight attendant. A partial reconstruction of what took place on board Flight 93 is possible because the four men and others used their cell phones, and also because some of the tape on the cockpit voice recorder has been salvaged, as CNN.com reported on September 22, 2001. The terrorists were armed with knives and box-cutters. Significantly, they appear to have been wearing red headbands, similar to those which had been worn nearly twenty years ago by the *basiji* suicide commandos of the Ayatollah Khomeini. At 9:15 A.M., according to the tape of a cockpit radio transmission obtained by Florida-based tabloid the *Star*, Jason Dahl, the pilot, was heard screaming, "Get out of here! Get out of here!" Jarrahi and the others struck ruthlessly, stabbing Dahl to death. Using the shock of their attack to force the passengers to do what they wished, the hijackers ordered twenty-seven of the forty-four passengers aboard to move to the front of the aircraft. Glick, Burnett, Beamer, and Bingham, with other passengers and five flight attendants, were forced to the back of the plane by one of the conspirators, who told them he had a bomb.

If the hijacking of Flight 93 is an example of the art with which the rest of the nineteen suicide commandos pirated the other three planes, then it seems like the terrorists followed rather closely the actions of the hijackers of more than twenty years before, such as those belonging to George Habash's Popular Front for the Liberation of Palestine and the other groups that made flying so perilous throughout Europe and the Middle East. It is perhaps more than ironic that the "new" group which had killed Israeli Tourism Minister Rehavam Zeevi on October 17, 2001, had adopted the name of Habash's organization. The tactics were almost identical: first a sudden act of violent terror, if deemed necessary, to cow the passengers and make further resistance unlikely; second, the bending of the passengers to the will of the terrorists. Did Atta, Moqed, Hanjour, and the rest have some training in their camps on how to hijack a plane? Clearly, taking over a jumbo jet with many passengers requires more instruction than, for example, getting a cup of morning coffee at the local java joint. Could they in fact have received deliberate teaching in how to take over a plane, sort of a "Hijacking 101" class? And if so, could their classroom mentors have been Palestinian renegades, who still thought the year was 1972? This is one of the mysteries of September 11 that will surely be on the agenda of the criminal investigation. Federal investigators believed as of October 19, 2001, that the terrorists had taken several airplane trips on Boeing 757s and 767s before September 11 to familiarize themselves with the interior of the planes.

To ensure that the terror of the moment be widespread on the ground, Jarrahi and company ordered their prisoners to make calls to their loved ones on their cell phones. The command to use the cell phones proved to be the undoing of their desperate mission. In their moment of exaltation, the *Shahid*, the martyrs, forgot that cellular phones make possible a two way communication. Up until now, the terrorists had kept up the ruse that they only intended to hijack the plane, not to destroy it and its human cargo. One of the hijackers (whose identity may remain an open question), speaking poor English with a heavy Middle Eastern accent, even pretended he was the pilot to allay the passengers' fears. He said, "there is a bomb on board. This is the captain speaking. Remain in your seat. There is a bomb on board. Stay quiet. We are meeting their demands. We are returning to the airport." According to Glick's family, he called his wife Lyzbeth around 9:40 A.M. and told her, "Honey, the plane's been hijacked." Apparently, Glick himself thought nothing more than that they had been indeed hijacked, which of course would be an occasion of fear in itself. However, while on the phone he seemed to hear other passengers talking excitedly about what their relatives told them about the catastrophe in New York City, which was unfolding at the same time. A senior American intelligence official told MSNBC that one of the flight crew up front turned on the microphone so that the passengers would hear what the terrorists were saying, perhaps hoping they would do something to help. Then Glick asked Lyzbeth, "did planes crash into the World Trade Center?" It was as if he wanted to confirm the rumors that were swirling among the anxious people around him. Lyzbeth told him yes. He said, "My God, we're next!" It is from the transmission from Glick's phone conversation that we know that the hijackers were wearing red headbands and carrying box cutters and knives. Glick also noted that they had a red box they claimed was a bomb.

At about the same time, Burnett was on the phone to his wife, Deena. He told her that somebody had been killed, presumably the pilot, and things looked "pretty bad." Bingham made a call to his mother, Alice Hogan, who lives in Sunnyvale, California. "I want you to know that I love you very much. I'm in the air. I'm calling on the air phone of the airplane. We've been taken over, there are three men that say they have a bomb." Another person on board, flight attendant CeeCee Ross-Lyles, called her husband in their home in Fort Myers, Florida. "We've been hijacked," she said. There were screams heard in the background, then her phone went dead. An unnamed United Airlines official told CNN that a flight attendant, probably CeeCee, had called her husband and said that three other flight attendants had been stabbed.

It appears from what happened next that Glick, Beamer, Bingham, and Burnett were already together and acting in concert. Glick, still on the phone to his wife, said that "we're just deciding whether we [perhaps Glick, Beamer, Burnett, Bingham] should do something, or are we better off not attacking them." Burnett told Deena, "I'm not giving up. We're getting ready to do something. A group of us. . . . I love you, honey." It was after this that the decision must have been made to act, as Burnett quickly ended his conversation. Beamer had reached GTE operator Lisa Jefferson on the airphone by his seat and said that they were going to "jump on" the terrorists. At the same time, Glick must have said to Lyzbeth, "we've taken a vote, and we're going to do something." It makes one almost smile to think that in the greatest peril of their lives, these men decided to solve things in the traditional, democratic American way: take a vote. Glick added, "our best chance is to fight these people, rather than to accept" being blown up. The last words Jefferson heard Beamer say were "let's roll!"

All four apparently dropped their phones, leaving the lines open. Richard Makely, Glick's father-in-law, heard, as the *Star* reported, "silence on board for a few minutes, followed by a series of loud screams, then several more minutes of silence, then more loud screams and turmoil in the background. Then silence." The report on CNN.com of September 22 confirms the account in the *Star*. CNN Washington correspondent Kelli Arena wrote that "officials familiar with the cockpit voice recorder on United Airlines Flight 93—the hijacked jet that crashed September 11 in western Pennsylvania— say there was a 'definite struggle' described as desperate and wild between hijackers and some of the passengers. An official has said there was some shouting, but it is not clear who was in control of the plane before it crashed. . . . Officials say the voice recorder was able to pick up scuffling sounds."

Knowing what we do about the four men, we can reconstruct what probably happened next. Burnett was 6 feet, 2 inches tall, and a former high school football quarterback. Bingham was an imposing 6 feet, 5 inches, and weighed 230 pounds. He was a rugby player who had played for the University of California and had once subdued a mugger. Glick himself was 6 feet, 1 inch tall, and had been a judo champion in college. In the words of the *Star*, "Glick and the other four men stormed from their seats and into history." Apparently, Burnett, Glick, Bingham, Beamer, and other passengers must have charged up the center aisle of the 757 like Theodore Roosevelt, one of Burnett's favorite presidents, did with his Rough Riders up San Juan Hill in the Spanish-American War. They rushed the terrorist who was guarding the front of the passenger cabin and overwhelmed him. Then they stormed into the locked cockpit. The struggle must have been intense. Dennis Fritz, director of municipal aviation at Johnstown, Pennsylvania, told the September 13 *Washington Post* that the director of the Federal Aviation Administration called him several times, warning him to evacuate the control tower because it looked like the plane might crash into it.[12] The chief executive of Flight Explorer corporation, Jeff Krawczyk, said his computer software firm used FAA data to track the flight. "It was going west, then took a turn to the north, and then went west again."[13] The plane headed toward Kentucky, and then south toward Washington. At that moment, FAA ground control in Cleveland lost contact with Flight 93 because somebody, accidentally or deliberately, had turned off the Boeing's transponder (the device which allows ground control towers to follow a plane's course). During the battle that followed, with nobody apparently flying the plane, Flight 93 lost control and plunged down toward the brown Pennsylvania earth. People living around Shanksville reported hearing a loud roar in the sky above them. Then, there was the sound of a loud crash as the Boeing 757 tore into the ground at about 450 miles per hour.

The plane gouged a twenty-five-foot-deep crater in the soil where it crashed on the reclaimed site of a former strip coal mine, not far from a copse of standing trees. There were few big pieces of wreckage. Pennsylvania State Trooper Tom Spallone said, "the biggest piece I saw was about one foot in diameter."[14] The field where the plane crashed was full of goldenrod and corn that was ready for the fall harvest. It was not, if one has to die, and all of us must, a particularly bad place to make the final journey. Somerset County, where Shanksville is located, is part of the Laurel Highlands of western Pennsylvania. Nearby is Mount Davis in the Allegheny Mountains, the highest point in Pennsylvania at 3,213 feet. The area is still so rural that some of the state troopers rode to the site on horseback. Somerset County is a place where streams with little waterfalls look as they must have when the first American settlers came into the region. Here the Allegheny Mountains soon make their graceful descent to the great middle plain of the United States, where rivers with names like the Muskigum and the Kanawha still remember the Indian tribes who lived there first. Kickenapauling's Town was the Native American settlement in Somerset County known to the arriving American colonists. It is still largely an area of small towns like Shanksville, where on Tuesday, October 23, 2001, the students at the Eagle View Elementary School remembered Flight 93 during a ceremony honoring the September 1787 signing of the U.S. Constitution, a document whose freedoms people like Osama bin Laden do not understand and so fear, but which the passengers on board the plane were ready to die to preserve. Already, in October 2001 the members of the Somerset County Historical Society were moving to gather whatever they could from the crash site to "secure, archive, and preserve items that could be damaged by the weather." The material would be kept as a permanent memorial to the people who died. A county memorial is to be constucted to honor the dead and, in American fashion, donations are being solicited.

Because of the heroism of Glick, Beamer, Burnett, Bingham, and their unknown compatriots, other American lives were saved. Based on American intelligence estimates, it is almost certain the hijackers had intended Flight 93 to fly like a guided bomb into the Capitol, the White House, or Air Force One as President Bush landed at Andrews Air Force Base. Like the American soldiers and marines who threw themselves on live hand grenades in World War II, the passengers on Flight 93 had given up their lives so that others might live. Vice President Dick Cheney said on *Meet the Press* on September 16 that "I think the Washington part of the attack was significantly interfered with. We know the plane crashed outside of Pittsburgh was headed for Washington. My guess is that the target was the Capitol building. The passengers were courageous when they made that decision, knowing that they were doomed. Without question, the attack would have been much worse if it hadn't been for the courageous Americans on United 93." To them, the vice president might truly owe his life.

At 9:25 A.M. on September 11, for the first time in American history, the Federal Aviation Administration closed all airports and ordered all civil airplanes to vacate the skies. As the day went on, and fear mounted that the country might be under attack, the Department of Defense in Washington took the unprecedented step of initiating measures for the defense of the country in case of war. From Norfolk, Virginia, at 1:44 P.M., two U.S. Navy aircraft carrier battle groups put to sea, those of the USS *John F. Kennedy* and the USS *George Washington*. In the most severe crisis the United States had faced since the Cuban missile crisis erupted in October 1962 when Kennedy was president, it seemed somehow fitting that a ship of war bearing his name would be one of those protecting the country. It was a double tribute, since

Kennedy had served in the U.S. Navy in World War II in the war against Japan as the captain of the PT-109 patrol torpedo boat. When the aircraft carriers left the harbor, they parted company with their battle groups; one steamed up the East Coast to New York and the other sailed up the Chesapeake Bay to provide protection for Washington. The entire East Coast was brought under the protective umbrella of the fighter squadrons at the ready on their massive flight decks. (The flight deck of the *Kennedy* is some 1,052 feet long by 252 feet wide.) In the carriers' battle groups sailed frigates and guided missile destroyers, armed with sea-to-air Sea Sparrow missiles, as are the *Kennedy* and the *Washington*. With the navy on a war footing, any unidentified planes that flew near the aircraft carriers would risk being shot down in flames by the air-to-air Sparrow missiles of the jet fighters that would be flying combat air patrol over the decks of the ships. David Alexander wrote in his book *Tomorrow's Soldiers*, "the all-weather F-14 Tomcats and F/A-18 Hornets fly their stations in a circular pattern, each keeping its nose to the other's [tail] so that their long-range threat-identification radars are always providing a full 360-degree coverage."[15] On board the two aircraft carriers and the battle groups were amphibious forces of U.S. Marines, ready for any emergency on shore.

When the FAA gave the surprise command to ground all civilian aircraft, Flight 77 was on its doomed journey. The employees at the Pentagon, the symbol of American military power since 1943, were watching on television the unbelievable sights unfolding before their eyes in New York City. Then, coming in from the west at 9:45 A.M., Flight 77 roared over the helicopter landing pad and tore into the Pentagon. Flight 77 had swooped in low over Arlington National Cemetery on its lethal approach. At the time of Flight 77's impact, army Maj. Jeff Mockensturm had been in a meeting in Room 3D450. Mockensturm later told a reporter it felt like the plane hit "right outside the window."[16] The rebuilding project that was then occurring at the Pentagon saved the lives of scores of people who otherwise would have been in the building that morning, since many were not at their desks. The plane hurtled like a guided missile through the three outer rings—E, D, and C—of the Pentagon "doughnut." Only the two inner rings, B and A, were undamaged. In the center of the building, the open air court was also intact. The peaceful tree-lined "hole" in the middle of the doughnut suddenly became a bloody triage site for the wounded. Jeff Garamone of the American Forces Press Service reported that the jumbo jet had "cut the building like a knife."

Tragically, the pilot of Flight 77, Charles Burlingame III, had spent ten years working in the Pentagon studying counterterrorism before retiring as a captain in the U.S. Navy. An unnamed army lieutenant colonel told Garamone that "we felt a thump and saw the flash. All of us and others gathered and went toward the site. We couldn't get close." With news reports of the disaster at the Pentagon, names of those interviewed are usually notable by their absence. Military censors kept their names secret due to concern about retaliation against these service personnel, especially as the anthrax scare began to sweep across the country in the first week of October. In interviews conducted aboard the aircraft carriers in the Arabian Sea, only the first names of service men and women were given for the same reason.

Those who could, immediately began to evacuate the scene as flames and smoke billowed from the bowels of the Pentagon. One worker threw his laptop computer out a window and hurried after it. Another clambered through the hole the plane had made. As the workers left the building, it was done in an orderly fashion, for all members of the armed forces are trained for disaster so many times that this day they were able to respond to the emergency almost without thinking, which was a blessing to them. Only when news of Flight 93, apparently also headed toward Washington, was reported did military and civilian police order the evacuees to hurry away from the damaged Pentagon.

When the second emergency over Flight 93 had passed, many returned to help in the mammoth search and rescue operation which had already begun. Firemen and emergency workers from Arlington, Virginia, were hard at work. An Arlington firefighter was Andrea Kaiser, who had worked six years prior for public television. Kaiser had been at a training session when she had received news of the plane crash. At the wheel of her fire engine number 101, she was one of the first rescuers on the scene. Kaiser told the *National Enquirer* on September 18, 2001, that she had seen "a mushroom cloud of smoke rising from the Pentagon like it had been hit by an atomic bomb." When she entered the smoking ruins "it was pitch black inside. Walls were crumbling, everything was scorched. It was like a war zone." Kaiser looked in vain but found nobody alive. The victims "never knew what hit them." Outside, doctors and medical teams established a triage center beyond the site of the helicopter landing pad. Stretcher bearers carried litters of injured people to the waiting ambulances, looking more like a scene from the battle for Okinawa in World War II than a morning in Arlington.

For years the 3rd U.S. Infantry Regiment, the Old Guard, which can trace its lineage back to the earliest days of the U.S. Army, has been renowned for the military dress parades its fife and drum corps has given in eighteenth-century American military uniforms. The Old Guard is to Washington what the Queen's Brigade of Guards is to London. All military ceremonies are conducted with infinite precision by the men of the regiment. When President Kennedy was assassinated in November 1963, it was the Old Guard millions of television viewers saw conduct the president's flag-draped coffin on the back of an artillery caisson to its final resting place at Arlington. The soldiers escorted a black horse with a pair of boots slung backward in the stirrups, the sign of a funeral of a leader since the time of Genghiz Khan. On September 11, the 3rd U.S. Infantry was called up for an even more mournful duty, going through the wreckage of the Pentagon in a search for survivors, with more military precision perhaps but no less grief than that being carried out by New York firemen at the same time. Sgt. Patrick Miller of C Company told interviewers from the Military District of Washington News Service that "it's horrible. We've briefed [the soldiers], but there's no telling how they'll react." Here, going through the Pentagon on a peaceful, sunny morning, they were encountering horrific injuries that an earlier generation in the U.S. Army had seen on Omaha Beach on D-Day in June 1944. In an eerie foretaste of what the nation would face a month after the attack, the soldiers entered the building wearing white biological protective suits with yellow Gortex boots. C Company was among 300 service personnel who worked around the clock in a vain search for life, but sadly, Miller and the other members of the company would find no survivors. On September 13, Defense Department officials reported that 126 service personnel were officially declared missing from inside the destroyed west wing. That number would later rise to 189.

In an unusual news story on this day of days, the *Toronto* (Canada) *Globe and Mail* carried a story about the Pentagon attack which mentioned that around the time Flight 77 crashed into the building "a number of unexplained explosions were reported close to the State Department and the Capitol. Reports also suggest that a second hijacked passenger plane headed for the Pentagon crashed near Camp David. While it is not known if it was shot down, F-16 fighter jets were headed in the plane's direction."[17] Whether this report was a confused reference to Flight 93, or actually referred to another unknown hijacking, whose details may remain classified, is one of the mysteries of September 11. Some who listened to the frantic talk on Flight 93 said that the transmissions ended with the sign of an explosion. We know that Glick said that the hijackers had a bomb in a red box. It is a possible scenario that the hijackers may have had bombs in all four of the planes which crashed that day. Wreckage from Flight 93 was allegedly found up to eight miles from the crash site near Shanksville. This would have been highly unlikely if the plane had crashed into the ground while still whole. However, if a bomb had exploded the plane in mid-air, then the wide dispersion of the wreckage would make sense. While admittedly speculation, the presence of the bombs on the other planes could help to explain why the Twin Towers had actually collapsed when Flights 11 and 175 tore into them. In what could prove to be a key part of the investigation, the Defense Department did reveal that the two "black boxes," the flight or data recorder and the voice recorder, had been retrieved from the wreckage of Flight 77. The recorders were handed over to the FBI, which took them to the National Transportation Safety Board in Washington for examination.

There was almost another victim in the state of emergency that blanketed the nation after the morning's bombings. Attorney General John Ashcroft had been flying toward a speaking engagement in the Midwest when the FAA had ordered all civilian aircraft to be grounded. Ashcroft's entourage veered east and began the return flight to Washington. His pilot was David Clemmer, a veteran of the Vietnam War. Clemmer had received a warning from the air traffic controller on the ground that he had to land his plane immediately, or risk being shot down by the air cover that now existed over Washington. He notified the air traffic controllers that he had Ashcroft on board, but the pilot and Ashcroft were still in danger. There was the possibility that the air traffic controller would not believe it was Ashcroft, or that the message would not get through to the armed forces commanders who now ruled the air space over the capital, or *they* would not believe it was the attorney general. In the atmosphere of the day, Clemmer wanted to take no chances that he and Ashcroft would die the victims of "friendly fire," shot down by a "Top Gun" navy pilot who would be taking no chances. Clemmer solved the dilemma by requesting for an F-16 to fly up—and escort them![18]

Over at the White House that morning, Vice President Dick Cheney was the man on the spot. President Bush was in Florida, so Cheney represented the visible government in Washington. Presumably, around the time that the planes hit the Twin Towers, Secret Service agents would have hurried

Cheney down to the subterranean "War Room," the Situation Room, where President John F. Kennedy presided during the Cuban missile crisis in October 1962. In a scene from a motion picture thriller, Secret Service agents burst into Cheney's office in the West Wing. Physically, they bundled him out of the office, saying "we have to move; we're moving now, sir."[19] With Cheney went Codoleezza Rice, Bush's national security advisor. However, the special edition of *Time* says they were hurried to "a bunker on the White House grounds."

Although such information is of necessity kept top secret, most likely Cheney was accompanied by a military attache with one of the "footballs," the attache cases which contain the nuclear launch codes by which a president can launch a full-scale thermonuclear retaliation if the country is under attack. With attacks already registered in the capital and in New York City, there was no reason not to believe that the assaults were the prelude to an all-out offensive against the United States. This was especially true when the White House was alerted that Flight 93 could be headed its way.

Thus, the emergency system known as "COG," for "continuity of government," got under way. All congressional leaders and other cabinet heads were taken to undisclosed places of safety. This was not done just to keep the government running but because, should both Bush and Cheney perish that day, the next chief executive would be chosen from among their number. Under the Presidential Succession Law of 1947, the third in line for the presidency would have been Speaker of the House of Representatives Denny Hastert and the fourth would have been the President Pro Tempore of the Senate, Strom Thurmond. After Strom Thurmond would come Secretary of State Colin Powell, and on through the cabinet to the Secretary of Veterans' Affairs Anthony Principi. (Powell might be disqualified, however, because he was not born in the United States.) A 1998 Brookings study titled "Atomic Audit: The Costs and Consequences of U.S. Nuclear Weapons since 1940" noted that "for continuity of government purposes, senior officials are divided into Alpha, Bravo, and Charlie teams, one would remain in Washington, another relocate to [location not revealed in this book], and the third disperse to other relocation sites. Officials at [location not revealed in this book] track the location of everyone designated to succeed the president twenty-four hours a day. Designated evacuees carry special identification cards, and regular briefings and drills are conducted. Officials are not allowed to bring their families."

When Cheney descended to the War Room under the White House, he entered one of the most secure locations in the United States. The War Room was designed, according to the best information available, during the Cold War with the Soviet Union. It is supposed to be able to withstand virtually anything short of a direct hit by a nuclear bomb. According to information available during the Cold War, the War Room, or a more extensive contiguous underground bunker, would have its own supply of emergency generators, air, food, water, and medicine. In the event of an attack, the War Room complex would have to be able to sustain the life of those inside until help could come. And in any attack on the capital, the rescue of those within the War Room would be priority number one. According to the Brookings document, a special air force emergency team "was trained to fly to the White House in the event of a nuclear attack, retrieve the president and first family, and relocate them to" underground command posts. "If the team should have difficulty reaching the White House before an attack, it carried specialized equipment to break into the bunker beneath the executive mansion; a backup unit with heavier equipment, including cranes, was also available if the damage proved more severe."

While Rice and Cheney were in the War Room, a different drama unfolded above them. With only the essential personnel moved down below, the rest of the White House staffers began an orderly evacuation of the executive mansion. There was no rush as they were escorted out of the building by the police and Secret Service agents. At this time, some of the Secret Service agents had started to get out their M-16s and kevlar vests from the arsenal which is located within the building. Although Pennsylvania Avenue had been blocked off for several years because of the danger of a terrorist car bombing, on this incredible morning it seemed like anything might be possible. There were other White House members working in the Old Executive Office Building across the street from the White House. These were watching the horrific scenes in New York City. Suddenly, Secret Service agents burst into their offices and, according to the *Philadelphia Inquirer*, told them that "the building is being evacuated. Please walk to the nearest exit." The staffers from the Old Executive Office Building joined the general exodus. Then, either an agent heard on his radio of a plane approaching the White House or saw Flight 77 on its mad dash to the Pentagon. Suddenly, the agents and police were crying for everybody to run for their lives. Women took off their high-heeled shoes and the whole crowd began a tumultuous dash for safety.

Even as late as September 30, the Secret Service could not permit the president and vice president to stay in the same room, for fear a surprise secondary attack could kill them both. A secondary attack was raised as a real possibility by Attorney General John Ashcroft, especially as the campaign against the Taliban and bin Laden gathered momentum. Warnings of another attack have been echoed by extremists throughout the Islamic world since September 11, and the government is taking such warnings deadly seriously. CBS Radio News announced on the night of October 4 that American intelligence sources considered that there was "a 100 percent" certainty of attack on American targets, either at home or overseas, if the United States invaded Afghanistan. Although our attack would come on October 7, 2001, as of February 2002, no further terrorist incidents had occurred on Amerian soil.

The morning of September 11, the president was speaking to Mrs. Sarah Kay Daniels's second grade students at the Emma E. Booker Elementary School in Sarasota, Florida. As soon as he arrived, he was taken off to a private room. National Security Advisor Condoleeza Rice was on the phone from the White House, telling him about the first plane crashing into the World Trade Center. Bush continued with his scheduled appearance, assuming perhaps the crash was a solitary occurrence. His meeting with the school children completed, he went on with what must have been the next scheduled part of his trip to the elementary school: a photo opportunity. Bush intended to pose for photographs with the school principal, teachers, and, being a father of two, most importantly the students themselves.

A presidential schedule is more tightly orchestrated than the troupe of the Russian Bolshoi Ballet performing Tchaikovsky's *Swan Lake*; every movement is choreographed by the presidential schedule-makers for the Oval Office. Yet, this day, Murphy's Law overawed the schedulers, even the chief of state of the most powerful nation in world history: "If things can go wrong, they will, and at the worst possible moment." Just as the president had regained his composure from hearing about the first plane hitting the World Trade Center, Andrew Card, his chief of staff, came into the room with even more dire news: Flight 11 had struck the WTC's north tower. The president left for more consultation.

Back in the room set up for the photos, some 200 people were waiting, now anxiously, for Bush to reappear. By this time, many congregating there would have heard at least of the first attack on the WTC. About thirty-five minutes later, Bush returned to the assembly. Instead of posing with school children, he had to make the most difficult address of his short presidency: "Ladies and gentleman, this is a difficult moment for America. I, unfortunately, will be going back to Washington." The president added with conviction, "terrorism against our nation will not stand."[20] With that, the Secret Service escorted him from the school and to the airport, where the president and his party boarded Air Force One. At 9:55 A.M., the presidential jet soared into the Florida skies.

That morning, First Lady Laura Bush was supposed to testify on Capitol Hill about education. She was a champion of her husband's national education reform package, which had been presented in the "No Child Left Behind" booklet. Being the First Mother as well, Mrs. Bush had adopted educational reform as her own program. When news came of the second plane hitting the Twin Towers that September morning, she decided to keep to her schedule. She spoke to Massachusetts senator Edward "Ted" Kennedy, in one of the first of the links between the Kennedys and the Bush administration that day. With her arm around his shoulders, they walked into the committee room where she was to testify. Senator Kennedy, with Sen. Judd Gregg of New Hampshire, Rep. John Boener of Ohio, and Rep. George Miller of California, chaired the joint House-Senate committee on education. The wife of the current president and the brother of a former president made joint statements about the acts of terror. Mrs. Bush said, "parents need to reassure their children everywhere in our country that they're safe." Undoubtedly, she was thinking of her two daughters, Barbara and Jenna. The *Philadelphia Inquirer* for September 14 reported that Senator Kennedy declared, "we are not going to see the business of America deferred because of terrorism." Just about then, news came of the strike at the Pentagon. Secret Service agents rushed to the First Lady's side to take her to a secure location. The area of Maryland and Virginia around Washington is honeycombed with such locales to be used in a national emergency. Some are ordinary buildings, while others are underground sites. At the same time, the agents with the Bushes' twin daughters, Jenna and Barbara, suddenly packed them into cars and took them off as well, presumably to where the Secret Service was guarding the First Lady. As was seen in the attempt on Ronald Reagan by John Hinckley, and the time Charles Manson follower Lynette "Squeaky" Fromme attempted to kill President Gerald Ford in California, the Secret Service agents are trained to protect the person whom they are assigned to guard with their lives. While Reagan lay on the street gravely wounded, agents covered the fallen president with their own bodies.

Then Senate Majority Leader, Trent Lott, was in his office when he saw smoke coming out of the stricken Pentagon. An aide later said, "we decided to get the hell out." Lott was taken to Andrews Air Force Base, most likely by helicopter. Meanwhile, concern gripped the rest of the House of Representatives and the Senate. Virginia senator John Warner joined a group on the steps of the Capitol to offer a brief prayer for those who had been killed in New York City at the time that Mrs. Bush and Senator Kennedy were appearing before the committee inside. Then somebody told him about the bombing of the Pentagon. Warner took a moment to reflect and then spoke to a reporter, memories of the greatest generation that had faced Pearl Harbor and World War II in his mind. "Now this generation is going to become the greatest generation," he prophesied, "if they have the same courage, commitment, and depth to pull together and lead this nation out of this." With the three attacks having taken place, the country seemed to be under a wider attack than that which had occurred on December 7, 1941. The only target the Japanese struck that day had been the base of the U.S. Pacific Fleet at Pearl Harbor. Later that morning, Lott and seventy other senators met secretly in the headquarters of the Capitol Police. Lott and Minority Leader Sen. Tom Daschle had both spoken to Dick Cheney at the White House, but they wanted to reach President Bush. An unidentified senator said, as *Newsweek*'s special September 11 edition quoted, "people were angry and full of questions." Then they saw Karen Hughes, Bush's counselor, appear on television. She would be the senior Bush administration official to appear in public that day. Another senator remarked in the *Newsweek* article, "we didn't need her to tell us that he was alright. We needed him to tell us that we were alright. They [the administration] missed the point." Now, with concern for the future of leadership of the country at hand, Capitol police and other security personnel rushed the Congressional leadership to a location some seventy-five miles outside Washington.

The "Atomic Audit" study by the Brookings Institute gives details about these underground locations. There are two in Virginia and one in West Virginia, and one is located near the Maryland-Pennsylvania state line. For security reasons, all details about these underground command posts will be kept vague. These facilities have all been declared closed, but with the announcement of the First Family and the Congressional leadership being evacuated to "secure locations" in "bunkers," in the national news media, then this information may be incorrect. One of these underground command posts in

Virginia was about seventy-five miles southwest of Washington, and would be the likely one to which the Congressional leaders were transported. The facilities were complete in every respect. All of them housed complete medical facilities. Some of them even had "pathological waste incinerators," a government euphemism for crematoriums. At least two of them cost $1 billion or more to build. The Brookings paper said that even the medical prescriptions for every member of Congress were kept in a special file. Fresh supplies were kept on hand. Central to all locales was the care and protection of the president, who would continue to function as the commander-in-chief in a national emergency, just like the one the United States faced on September 11, 2001.

At times, however, that morning President Bush himself seemed to be in jeopardy. From the White House "War Room," Dick Cheney relayed to the president aboard Air Force One as the plane was over Florida that the Secret Service feared that Air Force One itself could be under attack. It is here where the situation becomes murky. Interviewed by CBS News anchorman Dan Rather, correspondent Wayne Andrews told an unusual story. Speaking during a live interview on the afternoon of the catastrophe, Andrews apparently had been on Air Force One. Somewhere over northern Florida, Andrews recalled, a Secret Service agent looked out of the window of the jet and said, "there's a fifth plane [one not part of the convoy] out there." With that, Air Force One suddenly banked to the west and began what would be a flight to Barksdale Air Force Base, outside Shreveport, Louisiana. Although I have heard nothing more about the story, it does shed a sinister light on the warning the vice president gave about Secret Service concern of an impending attack on Air Force One itself. Based on the testimony of Florida congressman Dan Miller, as reported in the *Philadelphia Inquirer* Sunday, September 16, Air Force One was cruising over north Florida on its way to Washington. Suddenly, at 45,000 feet, Miller noticed the plane bank to the west.

Could there have been an unidentified, hostile plane nearing Air Force One on President Bush's flight back to a war-torn Washington? Based on informed speculation only, the answer must be a tentative yes. Since no planes are supposed to be near Air Force One while it is airborne, the flight controllers on the ground must know the flight path in advance so that they can keep a clear "air corridor" for Air Force One to insure against an accidental mid-air collision between the president's jet and any civilian commercial or private aircraft. The flight controllers must know the elevation and course of the presidential craft to be able to keep "open skies" around it during its journey. It has been discovered that Florida is the state where most of the hijackers like Atta had taken their flight training. From the outset of the investigation, the FBI warned that not all of the terrorists had been accounted for, and that some of them were definitely still at large. Was it possible that some other skyjackers had remained behind to launch a surprise air assault on Air Force One itself? The answer again must be a tentative yes.

It was public knowledge before the event that the president would visit Florida. On September 7, the Sarasota, Florida, *Herald-Tribune* published an article which read in part, "President George W. Bush will visit Sarasota on Tuesday to talk with students and teachers about 'his education and reading initiatives,' the White House said Thursday. The president plans to fly into Sarasota late Monday evening." Thus any would-be killers knew in advance that the president would be in the state on the day they planned for the attack, and beside Sarasota was the site of the flight school where Atta and al-Shehihi had trained. Could a different hit squad have possibly been able to listen in on the telecommunications traffic between Air Force One and the flight controllers on the ground? Unless the electronic communication was encoded, the answer again must be a tentative yes. Aboard Air Force One the Secret Service asked all the correspondents not to use cell phones so that nobody could track the plane by eavesdropping on cell phone communications, according to the *Time* magazine special edition of September 24, 2001. Moreover, they were requested, *Time* revealed in its special edition, "not even to turn them on—because the signals might allow someone to identify the plane's location." Thus, could it have been possible for other suicide commandos to plot a course to intercept Air Force One and kill all aboard, including President Bush, in a fiery kamikaze attack? The answer seems to be, unfortunately, again a tentative yes, certainly in view of the Secret Service warning against using cellular phones aboard the presidential craft.

One final piece of evidence needs to be factored in. According to the *Philadelphia Inquirer* for September 16, at 11:30 A.M., the president summoned the two Florida congressmen, Dan Miller and Adam Putnam, to meet with him on the plane. Bush told them that Cheney had called him and said that a definite threat had been received for Air Force One; moreover, whoever had called in the threat knew the secret code word for the plane, perhaps "ANGEL" as used here. Miller said later that Bush told them that "there is a credible threat on this plane, and we're going to an undisclosed location."

Further, he told the congressmen that six air force jet fighters and another plane were accompanying them. Whether the jet escort had been with Air Force One since it taxied off the runway or had been added while en route is not clear. The *San Francisco Chronicle* on September 12 would also observe that the big plane flew at "unusually high altitudes," possibly to get above the altitude ceiling of any private or commercial plane which might try to intercept it in the air.

Many compared bin Laden's surprise attack to that on the base of the American Pacific Fleet at Pearl Harbor by the Japanese fleet under Adm. Yamamoto Isoroku on December 7, 1941. They also recalled Yamamoto's words after the attack about the Pearl Harbor raid: "I am afraid we have awakened a sleeping giant and filled it with terrible resolve." But they do not recall how the admiral died. The story was told again on Air Force News.com as part of the Air Force's 50th Anniversary celebration in 1997. Station HYPO at Pearl Harbor, the main code-breaking section of U.S. naval intelligence in the Pacific, had broken the main Japanese naval code, JN [for Japanese Navy] 25. Two of the senior navy codebreakers were Joseph Rochefort and Joseph Finnegan, who would later be my father's commanding officer aboard the USS *Winston*. The breaking of JN-25 made possible U.S. Adm. Chester Nimitz's decisive victory over Yamamoto in the Battle of Midway in June 1942. In April 1943, the code-breakers had intercepted and decoded a dispatch which said that Yamamoto was set for an inspection trip by aircraft to the Japanese base at Bougainville Island in the Solomon Islands. What is now the 347th Air Force Wing was stationed at Henderson Field on Guadalcanal some 400 miles away. Acting on orders from Secretary of the Navy Frank Knox, the 347th in its twin-tailed P-38 Lighting fighters were ordered to intercept Yamamoto's "party and destroy it at all costs." Thus, on April 18, 1943, Capt. Thomas G. Lanphier in his P-38, avoiding the escort of Japanese fighters, shot down the "Betty" bomber on which Yamamoto was flying, killing the admiral. There seems to have been no reason that some other of bin Laden's suicide pilots might not have tried a similar mid-air strike against President Bush aboard Air Force One.

As the president flew over the United States, he was able to keep in constant communication with Cheney and Rice in the War Room back in Washington and American armed forces commanders throughout the world. The most sophisticated communications equipment possible has made Air Force One a true Oval Office on wings. Air Force One, according to the Web page hosted by the Boeing Corporation, is a Boeing 747-200B. Actually there are two Air Force Ones, codenamed ANGEL by the Secret Service, according to the www.2600.com site on the Internet (all Secret Service code names come from this source). Both were delivered by Boeing in 1990. When one is in use, a second plane is kept in a secure, remote location at Andrews Air Force Base, ANDY, under armed guard. As many already know, any plane the president is on actually becomes "Air Force One," but on the official aircraft, the president can be in touch about as quickly with a U.S. Navy "boomer," or nuclear submarine, cruising under the Arctic ice cap as he can be with First Lady Laura Bush. Although highly classified, it is surmised that Air Force One carries on board a large medley of evasive technology that can be employed if the plane is under attack from a missile or another plane, as was the fear on September 11. There are areas on board the presidential jet that are "off limits" to those without the proper security identification, where such defensive equipment is most likely located. The Boeing Web page on Air Force One does however state that the Boeing 747 has wiring that is "shielded to protect it from electromagnetic pulse, which is generated by a thermonuclear blast and interferes with electronic signals."

At 11:45 A.M. September 11, Air Force One taxied onto the runway at the Barksdale Air Force Base in Louisiana. As *Time* noted in its special edition, Air Force One landed "with fighters hovering beside each wing through the descent." If Air Force One did not have a fighter escort when it left Sarasota, it picked up one in mid-air in the flight over the Gulf Coast to Louisiana. The airmen at the base were ready for war: They were wearing their kevlar vests, "Fritz" style helmets, and were armed with M-16s. A cordon of the armed airmen immediately surrounded the presidential plane. Then, a motorcade carried the president to Building 245. Hurriedly, a room in Building 245 was made ready for a brief presidential speech. At 12:36, Bush spoke from a conference room, flanked by two American flags that had been brought quickly in for the occasion. Bush spoke tersely for about two minutes, but the tenor of the day was clear in one sentence: "Freedom itself was attacked this morning by a faceless coward."

After the sojourn of a few hours at Barksdale, Bush returned to Air Force One for a journey to Offut Air Force Base in Nebraska. Offut was the home for the Strategic Air Command, the nerve center for the nation's strategic air forces. It was from "SAC" that orders went out during the Cold War to the B-52 bombers that were in the air around the clock, ready for the command to launch an attack on the Soviet Union which thankfully never came. Until three years ago, SAC at Offut had housed the Doomsday Plane, a special classified plane which the president would use in the event of nuclear war. From Offut, Bush conducted a teleconference with the staff members back in Washington, undoubtedly with the vice president; Condoleeza Rice; and George Tenet, the director of the Central Intelligence Agency. Tenet, who had held his position during the Clinton administration, had agreed to keep it to help the new president. He had shown himself a capable steward of the CIA, and had helped it become wise in the newer ways of terrorism such as information warfare conducted by enemy hackers against the nation's computerized defense establishment. Never before did continuity in the nation's intelligence community mean so much as on September 11.

At 4:30 P.M., the president again took to the skies and flew eastward across a tormented nation to Washington. As he flew, a three-jet escort, probably provided at Offut, accompanied Air Force One back to Andrews Air Force Base. At Andrews, he boarded Marine One, the helicopter which would take him back to the White House. On this particular voyage, three identical choppers were flying with Marine One as decoys against any possible last minute coup against the president. Perhaps attack helicopters were flying a covering mission as well, but if this is the case such information has not been disclosed. The president arrived at the White House at 6:54 P.M. Around that time, Laura Bush and her two daughters were returned to the executive mansion, having been held under intense security by the Secret Service during the day. Almost immediately, the president held a meeting in the White House bunker with Cheney, Rice, Powell, Ashcroft, and the president's chief of staff, Andrew Card, who had been with them throughout the entire hectic day. "Make no mistake," Bush declared, "Understand my resolve, and all of your people need to understand this." Then the president threw himself into preparations for the address he was to give the nation at 8:30 P.M. from the Oval Office, where, during the Cuban missile crisis, Kennedy also held the fate of the United States in his hands. At no time since the missile crisis had a president of the United States faced a comparable challenge. Now, forty years later, President George W. Bush, at the same desk, would come into his own in a similar speech given to an equally shocked nation.

At the Capitol Building, the sense of emergency had passed. In the West Wing of the White House, Bush's speechwriters were putting the finishing touches to what the president knew would be the defining speech of the crisis. Karen Hughes, the president's counselor, was suddenly thrust into the position that Ted Sorenson had had during the missile crisis. It was up to her to get her crew of writers to craft a speech that would allay the nation's anxieties and at the same time send a message of firm resolve to the American people and the people who would be watching overseas. Some of these, in this age of instant communications, would be among bin Laden's strongest supporters. Like Kennedy before him, Bush had his own input into what he would say, as he did when Hughes's writers put together the address to Congress that the president gave later that same week. Condoleezza Rice played a role in crafting the speech to Congress, and may have done so on September 11 as well. At 7:30 P.M., the leadership of the House of Representatives gathered on the front steps of the capitol building. Republican Congressman Dennis Hastert, Speaker of the House of Representatives, gave an impromptu address. Next to him stood Dick Gephardt, a Democrat. Partisan politics, which are the necessary but irritating lubricant of a participatory government, were for the time forgotten. Hastert spoke: "when Americans suffer and when people perpetrate acts against this country, we as a Congress and as a government stand united, and stand together." Then the whole gathering joined together in a heartfelt singing of the United States' second national anthem, "God Bless America."

Darkness lowered its own soft shroud over the doleful remains of the day, as President Bush addressed a stricken nation from the Oval Office an hour later at 8:30. He told the waiting people of America,

> These acts of mass murder were intended to frighten our nation into chaos and retreat. But they have failed. Our country is strong. A great people has been moved to defend a great nation. Terrorist attacks can shake the foundations of our biggest buildings, but they cannot touch the foundation of America. These acts shatter steel, but they cannot dent the steel of American resolve. America was targeted for attack because we're the brightest beacon for freedom and opportunity in the world. And no one will keep that light from shining. . . . This is a day when all Americans from every walk of life unite in our resolve for justice and peace. America has stood down enemies before, and we will do so this time. None of us will ever forget this day, yet we go forward to defend freedom and all that is good and just in our world.[21]

When President Bush arrived at the Pentagon on September 12, part of the nose of the destroyed Boeing 757 was still in the cavern created by its crash. That morning, in defiance of the sneak attack, a huge American flag was lowered from the top of the injured building, while firemen and troops saluted. Great Old Glory stretched down nearly three stories.

While the crises of September 11 had unfolded before a national audience transfixed in front of their televisions, a live drama took place in Boston. Heavily armed police SWAT teams stormed into the Westin and Copley Place Hotels and the Park Inn in Newton, a Boston suburb. The police raid apprehended three men who were seen being hustled out of one of the buildings by the SWAT teams. The *Boston Globe* reported that the men had been arrested because of a credit card that tied them to the hijackers, presumably one which they had used to purchase airline tickets.

Incredible as it may seem now months after that ineffable morning of horror, several other terror hijackings appear in fact to have been averted. As reported in the *Fort Worth Star-Telegram* on September 21, 2001, the FBI also suspected that terrorists had been on American Flight 43, which had left Newark bound for LAX at 8:10 A.M. Responding to the grounding edict by the FAA, Flight 43 landed that morning at Cincinnati's airport at 10:23 A.M. Another flight that was headed from Newark to San Antonio, Texas, was also grounded on September 11 at St. Louis, Missouri. Later that day, two passengers aboard an Amtrak train from San Antonio to Fort Worth were arrested. They had been on the plane bound for San Antonio. Ayub Ali Khan and Mohamed Jaweed Azmath were taken into custody for allegedly carrying box cutters, hair dye, and between $5,000 and $10,000 in cash. The *Star-Telegram* disclosed on September 21 that both men were carrying false passports and one of them was using an assumed name. Moreover, for seven years previously they had both been living in Jersey City, New Jersey, across the river from the World Trade Center! They were, according to the September 14 *Star-Telegram*, originally picked up during a "routine drug search" on their train, the Texas Eagle. Their arrest was the first substantial break in the FBI investigation into the case, which bore the name Operation Penttbom, for the bombing of the Twin Towers and the Pentagon.

Atta and the other Muslim suicide commandos of September 11 would be looked on with the same mixture of awe and legend among many of their faith as the other suicide bombers of the *jihad*, those sent by Hamas and Hizbollah with bombs strapped to their chests in attacks on Israel. They would take their place in the hagiography of the *jihad* like the kamikaze flyers had taken on a special place in the mythology of Japan, where their spirits were enshrined in Tokyo's Yasukuni Shrine, dedicated to those who had died in battle for their country. The Japanese considered their suicide pilots as the *gyokusai*, the "broken gems," according to the *Book of the Northern Chi*, written during the time of the brief Chi Dynasty (550–77 C.E.). The book stated that "men of strength prefer to become gems to break into myriad fragments rather than to become roof tiles to live our their lives in idleness."[22] The same spirit of self-sacrifice was found throughout the Japanese Code of the Warrior, Bushido, which animated the samurai of Japan and was called upon again when the monarchy took control of the country in the Meiji Restoration of 1868, after Japan had been governed for centuries by the shoguns, or military leaders. In 1882, Emperor Meiji wrote in his Rescript to the men of the Imperial Japanese Army and Navy, "with a single heart fulfill your essential duty of loyalty, and bear in mind that duty is weightier than a mountain while death is lighter than a feather."[23] However, bin Laden and those in Hamas, Islamic *Jihad*, and Hizbollah who brought religious young men into special camps to indoctrinate them into becoming human bombs did not see the distinction that the spirit of Bushido inspired Japanese soldiers to offer up their lives while at war with the forces of the enemy, not in attacks on innocent men, women, and children going about their daily lives in peace.

During a year that President George Bush, Congress, and media pundits were debating the construction of an antimissile defense system against countries like North Korea and the Peoples' Republic of China, bin Laden's terrorists had struck the United States with terrible simplicity. They had commandeered four civilian jet passenger aircraft whose fuel tanks were loaded to near capacity for nonstop trips from the East Coast to the West. With devilish ease, they had transformed them into flying incendiary bombs, hurling them into the World Trade Center and the Pentagon. The Boeing 757, which was the airplane used on the attacks on the Pentagon (Flight 77) and the one that crashed near Shanksville, Pennsylvania (Flight 93), is powered by Rolls-Royce and Pratt and Whitney engines.* There are three planes in the Boeing 757 family, the 200 series, the 200-Freighter series, and the 300 series. Each has a maximum fuel capacity of over 10,000 gallons. Flight 77 and Flight 93

---

*For security reasons, more detailed information is not given here. This general information given is taken from Web pages of the Boeing Corporation.

were both from the 757–200 class. There are four members of the Boeing 767 family, the series 200, 300, 300-Freighter, and 400ER. Each one has a maximum fuel capacity of over 20,000 gallons. The Boeing 767 jets use a medley of General Electric engines, along with the Rolls-Royce and Pratt and Whitney of the smaller 757. The 767s on Flights 175 and 11 were from the Boeing 767–200 category.

Next to nuclear bombs, the most devastating weapon in the American or Russian arsenal is the "fuel air bomb," or fuel air explosive. A fuel air explosive, according to the Human Rights Watch report on the Internet for February 2000, was used by the Russians against the Islamic extremists in Chechnya. According to the Human Rights Watch, a fuel air bomb, "in its destructive capacity, . . . is comparable to low yield nuclear munitions." The fuel air bomb was first developed by the United States during the Vietnam War. According to Human Rights Watch, the bomb "consists of a container of fuel and two separate explosive charges. After the munition is dropped or fired, the first explosive charge bursts open the container at a predetermined height and disperses the fuel in a cloud that mixes with atmospheric oxygen (the size of the cloud varies with the size of the munition). The cloud of fuel flows around objects and into structures. The second charge then detonates the cloud, creating a massive blast wave." This is the sort of weapon made from skyjacked American jet planes that Osama bin Laden used against innocent American civilians on September 11, 2001. The effect on those in the Twin Towers and the Pentagon can only be imagined; to go into further detail would only make worse our grief and those of their survivors. It is no wonder that the rescue workers who went into the wreckage of the World Trade Center called the ruins "The Pit." It must have reminded them of a pit in Hell.

For days thereafter, the plume of smoke and fire marked the scene of the disaster in New York. A photograph from a satellite showed the cauldron from high up in the air, as the wind bore the smoky debris north over Long Island. The black spume looked like the cloud that must have hung over the German city of Dresden after the Americans and British had bombed it. Wrote David Irving in his *Destruction of Dresden*, "in Dresden, the arrival of dawn was hardly noticed: the city was still obscured by the three mile high column of yellow-brown smoke and fumes that characterised the aftermath of a fire storm."[24] Yet, almost miraculously untouched, the island near New York where the Statue of Liberty stands was undimmed by the doomsday cloud. The green area where the statue stands on Liberty Island, directly opposite the ruins of the World Trade Center, was as clear in the photograph as on an untroubled day. Perhaps it was a symbol for all Americans to cling to in this hour of trouble.

In the devastating aftermath of bin Laden's sneak attack, it was obvious to all that something had gone horribly wrong with the intelligence-gathering of the country. Despite the billions of dollars spent on our Intelligence community, a terrible tragedy had taken place without any warning. Aside from a generalized alert some months ago, when American ships were warned to leave Middle Eastern ports like Aden, where the USS *Cole* had been bombed, and our installations were put on heightened alert, we were taken totally by surprise.

The revelation that three of the skyjackers had also been enrolled at schools run by our Department of Defense came as a shocking revelation. According to the *Philadelphia Inquirer* for September 17, Mohammed Atta had attended the International Officers' School at Maxwell Air Force Base, Abdulaziz Alomari the Aerospace Medical School at Brooks Air Force Base in Texas, and Saeed al-Ghamdi had gone to the Defense Language Institute in Monterey, California. Atta had earned his place in infamy by being on the American Airlines Flight 11, which destroyed the north tower of the World Trade Center; Alomari was with him. Al-Ghamdi was on board United Airlines Flight 175, which had destroyed the south tower.

It would be interesting to know what type of background check was used by defense intelligence when these three candidates applied for admission to these Pentagon-run schools. The Defense Language Institute at the Presidio in Monterey, where al-Ghamdi studied at some period before his suicide flight, is officially known as the Defense Language Institute Foreign Language Center (DLIFLC). Its mission statement on the Internet states that it "conducts full-time foreign language resident training, exercising technical control of nonresident foreign language training in the Defense Foreign Language Program. The DLIFLC provides foreign language services to DOD [Department of Defense], government agencies, and foreign governments." Atta was listed as having attended the International Officers School (IOS), whose Internet mission statement states that the purpose of the school is to "educate and support international officers and their families and to manage international programs enabling [the U.S. Air Force] Air University to accomplish US security assistance objectives, support USAF international involvement, and build lasting military relationships." Those who attend the school, which is attached to the Air University, receive a student handbook, the text of which is on a Web page linked to the IOS. The introduction to the handbook reads in part, "This *International Officer Handbook* helps you prepare for your visit to the United States. It gives you information about your course of instruction while at International Officer School (IOS) and during your follow-on professional education. We have also included a section to help you better understand some of the cultural differences you are likely to find [in the United States]." In the handbook, a paragraph notes that "your ITO [International Travel Order] is the most important document to have in your possession. This is produced by official US representatives in the Security Assistance Office (SAO) in your country and is the official document for controlling all your training and entitlements while you are in the US."

Abdulaziz Alomari had been listed in the *Philadelphia Inquirer* as having attended the Aerospace Medical School, more properly the USAF School of Medicine. The primary Web page of the Aerospace Medical School says it is "the center for aeromedical education, training and consultation in direct support of USAF, DOD, and international aerospace operations. Provides peacetime and contingency support in hyperbarics, human performance, clinical and dental investigations, expeditionary medical support, and aeromedical evacuation." However, when I tried to access the Web links for the mission statement of the school or "requirements for international applicants desiring training," my computer received this notice: "Forbidden: your client is not allowed to access the requested object," apparently a warning put through by the school to my Internet service provider (ISP).

Although I am no expert on the subject, wouldn't it be elementary to thoroughly screen the foreign nationals who attend these schools before they come to study with "the best and the brightest" in our armed forces? Were these hijackers members of the armed forces of Arab countries friendly to the United States, like Saudi Arabia, Egypt, or Jordan? If a thorough background check in their countries had been undertaken by the U.S. Security Assistance Office, why were links not uncovered with extremist movements like the Islamic *Jihad*, the Muslim Brotherhood or, indeed, al-Qaeda?

Second, two of the three killers were already on a federal government "watch list" for potentially dangerous alien nationals. These were Khalid al-Midhar and Nawaf al-Hamzi, who were aboard American Airlines Flight 77. According to *Time* magazine for September 24, 2001, the CIA had tentative information linking both to al-Qaeda itself as early as the end of January 1999. In January 2000, al-Midhar was captured on videotape talking to some of the suspects who participated in the attack on the *Cole* in October 2000. In July 2001, they were actually in New York City, where they list their address on immigration documents as the "Marriott in New York City."[25] There are ten Marriott-run hotels in New York, including one at Three World Trade Center. A friend of mine attended a science fiction convention there year ago; she told me there was a wonderful view of the Twin Towers behind the hotel. It was a great place for the conspirators to stay to plan their mission. Yet it was not until August 23 that the CIA informed the FBI and the INS of their presence in the country, after which the FBI and the INS put them on a watch list. But it was too late: They had already gone to ground.

Of course, the value of such watch lists has been questioned in the past. Omar Abdul Rahman, "the blind shaikh," who played a major part in the previous attack on the WTC in February 1993, had been on a State Department watch list when he entered the United States from the Sudan, which was already controlled by the extremist imam Turabi. Rahman had already been implicated by the Egyptian government of President Hosni Mubarak in the killing of President Anwar Sadat in 1983. Rahman is currently serving a life sentence in a U.S. prison for his role in the first attack on the World Trade Center.

Not only was our intelligence community, among the hardest workers for our national security, found wanting in the events of September 11, but the security situation at our nation's airports was also revealed to be in dangerous shape. At Orly Airport in Paris, travelers are met by officers of the Gendermerie Nationale, the national police, armed with submachine guns and attack dogs. In Rome, the airport is watched by members of Italy's national police, the *Carabinieri*. Upon arrival at American airports, on the contrary, air passengers are greeted by "rent-a-cops" who are often paid only the minimum wage. Alan Bernstein, the chief operating officer of the large Wackenhut Security Corporation, told *Time* magazine that before bin Laden's attacks "the [airline] industry looked at security as a necessary evil that ate into profits."[26]

Argenbright is one of the country's foremost purveyors in the airport security industry. Among the airports that Argenbright was under contract to supply security to were Logan International Airport in Boston, from which Flights 11 and 175 took to the air, and also Dulles, from which Flight 77 began its deadly journey. In October 2000 Argenbright pleaded guilty to having hired untrained employees to work as security at Philadelphia International Airport from 1995–98. Some of these rent-a-cops had criminal records! Argenbright was fined $1.5 million. The news story received wide circulation among air industry publications. Airwise News on-line, for Friday, September 28, 2001, ran a similar story, which had first been reported on April 19, 2000. Airwise quoted U.S. Attorney Michael R. Stiles as saying, "Argenbright Holdings Ltd. and three former employees faced felony charges related to inadequate training, testing, and background checks of employees who staffed the airport security check points." The company provided "security and other services at more than 54 U.S. airports and 26 European airports." In an undated Internet piece accessed on September 20, 2001, CTSinc.net had written a "success story" about Argenbright's use of information technology in handling its growing business. The "success story" said, in part, "imagine if your company had to provide around the clock personnel, facility security, access control, personnel security checks, traffic and parking control and guard against fire, theft, sabotage, and safety hazards. Any organization would have a hard time handling those responsibilities while keeping a focus on their core business. That's why a number of companies call the facility services division of Argenbright Holdings Ltd. AHL's business is outsourcing security solutions." The CTSinc.net page also declared, "with the confidence that AHL has in CTSinc.net, the partners will soon be working together toward the next goal: providing a platform for future network infrastructure so that AHL can achieve their ultimate goal of providing the best security outsourcing solutions possible for their customers." Whether these development plans have been put "on hold" by the events of September 11, 2001, is unknown.

Argenbright apparently has no Web page of its own. However, information on the company was available through the Web page of the American Society for Industrial Security, especially its on-line Security Industry Buyers Guide. Argenbright is located in Atlanta, Georgia, and, according to the American Society for Industrial Security, the chairman and co-chief executive is Frank A. Argenbright Jr. Established in 1979, Argenbright's primary business "provides access control and security services, shuttle bus services, staffing services and background checks for corporations, office buildings, hospitals, universities, and retail facilities." However, in a few months, Argenbright will be without a major customer. CBS Radio News announced the night of October 4, 2001, that Philadelphia International Airport would terminate its contract for security services with Argenbright.

On-board the planes, security is not much better. An employee of an American airline once explained to me how easy it is to break into the cockpit of an American jet aircraft. After years of fighting terrorists, apparently only Israel had—at least until September 2001—addressed the vital question of the safety of the pilot and crew in the cockpit. El Al, the national airline of Israel, is the only airline that has "hardened" cockpits to protect the pilot and his coworkers from the sort of on-board attack that Atta and his comrades mounted on the American aircraft on the morning of September 11. Only once has an El Al jet been skyjacked; that was back in 1968. Apparently, El Al also uses armed sky marshals on its planes to discourage such attacks. In the wake of the disaster on September 11, this was a possible security development being discussed for the future on board American planes.

In the wake of "Black Tuesday," it is tragic to think of all the warnings that had been made in the previous years by the CIA, FBI, and private sources about threats to security at American airports and airlines. Unfortunately, the warnings appear to have been largely ignored. While in July 2001 the United States was celebrating the 225th anniversary of the signing of the Declaration of Independence, Israel was celebrating another anniversary. July 4, 2001, marked the twenty-fifth anniversary of "Operation Thunderbolt," the successful Israeli rescue of the hostages at Entebbe airport in Uganda. Given the lax security on American jets and at airports, the real surprise is not bin Laden's terror attack, but that such carnage did not take place many years sooner!

With seeming impunity, bin Laden's murder gang had gone about planning for its attack on America. From overseas, they had carefully infiltrated the country like the sleeper agents that they were. (In the language of intelligence, "a sleeper" is an agent who burrows himself into the society of the country which is his target and waits for orders to go into action.)

Several of the terrorists settled in Florida. An automobile driver's license was issued to Waleed al-Shehri in that state on May 4, 2001. (Spellings of the terrorists vary with every account consulted; the spellings used here are those used by *Time* magazine in its September 24, 2001, issue. Causes of the mispellings vary: one reason is that the terrorists may have mispelled the names themselves. The name on al-Shehri's Florida license is given as "Walfed M. Al Shehri." A possible cause for this being examined in the ongoing investigation is that they were not their real names, and therefore were easy to misspell.) The address for al-Shehri was given as an apartment complex in Hollywood, Florida. Hamza al-Ghamdi got his driver's license on June 26, 2001, in Florida. Again, the name on the license is different: "Hamzah Saleh Al

Ghamdi." Al-Ghamdi also apparently lived at an apartment, this one in Delray Beach, where Ahmed al-Haznawi and Ahmed al-Nawi also found lodgings. Nawaf al-Hamzi visited them in Delray. Throughout their whole operational time in the United States these men followed the spy's classic training: "Hide in plain sight." They paid in cash or by credit cards. There was no bouncing of checks reported due to insufficient funds to cover their purchases. And, although they were considered to be unfriendly neighbors, none had any brushes with the law, other than a motor vehicle incident described below. The conspirators followed the advice that al-Qaeda had given them in the terror handbook, *Military Studies in the* Jihad *against the Tyrant*: Blend in with the people you are going to kill until the time comes to kill.

Bin Laden's secret agents, for in truth that is what they were, followed the "hide in plain sight" scenario to its fullest. They dressed expensively and never seemed short of cash. Those who went to Florida were noted for their Gucci shoes and their expensive silk pants. They had a passion for late night action, hard drinking, and strip clubs, ignoring the injunctions of the Quran.

One of them, Atta, had an inordinate fondness for drinking vodka and orange juice. He and the others drank and at least once partied too hardy. On April 26, Atta was cited by the police in Broward County, Florida, on the peninsula's Atlantic coast, for not having a valid driver's license when he was stopped. According to some sources, he was stopped for being suspected of driving under the influence of alcohol. He was pulled over to appear in court but never did. A warrant for his arrest was issued but, since the lawmen had no reason to suspect him of anything more serious, no real effort was made to find him.

As the investigation deepened, it became apparent to the FBI that Atta was the paymaster of the operation in the United States. We know from the use of an ATM in Portland, Maine, that he had access to either a checking or a savings account in a bank. During the year before the terror strike, investigators believe that Atta received some $200,000 for use in his plans. The funds seem to have originated from a Saudi Arabian named Mustafa Ahmed, who appears to be the overall financial supervisor for bin Laden's al-Qaeda network. Ahmed operated from the United Arab Emirates (UAE) on the Persian Gulf. Ahmed left the UAE the day of the terror attack, and disappeared into Peshawar, Pakistan, the traditional gateway into Afghanistan. On September 4, Atta, al-Shehri, and al-Shehihi are believed to have sent money totaling $15,000 to Ahmed in the UAE. Investigators believe that this was the amount left over from the financing of the operation. However, there is more to this than making Atta seem like a trusted bookkeeper. In *jihad* suicide operations, the leaders promise to take care of the families of those who sacrifice themselves for the cause. The money could have been wired back to Ahmed to help take care of the families of Atta, al-Shehri, and al-Shehihi after their deaths.

The UAE is composed of seven federated shaikhdoms, Abu Dhabi, Ajman, Dubai, Ras al-Khaimah, Sharjah, and Umm al-Qaiwain. A main source of revenue for the UAE has always been the richly colored postage stamps they print for the international stamp-collecting market. The export of oil and natural gas deposits once dominated the economy, but in recent years Dubai has become a center of international banking. According to investigators, the somewhat lax banking laws in Dubai has made the UAE the financial focus of the investigation into the bombing. The *Philadelphia Inquirer* in its October 2 edition quoted a U.S. intelligence analyst as saying, "the UAE has been for a long time a good place for bin Laden to collect money, because the banking laws are very weak." The same article stated two of bin Laden's sisters wired money to him in the UAE, most likely as a transit point to reach him in his hideout in Afghanistan.

The FBI is using the same tactic against the terrorists that it used against the New York Mafia chieftain John Gotti, whom former New York Mayor Rudolph Giuliani fought when he was a federal prosecutor in the 1980s: "Follow the money." The UAE and Afganistan are both included on the Web site of transnationale.org, an Internet resource for the study of "offshore banking havens," locations whose opaque banking laws make them popular with the international narcotics trade, which, as mentioned earlier, has developed strong ties to international terrorism. According to the 1999 International Narcotics Control Strategy Report, which is specifically addressed toward money laundering and financial crimes, "drug traffickers, terrorists, money launderers, tax evaders and other criminals have found OFCs [offshore financial centers] a particularly inviting venue in which to conduct and conceal their nefarious activities." The UAE and Afghanistan are both on the transnationale.org map as havens for OFC activities.

Many factors go into making an OFC, and information on these is available in the 1999 State Department Narcotics Report as well as the transnationale.org site, both accessible through the Internet. Also on the Internet, offshore banking is touted as a way for its customers to enjoy freedom from outrageous taxation in their home countries. One Internet site is a clearinghouse for the creation of banking accounts in OFCs. One of its links assures prospective customers that "the banking laws in Eastern Europe, Luxembourg, the Middle East and several other tax havens do ensure high levels of privacy and security. Open your offshore banking account TODAY!"

The use of the United Arab Emirates as a way to fund bin Laden's terrorists is helped by a traditional Islamic system of banking known as *hawala*, where huge sums of money can be transferred with only trust as a guarantee between the two parties. A *hawala* (Hindi for "in trust") trader in one Islamic country is handed cash and simply e-mails another banker in a second Islamic country "who hands over the amount to the recipient there, leaving no paper or electronic money trails." In an October 2 *Philadelphia Inquirer* article titled "Emirates Officials Tell of Money Sent by Three Hijackers," Sudarsan Raghavan wrote, "*Hawala* traders in the UAE and Pakistan are major partners, often shifting thousands of dollars from the Afghan border town of Peshawar [in Pakistan] to Dubai." India's Rediff On The Net Web site tells how *hawala* bankers operating in India, according to the Indian government's Vohra Commission report, had helped to finance a web of drug smuggling, weapon smuggling, and narcoterrorism in India. The Vohra Commission blames the Pakistani ISI, which also has been the main support of the Taliban, for backing the *hawala* system within India as a way to destabilize the country. With special relevance for Atta's case, the Vohra Commission report also claims that the ISI is behind the growth of the *hawala* system in the United Arab Emirates.

❈ ❈ ❈

Atta and his fellow conspirators had learned to fly in the usual way: They took lessons at a school. This may be the reason that most of them came to the state of Florida. Florida, because of its postcard-perfect climate, is popular with those who wish to get their flying license in the least amount of time. Hundreds of hours behind the wheel are necessary for flight certification and Florida, along with Arizona and California, lead the nation in the number of flight schools because the climate makes possible many days of good flying weather. Flight schools in these states are not only popular with American students, but also with foreign students who wish to log the hours they need to fly in their own countries, especially for those who wish to get the coveted position of a pilot for a major airline.

Thus Atta and al-Shehihi signed up at the Huffman Aviation school, located between Tampa and Fort Myers on the Florida Gulf Coast. More than two-thirds of the students at the Huffman School are from foreign countries. There they trained on Cessna propeller-driven planes like the Cessna Skyhawk. According to *Time* magazine for September 24, 2001, flight training in a Cessna 150 was "$55 an hour, 40% less than what you might pay in a big city," so the $10,000 price tag for their courses of instruction was a bargain.[27]

Atta and al-Shehihi seemed to be focused on logging the hours necessary for flying the large commercial jets. An average airline would require at least 1,000 flying hours (hours spent actually piloting a plane) before even considering an applicant for a commercial pilot position. But the two were obviously in a hurry. They decided to try the sophisticated 727 flight simulator, which is very similar to an actual jet cockpit, to hasten their preparation time for flying the big jets. At the SimCenter in Opa-Locka, Florida, they rented six hours of time on the flight simulator for $1,500. Clearly, money was no object. Henry George, who runs the Opa-Locka school, had been interviewed by the British *Electronic Telegraph* newspaper for its September 14 Internet edition. George spoke of the men's time on the 727 simulator, saying that it would have given them only limited experience in the 757s and 767s which they turned into flying bombs. Said George, "I suppose Atta had just enough training to keep the plane in the air—how to make turns and move it up and down." That, sadly, is all the training Atta seems to have wanted.

There is some confusion as to why al-Shehihi went to such trouble, however. In 1997, he had graduated from Embry-Riddle Aeronautical University in Daytona Beach, Florida, with a degree in aeronautical science and a commercial pilot's license. Embry-Riddle has two campuses in sunshine states: the one in Daytona Beach and the other in Prescott, Arizona. More than 20,000 students are enrolled in both campuses. Barnstorming pilot John Paul Riddle and entrepreneur T. Higbee Embry had founded the Embry-Riddle Company in December 1925 at Lunken Airport in Cincinnati, Ohio. According to CNN.com for September 14, 12 percent of the university's students come from foreign countries. Of these, South Korea is number one, while Saudi Arabia stands in second place. Perhaps, with the assignment in mind, al-Shehihi enrolled at Huffman to refresh his professional knowledge. Abdulaziz Alomari told his landlord in Florida's Vero Beach that he was already a pilot for the Royal Saudi airline (as with other claims and information about the killers, this is also certainly part of the ongoing investigation).

Yet he, too, took classes, but at the Flight Safety Academy in Vero Beach, which relies on students from the Saudi airlines. In fact, Flight Safety Academy has a regular contract with the Saudi airlines, as a story in the September 14 *Washington Post* detailed.

Tragically, Embry-Riddle has another link with the September 11 catastrophe. In a letter to alumni, the university noted, according to the same story in the *Washington Post*, that David M. Charlebois, a 1983 graduate, had been the first officer on American Airlines Flight 77, which crashed into the Pentagon.

Flight training was indeed the common thread that linked all the conspirators. As far back as 1996, Hani Hanjour, who would be on Flight 77, had studied at the CRM Airline Training Center in Scottsdale, Arizona. In 1999, he was issued his commercial pilot's license; his only given address was a post office box in Saudi Arabia. (Alomari gave his address on federal aviation forms as Jiddah, Saudi Arabia. As the FBI investigation unfolded, as reported in its press updates, some nine of the nineteen hijackers killed on the flights appeared to have ties to Saudi Arabia.) Hanjour lived with two of the other killers in an apartment complex in San Diego, California, for much of 2001. There, the three of them spent many hours, according to their neighbors, playing flight simulator video games.

As the investigation deepened, it was revealed that they had additional help in their flight training. The London *Daily Telegraph* edition for September 29, 2001, carried the story of the Algerian Lotfi Raissi, who had been arrested in London as part of an international dragnet. According to his indictment in London as reported in the *Daily Telegraph*, Raissi was an Algerian pilot who had accompanied the murderers to the United States to insure they "were capable and trained" to carry out their mission. Raissi's mission particularly seems to have been to see to the training of Hanjour, who is believed to have been the pilot of Flight 77. Raissi himself had tried to get an American commercial pilot's license in 1997, but was being sought by federal authorities for falsifying information on his application by not mentioning that he had had surgery on his knee that could disqualify him in flight school and had been convicted for theft. He had, according to Mrs. Arvinder Sambei, who represented the United States at Raissi's London indictment, looked into some of the American flight schools that the skyjackers later attended. A videotape showed that he had traveled with Hanjour to Arizona. Mrs. Sambei said that Raissi had made "frequent trips to the US" between June 10 and July 11, 2001. At the time of his arrest, Raissi was beginning to study for a commercial flying license in England. American authorities are seeking to have the Algerian deported from the United Kingdom to the United States. Raissi's name was actually found in a car at Dulles Airport belonging to one of the terrorists who hijacked Flight 77 and flew it into the Pentagon. A stronger statement was made about Raissi by Arvinda Sambir, also representing the United States in London. Sambir declared that Raissi "was a lead instructor for four of the pilots responsible for the hijacking."

The investigation reached across the globe, on a scale that surpassed the hunt for Carlos the Jackal in the 1970s. South Africa's *Sunday Times* reported in its September 30 edition that the South African authorities had been given a list of some 200 names of possible accomplices to the September 11 terror conspiracy. (South Africa had previously helped the United States track down a suspected terrorist: Tanzanian national Khalfan Mohamed, who had sought sanctuary there after the bombings of the U.S. embassies in Tanzania and Kenya.)

Meanwhile, the police dragnet continued in England, bringing to mind the manhunt for Jack the Ripper in Victorian London. The London *Daily Telegraph* reported on September 30 that an Arab man, age thirty-six, had been held at Gatwick Airport under the Prevention of Unknown Terrorism Act as he tried to leave for the United States. Eleven of the nineteen terrorists on the death flights are believed to have entered the United States from the United Kingdom.

Indeed by September 30, 2001, it was possible to retrace much of the path that Atta, Hanjour, and the other conspirators had followed to reach the United States. Police raided a house in the Wood Green area of north London that belonged to another Algerian, Mustapha Labsi, who was believed to have trained the murderers in al-Qaeda camps in Afghanistan. Labsi apparently accompanied them to London, where he provided additional organizational support for their mission. In intelligence language, he appears to have been the "control officer" who had overall charge of their mission, at least as far as the United Kingdom is concerned. Determining whether there was another "control officer" active in the United States is something that must be high on the agenda of the FBI. Labsi has another link with bin Laden's terrorist activities in the United States: He is believed to have been involved in the planned millennium bombing plot to attack Seattle and Los Angeles. This was the plot for which a third Algerian, Ahmed Ressam, was apprehended. Scotland Yard's Special Branch also expressed interest in a British Muslim Omar Sheikh, who was suspected of also providing training for the skyjackers.

Before England, it appears that Germany was a primary stop for the terrorists. All over Europe and North America, they appear to have benefitted from the network of support groups outlined in earlier chapters which had been set up by Iran and other sponsors of terrorism. The September 30 edition of the *German Express* featured an article in which arrests had been made in Cologne of three men with ties to the "Kalifatsstaat" Islamic organization, which apparently had previously sent volunteers to fight in Afghanistan. Bin Laden went so far as to claim the German Muslims as brothers "with us in the fight against the Great Satan [the United States]."* The three suspects had weapons, ammunition, and plane tickets in their apartment when the police raided it.

Earlier, as *Time* magazine reported on September 24, attention had focused on Hamburg, Germany, as a spot where the terrorists had congregated. Unlike in Florida, here the terrorists had not tried to adapt to the ways of the country in which they were staying. They lived together in an apartment, where men were seen arriving in traditional Islamic garb, not the Western clothing worn by Atta, al-Shehihi, and the others in the United States. The men were heard reciting Muslim prayers and attracted the notice of neighbors by playing Arabic music loudly. Contrary reports described them as being exceptionally quiet tenants, even when they had a large number of visitors. Many of these would leave their shoes off outside as if they were going into a mosque during their visits, which were usually at night. Monika van Minden, a neighbor across the street, recalled that "the regular group was about seven people; other times there were more." They would sit in a circle on the floor praying. When they realized that she was watching, they installed blinds on the window.[28] As befitting good agents, they spoke German with hardly an accent, as another neighbor, Christian Schulz, said.

According to the *Philadelphia Inquirer* for September 14, 2001, Atta and al-Shehihi had been enrolled in the Technical Institute of Hamburg-Harburg. University president Christian Needess said Atta had been enrolled in the institute since 1992, a perennial student such as those who attend every Euro-

---

*All translations from German are by the author.

pean university. However, Atta earned the German equivalent of a Master's degree in construction engineering, a student said. (This is the same degree, coincidentally, that bin Laden had received in Saudi Arabia.) This would have given Atta the information on where to fly a plane into a building to cause the most destruction. It now appears, according to the investigation, that Hamburg was the first European stop for the conspirators, and from Hamburg they traveled to England. Atta and al-Shehihi disappeared suddenly from their Hamburg apartment in February 2001. From there, either individually or in small groups, the conspirators seem to have made their way to the United States. Possibly, some of the men, like Ahmed Ressam, the millennial bomber, came into the United State from Canada. Part of the global investigation focused on the possibility cells of supporters existed among the Muslim community in Canada. Much concern also would center on London, which appeared to be the point from which many of the plotters made their way to the United States.

It appeared as the investigation continued that any break might come from the personal fallibility of those involved. Even in a conspiracy as grandiose as that of September 11, there are members who should have remained in bed. One of these may have been Khalid S. S. al-Draibi. On September 11, he was seen speeding away from Dulles International Airport twelve hours after the suicide missions. Not only was he speeding, but he was driving with a flat tire! When police apprehended him in Manassas Park, Virginia, according to the *New York Times* for September 13, they found aviation manuals in his car. As in other instances of the investigation, he was quickly arrested on an immigration charge so the authorities could detain him for an investigation. In al-Draibi's case, the charge was lying about his citizenship: He was not an American citizen as he first claimed, but Saudi Arabian. Al-Draibi had taken flight lessons in Alabama and Kansas. Moreover, he was using a post office box in Anniston, Virginia, near an army depot where chemical weapons are stored. The FBI also circulated a list with the hijackers' names, including al-Draibi's, to banks, requesting them to advise the bureau if there was any activity in specific accounts. Radio talk show host Don Imus noted on air that some of the credit cards issued to the dead hijackers were still being used after September 11. Since most credit cards are issued by banks, this may be why the FBI issued the advisory to the banks.

One of the most intriguing figures that day was not on one of the planes, nor was he even arrested with incriminating material. He was Zacarias Moussaoui, who had been born in Morocco. As the investigation continued, the Moroccan became an "international man of mystery." Moussaoui had recently retired after a carreer with a French telecommunications company. He had been arrested by immigration authorities in Minnesota on charges of attempting to enter the United States illegally, according to the September 18 *Washington Post*. Moussaoui seemed to be the sort of man who is the intelligence services' dream. If he was supposed to be the twentieth hijacker, he certainly did not have much stealth. Moussaoui had attracted attention by asking to use a flight simulator similar to the one Atta had utilized in Florida. However, he only had a student pilot license. In May 2001, he had been enrolled in the Airman Flight School in Norman, Oklahoma, but left the program in a funk when trainers questioned his skills! Dale Davis, the director of operations, told the *Washington Post* that students at his school were usually able to fly a small plane after about thirty-eight hours in the sky. Moussaoui, however, could not master this skill even after he had spent some fifty-seven hours flying. Before trying out for a small plane license, he had requested training for a professional license to fly a commercial jet, but apparently lacked the $20,000 to pay for the course. Davis said, "I told him I had some concerns about his flying." However, after Memorial Day weekend, Moussaoui never returned.

This frustrated, would-be pilot did leave a paper trail behind him. The Airman Flight School had sponsored him on a visa from London, where he had e-mailed them for information about their flight program. When he arrived in the United States, however, he was using a French, not an English, passport. The odyssey of Mr. Moussaoui was further detailed in the September 21 *New York Times*. After the September 11 attack the London police raided an apartment he had lived in; however, he had left London nine months earlier. In fact, he had enrolled in the Oklahoma flight school on February 26. Meanwhile, the French counterterrorists, most likely the DST, had already compiled a dossier on him. In fact, *USA Today* reported on October 23 he had been on their watch list since 1999. He was known to have traveled to Pakistan and Afghanistan. Moussaoui may also have ventured to Chechnya and Kosovo. While apparently lacking the "right stuff" to fly a plane, Moussaoui apparently had made all the trips of a modern *mujahidin*. He may have been a brave fighter, a *bon barodour*, as the French Foreign Legion called a good warrior when he fought in Morocco and Algeria, but he did not have the makings of a man of intrigue. He attracted undue attention to himself in Paris by fanatically calling on other Muslims in the middle 1990s to "come and work for *jihad!*" Moussaoui was being held in jail in New York City for immigration violations. Charges were later brought against him in federal court in Virginia for the September 11 attacks, and his trial is scheduled to begin in August 2002.

In a related development, CBS Radio News broadcast on October 27 that some of those arrested in the dragnet that bagged Moussaoui had been detained because right after the September 11 atrocity they had been overheard by U.S. intelligence sources giving "congratulatory phone calls." This is interesting because it shows that the FBI and other federal agencies were using the highest level of technology in the pursuit of the September plotters. For several years, there has been talk of Project Echelon, a SIGINT system which gives the National Security Agency and its allies in Great Britain, Canada, Australia, and New Zealand (the countries of the old UK–USA alliance of World War II) the ability to listen in on conversations using electronic media like faxes, computers, e-mails, telex, and telephones, according to the final report that was delivered to the European Union Parliament. Echelon uses what are called "dictionary" search engines or processors to pick up words or phrases that are "red-flagged," perhaps words like "bomb," "terrorist," and "Osama bin Laden." The words are picked up from electronic communications by satellites. Once Echelon "hears" such words, it can allegedly begin recording the communication going on, including the names and telephone numbers of those communicating. PCWorld.com reported on March 19, 2000, that Echelon also contains "voiceprint technology to search telephone communications for targeted speakers," which may be how the federal government knew Osama bin Laden had called his stepmother before the September attack. The obvious question is, if Echelon exists, and a report by the European Union Parliament claimed that it did, how could it not have given warning about the attacks on September 11? IDG News Service carried a story on September 13 in which correspondent Rick Perera revealed that the National Security Agency had begun using Echelon some three weeks before the attack because, as the German newspaper *Allegemeine Zeitung* said, there were warnings that Arab terrorists would start to use hijacked airplanes as weapons against "prominent symbols of American and Israeli culture." American, Israeli, British, and German intelligence agencies, *Allegemeine Zeitung* claimed, had all received the warnings. Israeli intelligence, presumably meaning the Mossad, had been afraid that terrorists would seize an airplane and mount a Twin Towers–style attack in Tel Aviv or other Israeli cities. If *Allegemeine Zeitung*'s report is true, and Echelon failed, then one wonders about the funds being spent on such high technology programs in the first place. The final report on the Echelon system was given to the European Union Parliament on September 5, 2001—a week before the attacks on the World Trade Center and the Pentagon.

Zacarias Moussaoui highlighted again the London connection in the case. Interest centered around the so-called Shaikh Abu Hamza al-Masri, who the London *Daily Telegraph* on September 13 said heads the North London Central Mosque. Born Mustafa Kemal, he claimed to have lost both his hands and an eye fighting the Russians in Afghanistan. Through his Supporters of Shariah clique, he openly supported Islamic extremism. Al-Hamza's sermons were so incendiary that several British mosques took the extraordinary step of banning him from preaching in them. He entered England from Yemen, which has asked London repeatedly to extradite him there for accusations of terrorism. London has refused. His son and stepson are both imprisoned in Yemen for terrorist offenses. Three suspected terrorists, Moussaoui, Jerome Courtellier, and Djamel Beghal, are linked to his mosque. The latter two are under arrest in Paris for conspiring to blow up the American embassy there.

Since September 11, London Metropolitan Police, the respected Scotland Yard, has kept a uniformed presence outside al-Hamza's mosque. However, it is certain that the plainclothes Special Branch as well as MI-5 are monitoring events and visitors as well. Should al-Hamza be considered a threat, he could swiftly be picked up under the Prevention of Terrorism Act, which had been widely used as a weapon against the Irish Republican Army.

Another man of interest to the Special Branch is Abu Yahya, a firebrand who has received military training in a camp in Afghanistan near the Hindu Kush mountains. Yahya claims to have sent British Muslims to join the fight with the Taliban. Another radical is Shaikh Omar Bakri Mohamed, head of the al-Muhajiroun group. After the attack on the Twin Towers and the Pentagon, he gloated, "I am very happy today." Like the Taliban and al-Qaeda, Shaikh Omar is dedicated to creating a worldwide Islamic state, the *Daily Telegraph* said on October 19, 2000. The shaikh has the closest ties of any of the militants to bin Laden: The *Telegraph* pinpointed him as "a spokesman for the Islamic Political Front, the military wing of which was founded by Osama bin Laden." A sulphurous video features another performance by bin

Laden himself. Called "The State of the *Ummah*," or "Islamic community," it has sold widely from the Maktaba al-Ansaar bookstore in Birmingham, England. One scene pictures bin Laden saying that every Muslim man should be "a soldier for the glory of Allah." Bin Laden denounced all Americans and Jews as "monkeys and pigs." The bookstore was raided in 2000 under the Prevention of Terrorism Act, but no charges were filed.

All the Islamic militants mentioned here have sent Muslims from England off to the training camps in Afghanistan, where they undergo a rigorous regimen of preparation. The ability of the new recruits, according to American and British intelligence sources, is assessed with regard to carrying out terrorist activities. Some are considered not suited to the actual missions; these are used to provide support for the active terrorists, like procuring fake passports or creating safe houses. Others who have the motivation and strength are trained and are covertly sent back to their own countries or others to be ready for assignments. While it is known that Yahya and the others, like Shaikh Abu Hamza, have sent British Muslims to the camps, it is not known if they have been involved in planning or supporting terror missions. If investigation reveals that they have, their apprehension would be speedy.

While many Muslim nations were reticent or openly opposed to American action against Afghanistan, Turkey came out enthusiastically in support of the United States, long her ally in NATO. Reuters News Service carried a dispatch on October 2 concerning Turkey's response. An American delegation had visited Turkey on the same jaunt which had taken them to visit the exiled king of Afghanistan, Zahir Shah, in Rome. The United States viewed the eighty-three-year-old king as the only figure that all Afghans could rally around. As mentioned previously, Turkey has played a key role in the containment of Saddam Hussein in Iraq, pemitting American and British planes to fly from its air base at Incirlik. As long ago as the Cuban missile crisis, Turkey played an important part in the Cold War against the Soviet Union. (When President Kennedy got Soviet Premier Nikita Khrushchev to remove the Soviet missiles from Cuba, he later ordered the removal of out-of-date American Jupiter missiles from Turkey as part of a diplomatic compromise.) Turkey, which had already shared intelligence information with the United States, offered complete base facilities, as well as its armed forces, if the need arose in the war against the Taliban and al-Qaeda.

Meanwhile, as the investigation into the terrorist attacks stretched around the world, the United States began to marshal its forces for a possible invasion of Afghanistan. (Although the invasion did indeed occur, in the first weeks after the attacks such a move was not set in stone.) CBS Radio News on the morning of September 30 announced there were already 28,000 to 30,000 American troops standing off the Persian Gulf awaiting orders. Apparently however, American Special Forces and those of the British, particularly the British 22nd SAS (Special Air Service) Regiment, had already been active on the ground in Afghanistan. Whether they were pioneering routes for a possible ground attack, hunting for bin Laden, or both, was a closely guarded secret in Washington and London. There were reports in the *London Sunday Times* for September 30 of the SAS involved in a fight with Taliban soldiers on the outskirts of Kabul. The *Times* revealed that the SAS was active in Afghanistan, although first reports of the regiment's activity in the country had leaked out a week or more earlier, but were denied by the British Defense Ministry. Along with their military objectives, British soldiers were also hunting for any possible sites where bin Laden might be working on chemical, biological, or nuclear weapons. The possibility of joint cooperation among the special forces of the United Kingdom, United States, and France presented no problem. In fact, the special operations forces of all three had meshed well with each other during the 1991 Gulf War.

It is here where the elimination of the anti-Taliban chieftan Ahmed Shah Massoud fits into the picture. The operation on September 11 had been planned by bin Laden for at least a year, if not more, American intelligence analysts believe. Any such attack would almost certainly invite an armed response in Afghanistan, and Massoud was the likely linchpin of any such strategy. Hence, killing the "Lion of the Panjshir" would have been made a high priority by al-Qaeda, especially since Massoud stated his opposition to al-Qaeda in the *Newsweek* interview only two weeks before his death on September 9. The SAS appeared to have already linked up with Massoud's United Front, but its role in any anti–bin Laden campaign or move against the Taliban would be much reduced without Massoud's leadership. While Pakistan's president Gen. Pervez Musharraf offered bases in Pakistan to be used in military operations in Afghanistan, the fact that the first place that the SAS was sighted was up north with Massoud's force makes possible the suggestion that they had come from a former Russian base in Tajikistan.

Such early penetration missions have always been the strong point of the SAS in its operations. Before the British sent troops to drive the Argentinians off the Falkland Islands on May 21, 1982, during the Falklands War, teams of the SAS and its comrades in the Royal Navy's SBS (Special Boat Service) had already been in the Falklands since May 1 preparing invasion routes.[29] Indeed, it is possible that the SAS had been with the United Front for some time, perhaps even before the attack on the United States. Massoud apparently had close ties to the British, as journalist Michael Griffin revealed in *Reaping the Whirlwind: The Taliban Movement in Afghanistan*. From 1970 to 1976, the SAS fought in the Sultanate of Oman, next to Aden, to keep that principality from falling into the hands of a Communist insurgency. Based entirely on speculation, it would be wholly in keeping with British strategy if the SAS had been providing covert assistance to Massoud for some time before his assassination.

As ground operations were opened in Afghanistan and the grim recovery effort continued at the Pentagon and the World Trade Center, Americans began the doleful ritual of burying their dead. Memorial services, both public and private, blossomed like the red poppies which grew over the sad battlefields of World War I. The *New York Post* for September 16, 2001, devoted its entire final page to a photograph showing grieving firemen carrying a coffin bearing the body of Father Mychal Judge, the courageous firemen's chaplain who was killed ministering to a wounded fireman at the WTC. Services were held for the pilots of the doomed aircraft. Obituaries began to appear in newspapers across the country for those killed when the murderers hurled the planes into their targets.

All over the country, flags stood at half-mast outside federal government and other public buildings as a silent tribute to all of America's fallen, a number then estimated at 3,100. Sunday, September 23, was named the National Day of Mourning. Thousands gathered in Yankee Stadium in New York City during the day and later that night at Liberty State Park at Jersey City, New Jersey. The ceremony at Yankee Stadium was called "A Prayer for America," and fittingly began with the "Battle Hymn of the Republic," written by Julia Ward Howe.

The message of the assembly was delivered in the Lincolnesque voice of actor James Earl Jones. "Our nation is a symbol," Jones intoned, "of liberty, equality, opportunity, and democracy. This attack was an attempt to undermine these four pillars of our civic faith. It has failed. Our spirit is stronger than ever." The guest of honor was New York's mayor, Rudy Giuliani, who had shown throughout the whole ordeal the same fortitude that he had displayed when he was the Mafia-busting federal district attorney in New York City in the 1980s. It was fitting that the co-host of the affair, television personality Oprah Winfrey, had characterized Giuliani as "America's mayor." In a very real sense, Giuliani was. He was a born and raised New Yorker, the grandson of Italian immigrants. In 1986, Giuliani had been interviewed by *Time* magazine while he was fortifying himself for the epic battle against Mafia chieftain John Gotti. In the February 10, 1986, issue, he had summed up his philosophy of the gangsters he was fighting: "For purposes of ethics and law, we elevate human beings by holding them responsible. Ultimately, you diminish human responsibility and importance when you say 'Oh, you're really not responsible for what you did. Your parents are responsible for it, or your neighborhood is responsible for it, or society is responsible for it.' In fact, if you harm another human being, you're responsible for that."[30] What Giuliani had said about mobsters in 1986, the entire nation was feeling toward the butchers of September 11. No matter what the cause, or what the grievance, killing innocent people is murder, pure and simple. Yet, as with the people of London during the Blitz, the spirit of New Yorkers remained indomitable. As British Prime Minister Winston Churchill had spoken for all Londoners then, Mayor Giuliani spoke for all New Yorkers now. At the funeral for Fire Commissioner William M. Feehan on September 15, 2001, the mayor declared, "we're going to get through this. The Fire Department is going to get through it. The city is going to get through it."[31]

Yet as Giuliani would have been the first to say, the day belonged to those who died, and those who mourned for them. Alexander and Maureen Santora were at Yankee Stadium. After forty years with the New York City Fire Department, Alexander had retired as the deputy chief. They were there to mourn their son Christopher and his companions at Engine Company 54—all of them missing in the cavernous wreckage of the Twin Towers. Susan Brady, a nurse in Montclair, New Jersey, had been planning to marry her fiance, Gavin Cushing, on October 26, after which they planned to honeymoon in Greece. Now she was at a commemorative service for Gavin, missing and almost certainly dead. Susan said, "I'm planning a memorial service, but I was supposed to be planning a wedding."

The resonating themes of fortitude and shared sorrow also animated those who came to the evening's observance at Liberty State Park, an ideal place for the reaffirmation of what makes us Americans.[32] It stands on the Jersey City shore, within site of both the Statue of Liberty on Liberty Island and Ellis Island. It was past the Statue of Liberty and through the immigration center at Ellis Island that millions of the ancestors of today's Americans found their pathway to America and the very freedoms that Osama bin Laden and his Taliban allies would attempt to stamp out. (As a security measure, both Liberty Island and Ellis Island were temporarily closed in the wake of the attack by bin Laden's henchmen.) It is appropriate that the main highway through the park is called Freedom Way. The program was highlighted by two indomitable symbols of the American Spirit: Paralyzed actor Christoper Reeve proved that he was still "Superman" in his heart when he recited a speech, and blind singer Ray Charles led the crowd in "America the Beautiful." One attendee, Miguel Hernandez, had lost his daughter, Rosa Julia Gonzalez, at the age of twenty-four. Rosa had worked for the New York Port Authority. Looking over the thousands who had come to share his sorrow, Miguel remarked "it's beautiful, the response. It's beautiful that America unites." Karen Willoughby had not lost anybody to the terrorists' attack, but she had come that night to Liberty State Park to share her solidarity with those who had. Karen summed up the feelings of those who gathered with her that beautiful Sunday: "I wanted to continue on and not hide. That's what these terrorists want us to do, change our way of living, and we can't let them do that."

All over the country Americans of all colors and creeds joined together in mourning and commemorating our dead brothers and sisters. Some gave vent to the fires of hate. Sikhs, because they wear turbans and were thus assumed to be sympathetic to the terrorists, and Arabs were harassed throughout the country. One Sikh was shot to death in Arizona at a gas station where he worked because of his turban. Unfortunately, we shall always have among us those who turn to hate to fill the void in their lives. Yet these were, and always will be a minority. The vast majority, Christian, Jew, Sikh, Buddhist, Muslim, atheist, and others, joined together in the symbol of a nation in grief: crowds gathered together in public places holding lit candles, sharing their sorrow and at the same time their strength. If Osama bin Laden had launched his attack with the intention of terrorizing us, demoralizing us, and turning us against each other, he had proven himself wrong. In what he thought would be the hour of his greatest triumph, he suffered his worst defeat. The Boys Choir of Harlem had expressed the spirit of the entire American people when they sang the venerable civil rights hymn "We Shall

Overcome" at the ceremony that day at Yankee Stadium. The haunting, uniting chorus rang out as it had during the days of Martin Luther King Jr., and the crowd joined hands to sing: "Oh deep in my heart, / I do believe, / We shall overcome some day."

Another memorial to the victims would take place on Sunday, October 28, 2001. There in New York City, Mayor Rudy Giuliani, joined 9,200 mourners at Ground Zero, the site of the Twin Towers. For many of them, it was the first visit to the place where so many of their loved ones had gone on September 11, to work and later to save those who worked there, yet from which they had never returned. Of the gathering, Naomi Roman, whose sister-in-law had worked for Sandler, O'Neill & Partners, who had offices in one of the towers, told the *New York Times*, "it was something that thousands of people were waiting for. So many people got together. . . . It was a unity." "Amazing Grace" was sung. For only the second time since September 11, the recovery effort came to a halt. The first time had been for a moment of silence several weeks earlier. Firemen took mementos from the family members and placed them at the remains of the World Trade Center.

10

"Payback Is a Bitch"

In the weeks after the atrocity of September 11, as the nation mourned, American military forces slowly moved to the Arabian Sea to prepare the way for a counterattack against Osama bin Laden and the forces of terrorism. President Bush called it Operation Enduring Freedom; most Americans would probably call it Operation Enduring Vengeance. As always, it was the navy's aircraft carrier battle groups that put to sea first. The USS *Enterprise* and *Carl Vinson* were the first on the scene in the Arabian Sea. After ensuring that America was safe, the *Enterprise* had steamed majestically with its escort warships over 6,000 miles to carry the war to the enemy. During the week of September 30 the USS *Kitty Hawk* steamed west from its home port in Yokosuka, Japan, to add its firepower to Operation Enduring Freedom. There is no more powerful projection of military might than a U.S. Navy aircraft carrier battle group: Each is a fleet unto itself, more powerful than any fleet that ever sailed the seven seas. On October 17, CBS News reported that the good ship *Theodore Roosevelt* and its battle group had arrived at the seat of war in the Arabian Sea. The *Theodore Roosevelt* battle group contains the carrier, along with fourteen other warships, frigates, destroyers, and even submarines. It is somehow fitting that the carrier bearing the name of Thomas Burnett's favorite president joined the battle to avenge him. The United States Navy has twelve aircraft carrier battle groups, thus some 30 percent of the entire navy's carrier power was being deployed against Afghanistan. The main power that the carriers deliver is from the F-14 and F-18 jets that line their flight decks. The F-18 Hornet entered active service in 1980, according to the home page of McDonnell-Douglas, the company that makes the fighter. A Super Hornet began to fly in 1995. Hornets can do more than bomb targets: During the Gulf War in 1991 Hornets shot down two Iraqi Air Force MiG-21 jets in air-to-air combat. Grumman's F-14 Tomcat entered the navy to replace the F-4 Phantom, the main navy fighter of the Vietnam War; the F-14D made its debut with the fleet in 1990. All Tomcats and Hornets can fire missiles as well as drop bombs. The F-14, for example, can fire a volley of Sidewinder, Phoenix, or Sparrow missiles.

The Los Angeles class submarines with the battle group are hunter-killer subs, the great white sharks of the fleet. They are named for the first sub in the class, the USS *Los Angeles*, which was launched on April 6, 1974, at Newport News, Virginia. The Los Angeles class can fire torpedoes at hostile submarines as well as launch torpedoes and Harpoon missiles at enemy surface ships. The Los Angeles class of submarine can also fire Tomahawk cruise missiles, the TLAM, or "Tomahawk Land Attack Missile." The purpose of the destroyers with the aircraft carrier battle group is to protect the carrier. If necessary, a destroyer captain will risk his ship and the lives of himself and his crew to protect the carrier. When Japanese Vice Adm. Kurita Takeo attacked the American landing fleet in the Battle of Leyte Gulf on the morning of October 25, 1944, the destroyers sacrificed themselves to defend the American fleet. The destroyer USS *Hoel* made a direct attack on the battleship *Yamato*, the strongest battleship ever built, to attack it with torpedoes. The *Hoel* vanished under the counterbattery fire of the giant warship.[1]

As in World War II, Great Britain stood with the United States in this new conflict with tyranny. British missile-firing submarines, the *Triumph* and *Trafalgar*, would take part in any offensive against the Taliban. Sailing nearby off the coast of Oman, the British Royal Navy had put to sea the largest armada to fly the Union Jack since the Falklands War of 1982. The flagship was the aircraft carrier HMS *Illustrious*.

As always when a navy battle group takes to sea, it carries with it the sea soldiers of the U.S. Marines. Each battle group sails with its contingent of marines, as has every navy deployment since the founding of the marines and the navy in 1775 in Philadelphia during the American Revolution. The U.S. Navy now is basically divided into a "two-ocean" force, the Atlantic and Pacific Fleets. The marines on the carriers came from both of these, since the *Carl Vinson* and the *Kitty Hawk* are considered part of the Pacific Fleet based in Yokosuka, Japan, while the *Theodore Roosevelt* and the *Enterprise* are from the Atlantic Fleet. The usual number of Marines with the carrier battle groups could have been easily augmented by reinforcements for land combat purposes in Afghanistan into a marine expeditionary complement. In the Pacific Fleet, the USS *Pelelieu* already had on board her the U.S. Marines' 15th Marine Expeditionary Unit, whose Web page explains that the 15th is "special operations capable." (When I attempted to find more information about the *Pelilieu* for this work, the ship's Web page had the notice "many links deactivated until further notice," apparently as a wartime security measure. As of October 5, further updates on the *Kitty Hawk*'s Web page were also suspended.) As the American build-up continued, the number of troops, apparently army and marines, grew to some 28,000. As CBS anchorman Dan Rather put it, if the time came "to put boots on the ground," the men were ready and waiting.

As mentioned previously, British and American special forces had already been on the ground in Afghanistan for some time. And apparently, they owned it. After the first skirmish with the SAS, the Taliban troops showed no inclination to cross swords with the troops of the British and American special operations warriors. U.S. Navy SEALs would be attached to the carrier groups, while the Army Special Forces would be the 5th Special Forces Group, which is attached to the U.S. Army Central Command, with headquarters at MacDill Air Force Base in Florida. However, for Operation Enduring Freedom, the Prince Sultan base in Saudi Arabia is the forward command center for the Central Command. The 5th Special Forces has been the army's "weapon of choice" for special operations in the Middle East since it took part in some of the Operation Bright Star training exercises in Egypt in the 1980s.[2] The most elusive of America's special forces is of course the Delta Force, which is technically part of the army special forces troops. Delta Force worked with the British SAS during the Gulf War in the great hunt for the Iraqi SCUD missiles in the desert. Along with the rest of the army's special forces, the headquarters of Delta Force is at Fort Bragg, North Carolina. With the other special operations troops, Delta Force would avail itself of the services of the elite 160th Special Operations Aviation Regiment, whose mission is to get the special forces into—and out of—their area of operations.[3]

If the Delta Force is the army's newest counterterror force, then the U.S. Army 75th Rangers is considered the oldest. This unit was established on January 25, 1974, at Fort Stewart in Georgia.[4] However, the 75th Rangers trace their spiritual lineage to the famed rangers formed by Robert Rogers in the French and Indian War.

The main mission of the special forces would have been gathering information on prospective targets for any further offensive operations, such as air bases, radar installations, troop garrisons, command and control centers, and communication networks. The North Atlantic Treaty Organization (NATO), which directed the war in Kosovo against the Serbian dictator Slobodan Milosevic, calls these last three objectives, command, control, and communications, the C3. Information gathered, they would have sent back their "intel," their intelligence, through special "short burst" radio transmissions, where knowledge would be packaged into electronic chunks and sent off into the ether to be picked up by those at the receiving end. The dual purpose of short burst transmissions is that the special forces team would be on the air less time, frustrating efforts to pinpoint their location by enemy formations, and providing less opportunity for enemy SIGINT (signals intelligence) to attempt to pick up their messages. The special forces would also have access to satellite communications through the PRC-5 communications unit, which can encode its transmissions to frustrate enemy eavesdropping. Intelligence information would be passed to the rear in the "reach back" system to the Prince Sultan base, or even as far back as MacDill Air Force Base in Florida or American intelligence agencies. Gradually, the map of Afghanistan would fill up with possible targets, and information would be fed into computers to program the bombs and missiles that would carry the war to the Taliban and bin Laden in the first air campaign move of any military operation.

The special operations troops would seek to avoid—rather than to engage—the Taliban militia. Small in number until ground support began, the special forces would be exceedingly vulnerable to attack by larger Talib groups. Of course, if needed, they could call in jet fighter support from the aircraft carriers deployed offshore. At this early stage, the mission of the special forces was to gather intelligence information and most likely make contact with anti-Taliban forces in northern Afghanistan, the fighters of the United Front. A third goal would almost certainly have been to try to track down Osama bin Laden himself. Both American and British special forces are equipped with linguists trained in the languages they would encounter in Afghanistan, such as Pashtu, Dari, and Urdu. An unnamed Pentagon official interviewed in the October 8, 2001, issue of *Time* magazine said the goal of the forces was to help "get bin Laden—not to get bogged down."[5]

At the same time the special forces troops were gathering intelligence information on the ground, U-2 spy planes would be criss-crossing high overhead, out of range of most ground-to-air missiles. The U-2 began its spy missions in 1956, the year of the Soviet invasion of Hungary, at the height of the Cold War. The plane proved its mettle during the Cuban missile crisis. The U-2 was eclipsed for several years by the SR-71 Blackbird, although it appears that, for cost reasons, the Blackbird has been retired from active service. The Blackbird could fly at more than Mach 3, three and a half times faster than the speed of sound. The U-2's speed is given as .64 Mach, or roughly 475 miles per hour. The actual "ceilings," the altitudes at which these reconnaissance aircraft can fly, are classified, but available information imparts to the U-2 an altitude ceiling of above 70,000 feet, while the SR-71 is supposed to have a ceiling of above 100,000 feet. To keep up with changing times, a modern version of the U-2, the U-2S, took to the skies in 1994. Whether the supersecret Aurora spy plane, if indeed it exists, is being used over Afghanistan would be a closely guarded secret.

Below the manned spy planes, American forces would employ the Predator, the first unmanned American reconnaissance aircraft. According to Air Force News.com, the Predator began operations in 1996 over Bosnia in the Balkans. Although the Predator was the result of interservice cooperation and development, the air force, specifically the 11th Reconnaissance Squadron based at Nellis Air Force Base in Nevada, was charged with the operation of the Predator drone. Without worrying about a crew coming under hostile fire, the Predator can fly into the most heated areas of combat. Indeed, several Predators were shot down over Bosnia and later Kosovo. Imagery from the Predator is sent from the drone to its ground control, and from there by satellite to video units throughout the theater of operations. Commanders are able to see the Predator's images in about two seconds after the drone's sensors collect them, in what the armed forces call "near real-time."

Far above the Predator and even the spy planes, information about Afghanistan is collected by American spy satellites. On September 18, the British BBC News carried a story that American spy satellites had been reprogrammed to focus on Afghanistan in the hunt for bin Laden. "Retasking" satellites is no easy job, but the gravity of the attack on America ensured that it would be done. Two types of satellites were put on bin Laden's track. The first type are SIGINT satellites, whose task would be to intercept radio and mobile phone conversations from the region. In the past, bin Laden had been known to utilize high technology in his communications with his associates, including satellite communications and cellular phones. The

Trumpet communications satellite is especially gifted when it comes to hunting transmissions by cellular phones. The *Onion/Magnum* satellites are workhorses for many kinds of telecommunications intelligence. Although it is believed bin Laden has forsaken such means for fear of American electronic surveillance, there is always the hope that he or one of his senior commanders might "slip up," and do so—with fatal consequences.

The second type of spy satellite being used is one that transmits images back to the ground with a resolution that is less than a foot, meaning that the satellite can pick up objects smaller than the license plate of an automobile. The *KH Keyhole 11* satellite gives resolution in fact of five to six inches, although much of the information concerning the KH series, as reported in an MSNBC.com story on August 8, 1998, is classified "beyond top secret." The *Keyhole* satellites make possible the creation on the ground at the National Imagery and Mapping Agency (NIMA) actual three-dimensional animated views of what the satellite has broadcast; these are referred to as "envisions." These virtual reality animations, like those transmitted by the Predator, were first used in the fighting in Bosnia. There are five of these billion dollar "birds" overhead on any given day. The government is also requesting help from private companies to enlist their orbital "birds" in the war against terrorism. Using civilian satellites will enable the armed forces to keep a space eye on Afghanistan even when the orbits of the government intelligence satellites take them off to different areas. A new development in the government spy satellites and the private versions, like the *Orbview 4*, which was developed by the Orbital Imaging Corporation, is that they are "hyperspectral," they "allow . . . us to 'see' objects in colors that are normally beyond our range of vision."[6] These satellites will enable American forces to distinguish areas camouflaged by al-Qaeda and other hostile forces from the natural ground covering around them.

While American forces were gathering in the Arabian Sea like circling birds of prey, President Bush embarked on a campaign of building an international coalition against the Taliban and Osama bin Laden's terrorists, similar to the one his father cobbled together during the campaign against Saddam Hussein in the Persian Gulf War ten years earlier. Support came quickly from America's traditional allies, Great Britain, the democracies of Western Europe, and Japan. Soon after the attack on the World Trade Center and the Pentagon, for the first time in its history NATO invoked Article 5 of the NATO charter, which states that an attack on any one member nation constitutes an attack on them all. (The NATO charter was adopted on April 4, 1979.) Not quoted before in the present crisis, Article 5 minces no words: "The Parties [signatory countries] agree that an armed attack against one or more of them in Europe or North America shall be considered an attack against them all."

As America's traditional allies fell in beside her, great care was taken to reassure the countries in the Islamic world, in *Dar al-Islam*, like Egypt, Saudi Arabia, and Jordan, that the coming campaign would not be directed against them or against Islam. It would be nothing less than a war on terrorism, whoever the terrorists were and wherever they were hiding. For the Islamic countries that favored us, the coming situation would be like riding a tiger. In the Middle East, there are always, it seems, two rival governments, the one in the palace and the mob on the streets. Popular fervor was very pro–bin Laden in some countries. When news of the terror attacks on September 11 reached the West Bank, Palestinians responded by firing their AK-47s in the air for joy and riding around in trucks with their flag above their heads. Yassir Arafat, attempting to put a more moderate Palestinian face before the world, was photographed giving a pint of blood for the rescue effort. Police of the Palestinian Authority threatened television networks that they would not be responsible for their workers' safety if they filmed the pro–bin Laden street theater going on in the Gaza Strip or Hebron. Arafat was still very much interested in negotiations with the United States and Israel to cement his Palestinian state; the personal crusade of Osama bin Laden and al-Qaeda only made his position more difficult. In the weeks after September 11, the new situation had already exacted its price. The Bush administration had announced that before the attacks it was going to come out officially in favor of a Palestinian state, but the atrocities of September 11 made it decide to postpone the announcement indefinitely.

In Saudi Arabia, it was a foregone conclusion that if the United States went to war the Prince Sultan base complex would be the forward headquarters for the Central Command's offensive operations. The Saudi government in Riyadh was quick in issuing a condemnation of Black Tuesday. Almost immediately, the government information office had issued a statement posted on the official Saudi Arabian Information Resource page on the Internet. It read in part, "the Kingdom of Saudi Arabia strongly condemns such acts which contravene all religious values and concepts of civilized behavior and extends sincere condolences to the families of the victims, U.S.

President George W. Bush, and the U.S. people in general." The Saudi government confined its opposition to requesting that the American bases in the country not be used for any offensive actions against "Islamic countries." It was considered a given fact however that Prince Sultan air base would be used at least for the big "C3," command, control, and communications. The use of American bases in Saudi Arabia for assaults on Afghanistan remained problematic anyhow from the viewpoint of simple geography: Afghanistan was a much longer flight from the Arabian peninsula than Iraq had been in 1991. Nevertheless, the Saudi royal family still feared the brand of Wahabi extremism that Ibn Saud had unleashed to found his dynasty. Many of the September 11 terrorists had come from Saudi Arabia originally. In the Asir province on the coast of the Red Sea, one of the dominant tribes is that of the al-Shehihi; Marwan al-Shehihi and Waleed al-Shehri likely came from it, since their last names are derivations of the name of the tribe. Of interest is the fact that Asir province is the only region in the Muslim world west of Iraq where there is a large Shi'ite, as opposed to the dominant Sunni, Muslim population. To be on the safe side, the Saudi royal family left the country.[7] Saudi King Fahd as well as the Defense Minister Prince Sultan were reported as having flown with a convoy of eleven planes to Switzerland.

Pakistan was the country most on the front line in the worsening situation. Long before the attack on America, Afghan refugees were threatening to overwhelm Pakistan. In a dispatch dated November 10, 2000, the BBC News Online carried a story telling of thousands of refugees fleeing fighting between the United Front and the Taliban and the worst drought in memory in the country. At that time, the government in Islamabad estimated there were already some 3 million Afghans living in refugee camps in Pakistan. At that point, authorities in the North-West Frontier province, which Pakistan inherited from the British Empire when Pakistan and India became independent in 1947, wanted to close the border with Afghanistan to stem the tide. Pakistani Interior Ministry spokesman Hasan Raza Pasha told the BBC that "there has to be an end to the influx of foreigners, Afghan refugees, into Pakistan. It has created all sorts of problems, not just economic."

The main problem for Pakistan was security, not the economy. The presence of all the Afghan refuges had created an enormous "fifth column" of pro–bin Laden sympathizers who, it was feared, could raise havoc in the streets if General Musharraf openly came out in favor of American military action against the Taliban and al-Qaeda. BBC correspondents bore this out in a report on the night of October 7 from Quetta, a North-West Frontier province city not far from the Afghan border. A reporter told how bin Laden's face was everywhere in the city, on T-shirts and in shop windows. There was even a brand of nougat candy called "Osama," with his visage on the package. The company making it said it was hard on the outside, but soft on the inside. "Osama" had become the second most popular name in Pakistan. Furthermore, the Pakistani policy of supporting the Taliban had come back to haunt it. The Taliban had spun off its own fundamentalist movement in Pakistan, the Jehadi, or holy war movement, which was a direct threat to the stability of the country. Three weeks before September 11, Pakistan's Interior Minister Moinuddin Haider had warned against the danger of the Jehadis, in an interview with the *Pakistan Observer* on August 27, 2001. Some 300 Jehadis had been arrested in a recent police sweep for anti-government activity.

Nevertheless, American concern for Pakistan's stability took second place to the wrath that convulsed the United States after September 11. Soon after the attacks on America, Secretary of State Colin Powell made a speech in which he openly expressed the Bush administration's expectation that Pakistan would side with the United States against bin Laden and the Taliban. In the atmosphere after the attack on September 11, there was no more middle ground. After a day or two of agonizing, Musharraf closed the border with Afghanistan, effectively sealing the country. But the 3 million refugees remained a considerable threat to his government. He also quietly gave permission for the United States to use Pakistani air space in any attack on Afghanistan, which was essential in mounting any air assault from the carriers waiting in the Arabian Sea.

With the evolution of the crisis, Secretary of State Powell, as well as President Bush, reached new prominence. A career U.S. Army officer, Powell had had a central role in helping the elder President Bush formulate the strategy for the Persian Gulf War in 1991. As chairman of the Joint Chiefs of Staff, he had proven the most effective in that post since Gen. George C. Marshall in World War II. With care, Powell not only helped to deploy the American forces of the coalition united against Saddam Hussein but, like Marshall before him, had helped to oversee the growth of the coalition's armed forces into a united juggernaut which would roll over the Iraqi army. Now, facing war for the second time in a decade, this time as the Secretary of State, Powell was able to show the mastery of armed force—and the will to use it—which had characterized his earlier performance as the nation's chief soldier.

As with Powell, the crisis would be a testing time for other senior officials in the president's administration. Vice President Dick Cheney came into his own in the new Bush administration as well. As secretary of defense during the administration of the new president's father, he had critical experience in coalition warfare, expertise he could call on again. The fact that he was dealing with a part of the world with which he was most intimate in the Gulf War made his choice as current vice president a fortuitous one. Secretary of Defense Donald Rumsfeld was hardly a novice in the affairs of state, in the game of nations. He had been secretary of defense before, from 1975 to 1977, during the painful readjustment in the American armed forces after the Vietnam War. From 1973 to 1974, he had served as U.S. ambassador to NATO, gaining experience with the European armed forces that might join the United States in any invasion of Afghanistan.

Condoleezza Rice, the national security advisor, was the only one on the main Bush team not to have any previous experience at a senior policy-making level, military or political. However, she had been Thomas and Barbara Stephenson Senior Fellow at the Hoover Institution at California's Stanford University, where she had previously been the university provost. The Hoover Institution had been for over half a century one of the leading academic study centers for international relations in the United States. After a first Hoover appointment, Rice had gone to Washington during the Reagan administration to work on strategic nuclear planning at the office of the Joint Chiefs of Staff. Since her appointment as the national security advisor, she has gained respect for the collegial way in which she oversees the vital decision-making process at the top. Rice has a reputation for listening to all the points of view, and then leading the policy-makers to a decision. For Rice, America's own Afghan War would be her opportunity to make her mark on history.

As the noose tightened around Afghanistan, Pakistan became the center of allied efforts to reassure the Musharraf government of Pakistan's importance to the alliance. Visitors like Great Britain's Tony Blair came to Islamabad, attempting to shore up Musharraf against the feared pro-Taliban backlash in the streets. The official PakNews.com Internet site recorded on October 6 how Prime Minister Blair had visited the Islamic nation and expressed a hope that normal relations between the two countries, which had been disrupted after the October 1999 military coup that had brought Musharraf to power, would resume. Later, Blair flew on to consult with the Indian government of Prime Minister Atal Bihari Vajpayee in New Delhi.

Two days earlier Italian Foreign Minister Margherita Boniver had also paid a courtesy call on President Musharraf.

October 4 found U.S. Secretary of Defense Donald Rumsfeld on a whirlwind tour of state in the Middle East and the Persian Gulf in the continuing campaign to shore up support for any American counteroffensive. On that day, the secretary met with Sultan Qaboos of Oman, who was on an annual day-long retreat at a tent city built to recall when his ancestors lived in tents in the desert. (Like kings Hussein and Abdullah of Jordan, Qaboos also had been a student at the British military academy at Sandhurst.) As of the beginning of October, there were some 20,000 British troops on the ground in Oman. Prime Minister Blair visited them on his trip to the Middle East. Although in Oman for desert training (there has been a continual British presence in Oman since the Communist insurgency in the 1970s), they would be ready for any rapid deployment to Afghanistan. Later that same day, Rumsfeld continued on to visit with President Hosni Mubarak of Egypt. His tour would also encompass visits to Uzbekistan and Saudi Arabia. An article on the Department of Defense Internet news page, DefenseLink.com, for that day emphasized that the fight America was waging was against terrorism, not Muslim countries or the religion of Islam. Said Rumsfeld, "our discussion really ran to the fact that these people are trained to be terrorists and they then go about that activity. It's important for us to understand that that is totally apart from any faith."

An example of Afghan ferocity in battle occurred while the bombing of their country continued in October 2001. On October 26, the *New York Times* reported, Abdul Haq, a legendary *mujahidin* like Ahmed Shah Massoud, had been executed by the Taliban. He had entered Afghanistan from Pakistan in a hope of inciting an anti-Taliban revolt among the tribes. However, the Taliban found out he was in the country and, in spite of a daring intervention by U.S. Apache helicopters, Haq had been captured and put to death. Haq, who was a member of the Ahmadzai tribe, may have been betrayed as a result of a family feud within the tribe. However, he also had his faithful supporters. While the killing of Haq was a cause of rejoicing among the *talibs*, it remained to be seen if the murder might not have negative repercussions for the Taliban in the end. The same tribal principal of *badal*, revenge, which the Taliban may have used to catch Haq could boomerang against them. Should his supporters rally against the regime, it could prove bad for the *talibs*, because the tribe occupies a strategic area near the border with Pakistan.

Although Sunni Muslim, the Pashtuns of Afghanistan and the North-West Frontier shared in the same legacy of religious zealotry as the Shi'tes of Iran, since all arose from the same combination of Islam and central Asian ancestry. While not suicide warriors like the *basiji* whom Khomeini created in Iran, the Pashtuns had their religious warriors, the *ghazis*. In the 1897 British campaign to regain the Khyber Pass, Pashtun *ghazis* would even charge cavalry while on foot, armed with their *tulwars*, or sabers. While serving with the Malakand Field Force in the 1897 expedition, Winston Churchill's life was almost cut short in a skirmish with a *ghazi*. Coincidentally, Churchill also was serving as a war correspondent on the campaign, for the London *Daily Telegraph*. He would describe the Pathans as "wild, rifle-armed clansmen."[8] In *My Early Life: A Roving Commission*, Churchill wrote of how he had he had seen a *ghazi* attack a wounded adjutant: "The leading tribesman rushed upon the prostrate figure and slashed it three or four times with his sword. I forgot everything else at this moment except a desire to kill this man."[9] Although Churchill fired his .455 caliber Webley revolver several times at the *ghazi*, the tribesman ducked behind a boulder without Churchill knowing if his bullets had found their mark. Lt. P. C. Elliot of the Corps of Guides, the elite unit on the North-West Frontier, described the attack of the *ghazis*: "Bands of *Ghazis*, worked up by their religious enthusiam, would charge our breastworks again and again, leaving their dead in scores after each repulse."[10] The Pashtuns were also urged on by their Muslim *mullahs* in their battles with the British "unbelievers." The whole uprising had been inspired by the preaching of a Pashtun *mullah* named Sadullah, the spiritual progenitor of the Ayatollah Khomeini and the Mullah Omar.

Returning to our present Afghan problem, in the weeks after the September outrage Islamabad served as the unofficial White House pipeline to the Taliban. American warnings were relayed to Islamabad and Pakistan's President Musharraf passed them on to Mullah Omar and the Taliban leaders in Afghanistan. Regardless of the alarms, Omar and the others remained defiant. The *mullah* proclaimed to the Afghans that "the Americans don't have the courage to come here." Musharraf was interviewed by the BBC and the news of the interview was carried on the Pakistan News Service's Web page, Paknew.com, on October 2, 2001. Musharraf said that he felt any chances of the Taliban handing over Osama bin Laden were remote. "It appears that the United States will take action in Afghanistan," the president stated, "and we have conveyed this to the Taliban." When the BBC Television correspondent asked him if he felt the days of the Taliban were numbered, President Musharraf responded, "it appears so."

As the campaign to build up support for any action grew apace, the Bush administration began to share the intelligence information it had that proved bin Laden and al-Qaeda were behind the terror strikes of Black Tuesday. The information was shared with foreign heads of state, who accepted it and did not quibble about the blame being assigned to Osama bin Laden. On October 3, U.S. ambassador to Pakistan Wendy Chamberlin briefed Musharraf. A Pakistani source familiar with the briefing told the Pakistani News Service that "Chamberlin provided some of the substantiated evidence to General Musharraf on the alleged involvement of Osama bin Laden in terrorist attacks on the World Trade Center and Pentagon."

Allies in Western Europe like British Prime Minister Tony Blair were unequivocal in their acceptance of the evidence provided by the American government. Russian premier Vladimir Putin also accepted the evidence, as did most other heads of state contacted by Washington. Speaking in Belgium on October 2, where he was to meet with officials of NATO, Putin said that the evidence was convincing to him and to the Russian intelligence services. Putin noted, however, that while bin Laden's complicity was unmistakable, they could not pinpoint the degree to which he was involved. Putin denounced international terrorism, calling it "a bacteria that adapt by living off their host body." Later, after meeting with Belgian prime minister Guy Verhofstat, Putin declared that "the effort will never work unless we unite the whole international community in a common front against terrorism." Undoubtedly, Putin was thinking of the Russian war against the Chechen separatists, in which Western governments had sometimes scolded Russia for lack of respect for human rights. However, more recent intelligence information has confirmed how closely the fighters in Chechnya, including their leader Shamyl Beshayev, are linked with bin Laden's al-Qaeda. While foreign governments became privy to the information, the American news media was not included in the initial release of data. While the press bristled at these restrictions, the Bush administration said it was not divulging information to the general press for security reasons, apparently for fear that it would be noticed by the terrorists themselves. Another factor is possibly more important than the information itself: Intelligence analysts can sometimes track down the source of a piece of given information, the "leak," and thus put at risk an important source of intelligence that would be valuable for future use.

Eventually, central proof of bin Laden's criminality came in a major address given by Prime Minister Blair to the British Parliament on Thursday, October 4, *Time* magazine reported in its October 15 issue. Accompanying his speech, Blair had at his disposal a British Government White Paper which had been prepared with the quiet help of the White House, the CIA, and British intelligence, notably MI-6, which deals with intelligence outside England (MI-5 deals with intelligence in the United Kingdom). The "MI" designation comes from the fact that both were originally part of British military intelligence. When British and American special forces were deployed on the ground in Afghanistan, it was stated that officers of both countries' intelligence services accompanied the special operations troops "in country."

The White Paper alleges that one of bin Laden's "close associates" (who goes unnamed) planned the operation on September 11. In the weeks prior to the attack, bin Laden's top chieftains were all warned to return to Afghanistan by September 10. Before September 11, bin Laden asserted he was planning a major strike against the United States. The London *Daily Telegraph* quoted part of the White Paper in its October 5 edition: "There is evidence of a very specific nature relating to the guilt of bin Laden that is too sensitive to release." The White Paper noted that bin Laden was able to carry out his terror strikes from within Afghanistan because of his close relationship with the Taliban, which gave him the freedom to do so in return for his financial support of the Taliban and its struggle against the opposition Northern Alliance. In the text of the address carried by the *New York Times* on October 5, the conclusion was clear:

> The attacks of the 11 September 2001 were planned and carried out by Al Qaeda, an organization whose head is Osama bin Laden. That organization has the will, and the resources, to execute further attacks of similar scale. Both the United States and its close allies are targets for such attacks. The attack could not have occurred without the alliance between the Taliban and Osama bin Laden, which allowed bin Laden to operate freely in Afghanistan, promoting, planning and executing terrorist activity.[11]

The *Daily Telegraph* dispatch did not disclose the actual sources of the White Paper's information, but it can be stated again that the White Paper was most likely another "joint production" of American and British intelligence agencies.

Another piece of evidence arrived in a somewhat amusing package. Two days before the atrocity, a Western intelligence (whose country of origin is currently unknown) intercepted a rare phone call from bin Laden himself. As NBC News related the story, bin Laden had made a call to his stepmother in Paris in which he boasted that "in two days, you're going to hear big news, and you're not going to hear from me for a while." Before the East African attacks, bin Laden had been using a satellite phone, and his communications had been intercepted by the National Security Agency according to confidential CIA sources. When this SIGINT coup was leaked, he stopped using such sophisticated communications. However, apparently his gloating over the coming attacks on the "Great Satan" overcame his caution. Another such slip may truly be his last. After a major strike, like that of the East African bombings in 1998, it has been bin Laden's standard practice to go to ground for a while to avoid retaliation. However, he barely made it to safety after the 1998 embassy attacks. Enraged by the slaughter, President Bill Clinton had signed an executive finding, as CBS News told the tale, authorizing the killing of the archterrorist. However, at the last minute, the president grew concerned about incurring U.S. casualties in such an operation. He therefore ordered the CIA to use "cut outs," or foreign nationals, in the attempt. The cut outs, perhaps Saudis, actually made an attack on bin Laden's fast-moving caravan in Afghanistan, but did not succeed in slaying him.

While Putin accepted the evidence against bin Laden during his NATO visit, even more importantly he dropped any remaining opposition to American bases in the republics of the former Soviet Union (FSU). A pivotal republic was Uzbekistan, whose premier, Islam Karimov, knew well the problem of terrorists in his country. After the meeting with Secretary of Defense Donald Rumsfeld, Karimov gave permission to use bases in Uzbekistan in any campaign against the Afghans. However, mindful of the need not to antagonize the Uzbeks who support the Taliban, Karimov said that the bases could not be used in a combat role, although this may change as the situation evolves. Soon after, the U.S. Air Force moved 1,000 men into the central Asian republic. The air force deployment was to put close to the theater of operations ground rescue teams in case any American flyers were downed in the air war that began on October 7. However, many of those airmen deployed to Uzbekistan would be there to provide security to the installations to defend against any guerrilla attacks by pro-Talib Uzbeks. Such security would probably be furnished by the U.S. Air Force's Special Operations Wings, the air force component of the U.S. special forces community, which would also put into the theater extra special forces if the need for them arose. All-around base defense would be the permanent mission for the Air Force Security Police, who proved their mettle in the Vietnam War. Later, it was disclosed that the 1,000 troops were soldiers of the U.S. 10th Mountain Division, the only American army division with specialization in mountain war. Such expertise would be of much value if a prolonged ground campaign in Afghanistan were mounted. Putting "boots on the ground," as Dan Rather put it on October 7, is the only way that the United States will ever really have a say in shaping the destiny of a post-Taliban Afghanistan, as the British learned in the Afghan Wars of 1839 and 1878.

The republic of Tajikistan was already opposing the Taliban; the Russians had been using base facilities there for years to support the Northern Alliance forces of Gen. Ahmed Shah Massoud. As a terrorist revenge for the support of the Alliance, an official of the Tajik Culture Ministry was shot and killed a few days before September 11 in an ambush. The Northern Alliance had nevertheless established a government in exile in Tajikistan. It was to a Russian military hospital that Massoud was flown after the attack upon him early in September. Even earlier, in the 1990s, Russian troops had used Tajikistan as a base to support the forces opposed to the Taliban. Russia still retains a strong military presence in Tajikistan, according to reports by Radio Free Europe. Some 13,000 Russian troops guard the border with Afghanistan and the 7,000-man 201st Motorized Infantry Division guards the capital of Dushanbe. Even before the attack on America, the Tajik border with Afghanistan had been sealed to keep the impoverished central Asian nation from being overwhelmed with Afghan refugees as well as to prevent infiltration by the Taliban.

The Peoples' Republic of China also joined the coalition against the Taliban and al-Qaeda, responding to the support and training that the Uighur separatists in Xinxiang Province had received from the militants. The *New York Times* reported on October 5 that the Chinese increased surveillance over the Uighur population and that in the week before October 1 seven Uighurs were executed for "disrupting social order." Wang Jianping, an associate fellow with the Institute of World Religion at Beijing's Chinese Academy of Social Sciences interviewed by *New York Times* reporter Craig S. Smith, said that among the Uighurs "there could be as few as 100, or as many as 500" who had received military training in the camps in Afghanistan. Trying to prevent a replay of the September 11 plane hijackings in the United States, Xinxiang Airways now carries two armed guards on flights between Xinxiang, Russia, Islamabad, Moscow, and destinations in central Asia. Airport security has also been increased throughout the country. Mainland China has sealed its small border with Afghanistan and sent troop reinforcements to the frontier.

As the campaign to isolate Afghanistan and cause the Taliban to hand over bin Laden increased in intensity, there were signs of some anxiety within the country. Some fissures appeared in the religious community which had always been the staunchest supporter of bin Laden's brand of Islamic fundamentalism. On September 21, the *Los Angeles Times* carried a story about a convention of the *mullahs* gathered to, in the words of reporter Tyler Marshal, encourage bin Laden to "leave Afghanistan voluntarily." The gathering of *mullahs* voiced their position in a recommendation to Mullah Mohammed Omar, the virtual dictator of Afghanistan. "This religious council," the document read, "recommends to the political leadership of Afghanistan that it encourage Osama bin Laden to leave Afghanistan voluntarily in good time for another destination." The Afghan clerics, motivated by love for their own country, did not want to see fellow Afghans die for the crime perpetrated by Osama bin Laden and his fellow criminals of al-Qaeda. However, Omar remained steadfast in his defense of bin Laden and refused to carry out the advice of the religious leaders of his own movement.

George Bush remained just as steadfast in his demands that the Taliban surrender bin Laden. In an address to Congress September 13, 2001, the president remained adamant. He declared to the Taliban leadership, "Deliver to United States authorities all of the leaders of al-Qaeda who hide in your land. The Taliban must act and act immediately. They will hand over the terrorists, or they will share in their fate." But earlier in that day, the Taliban had given Bush an answer already. In a television interview with the Voice of America, the Taliban's ambassador to Pakistan said, "we will neither surrender Osama bin Laden nor ask him to leave Afghanistan. As hosts, we can only ask him to consider to leave but cannot and will not tell him to leave." The case of Osama bin Laden represented perhaps the first time in history where an international criminal had not only purchased asylum in a country, but also apparently bought the entire country and its leadership as well.

In the early morning hours of Sunday, October 7, 2001, CBS Radio News correspondents in Kabul reported that a serious case of war jitters had taken hold of the city. While Kabul is the capital, the real stronghold of the

Taliban was the old royal capital of Kandahar to the south. Several airplanes had been spotted in the sky over Kabul, and they did not belong to the Taliban's miniscule air force. Whether these were American Predator drones or other British or American aircraft is not evident, but it was apparent to the Kabulis on the ground that their purpose was not friendly. The anti-aircraft batteries around the city opened up on the planes, but with no perceivable effect. The agitated people of the capital feared that an attack was imminent. They were not wrong.

At about 12:30 P.M. on the afternoon of October 7, regular programming was interrupted on American television by a special report. President Bush appeared on the screen in the Oval Office of the White House. As if to underscore the importance of the address he was to give, he sat at the same desk from which President Kennedy had addressed a similarly anxious American people at the time of the Cuban missile crisis. Bush announced, "on my orders, the United States military has begun strikes against al-Qaeda terrorist training camps and military installations of the Taliban regime in Afghanistan. These carefully targeted actions are designed to disrupt the use of Afghanistan as a terrorist base of operations and to attack the military capability of the Taliban regime." The president went on to say that "more than two weeks ago, I gave Taliban leaders a series of clear and specific demands: close terrorist training camps. Hand over leaders of the al-Qaeda network, and return all foreign nationals, including American citizens unjustly detained in [their] country. None of these demands were met, and now the Taliban will pay a price." At the same time, Bush reassured the country that the attack was not against the Afghan people and that air drops of vitally needed food and medicine would be another part of the campaign. Again the president made clear that the battle was with terrorism, not Islam. "The United States of America," he proclaimed, "is an enemy of those who aid terrorists and of the barbaric criminals who profane a great religion by committing murder in its name." At last, after nearly twenty years of terror attacks by Islamic extremists stretching back to the suicide bombing of the marine barracks in Beirut in 1983, the United States was finally striking back!

The attack on Afghanistan was a combined sea and air assault of a magnitude that had not been seen in the world since the attack on Iraq in the Gulf War in Operation Desert Storm. Based on information gathered from Internet services, newspapers, and the press conference held the afternoon of October 7 by Defense Secretary Donald Rumsfeld, some twenty-five planes had swept off the decks of the aircraft carriers to fly into the night skies over Afghanistan. The BBC correspondent on board the USS *Enterprise* a few days later said that on every bomb was invisibly written "one word— revenge." B-52 bombers, still the warhorse of American offense, sailed from the British and American base on the island of Diego Garcia in the Indian Ocean. The Tomahawk cruise missiles, launched against bin Laden's camps in the wake of the 1998 embassy bombings in East Africa, again brought destruction to the terrorists from American submarines, surface ships, and bombers. It was made clear in Rumsfeld's briefing again that the target was the Taliban and al-Qaeda, not the Afghans who had suffered so much from two decades of war. The B-2 Spirit bomber, the stealth attack craft, was flown by the U.S. Air Force's 509th Bomb Wing all the way from the squadron's base at Whiteman Air Force Base, about seventy miles southeast of Kansas City, Missouri. The B-2 Spirits with their two-man crews dropped their bomb payloads on Afghanistan and then made the return flight to Missouri in one trip. Military targets were hit in Afghanistan's major cities: Kabul; Kandahar, the main base of the *talibs*; Herat; Jalalabad; and Mazar-i-Sharif. From the Northern Alliance positions over the hills from Kabul, American correspondents could see the flare of the bomb explosions in the Afgan capital. The fighters of the Northern Alliance/United Front had undoubtedly helped the Allied special forces build up knowledge of where the targets were in the days before the attack.

An unexpected item of dessert on the target menu were the warehouses where the Taliban stores its opium harvest. Although the Taliban had made headlines for banning the harvesting of opium, the ban seemed more a matter of public relations than of fact. The alliance of the Taliban and al-Qaeda rested on more than a mutual hatred of Western ways, or on the marriage of bin Laden's son to the daughter of his Egyptian lieutenant Ayman al-Zawahri. What also cemented this unholy alliance was the joint profiting of al-Qaeda and the Taliban from the narcotics trade, according to the CIA. Of all the material written about the alliance of drug traffickers and terrorists within this book, there is no more egregious example than that of the coalition between al-Qaeda and the Taliban. About 2:00 P.M. Eastern time, Britain's prime minster appeared on television from his official residence at 10 Downing Street in London to endorse the attack and announce it to the British people. In his address, the prime minister announced that "90 percent" of the heroin on British streets had its origin in the opium grown in Afghanistan.

During the coverage of the air war, CBS News broke away to telecast a prerecorded rant by Osama bin Laden. The broadcast originated with the Arabic-language al-Jazeera satellite television network in Qatar in the United Arab Emirates (UAE). Al-Jazeera has been for some time a conduit for bin Laden when he wanted to reach the West with some declaration. Osama appeared on television wearing a woodland camouflage jacket and the traditional white headgear of the *jihad*. The rocky background might have meant he was in the mountainous east of the country around Jalalabad. It is known that he learned about explosives in the al-Khabad training camp located in the Darunta region in the east. Although he claims to have adopted Afghanistan as his home, bin Laden's speech was still delivered in Arabic instead of one of the Afghan languages. His bodyguard of 3,000 to 4,000 fighters are all Arab-Afghans, and sometimes fight with the Taliban militia as the O55 Brigade.

The translation of his diatribe was given by somebody with a terrible grasp of English; the translator appeared to be beside Osama, but out of camera range. Based on the original translation and more provided later by various news sources, bin Laden expressed joy at the September 11 attacks on New York City and Washington. He declared that America was now afraid, "from north to south, from east to west, and that is a good thing." Bin Laden swore that the United States would never know peace until it ceased to support Israel in the struggle against the Palestinians and evacuated "the Land of Mohammed," Saudi Arabia. "To America, I say only a few words to it and its people. I swear by God, who has elevated the skies without pillars, neither America nor the people who live in it will dream of security before we live it in Palestine, and not before all the infidel armies leave the land of Mohammed, peace be upon him." He railed against the *kufr*, the unbelievers. The original translation did not include that he also denounced Americans as the *salibi*, the Crusaders, purposely equating his struggle with that waged by Islam against Christian Europe in the Middle Ages. The speech was a very intimidating performance, if one forgot that, as it was being telecast in the United States, bin Laden was most likely hiding from American bombs in one of his caves.

Regardless of bin Laden's saber-rattling, the air offensive continued over his head. Air raids at night merged into bombing around the clock. The Taliban denounced this bombing as "terrorist acts." Within three days of the beginning of the attack, Secretary of Defense Rumsfeld declared that the United States owned the skies over Afghanistan. Targets were chosen and bombed with impunity. No American planes were hit, and no casualties were suffered. The Northern Alliance, emboldened by the British and American presence, launched a counterattack against the Taliban forces. Over 1,000 of the best *talib* fighters, sent north to confront the Northern Alliance, went over to the other side. As the first week of the assault drew to an end, the bombings continued all over the country. Members of the Taliban leadership, relatives of Mullah Omar himself, were killed in the offensive. Ammunition dumps were destroyed near the Kabul airport. Rumsfeld told the press how he had seen videotape footage of the attack which showed the bombs going off, and "secondary explosions" from the detonating ammunition long after the bombers had flown away. As the bombing campaign continued, Afghan civilians were killed and injured, in spite of American efforts to avoid this "collateral damage" of war. A Red Cross facility was hit; a father and his children were killed by a bomb hitting their Kabul home. It was not for nothing that General Robert E. Lee had said during the Civil War after the Battle of Fredericksburg, "it is well that war is so terrible or we should grow too fond of it." Yet the United States had not struck first in this war—it took no military action until thousands of its civilians were killed in less than two hours. And even then the strike on Afghanistan was delayed until October 7, to give the Taliban time to hand over bin Laden and his al-Qaeda criminals.

Plans were being made to send in Blackhawk helicopters with American and British special forces troops on a massive scale to hunt down Osama bin Laden. Before the attack, U.S. Navy chiefs, the chief petty officers, had put an e-mail picture on the Internet. It showed a U.S. aircraft carrier with an American bald eagle glowering above it. The caption on the prow, the front, of the carrier read "payback is a bitch." Payback for those who were killed at the Pentagon and the World Trade Center, on the four hijacked planes, for the sailors on board the *Cole*, and for all those other innocent people who have fallen victim to terrorism had begun. And, as the navy chiefs had said, "payback is a bitch!"

Yet, within a month of the national keening over the destruction in Washington and New York, America faced another crisis. It began slowly at first in an amorphous form, and then took on more concrete substance. For years, the American intelligence community had been warning of the threat of biological warfare by terrorist groups. A main concern after September 11 was that al-Qaeda had obtained the means to carry out biological or chemical warfare against the United States. In mid-October, American intelligence agencies confirmed that bin Laden now had that capability. When the FBI examined the personal effects of Muhammad Atta after his suicide mission, the bureau found a manual on crop-dusting. For several days after the September onslaught, crop-dusters were banned from the skies by the FAA for fear the planes could be used to spread an aerosolized form of a biological warfare agent like anthrax over American cities. This was especially true since agricultural areas are still located close to many American cities and towns.

As the fires continued to smoulder at Ground Zero in New York City, it appeared that the warning had come true, and in the form of anthrax. In one of the ironies and coincidences with which this entire period of our national history has been rife, on September 1, 2001, the U.S. armed forces put up on the Internet a Web page entitled "What Everyone Needs to Know about the Anthrax Vaccine." The page read in part, "anthrax is the biological weapon most likely to be encountered."

The first casualty was Robert Stevens, a photography editor at American Media Inc. (AIM), in Boca Raton, Florida. American Media is known for publication of tabloids that have made a direct attack on Osama bin Laden and other terrorists in their sensational prose. Stevens died October 6, 2001, from the pulmonary form of anthrax, in which anthrax spores are inhaled and then pass into the lungs. Ernesto Blanco, an employee in AIM's mailroom, also contracted pulmonary anthrax, but because authorities were alerted by the experience of poor Stevens, he received treatment quickly and recovered. The investigation centered on mail being received in the mailroom where Blanco worked as the source of the infection. Anthrax, if diagnosed in time, is rarely fatal, and can be treated with the antibiotic Cipro (ciprofloxacin), as well as with doxycycline or penicillin, both of which are available in less expensive generic version equivalents. Thanks to Robert Stevens, the American medical community is now on alert, and many peoples' lives may be saved because of him. Although no proof has surfaced yet, the FBI feared the anthrax was another al-Qaeda terror attack.

Of many Web pages on the Internet, the one at Terrorismfiles.org gives an excellent overview of "Anthrax as a Biological Warfare Agent" for the general public. Anthrax is a naturally occurring disease caused by the bacterium *Bacillus anthracis*, and is found among all plant-eating animals, herbivores like sheep or cattle. It is especially common among people who work with sheep, and has for centuries been called "wool-sorters disease." In the natural world, intensive immunization of livestock has proven to be a good way to stop the spread of the infection at its source. Anthrax (there is only one anthrax bacterium, contrary to the impression given by some in the media), can be contracted by human beings in three ways: through cuts or breaks in the skin, which is called cutaneous anthrax; by eating diseased meat, gastrointestinal anthrax; or pulmonary anthrax, which is caused by inhaling the anthrax spores. This last is the most dangerous form, since it is inhaled directly into the lungs, and is the form that killed Stevens.

Soon, the danger spread to New York City, where a dust cloud still cast its emotional shadow over New Yorkers from the wreckage of the World Trade Center at Ground Zero. It was announced October 13 that a worker at NBC News tested positive for the disease after handling a letter for anchorman Tom Brokaw. The letter had scrawled upon it the message, "Death to America. Death to Israel. Allah is great." The New York City office of Governor George Pataki on Third Avenue in Manhattan was evacuated because of feared anthrax contamination. The governor announced on October 17 that although none of his New York staff had tested positive for anthrax, all of them, and the governor as well, were taking ciprofloxacin as a prophylactic. On October 18, Dan Rather also had the unpleasant task of announcing on the CBS Evening News that one of his assistants had become infected with anthrax while handling a letter addressed to him. At the same time, in the cruelest blow of all, the baby of an ABC News executive was found to have been exposed to anthrax after having been taken by his father on a trip to ABC News headquarters. On October 19, MSNBC verified the infection. At the *New York Post*, two workers were believed to have contracted cutaneous anthrax to exposure from contaminated mail.

The next battleground in this new kind of war was in Washington, D.C. As Dick Gephardt, the Majority Leader in the House of Representatives, declared, "we're in battle with terrorism, a new form of human warfare." A letter contaminated with the bacillus was received at the office of Tom Daschle, the Senate Majority Leader. The letter to Daschle contained the same inflammatory message as had that to Brokaw. Thirty-one Senate employees tested positive for anthrax contamination, a test administered usually through nasal swabbing. Twenty-three of those who were exposed belonged to Daschle's own staff; three were on the staff of Sen. Russell Feingold, whose office is next to Senator Dashcle's on the fifth floor of the Hart Office Building. Postal inspectors believe that a small rush of air that occurs in the mail sorting machines actually spread the spores. As October progressed, a total of some four buildings were feared to be befouled by anthrax contamination. A mail facility in the Dirksen Office Building was also found to be contaminated; as was a Capitol police office, which examines congressional mail; and the Ford Office Building, where employees sort mail destined for the House of Representatives. By October 22, two Capitol-area postal employees had succumbed to inhaled anthrax. A center of alarm was the Brentwood mail-processing plant that serviced the Capitol. Alarm spread further when the White House itself became the target of an anthrax probe, when on October 23 the news media reported that there had been suspected anthrax contamination at a mail-sorting facility for the White House located at Bolling Air Force Base; apparently some mysterious white powder had been found. The 120 workers at the plant had not been infected. At the White House, as the *New York Times* said on October 25, "some 200 workers who might have had contact with the mail were being treated with antibiotics protectively." Although Attorney General John Ashcroft made public efforts to downplay the danger in order to avoid panic, it was clear that the United States, as the intelligence agencies had feared, was now facing a biological warfare attack.

The words of Lt. Col. Terry Mayer offered a sound strategy to meet this new menace:

> The medical community should continue to work on biological warfare vaccinations that are broad-based, safe, and in sufficient quantities to inoculate those people most susceptible to biological warfare attacks. This daunting task will be even more challenging given the controversy about the vaccines administered during [Operation] Desert Storm and their suspected connection with the Gulf War Syndrome. Doctors should also strive to improve the post-attack treatment in terms of rapid diagnosis, effective medical treatment, and a responsive surge capacity to administer to large numbers of biological-warfare exposed patients.[12]

The man who found himself at the center of this new kind of combat was no stranger to war or danger. On Monday, October 8, Tom Ridge, former governor of Pennsylvania, had taken office as the new Cabinet-ranking director of the Office of Homeland Security. A personal friend of President Bush, Governor Ridge had been chosen by the president to coordinate the domestic defense of the United States in this time of danger. Ridge had received the Bronze Star for heroism in the Vietnam War. On October 19,

MSNBC carried the announcement that Ridge had declared that all the anthrax specimens gathered thus far in New York, Florida, and Washington originated from a single source. "The tests to date," Ridge explained, "have shown that the strains [of anthrax] are indistinguishable. It does appear that it may have come from the same batch. It may have been distributed to different individuals to infect and to descend into different communities." Fortunately, Ridge said there were no signs that the anthrax bacillus had been "weaponized" in a laboratory, which would have much increased its potency by treating it in such a way as to make it a more powerful biowarfare agent. On the same day, the *New York Times* announced that a letter had been received at its branch in Rio de Janeiro, Brazil, and preliminary analysis pointed to the presence of anthrax spores.

In the last week of October, anthrax spores were suspected to be present in the chambers of the U.S. Supreme Court. For the first time in sixty-six years, since the Court had moved into the building in 1935, the justices met outside their traditional court room. They heard cases in the nearby federal court building. At the same time, it was feared that mail contaminated with anthrax could be within the building housing the Department of Justice, where the FBI was leading the search for the anthrax conspirators. Contamination had been found in the Justice Department's mail center in Landover, Maryland, and the mailroom in the department was shut down. The mail had come to the Landover office from the contaminated Brentwood center.

Investigation was centered on the Trenton, New Jersey, area, since the bar codes and cancellation marks on the envelopes received by Daschle and Brokaw indicated that a mail distribution center there was at the center of the contamination attack. Ridge said in his remarks that the FBI had been able to pinpoint the site from which the contaminated letters had been sent to Brokaw and Dashcle, possibly by the same individual, because the same message had been scrawled on both of them. Ridge put it simply: "It was a mailbox." FBI agents were seen in what the bureau called "a full court press," removing several public letter boxes in the area for laboratory testing. A mail carrier, who was only identified in the news media as "Terri," had tested positive for exposure to anthrax, and the letter box in question was on the carrier's route; it had been carted away by the FBI for examination. As reported in the *Philadelphia Inquirer* for October 20, Terri was being treated for the cutaneous form of anthrax and was responding well to her antibiotic treatment.

Federal authorities made available the full text of the letters sent to

Daschle and Brokaw, both of which were dated September 11. The letter to Daschle read, "You can not stop us. We have this anthrax. You die now. Are you afraid? Death to America. Death to Israel. Allah the great." Brokaw's "poison pen" letter contained this text: "This is next. Take penicillin now. Death to America. Death to Israel. Allah is great." From the childish verbiage used on both letters it appears that they could have been written and mailed by the same terrorist. The printing on both envelopes also was similar.

Ridge said that there was no link at the time to the hijackings of September 11. However, as law enforcement authorities had warned all along, there was little certainty that all the members of the plot had been apprehended. In a conspiracy like that of September 11, terrorists are linked together in "cells," separate, discrete groups in which the members of one cell do not know the members of the others. Only a few key people know all the plotters. This was a system of organization that was first seen in the war which the Algerian FLN, the National Liberation Front, had fought against the French until Algeria was granted its independence in 1962. The FLN was formed into cells by leaders like Ali la Pointe and Saadi Yaacef during the Battle of Algiers, a massive counterterror operation mounted by the French under future General Marcel Bigeard, one of the architects of modern counterterrorism, along with another Frenchman, Major Roger Trinquier. Nevertheless, it was reported on Don Imus's national morning talk radio show on October 17 that Mohammed Atta had been seen meeting in Prague in the Czech Republic with an agent of Saddam Hussein's intelligence network. Atta was allegedly seen receiving two vials of white powder from the Iraqi spy. On October 24, the *New York Post* published a story that revealed Atta had made two trips to Prague in 2000. Atta met with Ahmed al-Ani, and possibly with Farouq Hijazi, who was a more senior officer in Saddam's intelligence corps. Al-Ani was later expelled from the Czech Republic for activities "incompatible with his diplomatic style," in other words, espionage.

Whether Atta received a white powder which was anthrax or not is a mystery that may never be solved. On the evening of October 19, CBS Radio News quoted Secretary of Defense Rumsfeld as saying that Afghanistan is not the only terrorist country that could be attacked. If laboratory tests show that the anthrax spores came from Iraqi laboratories, then it can be expected that retribution against Saddam Hussein will be as savage as that meted out to the Taliban in Afghanistan, where the bombing contributed almost without a pause after the air assault began on October 7.

DNA analysis can be used to "backtrack" a specimen of *Bacillus anthracis* and actually determine which laboratory was its point of origin. Further analysis has shown that the bacteria spores in the October attacks had a sophisticated coating which could only be manufactured in the United States, Russia, or Iraq. William C. Patrick III, who had worked with the American bacteriological warfare program before President Nixon banned it in 1969, told the *New York Times* on October 25 that the spores were believed to "have an additive that keep the spores from clumping, thus making it a more effective bio-weapon." If such testing determines that the anthrax used in the attacks on Americans had its origin in Iraq, through the contact in the Czech Republic, then, in the words of U.S. Navy Commander (retired) Richard Marcinko, who formed the navy's elite Red Cell counterterror squad, Saddam would indeed be a "canceled Czech."

In the week of October 22, there were fears that the terrorists' arsenal could expand to enfold the threat of smallpox, which had killed millions of people during its centuries-long reign of terror. In 1980, the World Health Organization declared the disease eradicated. However, the Soviet Bio-preparat combine kept a smallpox culture, as Dr. Ken Alibek testified to before Congress, and a culture was also kept by the United States. Thus a bacteriological "balance of terror" was maintained by the world's two most powerful countries. Unfortunately, as *Time* magazine informed the public in its October 29, 2001, edition, "there is evidence that Iraq, North Korea, and Russia researched ways to grow and deliver smallpox in large quantities and still retain undeclared stores."

The lethality of smallpox is considerably less than that of inhaled anthrax spores, which can kill some 90 percent of those infected if they are not treated speedily. Of those who contract smallpox, some 30 percent die if untreated. Smallpox is much more contagious than anthrax, however, because it can be passed from person to person like the common cold, while to be exposed to anthrax people must come in contact with the actual spores. This of course makes smallpox a more effective bioweapon to be spread in an aerosolized form, since it is already communicable through the air. However, fortunately, it is even harder to gain access to weapons-grade smallpox specimens than to such anthrax.

When a smallpox outbreak occurs, the common treatment protocol is to vaccinate all who may have come into contact with the virus. Currently, the government has about 15.4 million doses of the vaccine in secret locations,

CNN disclosed on October 14. Before the current anxiety, Don Imus's morning talk show reported that it would take until 2004 for significantly more doses of the vaccine to become ready. However, in the aftermath of the September 11 disaster, Secretary of Health and Human Services Tommy Thompson announced that a crash $1.5 billion program was starting for preparedness for bioterror attacks. As a stopgap measure, Dr. Anthony S. Fauci of the National Institute of Allergy and Infectious Disease debuted a program that would try to enlarge the nation's stock of smallpox vaccine by diluting the current dosage to increase the total number of vaccines ready for use. Hopefully, dilution will not render vaccine less effective. If successful, the program should be in full operation by the end of the year. A promising new treatment for smallpox is the antiviral drug Vistide, cidofovir, which was created by Gilead Sciences in Foster City, California. The Web page for Gilead noted Vistide had been approved in 1996 for treatment of an AIDS-related infection, but not as a treatment for smallpox. But Dr. Fauci said in *USA Today* on October 23 cidofovir was going to be tested as a back-up treatment.

Concerns about the safety of the anthrax vaccine have been raised, and indeed there are concerns about the safety of any vaccine. The *Philadelphia Inquirer* wrote of the efforts of Dr. Stuart Isaacs of the University of Pennsylvania in Philadelphia on October 22 to "prevent dangerous side effects that can come from vaccinating people against smallpox." While this book *in no way* pretends to offer medical advice on this current public health problem, it may be instructive to quote here what my grandfather, Joseph F. Nolan Sr., said about antibiotics, which are after all what is used to treat anthrax. My grandfather had been medical editor of the *Philadelphia Inquirer* until his retirement in 1958. He was one of the seminal medical journalists of the twentieth century. He counted among his personal acquaintances Sir Alexander Fleming, the discoverer of the first antibiotic, penicillin, still used as part of the treatment protocol for anthrax today. He also knew Jonas Salk, who invented the first vaccine for polio (poliomyelitis), and Albert Sabin, who later created an oral polio vaccination which was delivered on a sugar cube. When I was young, I was often sick, and compelled to take many antibiotics. My mother became concerned about my taking so much medicine. When she asked my grandfather his opinion, he replied that "every medicine and vaccine has its risks and side effects. But you have to balance the risks and side effects against the possible benefits of taking them." Currently, we are under anthrax attack, and we know the disease can kill, as can smallpox. Since the last smallpox vaccination program ended in 1971–72, even those who were vaccinated in childhood are again vulnerable to the disease. All those going over to Afghanistan have been vaccinated against anthrax as part of the medical program in the armed forces. Under the current circumstances, it seems that the danger from contracting smallpox and anthrax seems the greater danger than the risks and side effects of being inoculated against them.

There were some signs that the anthrax attack was mounted on a global scale. In October 2001, anthrax contamination was being reported in Nairobi, Kenya. About two days earlier, two members of the Israeli Knesset, or Parliament, Naomi Chazan and Yossi Sarid, both received letters with white powder on them. An Austrian Airlines flight to New Delhi was forced to turn back when a passenger found a quantity of white powder on a seat in the plane. Such global attacks are clearly possible with a network as widespread as al-Qaeda. After the attacks on the American embassies in East Africa, it has become clear that al-Qaeda is definitely an organization with terror cells in many countries of the world. Al-Qaeda must almost certainly have alliances with other terror organizations worldwide; as stated previously, American intelligence sources believed al-Qaeda merged with the Muslim Brotherhood in 1998.

On October 26, 2001, President Bush signed into law an omnibus bill to combat the growing menace of terrorism. With him were those on whose shoulders the counterterror effort would weigh most heavily: Attorney General John Ashcroft, Director of Homeland Security Tom Ridge, CIA Director George Tenet, and FBI Director Robert S. Mueller III. Among the provisions of the bill were new tactics to combat money-laundering and to provide "roving taps" for law enforcement to carry out surveillance of communications. Also included were provisions for enhanced coverage of computers and electronic mail. Another provision allowed, as the *New York Times* reported, "immigrants suspected of terrorist activities to be detained for seven days without charges, and in some cases held for an additional six months." A provision in the bill dealt with biological terrorism, high on the public agenda with the anthrax scare throughout the country. The bioterrorism provision makes it "illegal for people or groups to possess substances that can be used as biological or chemical weapons for any purpose besides a 'peaceful' one." At the signing, President Bush declared that the new law would "help law enforcement to identify, to dismantle, to disrupt, and to punish terrorists before the strike."

Such proactive measures were what the American people wanted during the anthrax plague that had struck them, in spite of isolated First Amendment protest demonstrations. Alistair Cooke, known by many Americans as the enduring host of *Masterpiece Theater* on the PBS television network, is a naturalized American citizen who contributes to the BBC Radio Network a weekly "Letter from America." On Sunday, October 28, he related how something as ordinary as going to the home mailbox had now become a trip fraught with fear and anxiety each day. In a weird fashion, the situation was similar to what Albert Camus described in Oran, Algiers, when bubonic plague, at least not yet used as a biological weapon against the American people, caused the city to be quarantined. Wrote Camus, "even the small satisfaction of writing letters was denied us. It came to this: not only had the town ceased to be in touch with the rest of the world by normal means of communication, but also—according to a second notification—all correspondence was forbidden, to obviate the risk of letters carrying infection outside the town."[13] In the United States at the end of October 2001, life seemed to be imitating art—in an extremely unpleasant way. Immediately after the signing of the antiterrorism bill, Ashcroft issued a statement that, as the *New York Times* stated, "directed all 95 United States attorney's offices and 56 Federal Bureau of Investigation field offices to start using the new law immediately."

❀ ❀ ❀

Worldwide, the antiterror campaign after September 11 carried to the farthest reaches of the globe. The Abu Sayyaf group in the Philippines is also an al-Qaeda affiliate. Only a few days after the September 11 carnage, the *Manila Times* for October 18 revealed, two Yemeni visitors had arrived to meet with Abu Sayyaf, according to the testimony of Joey Guillo, a hostage who had escaped from the clutches of the terrorists. On October 21, Filipino armed forces fought the Muslim extremists on Basilan and Jolo Islands. Sixteen guerrillas of Abu Sayyaf were killed on Jolo, while eight were slain on Basilan. Abu Sayyaf still holds eight Filipino hostages and two Americans, Martin and Gracia Burnham. The *Manila Times* for October 23, 2001, remarked that the Abu Sayyaf fighters were using heavy weapons against the troops. But Lt. Gen. Roy Cimatu, commander of the Filipino Army Southern Command, said, "the Marines and the Army special units are closing in." Given the close cooperation of American and Filipino armed forces, it would not be surprising if the Southern Command's action represents a "Filipino Front" in the war against terrorism. The *Manila Times* disclosed on October 15 that "as part of its international anti-terrorism campaign, the United States is sending military experts to the Philippines to help train and supply weapons" to the forces battling the Islamic extremists. The fact that only "the Marines and the Army special units" are now attacking Abu Sayyaf is very suggestive of the collaboration, since we likewise only used special operations forces when American troops finally put their "boots on the ground" in Afghanistan. The *Times* noted in a story dated October 21 that "a C-130 US military cargo plane landed . . . at the Ninoy Aquino International Airport and, without even cutting its engines, disgorged 30 military officers and personnel, as well as dozens of baggage and cargo, before flying back to an unknown base." The article continued to say that "the 30 Americans . . . would help the Armed Forces train special counter-terrorist troops and plot strategy against the extremist Abu Sayyaf" band.

❀   ❀   ❀

On October 19, the long-anticipated second phase of the invasion of Afghanistan began. Newspapers and radio news carried reports that night of an attack by U.S. Army Rangers on Kandahar, the main Taliban stronghold. Some 200 Army Rangers (although accounts vary) staged a dramatic night attack on a target near the city, using their night vision goggles to gain a decisive advantage. The attack had been mounted, according to the *New York Times*, from the flight deck of the carrier *Kitty Hawk*. It seems that both helicopters and C-130 transport planes were used, since a green-tinged night vision film showed troops jumping out of a plane in a parachute drop. The raid was an assault on the *talib* barracks at Qila Jadeed, about twenty miles northwest of Kandahar, Reuters News Service reported on October 20. U.S. Air Force C-130 Specter gunships appear to have provided massive covering fire from above. An Afghan refugee, Noor Mohammed, said in Pakistan that twenty-five of the Taliban militia had been killed. The Rangers were extracted from Qila Jadeed and returned to Pakistan by helicopter. When they departed the scene of battle, they left behind a reminder: a photograph of the New York firemen raising the Stars and Stripes over the ruins of the World Trade Center. Written over the photo were the simple words: "Freedom Endures." Tragically, two Army rangers, Spec. Jonn C. Edmunds and Pvt.

Kristofor Stonesifer, were killed in Pakistan, where their Black Hawk helicopter crashed on the return trip from Afghanistan.

Further details on the raid appeared in the *New York Times* for October 21. The raid had, in fact, also been directed at a command center belonging to Mullah Omar and the Taliban leadership, some sixty miles away from the first target. At the time of the raid, the targets were not at home. According to information supplied by the Afghan United Front, Omar and his leadership cadre had been attempting to avoid being found in such high-profile targets. For the first time on October 21, the Associated Press reported that Osama bin Laden had been a prime target in the raids. The Associated Press said that "US commandos are prepared to use deadly force on Osama bin Laden." Gen. Richard B. Meyers, chairman of the Joint Chiefs of Staff, said on the *This Week* show on ABC Sunday, October 8, that "if it's a defensive situation" when contact is made with bin Laden, "then bullets will fly, but if we can capture somebody, we'll do that." Meyers said the struggle against bin Laden and the Taliban is "a war we must win if we want to maintain our freedom." In the same terse style he had used when he was in General Meyers's position during the Gulf War, Secretary of State Colin Powell opined on CNN's *Late Edition* that "our mission is to bring him [bin Laden] to justice or justice to him." At the time of the raid, President Bush was in Shanghai, China, where he was attending an economic summit conference and working to enlist Asian nations in the war against terrorism. The president said about the American attack, "we are destroying terrorist hideaways. We are slowly but surely encircling the terrorists so that we can bring them to justice."

October 19 was an auspicious date to begin the ground combat in Afghanistan. On October 19, 1781, Gen. George Washington defeated the army of British general Lord Charles Cornwallis at Yorktown, Virginia, effectively winning the war of the American Revolution. Now, 280 years later in 2001, October 19 marked the beginning of the ground campaign that will ultimately bring victory in the war against terrorism. Yet, this time, as in the two world wars, American and British troops fight side by side. *USA Today* on October 23, 2001, said that British Defense Secretary Geof Hoon announced that British troops were ready to enter the fighting from their war games in Oman "at very short notice." In London the October 22, *Daily Telegraph* announced that the Paratroop Regiment and the Royal Marine commandos were on alert for deployment to Afghanistan. As October wound toward November, it appeared that, just like on D-Day in June 1944, in the words of William Shakespeare's warrior-king Henry V, it would be "once more into the breach" for the troops of the two allies.

At the time of the attack on America September 11, 2001, Osama bin Laden launched his suicide bombers with the smug sense of security that Americans lacked the courage to defend themselves. The world changed dramatically for bin Laden and those of his terroristic ilk when the skies opened up over Afghanistan on October 7 to rain down American bombs on al-Qaeda and Taliban targets. Terrorists the world over were brutally reminded the the arrows of war are clasped in one of the talons of the American eagle.

Supported by perhaps the largest American air offensive since the Vietnam War, the troops of the anti-Taliban Northern Alliance, buttressed by the elite American and British Special Forces, rolled back the vaunted al-Qaeda and Taliban fighters on all fronts. Kabul was captured before President George Bush even anticipated it. In November 2001, Hamid Karzai was appointed the interim leader of ravaged Afghanistan at a conference of anti-Taliban factions in Bonn, Germany. Within two months of the attack on the Twin Towers, Osama bin Laden, appearing in a videotape he released to be perhaps fatally ill, and his comrade criminal Mullah Omar, were being hunted by Northern Alliance forces and American and British special forces, supported by members of the Marine Expeditionary Unit from the USS *Pelilieu*. Indeed, they were being sought in the very Afghan border region with Pakistan's North-West Frontier in which the troops of British India like the Corps of Guides tracked dangerous bandits a century ago. If, as the ancient Greeks believedheels of justice grind slowly but truly, then the remnants of al-Qaeda and the Taliban were being ground into the dust of history.

On to Kabul!

W hen the hammer came down in Afghanistan, the blow was swift. For two months, the Taliban had seemed invincible. Stories were told of how they were victorious *mujahidin*, soldiers of the faith, ready to die for Islam and their spiritual leader, Mullah Mohammed Omar. Ali A. Jalali described the *talibs* as "a unique force of pickup truck cavalry, a mounted force of ideologically motivated and disciplined fighters."[1] The Northern Alliance was portrayed as unwilling to fight. There was already war-weariness in London and in Washington only a month after the bombing over Afghanistan had started. British Prime Minister Tony Blair was on his way to becoming the most unpopular speaker in England's historic houses of Parliament. Increasing concerns were being voiced over the civilian "collateral damage" caused by the massive B-52 bombing raids over Afghan cities. It appeared to be forgotten that the bombing had been caused by the Taliban's refusal to surrender Osama bin Laden, the mastermind of the September 11, 2001, attack on America.

Meanwhile, in the theater of war in Afghanistan, the warriors of the Northern Alliance were telling Western journalists that they were anxious to fight the Taliban and were waiting for the American bombers to make a path through the entrenched *talib* front line positions. Very few believed them. They were portrayed as a motley crew in flip-flop sandals and antiquated weapons, with no stomach for the fight. Then the American and British special forces, the first Allied forces to go into harm's way, joined the Northern

Alliance on the front. It was a warrior brotherhood, like that forged 120 years ago by the British soldiers of Kipling's India and the brave fighters of the Corps of Guides. With their sophisticated communications equipment, the Allied special ops troops were able to call down crushing air strikes on the enemy front lines. Huge BLU-82 "daisy cutter bombs," mammoth projectiles that are dropped by a parachute from a C-130 cargo plane, were used to pulverize the Taliban defenses.

Then on Monday, November 12, 2001, Veterans Day in the United States, two months plus one day after the terror strikes of September 11, the Northern Alliance troops charged forward like racing greyhounds. In the phrase of William Shakespeare in *Julius Caesar*, it was time to "cry 'Havoc!' and let slip the dogs of war!" Faced with the sudden Northern Alliance blitzkrieg, the vaunted Taliban frontline positions crumpled. The city of Mazar-i-Sharif, which, since before the time of Genghiz Khan had been the gateway to Afghanistan from the northwest, fell. Now, across the Amu Darya River, which had seen the passage of Alexander the Great and his conquering Macedonians, food could flow from Allied food dumps in Uzbekistan to the starving Afghans. The Bush administration, stunned by the speed of the Northern Alliance advance, advised the warriors to halt on the outskirts of the capital of Kabul so that plans could be made for a post-Taliban coalition government to be forged among the Uzbeks, Hazaras, and Tajiks of the north and the majority Pashtuns of the south. Yet, almost before the request could reach the attacking fighting men, they had conquered Kabul. Thousands of the gallant *talibs* were in full retreat, speeding southward. They were seen in headlong flight in their tanks, their armored personnel carriers—and their pickup trucks.

The people in the liberated cities rejoiced. Men threw the hated turbans the *talibs* had ordered them to wear into the gutters. The barbers became the most popular businessmen in town as the men lined up in droves to have the beards the Taliban had mandated shaved off. Women moved on the streets freely without their required male escorts. Loud music blared from windows in Mazar-i-Sharif and Kabul for the first time since the *talib* takeover, when the puritanic minions of Mullah Omar had forbidden all music except religious chanting. Along the path of conquest, the grim calculus of war was seen as news correspondents saw *talibs* hauled to the sides of the roads and shot by vengeful Northern Alliance soldiery. But this was Afghanistan at war, and the Taliban had done worse during its advance north, killing hundreds with the help of bin Laden's "foreigners." Special revenge was meted out to these Arab and Pakistani foreigners, who had brought on an invasion by a military great power upon the land of the Afghans for the second time in twenty-three years. The northern city of Kunduz was encircled by the Northern Alliance, trapping some of these Taliban fanatics within it. If they decided to die fighting, the commanders of the Alliance would oblige them.

Soon, the northern army was battling for Kandahar, the spiritual citadel of the Taliban movement. In an air raid on Kabul, Osama bin Laden's number three man, Mohammed Atef, believed now to have directly trained Mohammed Atta and the other suicide bombers, was reported killed. In the south, the Pashtun tribes joined the rebellion against the Taliban. With the road opened, American special forces surged from Pakistan into the city of Jalalabad, bringing provisions and the promise of more to the refugees. In one camp, a CBS News correspondent reported that the people had been without any food for four days. With the Northern Alliance and the Pashtuns closing in on the Taliban from opposite directions, the situation in Afghanistan was dire.

On November 16, as American bombs poured down like a lethal rain, Mullah Omar announced from Kandahar that he was willing to evacuate that city. The *mullah* said he was willing to retreat into the mountains after discussions with "close friends and army commanders." Apparently, the supreme military commander of the Taliban, who only two days earlier had told his men to stand and fight to the death, had decided that discretion was the better part of valor. Thus, as the first week of the ground offensive drew to a close, the Taliban was in flight. Osama bin Laden, whose plans for building nuclear weapons had been discovered partially burned in a cave, was already running and perhaps even out of the country. Yet, the battle for Afghanistan would continue, reduced to a guerrilla war fought from the mountains. The hunt for Osama bin Laden, an international criminal, would continue until, most likely, in the words of Thomas Friedman of the *New York Times* on the Don Imus radio show November 16, 2001, bin Laden would be found "dead—or dead."

On November 23, the London *Daily Telegraph* reported the peaceful surrender of Jalalabad. Three days later, the Pakistani *Frontier Post*, published in the historic city of Peshawar, carried notice of the fall of the strategic city of Kunduz to the British and American special forces and the troops of the Northern Alliance. The Taliban forces surrendered to the Northern Alliance's Gen. Ahmed Shah Dostum. The *Frontier Post* observed that Kunduz had been the last stronghold of the Taliban in the north.

As the war against al-Qaeda and the Taliban continued in Afghanistan, plans were afoot for the peaceful postwar rebuilding of the country, which had been at war virtually since the Russian invasion of December 1989. A conference was called in Bonn, the capital of Germany, among the anti-Taliban forces to draw up some frame of government for the crumpled Afghan state. Immediately, as in the days after the Russian evacuation, there was suspicion among the supporters of the Northern Alliance, which represented minority groups like the Tajiks in the north of the country, and those who were from the majority Pashtun tribes in the center and south of Afghanistan. The Bush administration applied great diplomatic pressure to keep this Afghan meeting from breaking up under clouds of squabbling and recrimination. Finally, Pashtun leader Hamid Karzai was chosen to lead an interim postwar government. Under the terms of the compact brokered at Bonn, CNN.com reported on December 23, 2001, that "the interim administration will be in power for six months, preparing the way for a provisional government that will rule for a year and a half. After that time, Afghanistan will hold democratic elections to choose new leadership." Ironically, Karzai, one of the "elder statesmen" of Afghanistan, had not been present at the Bonn talks, but had participated by his satellite phone! From 1992 to 1994, Karzai had served as Deputy Foreign Minister in the Afghan government that took office after the evacuation of the Russians in 1989. Karzai was an early supporter of the Taliban, according to CNN December 22, 2001. Initially, the *talibs* wished Karzai to represent Afghanistan at the United Nations. However, Karzai grew disenchanted with the Taliban movement "as he saw it being infiltrated and controlled by non-Afghans," which might be veiled reference to the role of the ISI, the Pakistani intelligence service, in attempting to gain dominance in Kabul. He and his father, Abdul Ahad Karzai, became critics of the Taliban. In 1999 in Quetta, Pakistan, Karzai's father was shot to death while walking home from a mosque. The family believe the Taliban were behind the shooting.

Upon the death of his father, Hamid Karzai assumed the leadership of the Popolzai tribe of Pashtuns in southern Afghanistan. The Popolzai Pashtuns played a hand in winning the war against the Taliban in southern Afghanistan. At the jirga which met in Bonn, Said Hamid Gailani, perhaps the most respected Pashtun leader within Afghanistan, had signed the agreement for his Pashtun tribesmen. When Karzai took over the caretaker regime in Kabul on December 22, 2001, he had the support of Afghanistan's last king, Mohammed Zahir Shah. Karzai is in fact a member of the same royal Durrani clan as the king.

The war had not ended, but victory was in sight in this new struggle against another tyranny that had attempted to enslave the bodies and minds of men and women. As Sir Winston S. Churchill said, "it was not the beginning of the end, but the end of the beginning." And, as in World War II, Americans and the British would triumph in the cause of freedom.

As a sign of the continued British commitment to the war effort, contingents of British Royal Marines had arrived in Kabul the evening before Karzai's inauguration as president. The Royal Marines were the first contingent of the International Security Assistance Force (ISAF), which was committed to maintaining order within post-Taliban Afghanistan. For the first time in twelve years, the United Kingdom opened the doors of its embassy in Kabul. The *Daily Telegraph* had announced on December 12, 2001, that the British would be the leaders of the new ISAF in Afghanistan.

Even as Hamid Karzai was taking the oath of office as the interim leader of his war-wracked nation, the troops of the Northern Alliance and the Pashtuns, backed by strong American and British special forces support, were scouring the mountainous region near Jalalabad near the Pakistan border and the North-West Frontier. It was here that, following Osama bin Laden and Mullah Omar, the remnants of the hard-core al-Qaeda and Taliban fighters had fled after Kandahar and the other main cities had fallen to the pincer movement of the Northern Alliance and the Pashtuns coming from the south. Over the entire war, however, the decisive factor in any engagement would be the overwhelming force of American air power, displayed in a way not seen since the bombing of North Vietnam in the Vietnam War.

As al-Qaeda and Taliban resistance crumbled in the rest of the country, the hard-liners had retreated to the Tora Bora region of the mountainous east of the country. There, vast cave complexes had been dug during the war against the Russians, and would now be used for a "last-ditch" stand by the supporters of Osama bin Laden and Mullah Omar. While the anti-Taliban forces converged on the Tora Bora region, forces continued to defect en masse from the dying regime of Mullah Mohammed Omar. On December 22, the day Karzai took the oath of office as Afghanistan's new president, Salam Abdullah Rockety, the Taliban commander in Jalalabad, agreed to surrender his 12,000 men and their weapons. The official acting for the new Karzai government in accepting Rockety's surrender was Said Hamid Gailani, who had signed the Bonn accord on behalf of the Pashtuns.

By the time that Karzai had been sworn in as the interim head of state, the battle for Tora Bora had been going on for days. On December 6, the London *Daily Telegraph* reported that "[anti-Taliban] Afghan tanks supported by American bombers opened the long-heralded offensive against Osama bin Laden's suspected [Tora Bora] mountain-top fortress yesterday." The *Daily Telegraph*'s correspondent Philip Smucker noted in a dispatch dated December 10, 2001, that American war planes "blasted the rocky eaves with a thunderous roar that rolled through the valleys of Tora-Bora." Smucker reported that American and British intelligence intercepts of communications picked up from the al-Qaeda die-hards revealed that "Arab and Chechen fighters inside the vast complex of eaves and tunnels were taking a beating." Without citing a definite source, Egyptians in the Tora Bora region claimed the intensive American bombing had already claimed some 150 lives of the al-Qaeda fighters. American and British special forces continued to "paint" al-Qaeda targets for devastating bombardment by laserguided bombs ("painting" means to shine a laser upon a target to serve as a "homing device" for laser-guided munitions).

On December 14, Hazret Ali, the local Northern Alliance commander, told Smucker that the al-Qaeda fighters "have refused our offers and now the final battle has begun." However, as Smucker recalled, Hazret Ali had "vowed two weeks ago to finish the battle for Tora-Bora in two days." Even though the Northern Alliance forces had reduced their estimate of the number of al-Qaeda warriors from 2,000 to 800, they still had not gone in for the kill. As Smucker wrote, "after more than a week of fighting, there has been little actual progress on the ground." It appeared that while battling with the Afghans supporting the Taliban, the Northern Alliance had done well. (Many *talib* commanders had, in fact, merely changed sides.) However, when faced by the fanatics of the "Arab Afghans" of bin Laden, the *mujahidin* of the Northern Alliance appeared notably reluctant to press for a final battle.

The impasse at the Tora Bora complex presented Gen. Tommy Franks, the U.S. Central Command commander, with the worst crisis of the Afghan campaign. Thus far, except for casualties from "friendly fire" and accidental deaths, there had been no American fatalities in the war. The worst incident of "friendly fire," that is casualties caused by American mistakes on the battlefield, took place in the fighting near Kandahar on December 5, 2001. According to the *Philadelphia Inquirer* (December 6, 2001), three American Special Forces soldiers, M.Sgt. Jefferson Donald Davis, Sgt. First Class Daniel Henry Petithory, and S.Sgt. Brian Cody Prosser were killed when an

American air strike had dropped bombs too near the Northern Alliance troops with whom the special forces soldiers were serving. The only American—or British—ground troops involved had been used for hunting down fleeing enemy groups, in hopes of capturing Osama bin Laden or Mullah Omar, or had been used to identify ground targets for American aerial bombardment, as were the three soldiers killed near Kandahar. On November 27, 2001, the *Daily Telegraph* had reported the first British Special Air Service (SAS) elite force casualties in combat with the al-Qaeda and Taliban forces. Now, the apparent distaste of Hazret Ali and his Northern Alliance fighters presented Franks with his worst-case combat scenario: the need to employ the British and American troops in close-combat fighting with the fanatics of al-Qaeda. What had thus far been a relatively bloodless war for the Americans and British could now become a truly sanguinary affair. For those military leaders in the Central Command, the prospect of committing American ground troops to the fight for the Tora Bora caves conjured up images of the savage fighting on the Pacific islands in the fight against the Japanese in World War II. From Guadalcanal in 1942 to Okinawa in 1945, fanatical Japanese soldiers had barricaded themselves in vast defensive cave systems, forcing American soldiers and marines to root out the defenders, often in hand-to-hand combat. Often, to save American casualties, combat engineers would simply shut the mouths of the caves with explosives, burying the fierce defenders alive. Now, the prospect for the same type of brutal combat loomed against the die-hards of al-Qaeda.

Faced with the prospect of potentially heavy American losses, Central Command planners decided to continue with the tactic of using Northern Alliance forces as ground troops, supported by the heavy "aerial artillery" of the American B-52 bombers flying high overhead. In spite of perhaps the heaviest American bombing since the attack on North Vietnam in the Vietnam War, the al-Qaeda fighters clung resolutely to their positions at Tora Bora. Smucker reported on December 15 that, even after American war planes staged a bombing assault on the al-Qaeda positions, "Arab snipers popped up amid clouds of dust, firing machine-guns and rockets at the enemy below" them.

Yet, the al-Qaeda fighting on December 15 seemed to be the movement's last hurrah. On December 17, the *Daily Telegraph* reported that some 2,000 al-Qaeda hard-liners were "on the run," indicating that the first estimate of 2,000 for bin Laden's followers had been correct after all. Standing at the foot of the Tora Bora mountains, the chief Northern Alliance commander in the eastern part of the country proclaimed, "this is the last day for al-Qaeda in Afghanistan." Osama bin Laden was believed to have fled the position he thought to have been impregnable on the night of December 16, 2001. Although their estimates could not be independently confirmed, Northern Alliance commanders boasted that they had killed about 200 al-Qaeda soldiers and taken some 25 alive.

To mark the rout of the last of the al-Qaeda forces, U.S. Secretary of Defense Donald Rumsfeld paid a surprise visit, the *Daily Telegraph* reported on December 17, to the American troops on the Tora Bora battle front. Meanwhile, the manhunt for Osama bin Laden, easily the most hunted man in the world, continued. The *Daily Telegraph* said in the same article that U.S. Secretary of State Colin Powell had told NBC news that "we will get bin Laden. Whether it's today, tomorrow, a year from now, two years from now, we will not rest until he is brought to justice or justice is brought to him." Although the main force of al-Qaeda and Taliban fighters appeared to have left the Tora Bora region, the search continued for "stay-behinds" who might want to launch hit-and-run attacks at American and British troops or the forces of Karzai's new government. Once again, the main concern was to avoid committing Allied troops to a possible meat grinder in a war of attrition for the caves. A plan to deploy some 500 army troops and marines from the fleet in the Arabian Sea was put on hold. Instead, as the *New York Times* said on December 27, 2001, American advisors were offering incentives "like weapons, money, and winter clothing" to the Afghan commanders in Jalalabad to send their men in instead for the dangerous hunt in the caves. A senior military official in Washington quoted in the *New York Times* said, "it is a matter of finding the right mix of incentives to get them to play a more active role" in the mopping-up of resistance in the Tora Bora area.

Meanwhile, on the day that Karzai was sworn in as Afghanistan's new leader, a new translation was made available of the tape bin Laden had had released on October 7, 2001, the day the American aerial offensive began. According to the *Daily Telegraph* for December 22, George Michael, one of the original British translators of the tape, found more damning evidence of bin Laden's complicity in the September 11 bloodbath. According to Michael, bin Laden had expressed delight at the effect of the planes colliding with the Twin Towers of the World Trade Center. Bin Laden said, "I said that the fuel on the plane would melt the iron and that the iron would lose its properties. Therefore the building would be destroyed from the point of impact upward. What actually happened [on September 11] was a lot more than we expected." When the new translation was released, it became evident that the manhunt would continue for bin Laden, in Powell's chilling words, "until he is brought to justice or justice is brought to him." Meanwhile, as if to show increased American resolve in the war on Middle Eastern terrorism, the headquarters of the U.S. Third Army, the main ground force component of the U.S. Central Command of General Franks, had been moved to Qatar in the United Arab Emirates. Some 24,000 American combat troops thus entered the region in the largest American troop deployment there since the Persian Gulf War of 1990–91. Meanwhile, within only days of the new translation of bin Laden's diatribe, another of his videos was made public by al-Jazeera. The tape, according to the *Daily Telegraph* for December 27, had been made on December 7, just as the American bombing campaign was reaching its crescendo over the Tora Bora range. In the new tape, bin Laden boasted that the West "condemns terror. We say our terror against America is blessed terror." Bin Laden continued, "it has become clear that the West in general and led by the United States are full of hatred for Islam."

Meanwhile, the hunt for Osama bin Laden and Mullah Omar intensified. On December 31, U.S. Marines from the 26th Marine Expeditionary Unit had been sent from their base at Kandahar airport to join in the hunt for Omar, who was believed to be headed to the province of Helmand, about 100 miles to the northwest of Kandahar, where American intelligence believed that pro-Taliban forces might be gathering strength for another stand. As winter began to assert its role in American strategy, the main target of the hunt, Osama bin Laden, remained as elusive as ever. Along their border with Afghanistan, Pakistani forces had joined the hunt for him, just as they had joined American forces in the hunt for Somali warlord Mohammed Aidid in October 1993, but there was still no sign as to where the most wanted man in the world could be.

As the war continued, there were ominous signs that it could spread beyond Afghan frontiers. As Taliban and al-Qaeda fighters sought refuge from the incessant pressure against them in Afghanistan, American intelligence, in the words of the London *Daily Telegraph* for January 11, 2002, "leaked details of what they said was information showing Iran had given safe haven to some al-Qaeda fighters fleeing across the border from Afghanistan." Historically, Iran had felt that its sphere of influence included western Afghanistan, if not indeed the entire country. And the Bush administration feared that Tehran would take advantage of the fragile Karzai coalition government to exert influence within Afghanistan. President Bush issued a clear warning to Tehran to keep out of Afghan affairs. Said Bush, "if they [the Iranians] in any way, shape, or form try to destabilize the government, the coaliton will deal with them." Apparently, President Bush's "shot across the bow" had the desired effect in Tehran. The February 6, 2002, *Philadelphia Inquirer* carried a statement from Iranian Foreign Minister Kamal Kharrazi about border-crossings by fleeing terrorists. Kharrazi said that the Iranian border authorities had taken strong measures "to prevent any abuse of our lands from Taliban and al-Qaeda members crossing."

As the war continued, the Americans had finally abandoned hope of using Northern Alliance or Pashtun troops to enter the Tora Bora cave region to search for any Taliban or al-Qaeda "stay-behinds." Philip Smucker related in the *Daily Telegraph* for January 15, 2002, that "America is using hundreds of its own troops to hunt al-Qaeda terrorists in eastern Afghanistan, spurning help from local warriors." The American troops had learned that some of the warlords they had used in December 2001 to go into the cave complex had "sent thousands of men into the mountains. But many al-Qaeda fighters, including Osama bin Laden, were allowed to escape."

The first sign in the new American strategy was the arrival on New Year's Day 2002 of American Special Forces by helicopter in Khost. Soon after the arrival of these Green Berets, some 200 U.S. Marines from USS *Pelilieu* arrived, apparently to launch ground attacks on the al-Qaeda Zawar Kili base. This seemed to be the first deployment in a long-range American strategy of using American Special Forces and regular troops to "mop up" any remaining pockets of al-Qaeda and Taliban resistance in the mountainous territory of eastern Afghanistan.

Meanwhile, plans were afoot to isolate the most fanatic of the followers of bin Laden and Omar from the rank and file of enemy prisoners. While hundreds of prisoners were being held at Kandahar airport, those deemed most dangerous were transferred via air-lift to the U.S. Marine Corps Base at Guantanamo Bay in Cuba. According to the January 11, 2002, *New York Times* the Pentagon would house the enemy in what was known as Camp X-Ray. Initial reports speculated that up to 2,000 Taliban fighters would be interned there. However, James Dao, writing for the *New York Times*, noted that "a Pentagon official said earlier in the week that the United States did not consider the detainees prisoners of war, but that they were still being afforded the protections under the Geneva Convention guidlines [regarding the treatment of prisoners of war]."

However, the situation at Camp X-Ray became the center of the first international incident to highlight the American conduct of the war. From the beginning, President Bush had maintained that the Taliban and al-Qaeda inmates did not deserve the status of prisoners of war, as the *New York Times* had remarked in its January 29, 2002, edition, and thus would not be granted the protection of the Geneva Convention. The president's stance had led to an outburst from among members of the anti-Taliban coalition like Saudi Arabia that the detainees of their countries ought to be treated with the protection of the Third Geneva Convention. With citizens of allied countries like Great Britain, Australia, France, Belgium, and Sweden among those being held at Camp X-Ray, the prisoner of war question loomed as a major foreign policy challenge to the American conduct of the war in Afghanistan.

Signed in 1949, and entered into force in 1950, the Third Geneva Convention was a way to prevent the barbarity perpetrated by the Germans and the Japanese on some prisoners of war during World War II. The president's position led the to the rare spectacle of a Secretary of State, Colin Powell, asking the president to reconsider his decision of January 18 denying POW status to the prisoners at Camp X-Ray. Katherine Q. Seelye and David E. Sanger wrote in the *New York Times* (January 29, 2002) that Powell and other military officers feared the president's position could set a "precedent that could put future American battlefield captives at risk." To defuse what was rapidly becoming an ugly international incident, President Bush stated "we're in total agreement on how these prisoners—or detainees, excuse me—ought to be treated. And they'll be treated well."

Yet, on February 7, 2002, President Bush issued another statement on the subject. As reported by the Associated Press on AOL News On-line, the president determined that while the Third Geneva Convention applies to "Taliban soldiers in Afghanistan," it would not apply to members of al-Qaeda. As terrorists who were not representatives of a legitimate government and whose targets were civilians, rather than military personnel or objectives, the al-Qaeda fighters themselves disregarded the rules of combat set forth in the Geneva Convention and so should not simultaneously be protected by its terms. According to the Associated Press's Ron Fournier, "the convention sets universal international standards for the humane treatment of prisoners of war." For example, "No physical or mental torture, or any form of coercion, may be inflicted on prisoners of war to secure from them information of any kind whatever." While *technically* excluding the al-Qaeda fighters from the terms of the convention, Secretary of Defense Donald Rumsfeld observed that "the United States has from the outset, is now and will in the future be treating [the al-Qaeda and Taliban detainees at Guantanamo Bay] in a way that is humane and consistent with the Geneva Convention."

One prisoner, John Walker Lindh, the "American Taliban," was destined for unusual treatment. Lindh, twenty years of age, who has often gone by the surname Walker, had been captured early in the war during the fighting for Kunduz. Raised a Roman Catholic, Walker converted to Islam in 1997. He later moved to Pakistan and entered the extremist *madrassah* religious schools. Ultimately, he joined the ranks of the Taliban. According to the indictment filed in the Federal District Court for the Eastern District of Virginia, Walker, "on or about December 9 and 10, 2001," was interviewed by an unnamed special agent of the FBI. During the questioning by the agent, Walker, who had taken the name Suleyman al-Faris, roughly translated as "Suleyman the Warrior," on his conversion, admitted that he had "in 1998 and again in early 2000 . . . traveled to Yemen to study Arabic and Islam." It was in 2000 that Walker apparently joined the ranks of Islamic extremism, perhaps having been exposed to al-Qaeda operatives during his time in Yemen. According to the indictment, based on the affidavit of FBI agent Anne E. Asbury, Walker then went from Yemen to Pakistan "to continue his studies" at a radical *madrassah*. Afterward, he joined one of the extremist groups which were fighting the Indians in Kashmir, the Harakat al-Mujahidin (HUM). Then Walker made the fateful journey "in or about June 2001," to travel "to Afghanistan to fight with the Taliban." The indictment details how, "from a Taliban recruiting center in Kabul, Afghanistan, Walker was referred to an Arabic *mujahideen* [*sic*] group that Walker was told was run by Usama bin Laden's al-Qaeda terrorist organization." At this, the al-Farooq training camp, Walker received "a seven week terrorist training program," during which time bin Laden visited the training facility. On at least one occasion while he was there, bin Laden "met Walker personally in a small group." Walker was captured and then imprisoned at Mazar-i-Sharif and was one of the prisoners interrogated by CIA officer Johnny Michael Spann before Spann was killed in rioting which convulsed the Mazar-i-Sharif facility on November 25, 2001.

After the uprising at Mazar-i-Sharif, which had been quelled only by fierce fighting, Walker was held briefly at the U.S. Marine Camp Rhino, near Kandahar. CNN reported on January 23, 2002, that Walker, a solitary prisoner, had been put on board a plane at Kandahar airport headed for the United States. On January 24, accompanied by two federal marshals, Walker made his first appearance in the U.S. Federal District Court in Virginia. The *New York Times* for January 25 disclosed that Walker faced four charges: (1) conspiring to kill Americans outside the United States, a crime which has a penalty of imprisonment for life; (2) belonging to the terrorist group Harakat al-Mujahidin, a charge which could carry with it a penalty of ten years in jail; (3) providing material support to al-Qaeda, a charge which could impose life in prison if Walker is convicted, due to the nature of the crimes attributed to al-Qaeda; and (4) providing goods and services to the Taliban, which carries a penalty of ten years. The *New York Times* article noted that the federal government had a month in which to decide upon indicting Walker for these offenses or not.

On February 6, 2002, the *Philadelphia Inquirer* carried the story that a federal grand jury had indicted Walker on all the charges contained in the original affidavit and on a new charge. According to *Inquirer* reporter Lenny Savino, the new charge states that Walker "was trained by Osama bin Laden's network and conspired with the Taliban to kill Americans." Attorney General John Ashcroft called the official grand jury indictment "an important step in securing justice." The critical charge of treason, which carries the death penalty, had not been laid on Walker, at least as of February 7, 2002. However, Paul McNulty, the U.S. Attorney for the Eastern District of Virginia, told reporters that "additional charges might be filed later."

As the the war continued through January and February against diehards of the Taliban regime, the chronic instability that has been the historic curse of Afghanistan reasserted itself. With the Taliban in eclipse, the traditional animosities and jealousies of Afghan society reasserted themselves. The fragile coalition of competing tribes and clans, Uzbeks, Tajiks, Hazaras, even competing clans of the Pashtuns, that had been so delicately pieced together at Bonn, seemed in danger of cracking apart. Even before Hamid Karzai had been sworn in on December 22, 2001, there was concern that the warlords in Afghanistan might not accept the agreement made by the diplomats in Germany. Already, the key posts of the Ministries of Defense, the Interior, and Foreign Affairs were held by Tajiks of the Northern Alliance, denying the Pashtun majority any hope of holding these vital positions.

As perhaps a portent of stormy times ahead, Ahmed Shah Dostum, the Northern Alliance chief who had captured Mazar-i-Sharif, announced he planned to boycott the entire new administration, according to the December 7, 2001, *Daily Telegraph*. Dostum, an Uzbek, was angered that he had only been offered the Ministries of Agriculture, Mining, and and Industry. Dostum said that the division of the spoils in Afghanistan was "a humiliation for us." Often during the war against the Russians from 1979 to 1989, the Afghan warlords like Dostum; Ahmed Shah Massoud, who had led the Northern Alliance before secret agents of al-Qaeda had killed him on September 9, 2001; and Golbuddin Hekmatyar had fought each other with a ferocity that surpassed that displayed toward the Russian invaders and their client government in Kabul. After the Russian withdrawal in 1989, the warlords had plunged Afghanistan into a condition of total anarchy as they fought among themselves for power. When the Northern Alliance had ruled from 1992 to 1996, the *Daily Telegraph* had reported it had been Dostum whose troops had laid waste to the city of Kabul. The savagery of this new civil war is what had led the Afghan people to initially welcome the Taliban when it came to power in 1996 as a way to bring peace and security to the ravaged country. Unfortunately, the Afghans had learned, as had the Germans who had welcomed Adolf Hitler and his Nazi party to power in 1933, that sometimes the price of such security was the rule of a harsh dictatorship! The Taliban, while freeing the country from the ravages of the warlords, had substituted its own harsh theocratic regime.

But the tenuous ability of Karzai's coalition to keep the peace in the postwar era had its worst test in the city of Gardez, south of the capital, Kabul. Two warlords, Saifullah, who like many Afghans goes by one name, and Padsha Khan Zadran had fought for the control of Gardez, which was the capital of the strategic Paktia province, located astride the historic trade route to Pakistan. American planes, while monitoring the situation from the air, remained neutral in the conflict.

At Gardez, Saifullah had taken control of the city, and Zadran was laying siege to it. At the end of the two-day engagement, the *New York Times* related on February 1, 2002, Zadran's forces simply disowned him and gave up the struggle. Nevertheless, by the time the guns fell silent, "perhaps 50 people had been killed, and dozens of others injured." The fight for Gardez gave a sharp reminder of the fragility of the peace agreement among the tempestuous tribal chiefs, and of the task which lay before the United States, Great

Britain, and the incoming peace-keepers of the international force in pre-venting post-Taliban Afghanistan from dissolving into a brutal civil war.

As a mark of the continued American involvement in Afghanistan in the post-Taliban era, Secretary of State Colin Powell visited Kabul, where he appeared with Hamid Karzai. Powell promised, according to the January 18, 2002, *New York Times*, that the United States would put forward "a significant contribution" to the $15 billion that international agencies like the World Bank and the International Monetary Fund had estimated would be needed to rebuild the virtually destroyed infrastructure and economy of Afghanistan. Further-more, Powell, in keeping with the tenor of his public statements since the attack on America took place on September 11, 2001, vowed that the United States would not cease its hunt for the al-Qaeda and Taliban terrorists. Said Powell, "we don't want to leave any contamination behind. That is in the inter-ests of the Afghan people and certainly the mission we came here to perform."

Earlier in January 2002, there had been signs that the American presence in Afghanistan and central Asia was becoming more permanent. The *New York Times* reported on January 9 that the United States and its allies were building a large airport in the central Asian republic of Kyrgyztan that could be used as the central point for American troops throughout the region. According to the article, "the base could house up to 3,000 troops and accommodate warplanes and support aircraft." Additionally, the Defense Department announced each of the armed forces had adopted a policy of rotating troops through the region, typically every ninety days to six months. The troop rotation policy being established for the central Asian region and the Arabian Sea was seen, in the words of the *New York Times*, as a sign that American armed forces were "set-tling in" for a stay of indefinite duration in the region.

Therefore, as February 2002 began, the interim government of President Hamid Karzai was in power in war-ravaged Kabul. While Osama bin Laden and Mullah Mohammed Omar had not been found, it was clear from what Secretary of State Powell had said that the hunt for them would never end. Yet while the Karzai adminstration was attempting to lay the foundation, with massive American and British assistance, for a new Afghanistan, the ghosts of the violent past emerged in the warfare in Khost and Gardez. How-ever, it appeared that the United States and the United Kingdom, the senior partners in the international force, were determined to not let the past repeat itself in Afghanistan.

As the future of Afghanistan began to take shape, there was something about it ineluctably reminiscent of the Afghanistan of a century ago and more. Once more, a regime in Kabul held tenuous control of the country, in the face of opposition from tribal warlords, all incredibly brave and virtually impossible to control. Again, it was Great Britain, this time with its ally and friend the United States, which alone possessed the military force to keep Afghanistan from dissolving into chaos. Now in 2002, the special forces of the English and American armies, allied with the Afghan forces of the Northern Alliance, hunted Osama bin Laden and Mullah Omar in the same rocky landscape as the British and their tribal levies in the North-West Frontier Scouts had hunted the Muslim extremist holy man, el Hajj Mirza Ali Khan, the Faqir of Ipi, in 1936.

Again, this time along with American special forces and marines, British troops would mount guard in Kabul and Kandahar, as they had under Gen. Lord Frederick Sleigh Roberts in the Second Afghan War (1878–80). The London *Daily Telegraph* was reporting the action of the campaign in 2002 as it had during the North-West Frontier Campaign of 1897, only now the war correspondent was Philip Smucker—not Winston Churchill. A photo of the prisoners of Zadran's force being held in the dungeon in Gardez published in the *New York Times* February 1, 2002, looked eerily similar to the photographs of Pashtun tribesmen of 100 years ago now in the National Army Museum in London. Indeed, the Pashtuns in jail in Gardez were literally the sons, grandsons, or great-grandsons of the tribesmen who had fought for—or against—the British during Great Britain's long years as the keeper of the peace along the North-West Frontier, a role now shared by the British with American troops. And today, commandos of the Pakistani Army, formed from the old British Indian Army at Pakistan's independence from England in 1947, were scouring the same North-West Frontier province in search of al-Qaeda and Taliban renegades. Indeed, looking at the columns of American and British Special Forces marching along the dusty Afghan plain on ABC, CBS, NBC, or CNN, one half expected to see them led by a column of Bengal Lancers, their red-over-white lance pennants fluttering in the breeze. People often have said that the past cannot repeat itself. Yet, for Afghanistan, Pakistan, and the fabled North-West Frontier at least, it seemed that the past does, in fact, live again!

12

Beyond the Fighting

I n early February 2002, the once-vaunted warriors of al-Qaeda and the Taliban were incarcerated, dead, or on the run from justice. Osama bin Laden, once the feared leader of al-Qaeda, was now the most wanted man in the world. Mullah Mohammed Omar, the charismatic leader of the Taliban, had last been seen fleeing on a motorcycle from the Tora Bora mountains.

Outside Afghanistan, the international war on terrorism was moving ahead on all fronts. Iran, which had been a sponsor of Islamic terrorism since the rise to power of the Ayatollah Ruhollah Khomeini in 1979, was now heeding American President George W. Bush's stern warning not to give sanctuary to al-Qaeda and Taliban refugees. In the February 9, 2002, *Manila Times* the president of the Philippines, Gloria Arroyo, defended the growing presence of American troops in her country as a welcome addition to the Filipinos' own war against Islamic extremism.

Within the Muslim world, the catastrophic defeat of the Taliban was having far-reaching effects. Turkey, the most moderate of the Muslim nations, was scheduled to take over command of the ISAF, the international peacekeeping force in Afghanistan, in six months' time, when leadership passed to the Turks from Great Britain. In Pakistan, the government of President Gen. Pervez Musharraf had seemed on the verge of collapse from the pro–bin Laden rioting in Quetta and Peshawar in September 2001. Now, in February 2002, Musharraf's regime was cracking down on the Islamic extremists who threatened the stability of Pakistan.

Within Afghanistan, the hard-pressed people of that brave nation face the first real prospect of peace since the overthrow of King Zahir Shah in 1972. The new adminstration of President Hamid Karzai has been promised more than $3 billion to restore Afghanistan, ravaged by over twenty years of war. However, more than money will be necessary to bring peace to the land of the Afghans. This will only come about through a long-term commitment of the United States to guarantee the stability of that troubled land. There can be no repeat of the quick American loss of interest in Afghanistan that followed the Russian withdrawal from the country in 1989. The price of our lack of support for the country was an era of civil war, and the rise of the Taliban which followed. And as we have learned all too well, what affects Afghanistan affects the rest of the region as well.

In the town of Ramallah on the West Bank of the Jordan River, Yassir Arafat, the chairman of the governing Palestinian Authority for two months has been confined in his residence by Israeli tanks.[1] Arafat, in spite of repeated protestations from Washington and Israel, has proven either unable or unwilling to curtail the activities of the extremist groups like Hamas that use Palestinian territory has a launch pad for terrorist strikes into Israel. There have been calls from Washington and Tel Aviv for Arafat to step down, and make room for a Palestinian leadership ready to confront the serious problem of the continued terrorist presence on the West Bank and in the Gaza Strip, areas now under Palestinian control.

The entire Middle East, in the wake of the attack on America in September 2001 and the subsequent invasion of Afghanistan in October, is in a state of flux. Paradoxically, the war against Islamic terrorism, which many feared could lead to a new crusade between the Christian and the Muslim worlds, may instead lead to an historic opportunity for peace for the entire region. The forces of Muslim extremism, which had threatened moderate Arab thinkers and regimes since the Ayatollah Khomeini, were for the moment in complete disarray following the rout of the Taliban and al-Qaeda in Afghanistan. Furthermore, a new generation of leaders, unmarked by the years and rumors of war, was taking power in the Muslim world. King Abdullah II in Jordan; Indonesian President Megawati Sukarnoputri; Pakistan's President Gen. Pervez Musharraf; Bashar Assad, the son of Hafez Assad of Syria; and Morocco's new king Mohammed VI, who succeeded to the throne on the death of is father Hassan II in 1999 are examples of this new generation of Arab and Muslim leadership. If Yassir Arafat is forced to step down from his position as chairman of the Palestinian Authority, he may be replaced by members of the Arab generation that has dedicated itself to the ongoing peace process with Israel, leaders like Hanan Ashwari, perhaps the leading Arab woman of her day, and Jordanian scholar Dr. Kamal Abu-Jaber, formerly of the Upper House of the Jordanian Parliament, who has close family ties with the United States. Indeed, in Israel, a new generation is beginning to take power unaffected by the defining moments of the *sabras*, the first generation of those born in Israel, named after the tough, enduring cactus which grows in the Negev Desert. These younger Israelis came to maturity without being directly affected by the savage wars of 1948, 1956, 1967, and 1973 that marked Israel's struggle for survival.

In the United States as well, a new president, George W. Bush, sits in the White House, with no ties to the Middle Eastern policies of his predecessor in office, President Bill Clinton. Since the ruthless attack on America on Black Tuesday, September 11, 2001, Bush has proved amazingly adept at proving to *Dar al-Islam*, the Muslim world, that the struggle has been against terrorism, not Islam. Moreover, Bush, ably seconded by Secretary of State Gen. Colin Powell, has succeeded in walking a fine line during the concurrent Second *Intifida*, or Palestinian uprising against Israel. While stoutly defending Israel's right to exist free from terror attacks, Bush and Powell have also succeeded diplomatically in parrying an overwhelming Israeli counterattack which may have destroyed the fledgling Palestinian state entirely.

Indeed, in the aftermath of the war in Afghanistan, the opportunity has come for an international conference to be called to discuss a peace settlement for the entire Middle Eastern region, from Israel to Afghanistan, and for central Asia as well, with which the Middle East has been inextricably linked since prehistoric times. The old ideas of the past, of political extremism on both sides, seem ready to be cast into the dust bin of Middle Eastern history, along with the artifacts of the ancient Philistines and Hittites. The Middle East has not known real peace since before the Arab riots against Jewish immigration in 1936. The time has come to break a vicious sixty-five-year cycle of fear and mistrust.

Of necessity, such a conference must be composed of all nations, both great and small, young and old, whose futures are linked to the Middle East and central Asia. The international congress must include strong powers like the United States, the People's Republic of China, Great Britain, and Russia, along with weaker nations like Kuwait and the United Arab Emirates. It must embrace new countries like Tajikistan and Uzbekistan in the same gathering with ancient nations like Egypt and Syria. And indeed, it must contain representatives of groups most of us might wish to exclude from such a conference. Representatives of Hamas and Hizbollah ought to be invited, along with delegates from Lebanon, Israel, and the Palestinian Authority. Delegates from the Kurdish PKK should be seated, as well as spokesmen for the Republic of Turkey. Members of the Taliban ought to be admitted as well as ambassadors from the Afghan government of Hamid Karzai. As U.S. Supreme Court Justice Robert H. Jackson once remarked, those whose cases have led to important Supreme Court decisions on civil liberties have not always been people that one would want to invite for dinner. The same principle must guide one for such an assembly. It is an old cliche that "one man's terrorist is another man's freedom fighter," but legitimate grievances are sometimes at the heart of the struggle of some terrorist groups. It is only by addressing these concerns that we can try to guarantee that the current generation of Middle East terrorist will be the last. We stand as the heirs of the first greatest generation, which brought peace to a war-ravaged Europe. We, as the second greatest generation, owe it to them as their legacy to bring peace to the Middle East.

The issues which would be confronted at such an international assembly are as complex as they are vital to the region's peace and security. Ever since Abraham made his journey to the land of Canaan, the Promised Land of the Bible, at the beginning of the second millennium B.C.E., natural resources like water have been a matter of survival for this often parched desert land. Since Nebuchadnezzar ruled Babylon in the beginning of the sixth century B.C.E., the waters of the Tigris and Euphrates rivers have been the life blood of Iraq. Yet, a large percentage of the Euphrates waters and a part of the main branches of the Tigris, the main source of water supply in Iraq, originate in neighboring Turkey. The current construction of the Turkish Ataturk Dam gives Turkey a potential stranglehold on Iraqi water in any period of tension between the two nations. In 1975, only two years after the Arab-Israeli War of 1973, Iraq and Syria almost went to war over the threat to Iraqi water resources from the construction of the Syrian al-Thawra Dam reservoir on the Euphrates River.

The oil and natural gas fields of central Asia, now in the early stages of production, stand to be the energy mother lode of the twenty-first century. With the oil reserves of the Persian Gulf now identified as finite, the rivalry for the energy bonanza of the central Asian region will only escalate. The realization of the importance of Persian Gulf oil to the economic life of the United States was a major consideration in the administration of the first President Bush in launching Operation Desert Storm against Saddam Hussein and Iraq in 1991. With Iraqi control of the oil fields of Kuwait and Saudi Arabia, the United States and the industrialized nations of the West, as well as Japan, would have been vulnerable to economic blackmail by Hussein. Now is the time for international agreements to be set in place to insure an equitable distribution of the energy wealth of central Asia before that area, like the Persian Gulf, becomes a flash point for future conflicts.

The rights of ethnic and religious minorities must also be brought to the conference table, whether they be the Kurds in Turkey, Iraq, and Iran; Shi'ite Muslims in predominantly Sunni Iraq; the eroding state of Christian communities in the Muslim world; or the Uighur population in the Chinese province of Xinxiang. All these secular and religious issues have led to bloodshed in the past and undoubtedly have the potential of doing so again in the future. The prospectus of future danger is even worse today, and more demanding of attention than in the past because, through the financial contributions of overseas members of many of these communities, it is now economically feasible for terrorist groups allied to these minorities to gain possession of nuclear, chemical, or biological weapons of mass destruction. One need only remember the chaos in Tokyo after the nerve gas attack by the Aum Shinrikyo cult in 1995. Even small groups these of terrorists, on the margins of society, can use these weapons of mass destruction to cause panic and fear out of all proportion to their numbers.

The most divisive problem of the Middle East, the seemingly endless feud between Israel and the Arabs, must have critical importance at any such international meeting. For over fifty years, the dispute between the Israelis and the Arabs has kept the Middle East in turmoil. The wars of October 1973 almost led to global catastrophe as the United States took the side of Israel and the Soviet Union supported its Arab allies. Nearly thirty years later, in 2001, Osama bin Laden used the continuing struggle between Israel and the Palestinian Arabs as part of his rationale for his campaign of terror against the United States and the West. The question of the establishment of a homeland for the Palestinian people must be addressed at such a conclave. According to United Nations estimates, some 480,000 Arabs were displaced from their homes during the foundation of the state of Israel. Even so, the right of the existence of the state of Israel must be fully acknowledged by all the parties to any agreement. The millions of Jews who died in agony in the German death camps during the Holocaust in World World II deserve nothing less as *their* legacy.

Ever since the partition of the British Indian Empire in 1947 into India and Pakistan, the province of Kashmir has been a serious point of friction between the two countries. The Kashmir issue has contributed to three wars between India and Pakistan, in 1947, 1965, and in 1971. Since both Pakistan and India became nuclear powers in 1998, the threat of another conflict between the two nations carries with it the specter of atomic war. Even at the height of the war in Afghanistan in December 2001, a crisis between the two nations over a raid on the Indian Parliament, blamed by the Indian government on Pakistani-backed Muslim militants from Kashmir, threatened to escalate into a wider conflict. Strong international pressure must be brought upon both India and Pakistan to permanently settle the Kasmiri problem—before a mushroom cloud of nuclear destruction spreads itself over the Indian subcontinent.

At the same time, the issues of international terrorism and the threat of weapons of mass destruction must stand at center stage in any such international conference. The savage attacks upon Washington, D.C., and New York City on the morning of September 11, 2001, show how the hatreds and animosities born in the Middle East can reach out to harm innocent people all over the globe. Material gathered by U.S. intelligence from al-Qaeda hide-outs during the Afghan campaign clearly shows how Osama bin Laden had been proceeding with plans to acquire weapons of mass destruction to further his own perverted version of *jihad*. U.S. Undersecretary of State John Bolton told CNN on January 25, 2002, that "I don't have any doubt that al-Qaeda was pursuing nuclear, chemical, and biological warfare capabilities. It's not our judgment that they were that far along [in their progress], but I have no doubt that they were seeking to do so. It underlines just how serious the threat of the use of these weapons of mass destruction could be, and why it's an important part of the global campaign against terrorism."

The most important decision that any such conference can make is a provision to protect the innocent people of the world from terrorist attack by adopting international protocols for the global prosecution of a campaign against terrorists and all those—nations as well as individual groups—who harbor them. In what future historians may refer to as the Bush Doctrine, George W. Bush gave eloquent expression to this ideal for the first time on

September 13, 2001, after the horrible attacks on the Pentagon and the World Trade Center: "Now that war has been declared on us, we will lead the world to victory. . . . Now is the opportunity to do generations a favor, by coming together and whipping terrorism." More than any heartfelt monument of stone or brick, such an international agreement for the relentless pursuit and bringing to justice of terrorists and those who support them would be the most fitting memorial to John O'Neill, Father Mychal Judge, and the thousands of other innocent victims of the attack on America on September 11, 2001.

APPENDIX I

Pitfalls on the Hunt for Bin Laden

Speech given at convocation at the U.S. Army War College, Carlisle Barracks, Pennsylvania,

by Dr. R. Don Green for John F. Murphy Jr.,

September 20, 2001.

(Special thanks to Dr. R. Don Green)

"Hostility toward America is a religious duty and we hope to be rewarded for it by God."
Osama bin Laden in an interview in *Time* magazine,
January 11, 1999

A s this is being written on September 14, 2001, it looks like the United States plans to go after the lion in his lair. It looks like we are planning to go after Osama bin Laden (finally) in his sanctuary in Afghanistan. And when we go in, it looks like we are planning to go in a big way. Secretary of Defense Donald Rumsfeld has already petitioned for the president to call up some 20,000 to 50,000 U.S. armed forces reservists. While these men and women themselves may not be targeted for any bin Laden offensive, they will probably be used state-side to release armed forces regulars for the big push. So this gives you some rough idea of the number of troops we plan to send in and get bin Laden. However, this may be a more difficult task than we anticipate.

Afghanistan is a wild and desolate country. It is a moonscape of deserts, mountains, and high mountain valleys. From December 1979 to 1989, it absorbed the best efforts of Russian troops to finally bring the country under the control of their proxy Najibullah in the capital of Kabul. Over 120,000 of the Soviet's best troops, including the 104th Guards Airborne Division, which had been the one to occupy the Prague international airport in the 1968 Soviet invasion of Czechoslovakia, were occupied in the war against the *mujahidin*, "the warriors of the faith." Osama bin Laden was one of the *mujahidin* commanders then fighting against the Russians. It is one of the prevailing myths that Najibullah's Marxist government collapsed when the main Soviet forces retreated over the Salang Pass into Soviet central Asia when Soviet leader Mikhail Gorbachev ordered the Soviet withdrawal in 1988. In fact Najibullah, receiving much Soviet covert assistance, managed to defy all efforts of the *mujahidin* to conquer him as long as the Soviets could send him aid. It was only when the Soviet Union collapsed around 1991 that the *mujahidin* were able to hang Najibullah in Kabul.

It is one of the great ironies of American history that Osama bin Laden and most of his chief followers received their training in the camps which our CIA set up in Pakistan and Afghanistan to train the *mujahidin* to fight the Russians. It gives an awful new meaning to the old saying of "biting the hand that feeds you"! Nevertheless, sad to say, it is the truth. Thus bin Laden knew which country to choose when he decided to begin his one-man war against the United States after, in his opinion, we polluted sacred Muslim soil when we sent troops to the defense of Saudi Arabia in 1990 when Iraq invaded Kuwait. Saudi Arabia is home to the most sacred of all Muslim shrines, the Q'aba in the holy city of Mecca.

For us, rather than the Russians, the gateway to any land operations in Afghanistan will lead right through Pakistan. During the war against the Russians, Pakistan, especially under General Mohammed Zia ul-Haq, did yeoman work as our main ally against the Russians, because General Zia realized (as did we) that if Afghanistan fell to the Russian Bear, then Pakistan would be next. The Pakistan intelligence service, the ISI, proved an invaluable ally to our CIA in the clandestine struggle against Moscow and its allies in Kabul. The ISI played an essential role in helping the CIA set up training camps in Afghanistan (and perhaps in Pakistan) as well as smuggle modern arms, including the Stinger ground-to-air missile, to the *mujahidin*. This is why Russian jet fighters began to attack Pakistan so furiously as the war in Afghanistan continued.

The only problem is, as the *mujahidin* have turned against us, eventually they have turned against Pakistan as well. It is pretty general knowledge that when the Taliban took power in Afghanistan after the death of Najibullah, they did so with the support of the Pakistani ISI. After the removal of the Russian forces, Islamabad, the Pakistani capital, seemed to think it could use the Taliban to create its own proxy state in Afghanistan. Unfortunately, to paraphrase Humphrey Bogart in the movie *Casablanca*, the Pakistanis were misinformed. Once in power in Kabul, the Talibani, so-called because they supposedly originated among students in Muslim *madrassas*, or religious schools, turned about and have tried to export their brand of Islamic extremism into Pakistan! Right now, the government of Pakistan, under President Gen. Pervez Musharraf, is under siege from the very same breed of *mujahidin* inspired by bin Laden as the suicide pilots who dove into the World Trade Center and the Pentagon on September 11, 2001. In the Pakistan *Observer*, which is published in Islamabad, for August 27, 2001, Pakistani Interior Minister Moinuddin Haider warned of the growing Islamic factionalism which is threatening to tear Pakistan apart. In a recent police sweep, some 300 of these Jehadis were arrested throughout the country. The Jehadis are those who wish to bring the Taliban form of the Islamic *jihad*, or "holy war" into Pakistan. According to an Indian reporter at Secretary of State Colin Powell's press conference on September 13, the Indian government has intelligence that the Taliban already has training camps within Pakistan. So concerned is General Musharraf about the internal security situation in Pakistan that he has made new overtures to the Indian government in New Delhi to settle the long-festering dispute between the two countries over Kashmir.

The Bush administration has served notice on Pakistan that it expects its cooperation in our hunt to get Osama bin Laden. This has put the government of Pakistan on the horns of a terrible dilemma. If Pakistan's President Musharraf resists our attempts to use his country as a passage to the Afghans, considering our current frame of mind we will simply make his country and army into roadkill. And he knows this. However, if Musharraf is seen to capitulate to American pressure, then the very Islamic extremist forces which established the Taliban and support Osama bin Laden in Afghanistan might succeed later in bringing down Musharraf's government in Islamabad. That, if possible, would only make our current situation even more troubling. In spring 1998, Pakistan, along with its old enemy India, became a card-carrying member of the nuclear bomb club. If the Jehadis succeed in toppling

Musharraf from power, and hanging him like the *mujahidin* hung Najibullah in Kabul, then for the first time Osama bin Laden or his successors will have direct access to a modern nuclear arsenal that not only includes nuclear warheads but also the ballistic missiles with which to launch them.

The concept of revenge for a wrong is well-established among the Pashtun tribes which make up so much of the population of Pakistan and Afghanistan, the lair of bin Laden. In the villages of the Pashtuns in the North-West Frontier of India and in Pakistan, feuds between Pashtun clans have been passed on from generation to generation like their prized rifles. Even Osama bin Laden and those others who are behind the terror bombings in New York and Washington understand this, and expect us to come after them. This is why on September 9, two days before the atrocity on September 11, a suicide bomber sent by bin Laden made an attempt on Ahmed Shah Massoud, the famous Lion of the Panjshir Valley, in his stronghold in northern Afghanistan. Massoud, who has been fighting the Taliban as he fought the Russians before, would be the linchpin of any American ground strategy in Afghanistan. Hopefully, Massoud survived the attack. If we do not take after Osama bin Laden, he and his supporters will doubt our manhood, and feel it will be safe to strike us again.*

However, we must do so in such a way that will not destabilize Pakistan any further. Once before in 1979, we entered this part of the world against the Russian invaders of Afghanistan without looking at the long-range consequences. What happened was that the *mujahidin*, after savoring the victory of their *jihad* when the Russians pulled out, looked for other infidels to fight. The Muslim veterans of the war, the Afghanis as they were called, became the shock troops of every Muslim extremist movement ever since, from Bosnia in the Balkans to the struggle in Chechnya against the Russians, not to mention of the Taliban's conquest of Afghanistan. And the largest infidel nation of all was the United States, their former benefactor, already demonized as the Great Satan by the extremists of Iran's Ayatollah Khomeini. Even the bombers of the USS *Cole* in Aden harbor in October 2000 had received their training in the camps that bin Laden had established in Afghanistan. For all we know, they were the same camps we had first built to train Osama and the Afghanis in the struggle against the Soviets.

---

*Massoud died from his injuries, and an attack by the United States was launched October 7, 2001.

Therefore, go after Osama bin Laden and the infrastructure of his terror network, al-Qaeda, we must. But we must do so in a way that does not cause fragile Pakistan to fall into the hands of his Pakistani allies who are already waiting to take over the country. If we do so, just as in 1979 we will sow dragon's teeth, as Jason did in the Greek myth of the Golden Fleece. For if we destroy the tottering government of Pakistan in the process, the next generation of *mujahidin* which will take power in Islamabad will inherit the very nuclear weapons of mass destruction which we fear that they will one day possess. According to the great English poet Rudyard Kipling, there stands a tombstone near the Khyber Pass over the grave of an anonymous Englishman. The inscription on the tombstone reads, "here lies a fool who tried to hustle the East." We cannot afford to make the mistake of moving into Afghanistan a second time before analyzing under a microscope the possible consequences first.

BIBLIOGRAPHY

Edwardes, Michael. *Playing the Great Game*. London: Hamish Hamilton, 1975.

Hopkirk, Peter. *The Great Game: The Struggle for Empire in Central Asia*. New York: Kodansha USA, 1994.

Klass, Rosanne. *The Great Game Revisited*. New York: Afghan Freedom House, 1994.

Margolis, Eric S. *War at the Top of the World: The Struggle for Afghanistan, Kashmir, and Tibet*. New York: Routledge, 2001.

Meyer, Karl E., and Shareen Blair Brysac. *Tournament of Shadows: The Great Game and the Race for Empire in Central Asia*. New York: Counterpoint Press, 2000.

Murphy, John F., Jr. Personal interviews with Arab-Americans and Palestinians, 1991–2001.

———. Personal interviews with supporters of Afghan *mujahidin* resistance, 1993–96.

———. "The Story of Two Frontiers: The Northwest Frontier of British India and the American West." Unpublished ms., National Army Museum, London.

Rashid, Ahmed. *The Taliban*. London: Tauris, 2000.

———. *The Resurgence of Central Asia: Islam or Nationalism?* London: Zed Books, 1994.

Roy, Olivier. *Afghanistan: From Holy War to Civil War*. Princeton, N.J.: Princeton University Press, 1995.

APPENDIX II

Terrorism
Time for a Change

John F. Murphy Jr. and Dr. R. Don Green

"Oh, East is East, and West is West, and never the twain shall meet,
Till Earth and Sky stand presently at God's great Judgment Seat;
But there is neither East nor West, Border, nor Breed, nor Birth,
When two strong men stand face to face, though they come from the ends
  of the earth!"
    —Rudyard Kipling, "The Ballad of East and West"

T he past few months have sounded like the continuous playing of Taps at a military funeral: the bombing of the American armed forces compound at Dhahran in Saudi Arabia in June, the downing of TWA Flight 800 in July, and the bombing at the [1996] Summer Olympic Games at Atlanta. Tragically, this year has shown us that our "age of innocence" is over, that we are every bit as vulnerable to terrorism, foreign or domestic, as Italians in Milan or Israelis in a kibbutz on the borders of southern Lebanon. As the last of the personal effects are being returned in November to the families of those killed aboard TWA Flight 800, it is clear that the United States is now on the front line of the war against international terrorism.

In the wake of such national mourning, it is time to take a hard, and difficult, look at the situation to see how we, like the Israelis, can try to make sure that such terrible events happen "never again" to our fellow Americans. Two inescapable lessons still are forgotten time after time, so that they must

---

Originally titled "On Terror's Front Line," this article is reprinted courtesy of *Officer Review* magazine, May 1997, vol. 36, no. 6, The Military Order of the World Wars.

be learned horribly all over again in some different city, or on another airliner. The first of these is how to respond to terrorist attacks and, second, the real identity of the terrorists and why they have declared war on us—for, as columnist Joseph Krauthammer wrote in the *Philadelphia Inquirer* on August 12, this is definitely what has happened.

The first lesson is that we already have on hand a vast and highly potent response to international terrorists who prey on innocent American citizens or American servicemen and -women overseas. And, as Krauthammer writes, it is not some passive defense such as improving airport security or issuing condemnations of the terrorists at solemn conferences. Over the past years, especially since the debacle of the American hostages in Iran during the Carter administration—surely no president ever personally suffered more of a tragic burden than Jimmy Carter—the United States has built up a considerable force of highly trained personnel who are trained to provide an armed response in just such terrorist situations, just as the British Special Air Service (SAS) Regiment did during the siege of the Libyan Embassy in Prince's Gate in London in 1980, in which a British policewoman was slain. These forces, such as the Delta Force, the Navy SEALs, or the Army Special Forces, the "Green Berets," along with being highly trained in warfare, bear this role of acting in a terrorist situation. Now, such special operations forces have their own unified command, the USSOC, the United States Special Operations Command. They are specially trained to both eliminate terrorists and save hostages' lives, in any type of terrorist incident.

Terrorism is performed to produce just the frightened feeling that we have felt this year, that is, after all, why it is called terrorism and not softball! The best antidote to terrorists is to realize that we have elite forces trained to fight, and beat them, at their own game, providing the executive branch has the political will to initiate such action. Robert Kupperman and Jeff Kamen wrote in their *Final Warning: Averting Disaster in the New Age of Terrorism* (1989), such a "backpocket military option keeps the terrorists off balance, forcing them to devote far more attention and resources to protecting themselves than to planning new attacks." Our counterterrorist (CT) forces regularly train with those of our allies, such as the Italian 9th Incursori Parachute Regiment (*Incursori* means "raiders" in Italian), a special forces group which has seen duty in Bosnia, and the German Grenzchutzgruppe-9, G-9, the German counterterror force. Another significant Western counterterror contingent is the French GIGN, the Groupement d'Intervention de la Gendarmerie Nationale, the crisis intervention unit of France's Gendarmerie Nationale; the GIGN makes heavy use of special motorbikes to strike swiftly. The British special forces Special Air Service Regiment, first formed to combat the German Afrika Korps in World War II, has already been mentioned here.

Considering how to guard *against* terror attacks, too often security is not the main importance at airports, where the desire to keep down costs and keep profits high is pushed by the highly competitive air traffic market today. At almost all airports in the United States, security is provided by privately contracted security policemen, known to American "special operations" personnel sarcastically as "rent-a-cops." Indeed, in trying to fight professional terrorists, a task they are thoroughly untrained to do, they may indeed heighten the threat to the passengers. (When the Echelon Mall was robbed in Deptford, New Jersey, in August 1996, two of those killed were innocent mall shoppers, at least one by an armored car guard's bullet!) Security in most airports in the United States is really just a pious hope. Considering these factors, it would not be too premature to consider having airports, at least critical ones which handle a large volume of overseas passengers, to be guarded by military personnel. Using regular armed forces troops would be, at least under current federal law, impossible, but there would be nothing to prevent National Guard troops from the various states from taking on the same role. (However, early in his administration President Clinton signed Presidential Decision Directive No. 25, some portions of which are still classified, which allows U.S. troops to be used inside the United States.) Italy, which saw much terrorism in the 1970s, has its airports guarded by the Italian *Carabinieri*, the national police, armed with submachine guns and large guard dogs stationed throughout their airports and outside them as well. (The *Carabinieri* have their own special counterterrorist group, the Groupe Interventional Speciale, the GIS.) In this job, they are also helped by the equally capable (and heavily armed) Financial Police. There is no doubt that our different state National Guards, given training by the appropriate U.S. armed forces special operations groups, could in time function just as well here in the United States. The Delta Force already appears to be involved in some training activities in the country already.

Along with the use of appropriate armed force, there are many other positive steps which can be taken at American airports to combat the threat of terrorism. Much more sophisticated baggage-searching can be done to prevent bombs being smuggled aboard airplanes, especially those destined for foreign shores. Special attention, perhaps even special reception areas separated from domestic travel, can be used for those arriving from foreign countries. TWA Flight 800, for instance, had just flown in from Athens, Greece, a terrorist hot spot, before it embarked on its ill-fated trip to France. There are also many other security measures, rightly classified as top secret, which can be borrowed from those countries, such as Israel, which have unfortunately had a far longer history of terrorist attack than ourselves. A major objection to such measures is that American air travelers are too impatient to want to take the time to submit to such more complicated security checks. This assumption, if it was ever true, certainly is no longer true after the crash of Flight 800 on July 17.

Another positive step that can be taken is that we finally begin to learn from our mistakes in the past. This has been one of the weakest points in the protection of Americans from terrorists, especially those stationed overseas. The tragic bombing of the U.S. armed forces compound in Dhahran, Saudi Arabia, on June 25, was simply a rerun of the earlier bombing in 1983 of the U.S. marine barracks building in Beirut on October 23, 1983. In an area known for terrorism, the troops ought to be dispersed, not clustered together in motel-like buildings! Had the Americans in these instances been housed in the old types of barracks buildings, or even tents or World War II–type Quonset huts, the number of deaths would have been a fraction of what they were.

Furthermore, the security in the barracks areas at Dhahran and Beirut was tragically insufficient. American marine guards at Beirut were even forbidden to carry loaded M-16s ready to fire for fear it would be considered a hostile act by one or other of the warring factions! Had the "leatherneck" sentry who saw the suicide truck driver approaching the barracks been able to fire at him, the entire tragedy might have been averted by a few 5.56 mm caliber bullets. Furthermore, effective roadblocks should have been in place around the barracks to prevent the truck bomber from getting so close to the marines in the first place. By the same token in Dhahran in spite of an earlier terrorist attack aimed at American military personnel, and explicit threats had been made by anti-American groups, security precautions were sadly lacking at the barracks, with devastating results. (A colleague of mine, an army officer, tells of the great ease in entering the same building, and the same minimal security—during the Gulf War!) The lessons bloodily learned at Beirut were simply forgotten, or never learned at all. Now, after the tragedy at Dhahran a massive installation is being constructed at the remote Prince Sultan Saudi Air Force base to house American personnel, considered an easier spot to defend than barracks in cities like Dhahran. One only hopes it will not be another "motel!"

Another critical factor is to take advantage far more of intelligence-gathering, either done by the CIA or by these special operations formations, who sometimes perform perilous missions, covertly, in hot spots around the globe. Navy Commander Richard Marcinko, probably the best "spec ops" warrior ever seen in this country, writes in his *Rogue Warrior* memoir how his SEAL Team 6 had been tasked with investigating the security at the American Embassy in Beirut, during the same American intervention that resulted in the bombing of the marine barracks. When Marcinko presented the results of his security study, a senior American diplomat refused point-blank to implement any of the professional suggestions that Marcinko made, claiming such security "hardening" was totally uncalled-for. Several weeks later, the embassy was bombed on April 18, 1983, using one of the open routes that the Navy SEALs had discovered. In the sixth century B.C.E., the Chinese warlord and philosopher Sun Tzu wrote "the means by which enlightened rulers [or in this case, U.S. foreign service officers] and sagacious generals moved and conquered others, that their achievements surpassed the masses, was advance knowledge." How sad to have such "advance knowledge" and refuse to use it!

Writing long before the era of terrorism, General Sun, in his classic *Art of War*, made an observation which is as apt as ever: "thus it is said that one who knows the enemy and knows himself will not be endangered in a hundred engagements." This statement applies not only to the usual conception of "advance knowledge" of what terrorists may do, but also of an attempt to understand the mind of the terrorists, and why they engage in their struggle, so as to possibly prevent terrorist actions in the future. For, while writing about the ways a general can win in war, Sun still considered the best of all generals he who could win a war without ever having to *fight* a battle.

Probably the first question that we should be asking ourselves is *why* the terrorists—in almost all cases Islamic fundamentalists—are now attacking *us*. The most obvious reason is that the terrorists feel that we have taken the side of Israel against the Arab states since the birth of the state of Israel. The second reason is that they, and I am speaking of most Arabs, whether supporters of fundamentalist causes or not, in both cases feel that we support corrupt and dictatorial regimes in countries in the Middle East because these nations support us. The two Middle East nations most often mentioned to me have been Egypt and Saudi Arabia. The third is that they see in the "decadent West" a dangerous threat to the simple—meaning in no pejorative sense here—and traditional values which they had kept, since they were written down in the Quran and the book of the sayings of the Prophet Mohammed, the *Hadith*. This is the reason Americans have consistently misunderstood, and done so with tragic results. In a country like ours where for too many religion is just a-once-a-Sunday event—if that—the Islamic fundamentalists have a fiercely devout belief in their faith that causes them to even actively seek martyrdom by dying in its cause! Nobody has stated this belief more clearly than the Ayatollah Khomeini, leader of the first fundamentalist Islamic state, Iran: "Victory is not achieved by swords; it can be achieved only by blood. Victory is not achieved by large populations; it is achieved by strength of faith." And because of these reasons, we have heard, they have declared a *jihad*, or holy war, against us, the Great Satan America. And the fighters in this holy war call themselves the *mujahidin*, the soldiers of the faith (*din* meaning "faith" in Arabic.)

It is important as you read this that this is a creed that the fundamentalist Muslims, and to a lesser degree, moderate Muslims, believe in the Middle East, and also here in the United States. The [1993] bombers of the World Trade Center in New York City were followers of one of the most traditional-minded Muslim, and influential, teachers in the Middle East, Omar Abdel Rahman, spiritual advisor to the Egyptian fundamentalist soldiers who shot [Anwar] Sadat in 1981. Many of the fundamentalist Muslims now fighting against us and Israel are veterans of the war in Afghanistan against the Soviet Union; for this reason the Muslims themselves refer to these holy warriors as the *Afghanis*, those who had fought in the Afghan War. Even today, *Afghanis* have been left behind in Bosnia to carry on a guerrilla war if necessary against us and the rest of the NATO peace-enforcing expedition. It is one of the highest ironies of the Cold War that we actually trained these *Afghanis* to fight the Russians, and now their military skills are being turned against us—it reminds you of the gravestone epitaph that the British writer Rudyard Kipling wrote of the man who thought "that he could hustle the East!" The fact is that they honestly and sincerely believe that they are fighting a holy war—no different in their eyes than to our ancestors who went to fight our holy wars, the Crusades, against the Muslims in the Holy Land nearly 1,000 years ago. To miss this point is not only to make a terribly foolish mistake, but to court disaster as well. How can you hope to cope with an enemy, let alone defeat him if it comes to that, if you dismiss him with contempt? One only has to remember the defeat of Gen. George Armstrong Custer at the Little Bighorn River 120 years ago . . . to see down what road such foolish short-sightedness can take us.

Another factor which inflames Arab opinion—among Christian Arabs and Muslims (yes, there are Christian Arabs, not only in Syria and Lebanon, but in Egypt as well) is the defamatory image of Arabs which continually appears in American books, newspapers, on television, and in the movies. This is as true with Arab-American citizens here in the United States as gold merchants in the *souks*, or open air markets, of Cairo. The thoughtless stereo-typing of Arabs in motion pictures as rabid religious fanatics, caring nothing for human lives, has angered and humiliated Arabs both here and abroad. Anyone seeing such films could easily believe that Islam gives its blessings to the acts of the terrorists who act in its name!

There are many Americans of Middle Eastern descent who have united to defend against such stereotyping aimed at the Arab world. One of the leaders of this movement has been former U.S. senator James Abourezk. Arab-Americans, and other ethnic groups in the Middle East who are not racially Arab at all, like the Lebanese, Turks, and the Iranians, are proud of their heritage and of the contribution they make to this country. They take deep offense and personal hurt at such stereotyping—as would any other ethnic group in the United States, whether Polish-American, Irish-American, or African-American!

Thus, we have the collision of two peoples and of two stereotypes, the greedy "towel-heads" of the Middle East and the "Great Satan" of the United States. Certainly, another factor, in the eyes of the people from the Middle East I have interviewed, from moderates to supporters of the most extreme groups, is the belief that the United States has always favored the state of Israel at the expense of Arab interests. To the Arabs, Israel has been the country which, at its birth in 1948, took the land of Arabs who had lived there since the time of Abraham, and still seeks to dominate militarily the entire Arab world. Some 480,000 were dispossessed from their homes at the founding of the state of Israel.

These, then, are the reasons behind the upsurge of Islamic "fundamen-talism" and the terrorism connected to it. Yet, while we and the Israelis suffer from the threat of terrorism, it should be remembered that the people most at risk now from the fundamentalists are those Arabs who have participated in the peace process with the Israelis. Noteworthy among these are the Palestinian peace negotiators, especially Yassir Arafat, the old-line head of the Palestine Liberation Organization, the PLO, the first group to begin the armed struggle against Israel after the Six Day War in 1967, and now president of the new Palestinian state on the West Bank of the Jordan and the Gaza Strip, and Hanan Ashwari, a Palestinian woman who has contributed greatly to the peace initiative. These are the ones regarded by many as traitors to the Arab cause, and are in great danger from extremists like the followers of Islamic *Jihad*, Hamas, and Hezbollah. Many young Arabs who support the fundamentalists see Arafat as nothing but a pawn of the Israelis, "an Israeli in a green [Muslim] uniform," as one Arab youth, Abdul al-Fatah, a Syrian engineer student, told me. (Green was the color of the Prophet Mohammed's flag and is thus considered the traditional Islamic color). With all the praise that has gone to the Palestinian peace negotiators, due recognition should be given to those Jordanian diplomats who were the first ones to bravely open the lines of communication with the Israelis to begin the peace process in the first place. If true peace ever comes to the Middle East, these brave diplomats, especially one whose name I cannot mention here, will be the true unsung heroes! Every peace negotiator, both Israeli and Arab, is in danger of assassination from their own extremists; one can never forget the murder of Israeli Prime Minister Itzhak Rabin in 1995 or that of Egyptian President Anwar Sadat in 1981, the first Arab world chief of state to sign a peace pact with Israel in 1979 at Camp David.

What then, can be done to try to bring to an end this violent spiral of ignorance and terrorism, before even more innocent lives are snuffed out? First, we and the Arabs can begin a major effort to see each other clearly, without the distorted lens of prejudice and stereotyping. We can start to see Arabs as they really are, not sheikhs out to pillage us and rob us of our oil, but as sophisticated, educated people, the same as we are. Most people in the Arab world today have never even been in the desert, let alone live in a tent or ride a camel. They go to movies, eat at restaurants, and watch television like Americans. We, on the other hand, are not "great Satans," and many Americans, in fact, beginning with missionaries and educators going well back in the nineteenth century, have spent their lives and careers in the Arab world, selflessly devoting themselves to the Arab people. The American University in Beirut is the greatest symbol of the link forged between the United States and the Arab world.

The next step is to realize what, basically, Americans, Arabs, and Israelis, too, share in common, as Dr. R. Don Green, the co-author, has observed. All want to have a better life for themselves and their children in the future. They want an equal opportunity to develop their lives and the chance to better themselves through education and hard work. All three groups want to live in peace, and to live to enjoy that peace! This common ground exists in spite of all the harsh feelings and suspicions. It exists at the deepest level, too, for all of us, American, Arab, and Israeli, share the same common religious heritage, which teaches us the greatest truth of all: to love ourselves, and to love our neighbors, whether in the Muslim Quran, the Jewish Talmud, or the Christian Bible.

Most of all, we can continue to support the on-going peace process in the Middle East, for this represents the best hope of a stable peace in the region since the current unrest began some fifty years ago, with the birth of Israel in 1948. There is no way that a resumption of hostilities can be a realistic option—not when both sides have the capacity to extinguish each other. Not when Israel has the atomic bomb, and the Islamic countries may have it soon. If a serious crisis breaks out again over Jerusalem or the West Bank of the Jordan, the heart of the new Palestinian State, this time no one knows where it will end. And as a relative of one highly placed Arab official told me, the Arabs have agreed to make peace out of a genuine desire for peace, "not out of any feeling of weakness toward Israel."

With peace negotiators fearing their work is unraveling, it is time for us to take the role we have in the past, to act, in President Theodore Roosevelt's phrase, as "the honest broker," as President Jimmy Carter played when he brought Anwar Sadat and Israel's prime minister Menachem Begin together at Camp David in 1979. Like it or not, we are the only country in the world which has the influence with both sides to do this again. Like it or not, we have no choice, for with the arsenals on both sides in the Middle East at this time, a war could lead to a catastrophe for everyone.

For those who seek, regardless of our efforts to bring about a peaceful settlement, to harm innocent American lives we have a very effective armed response, gallant men dedicated to die if necessary in defense of our country and its citizens. But to those, Arab and Israeli alike, who seek to bring about an end to fifty years of war and mistrust, let us in President John F. Kennedy's words, "bear any burden" in bringing about peace in the land which Christians believe is the birthplace of the Prince of Peace, Jesus Christ.

Even many of those who support the fundamentalists, like Abdul al-Fatah, yearn for peace in the Middle East, if they can believe that it will be "an honest one," kept by both sides. Christ himself said in his Sermon on the Mount, "blessed are the peacemakers, for they shall be called the children of God." And Mohammed, who had as much reverence for the teachings of Christ and Moses as any Christian or Jew, put into the Quran, which Muslims believe is as divinely inspired as the Bible, "remember Allah's favor unto you: how ye were enemies and He made friendship between your hearts so that ye became as brothers by His grace; and how ye were upon the brink of an abyss of fire, and He did save you from it."

We quoted a Chinese philosopher, Sun Tzu, near the beginning of this article concerning the ability to wage war. It is only fitting that we quote another Chinese philosopher on the need to seek peace: Confucius. It was Confucius who said that the "journey of a thousand miles begins with a single step." In the journey in search of peace in the Middle East, the only thing we have to lose is war.

Osama and the Jihad

Much has been made since the attack on America in September 2001 of the concept of the Islamic holy war, or *jihad*. The idea of *jihad*, as preached since 1998 by Osama bin Laden, has been that of a merciless struggle against the *kufr*, the "nonbelievers" or "unbelievers." According to Osama, the two greatest enemies of Islam are the Crusaders and the Jews, meaning the Western countries, specifically the United States and Israel. Indeed, in the video first shown on the Arabic-language satellite television station al-Jazeera, located in Qatar in the United Arab Emirates, and broadcast into American homes the day of the opening of hostilities against Afghanistan on October 8, 2001, bin Laden attempted to unite all of Islam in a new *jihad* against the *salibi*, the Crusaders, and the Jews.

However, bin Laden in fact lacked the requisite religious training and experience usually considered necessary to declare a *jihad*, or to pronounce a *fatwa*, or religious decree. This religious background is considered to belong only to Muslim holy men, *mullahs* or *ayatollahs* for example, or to particularly learned laymen like some tribal shaikhs—not to an ordinary Muslim layman like Osama bin Laden.

Furthermore, the extremist view of the *jihad* as pronounced by bin Laden appears to be the direct opposite of the conception of the *jihad* as preached by the Prophet Mohammed. While a *jihad* could be pronounced (before the abolishing of the caliphate in 1924) by the caliph, or the "leader of the faithful," the *jihad* was first and foremost a "holy war" undertaken, ideally at least, in the name of God and not for the aggrandizement of some Arab dynasty. Since the *jihad* was fought in the name of a God who loved the men and women he had created, it could not very well be waged for the utter destruction of those men and women, a goal bin Laden so savagely carried out in his attacks on Washington, D.C., and New York City on September 11, 2001.

Guidance in the prosecution of a *jihad* can be found within the *surahs*, the chapters of the Quran. First and foremost, a *jihad* could only be decreed if Islam was endangered, or if the caliph wished to fight such a war among the *kufr*. Selections from the Quran can be interpreted to show that continued war between believer and unbeliever was not considered to be in the divine plan for mankind. For example, Surah 5:48 states, "To everyone we have given a law and a way. . . . And if God had pleased, he would have made you all one people. But he hath done otherwise, that He might try you in that which he have severally given unto you: wherefore press forward in good works. Unto God shall ye return, and He shall tell you that concerning which ye disagree." This could be interpreted to mean that when a *jihad* had not been ordained, although all were not "one people," the foremost goal was to love one's fellow men and women, no matter what their religious creed. Far better to "press forward in good works," with them and for them!

Further guidance in relations with those who had not accepted Islam is found in Surah 8:61: "And if they [the *kufr*] incline to peace, incline thou also to it, and trust in Allah. Lo! He is the Hearer, and the Knower!" Indeed the simplicity of the message reminds one of the Sermon on the Mount given by Jesus Christ to his disciples: "blessed be the peacemakers, for they shall be called the children of God!" It is not the fault of the prophets that the divine message of peace which they carried to men and women has been ignored, either by the Christian followers of Serbian leader Slobodan Milosevic in Kosovo in 1999 or the Muslim suicide bombers of Osama bin Laden in New York in September 2001.

An important factor in the case of one who has decided to become a *shahid*, or martyr, for Islam is that the decision for martyrdom be given voluntarily and knowingly. This is another tenet of the *jihad* in which bin Laden seriously erred. In the second video that he made that was released by al-Jazeera in December 2001, bin Laden joked about how some of those who had become *shahidin*, martyrs, on September 11, Mohammed Atta and the others, had not known beforehand that their missions would end in their deaths. Thus, not only were his terror attacks against the spirit of *jihad*, but he had deceived some of those who had participated in the missions as human bombs by sending them to their deaths unknowingly and without giving them the opportunity to make such a drastic decision of their own free will. By doing so, bin Laden may have committed the sin of blasphemy, one of the few crimes for which the Islamic law, or *sharia*, prescribes the penalty of death. It was for blasphemy that the Iranian ayatollahs issued their death sentence against Muslim author Salman Rushdie, for ridiculing the Prophet Mohammed in his novel *The Satanic Verses*. It would be ironic if, while the United States searches for Osama bin Laden to bring him to justice for the crime of terrorism against the United States, some Muslim brings him to justice first for sinning against Islam.

Glossary

Alim. See *Ulema*.

Ashura. The yearly feast held by Shi'ite Islam to commemorate the death of Caliph Hussein at Qarbala in 680 C.E. In Shi'ite theology, Hussein was the last caliph to be of true spiritual descent from the Prophet Mohammed. See also *Shi'ia/Shi'ite*.

Assassins. The secret order of killers apparently founded by Hasan-i-Sabah, who was born in the eleventh century C.E. in the Shi'ite religious center of Qum. The order was originally known as the *Hashishin*, from the belief that potential recruits were drugged with hashish to make them more willing to act by inducing in them visions of paradise. Members of the Order were known as *rafiq*, which can mean "brother" or "comrade." In 1256, the order was destroyed and the last grand master killed by the Mongol armies of Hulagu Khan.

Atabeg. One of the many administrative titles in the Ottoman Empire. Although not in current usage, during the time of the Crusades it could mean either a military commander or the holder of a political post, such as the governor of a town or province.

Ayatollah. A title used for an especially enlightened religious ruler, parcitularly in Shi'ite Islam. The term means the "enlightened one," or "the anointed of God."

Basiji. The term for those who offered up their lives for the Ayatollah Ruhollah Khomeini's Iran in the 1980–88 war against Iraq and Saddam Hussein. The *basiji* were seen by Iranians as modern incarnations of the *shahidin* (see below) who died for the holy *jihad*.

Beg (bey). An Ottoman title very similar in meaning to *atabeg*.

Burqa. Covering (veil) worn by Muslim women in public. See also *chador*; *purdah*.

Caid. North African Arabic expression for "chief" or "*shaikh*," possibly derived from the noun *qadi*, an Islamic judge.

Caliph. See *Khalif.*

Caliphate. In the English language, the belief that the rulers of Islam were both the temporal and spiritual custodians of the Muslim community on earth. It may be possible that Mohammed absorbed this belief himself from the Christians he met during the years he spent as an operator of a caravanserai, or business catering to camel caravan trade, in the Holy Land. The ruler of each dynasty, Abbasid, Umayyad, and later Fatimid, in Muslim history claimed the title of khalifa, or caliph. When the Ottoman sultans emerged supreme in the Muslim world when Mehmed II conquered Constantinople in 1453, the title of caliph—and with it the idea of the caliphate—merged with the Ottoman sultanate. In March 1924, after having abolished the office of sultanate, the reforming Turkish National Assembly abolished the caliphate as well.

Chador. Veil worn by Muslim women in public, less confining than a *burqa*.

Dar-al-Harb. In Muslim thought, "the world of war"; that part of the world still inhabited by the *kufr*, the "unbelievers." It was the duty of every Muslim to contribute in any way he or she could to spread *jihad* to the *Dar-al-Harb* until the whole world had submittted to the will of Allah.

Dar-al-Islam. In Muslim thought, "the world of Islam," that part of the world which had already made its submission to the will of Allah by converting to Islam, the religion of the faithful.

Darwish (Dervish). A mystical Sufi religious sect. Held in suspicion in the Ottoman Empire for their religious views, believing it was only through personal communion with the deity that religious truths could be revealed, the reputation of *darwishes* was rehabilitated in large part when Sultan Bayezid II became a *darwish* himself. The "whirling" dances of the *darwishes* are still performed each Friday in Istanbul, and are enacted as a way of gaining ecstatic unity with God.

Devshirme. The human tribute exacted from the Christian population of the Balkans in the Ottoman Empire. The *devshirme*, which was the most hated part of Ottoman rule, had two purposes: to recruit the best of Christian youth to serve in the *yeni cheris*, or Janissaries, but also to deny the Christian community a reservoir of possible resistance fighters against Ottoman rule.

Druze. A warrior community of Muslims now found largely in Lebanon, although Druze communities also exist in the United States, Canada, and the United Kingdom. Founded in the eleventh century, around the time of the First Crusade, the Druze were first heard of in Egypt. They may have arrived in the Holy Land in the ranks of the Egyptian Fatimid army which had conquered Jerusalem only months before the European Christian Crusaders seized it in 1099. The Druze espoused heterordox views in Muslim theology, especially the belief that Jewish and Christian prophets were worthy of veneration. Their religious nonconformity forced them to adopt the position of warriors in Islam to protect their communities from attack from more orthodox Muslim neighbors.

Faqir (Fakir). A wandering Muslim holy man; the term *faqir* can be translated from Arabic as a "poor man," since the *faqir*, like the *marabout* (see below) depended on the generosity of the *ummah*, the Muslim community, for his sustenance. Unlike *marabout*, the term came into disrepute since many *faqirs* became little more than amusement attractions in the local *souq* or town square. The *faqirs* were among the first to practice amusements like the Indian rope trick or charming snakes.

Fatwa. A religious decree in Islam issued usually on a matter of theology or Islamic policy. Because of the decentralized nature of Islam, many religious scholars have felt able to issue binding *fatwas* on the entire Islamic community, or *ummah*. Sometimes, as in the case of Osama bin Laden, a layman, without proper religious authority, has taken on himself the authority of giving a *fatwa* when it was not within his power to do so.

Fedayeen. A term which has been translated as "warriors of the faith," similar to *mujahidin*. However, *fedayeen* came to mean almost solely the fighters of the Palestinian Liberation Organization, and thus early on took a political coloration which never affected those who were the religious *mujahidin* in the war in Afghanistan.

Firman. An imperial decree or commission issued by one of the Ottoman sultans in Constantinople. Because of the power of the sultans, a *firman* was usually accepted throughout the Ottoman world. In this way the Ottoman *firman* was similar to the *ukase*, or imperial decree, of the tsars of Imperial Russia.

Ghazis. Tribal religious warriors encountered by the British and their Indian allies in their wars against the Afghans and the Pashtuns during the nineteenth and twentieth centuries. The *ghazis* were considered similar to the fierce *"berserker"* warriors of the medieval Vikings. Some of the British who wrote of their encounters with the tribal *ghazis* felt that their religious zeal was at least partly enhanced by the use of hashish before battle.

Hadith. A collection of wise sayings attributed to the Prophet Muhammed apparently first collected before his death in 632 C.E.

Hajj. The pilgrimage which every devout Muslim hopes to make to Mecca at least once during his lifetime. Those who make this epochal religious journey are permitted from then on to add the title *al-Hajji* to their names.

Harem (Harim). Extensive women's quarters that were part of a sultan's household. See also *purdah*.

Hashishin. See *Assassin*.

Hawala. The ancient Arabic system of banking in which large sums of money, sometimes in the form of cash, pass among the *hawala* bankers simply on the mutual trust held among them. However, since the terror attacks on the United States in September 2001, the *hawala* system has come under increasing scrutiny by federal investigators as a way of covertly funneling money to terrorists.

Hijra (Hegira, Hejira). The journey which Mohammed Mustafa, the Prophet, made from Mecca to Medina in 622 to escape persecution. Muslims date the beginning of their calendar from the year of Mohammed's *Hijra*, thus 632 C.E., the year of Mohammed's death in the Christian calendar, is the year 10 in the Muslim calendar.

Imam. A Muslim cleric believed by the faithful to be divinely guided to lead them. This is especially true in the Shi'ite division of the Muslim faith.

Islam. The third great desert monotheistic religions, after Judaism and Christianity. Devout Muslims believe that the teachings of Islam, ultimately recorded in the Holy Quran, were handed down to the Prophet Mohammed by the Angel Gabriel (*"Jibril"* in Arabic). The word *Islam* comes from the Arabic word meaning "submission" to the word of God, or Allah.

The practice of Islam rests upon the "five pillars of the faith," which are generally conceived to be (1) *shahada*: the belief that there is no God (Allah) but God and Mohammed is his messenger; (2) *salat*: the worshipping of God five times a day, at dawn, noon, midafternoon, sunset, and nightfall; (3) *sawm*: to abstain from food and drink from sunrise to sunset during the Holy Month of Ramadan, the ninth month of the Islamic calendar; (4) *zakat*: to give alms to the poor, which according to American Arab sources amounts to about 2 percent of an Arab's annual income; and (5) *hajj*: the taking of the holy pilgrimage to Mecca at least once in a Muslim's life.

Janissaries. See *yeni cheri.*

Jihad. The concept of a "holy war" waged either to further the cause of Islam or to defend it from agressors. The justifications for *jihad* are found in the words of the Holy Quran and the *hadith* attributed to the Prophet Mohammed. Great controversy has raged throughout the history of Islam over such Quranic concepts as the degree of total war which can be justified in a *jihad*, as well as who among the enemy should be slain or spared. The nature of *jihad*, and the conditions under which it can be waged, is still a flammable issue among the world's Muslims.

Khalif (Khalifa, Caliph). A Muslim religious title which often is translated as "leader (or commander) of the faithful," i.e., the Muslims. The first *khalif* was Abu Bakr, chosen by the Prophet Mohammed to succeed him as leader of the Muslims (in this sense, khalif also can mean a "successor"). From the time of the Ottoman conquest of Constantinople, the office of *khalif* was virtually merged into that of the sultan of the empire. Among Sufi mystics, a *khalifa* was a disciple who gained enough in wisdom to be able to take the place of his master, often a shaikh, and instruct new students in Sufism's esoteric teachings.

Koran. See *Quran*.

Kufr. The Islamic term for "unbelievers" or "infidels." Injunctions to fight the *kufr* can be found in many of the *surahs*, or chapters, of the Quran. For example, *Surah* 9 reads in part, "fight those who believe not in God or the Last Day."

Madrassah. The primarily religious schools which exist throughout the Muslim world. Unlike the secular schools mandated by the governments, the *madrassahs* are religious schools whose entire curriculum seems to revolve around the recitation and memorization of the Quran. The students at the *madrassahs*, the *talebas* or *talibs*, provided a ready reservoir of religiously indoctrinated recruits for Osama bin Laden's al-Qaeda and the Taliban in Afghanistan.

Mamlukes. Originally "soldier slaves" who were brought to the Islamic kingdom of Egypt as mercenaries. Eventually, about 1250, through their military training and *esprit de corps*, the Mamlukes were able to overthrow the civil rulers and govern Egypt in their own right. The power of the Mamlukes in Egypt was not effectively broken until Napoleon and his French expeditionary army defeated them at the Battle of the Pyramids in 1798.

Marabout. A wandering saint or holy man in the Muslim world who depended upon the alms given by believers for his livelihood. Some *marabouts* were esteemed for their wisdom and spirituality.

Minaret. The high tower in the mosque from which the *muezzin* issues his call to prayer to the Muslim faithful. In the great mosque built by the Abbasid Dynasty at Samarra, the minaret stands over 150 feet tall.

Moslem. See *Muslim.*

Mosque. From the Arabic term *"masjid,"* the building where Muslims hold their religious worship. In Islam, Friday is the great day of communal prayer held by the Muslim *ummah*, or community, in the mosque. Muslim rulers lavished great wealth upon the building of mosques, as contemporary Christian rulers did on the construction of cathedrals.

Muezzin. The Muslim cleric who ascends to the top of the minaret to offer the call to prayer. In times past, the *muezzin* had to rely on the strength of his voice to utter his summons to the faithful. Microphones have now been installed at the tops of the minarets to carry farther the call to prayer. The muezzin offers the summons to prayer at the five times daily set aside by Islam.

Mujahidin (mujahiddeen). Roughly translated as "warriors of the faith," the term dates from the beginning of the Russian invasion of Afghanistan in December 1979 to denote those who waged the *jihad* against the Russian infidel Communists.

Mullah. A Muslim religious leader in the Sunni faith corresponding roughly to the *imam* of the Shi'ites.

Muslim. One who has made his "submission" to the will of God, or Allah, and who has become a member of the faith of Islam.

Pasha. A military title denoting a senior rank in the army of the Ottoman Empire. As with *atabeg* and *beg* (*bey*), the term *pasha* is difficult to locate in modern Turkish dictionaries.

Punktunwhali. The ancient code of honor among the Pashtun (Pathan) tribes in Afghanistan and the North-West Frontier region of the (now) Pakistani frontier which enjoins the tribesmen to offer hospitality and protection to even their worst enemies.

Purdah. The condition of isolation of women in Muslim society. Literally, the term means "the veil," or being "behind the veil." While women seem to have associated on almost terms of equality with men in Islamic society in the time of the Prophet Mohammed, by about the tenth century C.E. they seem to have become isolated from general society, and housed in almost "women's quarters" in a Muslim household. Purdah appears to have been a concept which the conquering Arabs picked up from Persian (Iranian) society in the seventh century. Women would usually only be allowed out in public with male members of their household or special escorts. Even the mosques had special closeted areas for the women to pray in, apart from the male population.

The tradition of purdah gave rise to the idea of the *harem*, or harim, the extensive "women's quarters" which were part of the household of the Ottoman sultans. Harems were also held by the caliphs before the Ottoman rulers. as well as by tribal *shaikhs*. Guarded by castrated male guards, or eunuchs, the women of a harem lived a life virtually cut off from the outside world. However, the harem could be an arena of great political intrigue where a strong-willed woman might scheme to have the sultan or ruler's first-born son supplanted on the throne by her own.

Supporters of purdah feel it helped to preserve the honor and dignity of Muslim women, while its critics believe it oppressed them. In reforming Muslim societies like the Turkey of Kemal Ataturk in the 1920s, the condition of purdah was publicly abolished, as was the wearing of the *chador* or *burqa*, the veils Muslim women were forced to wear when in public. As a rough rule, the *chador* was less confining than the *burqa* and permitted the Muslim woman better vision. Now, as part of the Islamic revival, *burqas* and *chadors* are being seen more in Islamic countries than at the time of World War II, especially in societies where the presence of religious extremists like the Taliban predominates. The wearing of the *chador* is enforced by the religious police in Saudi Arabia, the first modern Islamic fundamentalist state.

Qadi. An Islamic judge who can render judgments upon interpretations of the Islamic law, the *sharia*.

Quran. The Holy Book of the Muslims, corresponding to the Holy Bible of the Christians and the Torah of Judaism. Muslims believe that the Quran was divinely inspired and that the religious truths were passed down to the Prophet Mohammed by the angel Gabriel, "Jibril." The Quran is divided into *surahs*, as the Holy Bible is divided into books.

Salibi. Muslim term for Christian crusaders from the period of the traditional Crusades of the Middle Ages (1096–1270).

Shahidin. Those killed in the prosecution of *jihad*. It was believed that the the souls of the *shahidin* would ascend immediately to paradise as a reward for their act of sacrifice. The singular form of *shahidin* is *shahid*.

Shaikh (Sheikh). The traditional leader of the tribes which made up the greater part of the Arab community. Not only were *shaikhs* the political and military leaders of their tribes, but some, because of their religious wisdom, were also considered qualified to hand down *fatwas*, or religious decrees. In Sufism, a shaikh is a learned teacher who passes on the teaching of mysticism to his disciples.

Sharia. Over the years, the body of Muslim religious thought, beginning with the Holy Quran and the *hadith*, became codified into a body of sacred texts and decisions known as the *sharia*. Although the *sharia* has been open to interpretation, the *sharia* is most often considered as being the "final authority" in Muslims' questions of theology.

Sheikh. See *Shaikh*.

Shi'ia/Shi'ite. One of two major sects within Islam (the other is Sunni); the word *Shi'ite* had its origin in the Arabic word for "sect" or "party." The great schism between Sunni and Shi'ite Muslims stems from the death of the Prophet's grandson, the Caliph Hussein, in the battle of Qarbala in Iraq in 680 C.E. The Shi'ites regard Hussein as the last legitimate caliph to rule Islam after Mohammed. The Shi'ites remember the slaying of Hussein in bitter mourning each year in the Feast of Ashura, where Shi'ite men slice themselves with knives, and Shi'ite mothers do the same with their sons, in memory of what they consider the martyrdom of Hussein.

Souq (Souk). The traditional market of Arabic towns and cities, where produce as well as news and gossip could be found. Even in the twenty-first century, the *souq* can still be found in most population centers in the Arab world.

Sufism. The mystical source for the search for the essence of communion with Allah, seen as the heart of Islam by Muslim mystics. In Sufism, the path to spiritual wisdom is called the *tasawwuf*. As in orthodox Christianity, Muslim mystics have always been viewed with concern by the forces of orthodoxy because their ideal of personal, ecstatic union with the divine is seen as "beyond the pale" of traditional religious practice. It was because of their link with Sufism that the various orders of *darwishes* were viewed with mistrust.

Sultan. The title, derived from the Arabic word for "power," which was granted to the ruler of the Ottoman Empire, especially after the conquest of Constantinople in 1453 by the Sultan Mehmed II.

Sunni. The majority sect within Islam. The term is derived from the Arabic word for "pillar"; the Sunnis believe themselves to be the main "pillar" or support of Islam. Sunni Muslims are in the majority of most Muslim countries, with the exception of Iran, where Shi'ite Islam is the dominant sect.

Talib (Taleba). The students at the *madrassahs*, or religious schools, in Islamic countries. It was from the ranks of *talibs* that the Taliban movement, "the student movement," which completed its conquest of Afghanistan in 1996, gained its strength. Foreign sources, particularly Indian intelligence, believed that the Taliban was simply a Trojan Horse used by the Pakistani intelligence agency, the ISI, to extend Pakistani control into Afghanistan with a view to gaining at least partial control over the expected bonanza in central Asian natural gas and oil. The Taliban established a harsh, purtitanic rule in Afghanistan, which was quickly destroyed when troops of the anti-Taliban Northern Alliance, or United Front, supported by British and American power, swept through the country in October and November 2001.

Taqiyya. In traditional Shi'ite belief, *taqiyya* was a religious dispensation which permitted a member of the Shi'ite sect to conceal the nature of his belief from the members of the Sunni majority. However, in the hands of unscrupulous leaders like Hasan-i-Sabah, this Shi'ite belief was perverted into a justification for political intrigue and murder wholly at odds with the morality of most members of the Shi'ite creed.

Ulema. The body of men learned in Islamic jurisprudence and theology who could render opinions based on their study of the Quran and the other texts of the *sharia*. Singular form of *ulema* is *alim*.

Ummah. The generic term used for the "communion of the faithful" in *Dar-al-Islam*, the "world of Islam."

Yeni cheri. Turkish for the "new corps," the *yeni cheris*, or Janissaries, were the elite troops of the Ottoman Empire which were chosen from the captive Christians of the Balkans to serve the sultan. Nothing served to crystallize the opposition of the Balkan Christians to their Ottoman lords more than the raising of the *yeni cheri* through the system of the *devshirme*.

Notes

INTRODUCTION

1. Joseph Conrad, *Heart of Darkness and the Secret Sharer* (New York: Signet Books, 1950), p. 158.

CHAPTER 1

1. The information on the USS *Cole* is based on the official U.S. Navy Web pages concerning U.S. Navy destroyers and the *Cole* in particular. These pages, accessible on the Internet through the U.S. Navy home page (www.navy.mil/), are invaluable to anyone writing about this incident.

2. Douglas Waller, "The Hunt for Osama," *Time*, December 21, 1998.

3. The information about Osama bin Laden is taken from the Heritage Foundation's Web page on the Internet (www.heritage.org), as well as my own research into bin Laden and Arabic tribal society.

4. Frank Richards, *Old-Soldier Sahib* (London: Faber and Faber, n.d.), pp. 334–35.

5. Information on Yemen is from the *Proceedings of the British-Yemeni Society*. Some of the issues of the *Proceedings* have been put on the Internet (www.al-bab.com). They provide an excellent look at the Imperial sunset in a corner of an empire upon which the sun once never set. East of Yemen, in allied Oman, the British Lion continues his presence, guarding the entry to the Arabian Sea.

6. H. H. A. Cooper and Lawrence J. Redlinger, *Making Spies: A Talent Spotter's Handbook* (Boulder, Colo.: Paladin Press, 1986), p. 78.

7. The reconstruction of the bombing of the *Cole* is based on the official U.S.

Navy Web page account of the tragedy, as well as reports in the *Washington Post*, the *New York Times*, and the *Philadelphia Inquirer*. I have also used my personal knowledge of the U.S. Navy to supplement these sources. My father, John F. Murphy Sr., retired as a captain after a thirty-five-year career in the U.S. Navy and the U.S. Navy Reserve.

CHAPTER 2

1. The definitive source for the account of the Omdurman campaign is still Winston Churchill's *The River War* (New York: Award Books, 1964). The book is a classic in war reportage a century after he wrote it. Another, more modern account, is Phillip Ziegler's *Omdurman* (New York: Hippocrene Books, 1988).

2. Robert Kaplan, *The Arabists: The Romance of an American Elite* (New York: The Free Press, 1993) p. 186.

3. An interesting look at Soviet policy toward the Arabs and Israel in this crucial time frame can be found in Walter Laqueur, *The Struggle for the Middle East: The Soviet Union in the Mediterranean, 1958–1968* (New York: Macmillan, 1969). Laqueur commented that "the Soviet decision in 1947 to vote at the United Nations for a Jewish state came as an agreeable surprise to Zionists" (p. 43). *Zionists*—in the context of modern historiography refers to those followers of Theodore Herzl, who sought a modern homeland for the Jewish people, long dispossessed from the home of their ancestors in the Middle East.

4. Of the many books available on this tumultuous era, two of the best are Chaim Herzog, *The Arab-Israel Wars* (New York: Vintage Books, 1984) and Benny Morris, *Righteous Victims: A History of the Zionist-Arab Conflict, 1881–1999* (New York: Alfred A. Knopf, 1999).

5. Lt. Col. Terry N. Mayer, "The Biological Weapon: A Poor Nation's Weapon of Mass Destruction," in *Battlefield of the Future: 21st Century Warfare Issues*, ed. Barry R. Schneider and Lawrence E. Grinter (Maxwell Air Force Base, Ala.: Air University Press, 1995).

6. Claire Sterling, *The Terror Network: Secret War of International Terrorism* (New York: Holt, Rinehart, and Winston, 1981), p. 125.

7. The account of Carlos the Jackal is based primarily on Claire Sterling's portrait of him in *The Terror Network*, pp. 131–49, and my own research. In 1997, I did volunteer research on the case of the Jackal as it impacted the case of Ira Einhorn, the Philadelphia hippie guru who had killed his lover Holly Maddux in September 1977. On April 28, 1979, her remains were found in a steamer trunk in Einhorn's apartment. He fled Philadelphia in January 1981 to avoid prosecution. When the office of District Attorney Lynne Abraham finally located him in France in 1997, twenty years after Holly's murder, the French were reluctant to extradite him because he had been

sentenced to death in absentia in Philadelphia. The French authorities refused to extradite him without promise of a new trial. This was similar to the situation with the Jackal when he was living in the Sudan. Ironically, Carlos was also tried and sentenced in 1997 to life in a French prison. Rick DiBenedetto was the extradition officer who had handled the Einhorn case for the district attorney's office. I researched the case of the Jackal for DiBenedetto to provide some background for the efforts of the district attorney's office to bring back Einhorn to face justice in the United States. For more on the case of Ira Einhorn, see Steven Levy, *The Unicorn's Secret: Murder in the Age of Aquarius* (New York: New American Library, 1988); for Rick DiBenedetto's role, view pp. 371ff.

8. Roger Faligot and Pascal Krop, *La Piscine: The French Secret Service since 1944*, trans. by W. D. Halls (New York: Basil Blackwell, 1989), pp. 258–59.

9. Ibid., p. 258.

10. Ovid Demaris, *Brothers in Blood: The International Terrorist Network* (New York: Scribner's, 1977), p. 21. The allegation regarding the Jackal working for the PFLP is from Jay Robert Nash, *Terrorism in the 20th Century* (New York: M. Evans and Company, 1998), pp. 215–16.

11. Faligot and Krup, *La Piscine*.

12. Ibid., p. 260.

13. Quoted in Patrick Goodenough interview, Conservative News Service (CNS.com) December 1999. Abu Daoud's book was published in the United States as *Memoirs of a Palestinian Terrorist*, with Gilles du Jonehay (New York: Arcade Books, 1999).

14. Ahron Bregman and Jihan El-Tahri, *Israel and the Arabs: An Eyewitness Account of War and Peace in the Middle East* (New York: TV Books, 2000), p. 192.

15. Samuel M. Katz, *The Night Raiders:Israel's Naval Commandos at War* (New York: Pocket Books, 1997), p. 210.

16. William Stevenson, *90 Minutes at Entebbe* (New York: Bantam Books, 1976). A story connection with the Israeli raid on Entebbe is that one of the commandos drove out of one of the transports dressed as Idi Amin himself, to confuse the guards.

17. Sandra Mackey, *Lebanon: Death of a Nation* (New York: Anchor Books, 1991), p. 142. For more information, see also Peter Mansfield, *A History of the Middle East* (New York:Viking, 1991), pp. 307–18.

18. Bregman and El-Tahri, *Israel and the Arabs*, p. 201.

19. Bob Woodward, *Veil: The Secret Wars of the CIA, 1981–1987* (New York: Pocket Books, 1987), p. 320. Woodward is the principal source for the following discussion of the events, pp. 320ff.

20. Ibid., p. 456.

21. Bregman and El-Tahri, *Israel and the Arabs*, p. 231. An additional perspective on the Palestinian uprising, or the First *Intifida*, is found in Charles D. Smith, *Palestine and the Arab-Israeli Conflict*, 2d ed. (New York: St. Martin's Press, 1992), pp. 290–92. An early Palestinian view is Edward Said, one of the preeminent scholars of the Arab-Israeli Conflict, in *The Question of Palestine* (New York: Vintage Books, 1979).

22. Galia Golan, "Gorbachev's Middle East Strategy," *Foreign Affairs* (Fall 1987) p. 46.

CHAPTER 3

1. Francis Woodman Cleaves, trans. and ed., *The Secret History of the Mongols* (Cambridge, Mass.: Harvard-Yenching Institute, 1982), p. 200.

2. Mahmud Shaltut, "A Modernist Interpretation of Jihad," in *Jihad in Classical and Modern Islam*, ed. Rudolf Peters (Princeton, N.J.: Markus Wiener, 1996), p. 74.

3. Robert Payne, *The History of Islam* (New York: Dorset, 1987).

4. Taqi al-Din Ahmad Ibn Taymiyya, "The Religious and Moral Doctrine of Jihad," in Peters, *Jihad in Classical and Modern Islam*, p. 48.

5. Rene Grousset, *The Epic of the Crusades*, trans. Noel Lindsay (New York: Orion Press, 1970), p. 50. Grousset's work, in addition to Steven Runciman's massive three-volume history of the Crusades are still the standard histories from the Western point of view. See Runciman, *A History of the Crusades* (Cambridge: Cambridge University Press, 1952). A welcome addition to crusading literature is Francesco Gabrieli, *Arab Historians of the Crusades* (New York: Dorset Press, 1989). Zoe Oldenbourg produced an excellent one-volume history of the crusading era, *The Crusades* (New York: Pantheon Books, 1966). An excellent history of the art of war during the Crusades is R. C. Smail, *Crusading Warfare, 1097–1193* (Cambridge: Cambridge University Press, 1972). Smail's book was supplemented by John France, *Western Warfare in the Age of the Crusades*, 1000–1300 (Ithaca, N.Y.: Cornell University Press, 1999). Every year, more books are published on the Crusades, making it one of the most popular fields of historical research, representing the fact that events in the Middle East are as important to us now as they were when the Crusades began, some 900 years ago.

6. Quoted in Grousset, *The Epic of the Crusades*, p. 69.

7. Grousset, *The Epic of the Crusades*.

8. For more information, see James Wasserman, *The Templars and the Assassins: The Militia of Heaven* (Rochester, Vt.: Destiny Books, 2001), p. 156. One of the first modern histories of the Knights Templars to be published was in London

in 1842, Charles G. Addison, *The History of the Knights Templars* (reprint ed. Kempton, Ill.: Adventures Unlimited Press, 1997).

9. The classic account of the Assassins is that given in Bernard Lewis, *The Assassins: A Radical Sect in Islam* (London: Weidenfeld and Nicolson, 1967). Another treatment comparing the Knights Templar and the Assassins is Paul Elliot, *Warrior Cults: A History of Magical, Mystical and Murderous Organizations* (New York: Sterling, 1998), pp. 59–90.

10. Gabrieli, *Arab Historians*, p. 269.

11. Quoted in M. R. B. Shaw, trans. and ed., *Chronicles of the Crusades: Joinville and Villehardouin* (New York: Barnes & Noble, 1993).

12. Harold Lamb, *The March of the Barbarians* (New York: Literary Guild of America, 1940), p. 245. The barbarian, or at least comparatively uncivilized, tribes emerging from the steppes of central Asia to disrupt existing cultures has been a recurring theme in scholarship. Additional information on these tribes and their role in history can be found in Rene Grousset, *Empire of the Steppes: A History of Central Asia*, trans. Naomi Walford (New Brunswick, N.J.: Rutgers University Press, 1970); Luc Kwanten, *Imperial Nomads: A History of Central Asia, 500–1500* (Philadelphia: University of Pennsylvania Press, 1979); and Erik Hildinger, *Warriors of the Steppe: A Military History of Central Asia, 500 B.C. to 1700 A.D.* (Cambridge, Mass.: Da Capo/Perseus, 1997).

13. C. Max Kortepeter, *Ottoman Imperialism during the Reformation: Europe and the Caucasus* (New York: New York University Press, 1972), p. 214.

14. Hans E. Tutch. "Arab Unity and Arab Dissension," in *The Middle East in Transition*, ed. Walter Z. Laquer (New York: Praeger, 1958), pp. 23–25.

15. Philip Mansel, *Constantinople: City of the World's Desire, 1453–1924* (New York: St. Martin's Press, 1998).

16. Ibid., pp. 38–39.

CHAPTER 4

1. C. Max Kortepeter, *Ottoman Imperialism, during the Reformation: Europe and the Caucasus* (New York: New York University Press, 1972), p. 220.

2. Bernard Lewis, *The Middle East: A Brief History of the Last 2,000 Years* (New York: Simon & Schuster/Touchstone, 1995), p. 284. This period also saw the beginning of the great Russian expansion into central Asia, which brought the Russians ever closer to the British in India. The brief Russian occupation of Herat in Afghanistan in 1885 brought the British and the Russians perilously close to war.

3. Charles Mercer, *Legion of Strangers: A Vivid History of a Unique Military Tradition, the French Foreign Legion* (New York: Holt Rinehart and Winston, 1964), p. 33.

4. Brian Bond, ed., *Victorian Military Campaigns* (New York: Praeger, 1968), p. 274.

5. George Antonius, *The Arab Awakening* (New York: Capricorn, 1965), p. 94.

6. Ibid., pp. 230ff.

7. T. E. Lawrence, *The Essential T. E. Lawrence*, ed. David Garnett (New York: Oxford University Press, 1992), p. 218.

8. B. H. Liddell-Hart, *Colonel Lawrence: The Man behind the Legend* (New York: Dodd, Mead, 1935), pp. 278ff., for Lawrence's pursuit of the Turkish Fourth Army.

9. Antonius, *The Arab Awakening*, p. 225.

10. T. E. Lawrence, *The Seven Pillars of Wisdom: A Triumph* (New York: Anchor/Doubleday, 1991).

11. The text of the Balfour Declaration can be found in Peter Mansfield, *A History of the Middle East* (New York: Viking, 1991), pp. 159–64 and Antonius, *The Arab Awakening*, pp. 258–73.

12. Lawrence, *The Essential T. E. Lawrence*, pp. 73–74.

13. The best source for the diplomatic aftermath of World War I remains David Fromkin's *A Peace to End All Peace* (New York: Avon, 1989). Once again, save for the influence of the Wahabis in Ibn Saud's kingdom, the entire struggle was for Arab nationalism, not Islamic extremism. Prince Faisal was a political pragmatist, not an ideologue. In Paris for the peace conference, he met with leaders of the Zionist community in Europe to try to arrange a peaceful solution to the Arab-Zionist problem. This was, of course, occasioned by the British promising Palestine to both Jew and Arab during the war. For more on the Ikhwan and Ibn Saud's campaign of conquest, see Robert Lacey, *The Kingdom: Arabia and the House of Saud* (New York: Avon Books, 1981), pp. 141–50, and Mansfield, *History*, pp. 184–85.

14. For more information, see Anthony Cave-Brown, *Treason in the Blood: M. St. John Philby, Kim Philby, and the Spy Case of the Century* (New York: Houghton Mifflin, 1994), p. 36.

15. Charles E. Farah, *Islam* (New York: Barron's, 2000), p. 370.

16. William Seabrook, *Adventures in Arabia* (New York: Harcourt, Brace, 1927), p. 52.

17. Lacey, *The Kingdom*, p. 185.

18. Steven Emerson, *The American House of Saud: The Secret Petrodollar Connection* (New York: Franklin Watts, 1985), p. 24.

19. Antonius, *The Arab Awakening*, p. 409.

20. Somerset de Chair's *The Golden Carpet* has most recently appeared in paperback edition (New York: Bantam Books, 1984).

21. Yigael Allon, *Shield of David: The Story of Israel's Armed Forces* (New York: Random House, 1970), p. 114.

CHAPTER 5

1. Morris Beckman, *The Jewish Brigade: An Army with Two Masters, 1944–45* (Rockville Center, N.Y.: Sarpedon, 1998), p. 99. The origins of the Irgun and the Leuchi are traced in Yigael Allon, *Shield of David: The Story of Israel's Armed Forces* (New York: Random House, 1970), pp. 100–101; Tom Segev, *One Palestine Complete: Jews and Arabs under the British Mandate* (New York: Metropolitan Books, 2000), pp. 381–85; and Benny Morris *Righteous Victims: A History of the Zionist-Arab Conflict, 1881–1999* (New York: Alfred A. Knopf, 1999).

2. Leon Uris, *Exodus*, (New York: Bantam Books, 1958), p. 352.

3. Roland Dallas, *King Hussein: A Life on the Edge* (New York: Fromm International, 1999), p. 41.

4. Quoted in ibid., p. 12.

5. Jillian Becker in Benjamin Netanyahu, *Terrorism: How the West Can Win* (New York: Avon Books and the Jonathan Institute, 1986), p. 99.

6. Janet Wallach and John Wallach, *Arafat: In the Eyes of the Beholder* (New York: Carol Publishing Group, 1990), p. 102.

7. Edmund Taylor, *The Real Case against Nasser* (Cleveland: Zubal Books, 1956), p. 34.

8. George E. Kirk, *A Short History of the Middle East* (New York: Praeger, 1959), p. 21.

9. Philip Mansel, *Constantinople: City of the World's Desire, 1453–1924* (New York: St. Martin's Press, 1998), p. 293.

10. "Ataturk, Mustafa Kemal, Strides in Education," www.ataturk.com.

11. "The Era of Reza Shah, 1921–41," www.cyberiran.com; Gamel Abdel Nasser, *Egypt's Liberation: The Philosophy of the Revolution* (Washington, D.C.: Washington Public Affairs Press, 1955), p. 113.

12. Efraim Karsh and Inari Karsh, *Empires in the Sand: The Struggle for Mastery in the Middle East, 1789–1923* (Cambridge, Mass.: Harvard University Press, 1999), p. 48.

13. Nasser, *Egypt's Liberation*, p. 113. The best single-volume account of the Suez Crisis remains Hugh Thomas, *Suez* (New York: Harper and Row, 1967); see also Peter Mansfield, *A History of the Middle East* (New York: Viking, 1991), pp. 257–60; for military operations see Chaim Herzog, *The Arab-Israeli Wars* (New York: Vintage Books, 1984), pp. 111–41.

14. Daniel Lerner, *The Passing of Traditional Society: Modernizing the Middle East* (New York, The Free Press, 1958), p. 93.

15. Ibid., p. 237.

16. Ibid.

17. Ibid., p. 239.

18. Sylvia G. Haim, trans. and ed., *Arab Nationalism* (Berkeley, Calif.: University of California Press, 1962), p. 243.

CHAPTER 6

1. William Dalrymple, *From the Holy Mountain: A Journey among the Christians of the Middle East* (New York: Henry Holt, 1997), p. 92.

2. Ibid., p. 441.

3. Ibid., p. 433.

4. Wilfred Cantwell Smith, *Islam in Modern History* (New York: Mentor Books, 1957), p. 106.

5. Quoted in ibid.

6. Thomas W. Lippman, *Understanding Islam: An Introduction to the Muslim World* (New York: Mentor, 1990), p. 164.

7. Albert Camus, *The Rebel: An Essay on Man in Revolt*, trans. by Anthony Bower (New York: Vintage Books), p. 123.

8. Ibid., p. 124.

9. Samuel P. Huntington, *Political Order in Changing Societies* (New Haven: Yale University Press, 1968), p. 246.

10. Graham E. Fuller, "The Emergence of Central Asia," *Foreign Policy*, no. 78 (spring 1990): 56.

11. Ibid., p. 55.

12. Robin Wright, *Sacred Rage: The Wrath of Militant Islam* (New York: Simon & Schuster, 1986), p. 32.

13. Ibid., p. 33.

14. Sayyid Husayn Nasr, trans. "Allamah Sayyid Husayn Tabatabai, *Shi'a*," www2.mozcom.com~habibislamstu.htm.

15. Wright, *Sacred Rage*, p. 37.

16. Harold Lamb, *Genghiz Khan: Emperor of All Men* (New York: Bantam Books, 1962), p. 110. A more scholarly life of the "emperor of all men" is Rene Grousset, *Conqueror of the World: The Life of Chingis-Khan*, trans. Marian McKellar and Denis Sinor (New York: Orion Press, 1966).

17. Maxime Rodinson, *Israel and the Arabs* (New York: Pantheon, 1968), p. 102.

18. Mark Huband, *Warriors of the Prophet: The Struggle for Islam* (Boulder, Colo.: Westview, 1998), p. 57.

19. Ibid., pp. 58–59.

20. Judith Miller, *God Has Ninety-Nine Names: Reporting from a Militant Middle East* (New York: Touchstone, 1996), pp. 180–81.

21. Albert Camus, *The Plague*, trans. by Stuart Gilbert (New York: Penguin Books, 1971), p. 148.

22. Jay Robert Nash, *Terrorism in the Twentieth Century* (New York: Evans, 1998), p. 257.

23. In a June 22, 2000, press briefing, Pino Arlacchi, executive director of the UN Office of Drug Control and Crime Prevention, stated that "there had been a dramatic increase in the trafficking of drugs and weapons . . . because of the growth of organized crime in the region" (www.un.org/news).

24. Peter Hopkirk's *Setting the East Ablaze: Lenin's Dream of an Empire In Asia* (New York, Norton, 1984), is the best guide to this tumultuous period in central Asian history.

25. Smith, *Islam in Modern History*, pp. 73–74.

26. Yossef Bodansky, *Target America: Terrorism in the US Today* (New York: SPI Books, 1993), p. 335.

27. Ibid., p. 301; *Ma'riv* (Israel), August 25, 1989.

28. Bodansky, *Target America*, p. 322.

29. *Under Siege*, bulletin of the Islamic Center, Washington, D.C., August 20, 1986.

30. Bodansky, *Target America*, p. 335.

31. Ibid., p. 343.

32. W. R. Farrell, *Blood and Rage: The Story of the Japanese Red Army* (Lexington, Mass.: D. C. Heath, 1990), p. 210; Bodansky, *Target America*, pp. 343–44.

33. Quoted in James Sanders, *The Downing of TWA Flight 800* (New York: Zebra Books, 1997), p. 52.

34. Further support for this terrible idea comes from an article by Howard Altman, "The Deadly Parakeet" *Philadelphia City Paper* (July 25–August 1, 1996). In the article, Altman quoted U.S. Assistant Attorney William Schaeffer as saying "the method of delivery suggests that this is not the first time that something like this ever occurred." Schaeffer expressed the fear to Altman that—to quote Altman's words—"an unknown quantity of Red Parakeets and other Chinese munitions are floating around this country and elsewhere." Schaeffer further stated that Ku intended to sell his cache of weapons within the United States, as Altman put it, to "Chinese street gangs and terrorist groups."

35. Huband, *Warriors of the Prophet*, p. 155.

36. Miller also notes that "the forced Islamization of non-Muslim children was one of many heart-breaking facts of life in Hasan Turabi's putative Islamic regime," *God Has Ninety-Nine Names*, p. 129.

37. Laslo Havas, *The Plot to Kill the Big Three* (New York: Bantam Books, 1971), p. ix.

38. Growing American pressure from the State Department and the DEA has made the Golden Triangle route less profitable because of efforts to make the government of Thailand take a more aggressive role in the "war on drugs." Khun Sa himself, the great Chinese drug lord, was forced to surrender to the Burmese government, although it is thought the Burmese regime has taken over his part in the drug trade!

Of course, the pure opium gum, after the poppy is harvested, has to be taken out of the countries like Afghanistan before it can be refined into heroin for the drug trade. As in many cases, the Third World supplies only the raw materials; the opium gum or paste is refined into heroin in the laboratories of the countries of the Second and First Worlds. Not only are laboratories available in First World countries like France (in Marseilles) but some Second World nations like Thailand can now refine the gum as well, after it arrives on mule caravans from the poppy fields in Burma.

It was during the Napoleonic Wars that the modern development of the opium trade began. In 1805, morphine was first extracted from the poppy's sap. E. Merck and Company of Darmstadt, Germany, began to manufacture morphine in 1827, with a large surge in production with the invention of the hypodermic needle in the 1860s. In 1874, according the somewhat paranoid Alfred W. McCoy's *The Politics of Heroin: CIA Complicity in the Global Drug Trade*, "the English researcher C. R. Wright synthesized heroin, or diacetylmorphine, for the first time when he boiled morphine and a common chemical, acetic anhydride, over a stove for several hours. . . . In 1898, however, the Bayer Company of Elberfeld, Germany, began mass production of diacetylmorphine and coined the trade name heroin to market the new remedy." The rest, as they say, is history.

39. Glen E. Schweitzer, with Carole C. Dorch, *Super-Terrorism: Assassins, Mobsters, and Weapons of Mass Destruction* (New York: Plenum, 1998), p. 170.

40. Sen. John Kerry and Sen. Hank Brown, *The BCCI Affair: A Report to the Committee on Foreign Relations* (Washington, D.C.: U.S. Senate, 1992). The Executive Summary of the Kerry-Brown report credits New York District Attorney Robert Morgenthau with initiating the investigation in 1989 with "materially [contributing] to the chain of events that resulted in BCCI's [global] closure" on July 5, 1991.

41. Ibid., chap. 11.

CHAPTER 7

1. Dietl Wilhem, *Holy War*, trans. Martha Humphreys (New York: MacMillan, 1984), p. 226.

2. Roland Dallas, *King Hussein: A Life on the Edge* (New York: Fromm International, 1999), p. 259.

3. David Shearer, "Outsourcing War," *Foreign Policy* (fall 1997).

4. Ehud Sprinzak, "The Great Superterrorism Scare," *Foreign Policy* (fall 1998).

5. Ibid.

6. Christopher Dickey, Gregory L. Vistica, and Russell Watson with Joseph Contreras, "Saddam + Bin Laden?" *Newsweek*, January 11, 1999.

7. Benjamin Netanyahu, *Terrorism: How the West Can Win* (New York: Avon, 1986), p. 10.

8. "Biological Warfare: An Historical Perspective," *Journal of the American Medical Association* (August 1997).

9. Robert L. Sherrow, "Better Killing through Chemistry," *Soldier of Fortune* (September 1998).

10. "Conversation with Terror," *Time*, January 11, 1999, p. 38.

11. Bruce W. Nelan, " The Price of Fanaticism," *Time*, April 3, 1995.

12. Stansfield Turner, *Secrecy and Democracy: The CIA in Transition* (Boston: Houghton Mifflin, 1985), p. 91.

13. David E. Mark, "Eurasia Letter: Russia and the New Transcaucasus," *Foreign Policy* (winter 1996–97).

14. According to *Periscope*, the newsletter of the United States Association of Former Intelligence Officers (AFIO), in edition number 4 for 1998, a precedent already exists for this cooperation.

15. Michael Ledeen, "Soviet Sponsorship: The Will to Disbelieve," in Netanyahu, *Terrorism: How the West Can Win*, pp. 87ff.

16. Jay Scott, *Army War Heroes* (Derby, Conn.: Monarch Books, 1963), pp. 46ff.

17. Stewart Steven, *The Spymasters of Israel* (New York: Ballantine, 1980), pp. 156–86. The plan to stop the German rocket experts was perceived by Israel as vital to its survival. One of those whom Nasser had recruited was Paul Goerke, who had worked for Hitler's rocket program at Peenemunde, the launch site of the V-1 rockets targeted at London. Although the Mossad's plan to drive the Germans out of Egypt, Operation Damocles, was ruthlessly successful, it inadvertently led to the resignation in March 1963 of Isser Harel, the Mossad's chief.

18. George Carpozi Jr., *Nazi Gold: The Real Story of How the World Plundered Jewish Treasure* (Fair Hills, N.J.: New Horizon Press, 1999).

CHAPTER 8

1. Project Megiddo of the FBI is probably the best account of Christian apocalyptic groups at work in the United States. It first appeared in 1999, and was immediately put up on the World Wide Web by the Federal Bureau of Investigation.

2. Gershom Gorenberg, *The End of Days: Fundamentalism and the Struggle for the Temple Mount* (New York: Free Press, 2001), pp. 212–13.

3. Ironically, the Senate testimony of Tenet was found on the Internet at the Russian Internet site, agentura.ru, which many in American intelligence believe is linked to the Russian intelligence services!

4. Ahron Bregman and Jihan El-Tahri, *Israel and the Arabs* (New York: TV Books, 2000), p. 249.

5. Fitzroy MacLean, *Eastern Approaches* (New York: Time-Life Books, 1964), p. 168.

CHAPTER 9

1. "Bush: 'We're at War,'" *Newsweek*, September 24, 2001, p. 32.

2. Johanna McGeary and David Van Biema, "The New Breed of Terrorists," *Time*, September 24, 2001, p. 36.

3. Tim O'Brien, "Wife of Solicitor General Alerted Him of Attack from Plane," CNN.com (www.cnn.com), September 12, 2001; Matthew P. Blanchard and Kayce T. Ataiyero, "Magnitutde of Tragedy Unfolds in Lost Lives," *Philadelphia Inquirer*, September 12, 2001, pp. A1, A17.

4. Alfred Lubrano, "In Seconds a Confident NY Is Shaken," *Philadelphia Inquirer*, September 12, 2001, pp. A8–A9.

5. Ibid., p. A8.

6. Ibid.

7. Nancy Gibbs, "If You Want to Humble an Empire," *Time*, September 24, 2001.

8. Carol Eustice, "Disabled Helped to Safety in WTC Tragedy," www.arthritis.about.com, accessed March 3, 2002.

9. Lubrano, "In Seconds," pp. A8–A9.

10. Ibid., p. A9.

11. Information on Flight 93 has been derived from the following sources: Thomas Fitzgerald and Diane Mastrull, "Crash in PA: 'We Are Being Hijacked!'" *Philadelphia Inquirer*, September 12, 2001, p. A3; Rose Ciotta and Craig R. McCoy, "On Flight 93, Defiant Voices," *Philadelphia Inquirer*, September 13, 2001, pp. A1, A8; "Facing the End: The Fight for Flight 93," *Time*, September 24, 2001, pp. 68–77; Charles Lane and John Mintz, "Bid to Thwart Hijackers May Have Led to Pa. Crash," *Washington Post*, September 12, 2001, p. A1.

12. Thomas Fitzgerald and Diane Mastrull, "'Black Box' from Jet That Hit in Pa. Might Be the Key," *Philadelphia Inquirer*, September 13, 2001, p. A6.

13. Lane and Mintz, "Bid to Thwart Hijackers," p. A1.

14. Fitzgerald and Mastrull, "Crash in Pa.," p. A3.

15. David Alexander, *Tomorrow's Soldiers* (New York: Avon, 1999), p. 174.

16. Gerry J. Gilmore, "Alleged Terrorist Airliner Attack Targets Pentagon," American Forces Information Service, www.defenselink.mil/news/, September 11, 2001.

17. CTVNews.com staff, "Terrorist Attack Declared New 'Pearl Harbor,'" *Toronto Globe and Mail* on-line (www.theglobeandmail.com), September 11, 2001.

18. "Bush: 'We're at War,'" p. 29.

19. "Inside Cheney's Bunker," *Newsweek*, December 31, 2001, p. 48.

20. *Atlantic City Press*, September 16, 2001.

21. The full text of Bush's speech is available in many sources, for example, the *Buffalo News*, September 12, 2001, p. A8; or on-line at the Toronto Globe and Mail Web site (www.theglobeandmail.com).

22. Quoted in Denis and Peggy Warner, *The Sacred Warriors: Japan's Suicide Legions* (New York: Avon Books, 1984), p. 40.

23. Quoted in ibid., p. 42.

24. David Irving, *The Destruction of Dresden* (New York: Ballantine, 1964).

25. McGeary and Van Biema, "New Breed of Terrorist," p. 34; "Bush: 'We're at War,'" p. 33.

26. Daniel Eisenberg, "How Safe Can We Get?" *Time*, September 24, 2001, p. 88.

27. McGeary and Van Biema, "New Breed of Terrorist," p. 32.

28. Ibid., p. 33.

29. Steve Crawford, *The SAS Encyclopedia* (Miami: Lewis International, 1998), pp. 90–91.

30. Richard Stengel, "The Passionate Prosecutor: Rudolph Giuliani Snares Mobsters and Headlines," *Time*, February 10, 1986, p. 53.

31. Robert D. McFadden, "For the Fire Department, the First Three Farewells," *New York Times*, September 16, 2001, p. A11.

32. Information on the memorial held at Liberty Island comes from Frances Robles, Elisa Ung, and Jennifer Autry, "Our Spirit Is Stronger Than Ever," *Philadelphia Inquirer*, September 24, 2001, p. A9.

CHAPTER 10

1. Masanori Ito, *The End of the Imperial Japanese Navy* (New York: Jove, 1986), p. 162.

2. David Miller and Gerard Ridefort, *Modern Elite Forces* (London: Salamander Books, 1991), p. 119.

3. Tom Clancy, with John Grisham, *Special Forces: A Guided Tour of US Army Special Forces* (New York: Berkley, 2000), p. 166.

4. John D. Lock, *To Fight with Intrepidity: The Complete History of the US Army Rangers from 1622 to the Present* (New York: Pocket Books, 1998), p. 440.

5. Joshua Cooper Ramo, "In Hot Pursuit," *Time*, October 8, 2001, p. 57.

6. Dawn Stover, "Nowhere to Hide," *Popular Science* (August 2001): 64.

7. *New York Post*, October 2, 2001, p. 6.

8. Quoted in Charles Miller, *Khyber: British India's Northwest Frontier* (New York: Macmillan, 1977), p. 627.

9. Sir Winston S. Churchill, *My Early Life: A Roving Commission* (New York: Manor Books, 1972), p. 141.

10. Quoted in Miller, *Khyber*, p. 269.

11. Patrick E. Tyler, "British Detail bin Laden's Link to U.S. Attacks," *New York Times*, October 5, 2001, p. A1.

12. Lt. Col. Terry Mayer, "The Biological Weapon," in *Battlefield of the Future: 21st Century Warfare Issues* (Maxwell Air Force Base, Ala.: Air University Presss, 1995).

13. Albert Camus, *The Plague*, trans. by Stuart Gilbert (New York: Penguin Books, 1972), p. 58.

CHAPTER 11

1. Ali A. Jalali, "Afghanistan: The Anatomy of an Ongoing Conflict," *Parameters*, journal of the U.S. Army War College (spring 2001).

CHAPTER 12

1. *Philadelphia Inquirer*, February 6, 2001.

Selected Bibliography

Aburish, Said K. *The Rise, Corruption, and Coming Fall of the House of Saud*. New York: St. Martin's, 1996.

Ajami, Fouad. "Iran: The Impossible Revolution." *Foreign Affairs* 67, no. 2 (winter 1988/89).

Alexander, David. *Tomorrow's Soldiers*. New York: Avon Books, 1999.

Alibek, Ken [Alibekov], with Stephan Handleman. *Biohazard*. New York: Random House, 1999. Born Alibekov in Soviet Kazakhstan, Alibek was the First Deputy Chief (1988–92) of the Russian biological warfare combine, Biopreparat, before his defection to the United States in 1992. This is his inside account of the workings of Biopreparat.

Allon, Yigael, ed. *The Making of Israel's Army*. New York: Ballantine, 1970.

———. *Shield of David: The Story of Israel's Armed Forces*. New York: Random House, 1970.

Antonius, George. *The Arab Awakening*. New York: Capricorn, 1965.

Barthorp, Michael. *The North-West Frontier, British India and Afghanistan: A Pictorial History, 1839–1947*. New Orchard, U.K.: Blandford Press, 1982.

Beckman, Morris. *The Jewish Brigade: An Army with Two Masters, 1944–5*. New York: Sarpedon, 1998.

Betser, Colonel Muki, with Robert Rosenberg. *Secret Soldier: The True Life Story of Israel's Greatest Commando*. New York: Atlantic Monthly Press, 1996. The story of the author's adventures with the Sayaret Matkal.

Bin Sayeed, Khaled. *Western Dominance and Political Islam*. Albany: State University of New York Press, 1995.

Bodansky, Yussef. *Target America: Terrorism in the US Today.* New York: SPI Books, 1993.

Bond, Brian, ed. *Victorian Military Campaigns.* New York: Praeger, 1967.

Border, Jack. *Nazi Gold: The Full Story of the Fifty-Year Swiss-Nazi Conspiracy to Steal Billions from Europe's Jews and Holocaust Survivors.* New York: Harper-Collins, 1997.

———. "Taliban Turnaround: The Rise and Fall of Afghanistan's Islamic Militia." *Soldier of Fortune* (February 1999).

Bregman, Ahron, and Jihan El-Tahri. *Israel and the Arabs: An Eyewitness Account of War and Peace in the Middle East.* New York: TV Books, 2000. An eyewitness account compiled to accompany the multipart series hosted by PBS televion network.

Bresler, Fenton. *The Chinese Mafia.* Briarcliff, N.Y.: Stein and Day, 1981.

Brock, Ray. *Blood, Oil and Sand.* Cleveland: The World Publishing Co., 1952.

Brooksmith, Peter. *Biohazard: The Hot Zone and Beyond.* New York: Barnes & Noble, 1997.

Burnaby, Capt. Frederick. *On Horseback through Asia Minor.* New York: Oxford, 1996.

———. *A Ride to Khiva.* New York: Oxford, 1997. Burnaby traveled through central Asia to the fabled city of Khiva in 1875, one year before he made his trip to Asia Minor. Although gazetted as a captain in the prestigious Royal Horse Guards, these expeditions on the borders of the Russian Empire, when Russia was England's main rival in central Asia, makes one believe that Burnaby was one of those many British traveling officers like "Bokhara" Burnes who performed more service for the British and Indian secret services than they did for the British or Indian armies!

Burrows, William D. *Deep Black: The Startling Truth behind America's Top-Secret Spy Satellites.* New York: Berkley, 1986.

"Bush: 'We're at War.'" *Newsweek,* September 24, 2001, pp. 26–40.

Bushart, Howard L., John R. Craig, and Myra Barnes. *Soldiers of God: White Supremacists and Their Holy War for America.* New York: Kensington, 1998.

Camus, Albert. *The Plague.* Translated by Stuart Gilbert. New York: Penguin Books, 1972.

———. *The Rebel: An Essay on Man in Revolt.* Translated by Anthony Bower. New York: Vintage Books, 1956.

Carpozi, George, Jr. *Nazi Gold: The Real Story of How the World Plundered Jewish Treasure.* Fair Hills, N.J.: New Horizon Press, 1999.

Cave-Brown, Anthony. *Treason in the Blood: M. St. John Philby, Kim Philby, and the Spy Case of the Century.* New York: Houghton Mifflin, 1994.

Churchill, Sir Winston. *My Early Life: A Roving Commission.* New York: Manor Books, 1972.

———. *The River War.* New York: Award Books, 1964.

———. *The Story of the Malakand Field Force.* New York: Barnes & Noble, 1993.

Clancy, Tom, with John Grisham. *Special Forces: A Guided Tour of US Army Special Forces.* New York: Berkley, 2000.

Cleaves, Francis Woodman, trans. and ed. *The Secret History of the Mongols.* Cambridge, Mass.: Harvard-Yenching Institute, 1982.

Clover, Charles. "Dreams of the Eurasian Heartland: The Reemergence of Geopolitics." *Foreign Affairs* (March/April 1999).

Collins, Larry, and Dominique Lapierre. *O Jerusalem!* New York: Pocket Books, 1972.

Conrad, Joseph. *Heart of Darkness and the Secret Sharer.* New York: Signet Books, 1950.

Cooper, H. H. A., and Lawrence J. Redlinger. *Catching Spies: Principles and Practices of Counterespionage.* New York: Bantam Books, 1990.

———. *Making Spies: A Talent Spotters Handbook.* Boulder, Colo.: Paladin Press, 1986.

Crawford, Steve. *The SAS Encyclopedia.* Miami: Lewis International, 1998.

Dallas, Roland. *King Hussein: A Life on the Edge.* New York: Fromm International, 1999.

Dalrymple, William. *From the Holy Mountain: A Journey among the Christians of the Middle East.* New York: Henry Holt, 1997.

Dayan, Moshe. *The Story of My Life.* New York: Da Capo, 1992.

Deacon, Richard. *The French Secret Service.* London: Grafton Books, 1990.

De Chair, Somerset. *The Golden Carpet.* London: Faber, 1944. (In paperback, New York: Bantam Books, 1984).

Demaris, Ovid. *Brothers in Blood: The International Terrorist Network.* New York: Scribner's, 1977.

Dietl, Wilhem. *Holy War.* Translated by Martha Humphreys. New York: Macmillan, 1984.

Donia, Robert J., and John V. A. Fine Jr. *Bosnia and Hercegovina: A Tradition Betrayed.* New York: Columbia University Press, 1994.

Eisenberg, Daniel. "How Safe Can We Get?" *Time,* September 24, 2001, pp. 85–91.

Eisenberg, Dennis, Uri Dan, and Eli Landau. *The Mossad: Israel's Secret Intelligence Service.* New York: Signet, 1979.

Emerson, Steven. *The American House of Saud: The Secret Petrodollar Connection.* New York: Franklin Watts, 1985.

Esposito, John L. *The Islamic Threat: Myth or Reality?* New York: Oxford, 1992.

Faligot, Roger, and Pascal Krop. *La Piscine: The French Secret Service since 1944.* Translated by W. D. Halls. London: Basil Blackwell, 1989.

Farago, Ladislas. *Aftermath.* New York: Avon Books, 1974. Details the hunt for Martin Bormann in Latin America.

Farah, Charles E. *Islam.* New York: Barron's, 2000.

Farrell, W. R. *Blood and Rage: The Story of the Japanese Red Army.* Lexington, Mass.: D. C. Heath, 1990.

Featherstone, Donald. *Khaki and Red: Soldiers of the Queen in India and Africa.* London: Arms and Armour Press, 1995.

Finckenhauer, James O., and Elin J. Waring. *Russian Mafia in America: Immigration, Culture, and Crime.* Boston: Northeastern University Press, 1998.

Fletcher, Richard. *Moorish Spain.* Phoenix: University of Arizona Press, 1994.

———. *The Quest for El Cid.* New York: Knopf, 1990.

Follain, Jack. *Jackal: The Complete Story of the Legendary Terrorist Carlos the Jackal.* New York: Arcade, 1998.

Forbes, William H. *Fall of the Peacock Throne: The Story of Iran.* New York: Harper and Row, 1980.

France, John. *Western Warfare in the Age of the Crusades, 1000–1300.* Ithaca, N.Y.: Cornell University Press, 1999.

Freemantle, Brian. *The Octopus: Europe in the Grip of Organized Crime.* London: Orion, 1995.

Fromkin, David. *A Peace to End All Peace.* New York: Avon, 1989.

Fuller, Graham E. "The Emergence of Central Asia." *Foreign Policy,* no. 78 (spring 1990).

Gabrieli, Francesco. *Arab Historians of the Crusades.* Translated by E. J. Costello. New York: Dorset, 1989.

Gaury, Gerald de. *The Rulers of Mecca.* New York: Dorset, 1991.

Glubb, John Bagot (Pasha). *The Great Arab Conquests.* New York: Barnes & Noble, 1995.

Golan, Galia. "Gorbachev's Middle East Strategy." *Foreign Affairs* (fall 1987): 41–57.

———. *The Soviet Union and the Palestine Liberation Organization.* New York: Praeger, 1980.

Gorenberg, Gershom. *The End of Days: Fundamentalism and the Struggle for the Temple Mount.* New York: Free Press, 2001.

Graz, Liesl. *The Turbulent Gulf: People, Politics, and Power.* New York: Tauris, 1992.

Green, Peter. *Alexander of Macedon, 356–323 BC: A Historical Biography.* Los Angeles: University of California Press, 1991.

Grousset, Rene. *The Empire of the Steppes: A History of Central Asia.* Translated by Naomi Walford. New Brunswick, N.J.: Rutgers University Press, 1970.

————. *The Epic of the Crusades.* New York: Orion, 1970.

Guillaume, Alfredo. *Islam.* New York: Penguin, 1990.

Haim, Sylvia G., trans. and ed. *Arab Nationalism.* Berkeley: University of California Press, 1962.

Herzog, Chaim. *The Arab-Israeli Wars: War and Peace in the Middle East from the War of Independence through Lebanon.* New York: Vintage Books, 1984.

————. *War of Atonement.* Boston: Little, Brown, 1974. The October Middle East War of 1973. Chaim Herzog was president of Israel when he died in 1998. Born Vivian Herzog, he was a former officer of the British army who then served as a master intelligence officer of the Israeli Haganah in the 1948 war.

Hiro, Dilip. *Between Marx and Mohammed: The Changing Face of Central Asia.* New York: HarperCollins, 1995.

————. *Holy Wars: The Rise of Islamic Fundamentalism.* New York: Routledge, Chapman, and Hall, 1989.

Hitti, Philip. *Syria: A Short History.* New York: Collier Books, 1962.

Hopkirk, Peter. *The Great Game.* New York: Kodansha, 1992.

————. *Setting the East Ablaze: Lenin's Dream of an Empire in Asia.* New York: Norton, 1984.

Horne, Alistair. *A Savage War of Peace: Algeria, 1954–1962.* New York: Penguin Books, 1987.

Hourani, Albert. *A History of the Arab Peoples.* Cambridge, Mass.: Harvard University Press, 1991.

Huband, Mark. *Warriors of the Prophet: The Struggle for Islam.* Boulder, Colo.: Westview, 1998.

Huntington, Samuel P. *Political Order in Changing Societies.* New Haven: Yale University Press, 1968.

Ibn-Khaldun, Abd al-Rahman. *The Muqaddimah: The Philosophy of History.* Translated by Franz Rosenthal, abridged and edited by N. J. Dawood. Princeton, N.J.: Princeton University Press, 1989.

"Inside Cheney's Bunker," *Newsweek,* December 31, 2001, p. 48.

Irving, David. *The Destruction of Dresden.* New York: Ballantine Books, 1964.

Ito, Masanori. *The End of the Imperial Japanese Navy.* New York: Jove, 1986.

Joinville, Jean de, and Geoffroi de Villehardouin. *Chronicles of the Crusades.* Translated by M. R. B. Shaw. New York: Barnes & Noble, 1993.

Josephus, Flavius. *The Works of Josephus.* Translated by William Whiston. New York: Hendrickson, 1987.

Julien, Robert M. *A Primer of Drug Action.* New York: Freeman, 1998.

Kann, Robert A. *A History of the Habsburg Empire, 1526–1918*. Berkeley: University of California Press, 1974.

Kaplan, Robert D. *The Arabists: The Romance of an American Elite*. New York: Free Press, 1993.

———. *The Ends of the Earth: A Journey to the Frontiers of Anarchy*. New York: Vintage, 1996.

———. *Soldiers of God: With the Mujahidin in Afghanistan*. Boston: Houghton Mifflin, 1990.

Karsh, Efraim, and Inari Karsh. *Empires in the Sand: The Struggle for Mastery in the Middle East, 1789–1923*. Cambridge, Mass.: Harvard University Press, 1999.

Katz, Samuel. *Battleground: Fact and Fantasy in Palestine*. New York: Shapolsky, 1985.

Katz, Samuel M. *The Elite: The True Story of Israel's Secret Counterterrorist Unit*. New York: Pocket Books, 1992. A history of the Israeli Sayaret Matkal.

———. *The Night Raiders: Israel's Naval Commandos at War*. New York: Pocket Books, 1997. An account of Israel's naval commandos, now known as Force 13.

Kinross, John Patrick Douglas Balfour, Baron. *The Ottoman Centuries: The Rise and Fall of the Turkish Empire*. New York: Quill, 1977.

Kirk, George E. *A Short History of the Middle East*. New York: Praeger, 1959.

Klass, Rossanne. *Afghanistan: The Great Game Revisited*. New York: Afghan Freedom House, 1989. Rossanne Klass and John Walker rank as the leading scholars in the United States on Afghanistan.

Kortepeter, C. Max. *Ottoman Imperialism during the Reformation: Europe and the Caucasus*. New York: New York University Press, 1972.

Kronenwetter, Michael. *The War on Terrorism*. Englewood Cliffs, N.J.: Messner/Simon & Schuster, 1988.

Krott, Rob. "Genocidal *Jihad*: SOF's Sudanese Summer Vacation." *Soldier of Fortune* (October 1998).

Lacy, Robert. *The Kingdom: Arabia and the House of Saud*. New York: Avon, 1981.

Lamb, Harold. *Genghiz Khan: Emperor of All Men*, New York: Bantam Books, 1962.

———. *The March of the Barbarians*. New York: Literary Guild of America, 1940.

Lamy, Philip. *Millennium Rage: Survivalists, White Supremacists, and the Doomsday Prophecy*. New York: Plenum, 1996.

Lapidus, Ira M. *A History of Islamic Societies*. New York: Cambridge University Press, 1988.

Laqueur, Walter. *The Struggle for the Middle East: The Soviet Union in the Mediterranean, 1958–1968*. New York: Macmillan, 1969.

Lawrence, T. E. [Lawrence of Arabia]. *The Essential T. E. Lawrence.* Edited by David Garnett. New York: Oxford University Press, 1992.

————. *The Seven Pillars of Wisdom: A Triumph.* New York: Anchor/Doubleday, 1991.

Ledeen, Michael. "Soviet Sponsorship: The Will to Disbelieve," in *Terrorism: How the West Can Win,* edited by Benjamin Netanyahu. New York: Avon Books and the Jonathan Institute, 1986.

Legg, Stuart. *The Barbarians of Asia: The Peoples of the Steppes from 1600 BC.* New York: Dorset Press, 1990.

Lerner, Daniel. *The Passing of Traditional Society: Modernizing the Middle East.* New York: The Free Press, 1958.

Leulliette, Pierre. *The War in Algeria.* New York: Bantam Books, 1987. A French parachutist's eyewitness account of the war against the Algerian FLN, formerly published as *St. Michael and the Dragon.* St. Michael is the patron saint of all French paras; his wing and sword comprise the emblem on their distinctive beret badge.

Levenda, Peter. *Unholy Alliance: A History of Nazi Involvement with the Occult.* New York: Avon Books, 1995.

Lewin, Ronald. *The American Magic.* New York: Penguin, 1982.

Lewis, Archibald R. *Nomads and Crusaders, AD 1000–1368.* Bloomington: Indiana University Press, 1988.

Lewis, Bernard. *The Arabs in History.* New York: Oxford, 1993.

————. *The Assassins: A Radical Sect in Islam.* London: Weidenfeld and Nicolson, 1967.

————. *The Middle East: A Brief History of the Last 2,000 Years.* New York: Simon & Schuster/Touchstone, 1995.

Liddell-Hart, B. H. *Colonel Lawrence: The Man behind the Legend.* New York: Dodd, Mead, 1935.

Lippman, Thomas W. *Understanding Islam: An Introduction to the Muslim World.* New York: Mentor, 1990.

Lloyd, Mark. *Special Forces: The Changing Face of Warfare.* New York: Arms and Armour Press, 1995.

Lock, John D. *To Fight with Intrepidity: The Complete History of the US Army Rangers from 1622 to the Present.* New York: Pocket Books, 1998.

Long, Robert Emmet. *Banking Scandals: The S&LS and BCCI.* New York: Wilson, 1993.

Lunt, Maj. Gen. James D. *Bokhara Burnes.* London: Faber and Faber, 1969. Alexander "Bokhara" Burnes was one of the only players of the "Great Game" who ever saw the Russian threat up close. Captain Vitkievitch, aide-de-camp to the tsarist governor-general of Orenburg, visited Kabul, the capital of Afghanistan, on Christmas Eve, 1837. Burnes had him as a guest for Christmas dinner. Later, Burnes would be savagely murdered by the Afghans in their rebellion against the British rule in November 1841. Burnes had visited Bokhara, then an independent khanate in central Asia, in June 1832. He returned to London in 1833, well-earning his nickname "Bokhara" Burnes. His famous *Travels in Bokhara* was published in London in 1834. Major General Lunt, like Burnes, served in the old British Indian army; Burnes served while it was still the army of the Honourable East India Company.

Lyons, Malcolm Cameron, and D. E. P. Jackson. *Saladin: The Policies of the Holy War*. Cambridge: Cambridge University Press, 1982.

Maalouf, Amin. *The Crusades through Arab Eyes*. New York: Schocken, 1984.

Mackey, Sandra. *Lebanon: Death of a Nation*. New York: Anchor Books, 1991.

———. *Saudis: Inside the Desert Kingdom*. New York: Signet, 1990.

MacLean, Fitzroy. *Eastern Approaches*. New York: Time-Life Books, 1964.

Mansel, Philip. *Constantinople: City of the World's Desire, 1453–1924*. New York: St. Martin's Press, 1998.

Mansfield, Peter. *A History of the Middle East*. New York: Viking, 1991.

Mark, David E. "Eurasia Letter: Russia and the New Transcaucasus." *Foreign Policy* (winter 1996–97).

Matthews, Owen. "Afghanistan: Another Kind of War." *Men's Journal* (August 1998).

Mayer, Lt. Col. Terry N. "The Biological Weapon: A Poor Nation's Weapon of Mass Destruction." In *Battlefield of the Future: 21st Century Warfare Issues*. Edited by Barry R. Schneider and Lawrence E. Grinter. Maxwell Air Force Base, Ala.: Air University Press, 1995.

McDowall, David. *A Modern History of the Kurds*. New York: St. Martin's Press, 1996.

McGeary, Johanna, and David Van Biema. "The New Breed of Terrorist," *Time*, September 24, 2001, pp. 28–39.

McNally, Raymond T., and Radu Florescu. *Dracula, Prince of Many Faces: His Life and Times*. Boston: Little, Brown, 1989.

Mercer, Charles. *Legion of Strangers: A Vivid History of a Unique Military Tradition, The French Foreign Legion*. New York: Holt, Rinehart, and Winston, 1964.

The Middle East Magazine (March 1999), special articles on Jordan after King Hussein, and the upcoming Algerian and Turkish elections.

Miller, Charles. *Khyber: British India's Northwest Frontier*. New York: Macmillan, 1977.

Miller, David, and Gerard Ridefort. *Modern Elite Forces*. London: Salamander Books, 1991.

Miller, Judith. *God Has Ninety-Nine Names: Reporting from a Militant Middle East.* New York: Touchstone, 1996. Miller is an intrepid reporter for the *New York Times*. Miller's title comes from a Muslim fable dating from the time of the Prophet. According to the story, God had 100 names, not ninety-nine as Miller states. Men only knew ninety-nine of them. The camel was the only beast that knew God's—Allah's—one-hundredth name, and that was why the camel always had such a smug look on its face!

Mizell, Louis R., Jr. *Target USA: The Inside Story of the New Terrorist War*. New York: Wiley, 1998.

Morris, Benny. *Righteous Victims: A History of the Zionist-Arab Conflict, 1881–1999*. New York: Alfred A. Knopf, 1999.

Murphy, John F., Jr. "A Tale of Two Frontiers: The American West and the Northwest Frontier of British India." Unpublished ms. London: National Army Museum.

Nash, Jay Robert. *Terrorism in the 20th Century*. New York: M. Evans and Company, 1998.

Nasser, Gamal Abdel. *Egypt's Liberation: The Philosophy of the Revolution*. Washington, D.C.: Washington Public Affairs Press, 1955.

Nelan, Bruce W., "The Price of Fanaticism," *Time*, April 3, 1995.

Netanyahu, Benjamin. "Defining Terrorism," in *Terrorism: How the West Can Win.* New York: Avon Books and the Jonathan Institute, 1996. The Jonathan Institute was named for Netanyahu's brother Jonathan "Yonni" Netanyahu, the only Israeli fatality in the 1976 Israeli raid on Entebbe airfield in Uganda. Both brothers, like former Israeli prime minister Golda Meir, were born in the United States; Mrs. Meir had been a school teacher in Chicago. The Netanyahus' father is a distinguished professor at an American university.

———. *Fighting Terrorism*. New York: Farrar, Straus, and Giroux, 1995.

Nicolle, David. *The Muslim Warlords: Genghiz Khan, Kublai Khan, Hulegu, Tamerlane*. New York: Firebird/Stirling, 1990.

Nugent, Rory. "The March of the Green Flag." *Spin* (May 1995).

Nutting, Anthony. *Lawrence of Arabia: The Man and the Motive*. New York: Signet, 1962.

O'Ballance, Edgar. *The Arab-Israeli War, 1948*. New York: Praeger, 1957.

Oldenbourg, Zoe. *The Crusades*. New York: Pantheon Books, 1966.

Paret, Peter. *French Revolutionary War from Indochina to Algeria: The Analysis of a Political and Military Doctrine*. New York: Praeger, 1964.

Payne, Robert. *The History of Islam*. New York: Dorset, 1987.

Payton-Smith, D. J. *Oil: War-Time Policy and Administration*. London: H.M.S.O., 1971.

Peres, Shimon. *David's Sling*. New York: Random House, 1970.

Peters, Edward, ed. *The First Crusade: The Chronicle of Fulcher of Chartres and Other Source Materials*. Philadelphia: University of Pennsylvania Press, 1998.

Peters, Rudolph. *Jihad in Classical and Modern Islam*. Princeton, N.J.: Markus Wiener, 1996.

Pickthall, Marmaduke. *The Meaning of the Glorious Koran*. New York: Mentor Books, 1991. All Quranic quotations are from Pickthall's translation.

Plutarch. *Lives of the Noble Greeks*. New York: Dell Books, 1961. Specifically, Plutarch's "Life of Alexander." There are many editions of Plutarch's biographies in print.

———. *Lives of the Noble Romans*. New York: Dell Books, 1961.

Polk, William R. *The Arab World Today*. Cambridge, Mass.: Harvard University Press, 1991.

Posner, Gerald L. *Warlords of Crime: Chinese Secret Societies: The New Mafia*. New York: Penguin, 1988.

Ramo, Joshua Cooper. "In Hot Pursuit," *Time*, October 8, 2001, pp. 54–58.

Rashid, Ahmed. *The Resurgence of Central Asia: Islam or Nationalism?* London: Zed Books, 1994.

Richards, Frank. *Old-Soldier Sahib*. London: Faber and Faber, n.d.

Ridgeway, James. *Blood in the Face: The Ku Klux Klan, Aryan Nations, Nazi Skinheads, and the Rise of a New White Culture*. New York: Thunder's Mouth Press, rev. ed. 1995.

Riley-Smith, Jonathan, ed. *The Oxford Illustrated History of the Crusades*. New York: Oxford University Press, 1995.

Rodinson, Maxime. *Israel and the Arabs*. New York: Pantheon, 1968.

Runciman, Sir Steven. *The Fall of Constantinople, 1453*. New York: Canto/Cambridge University Press, 1995.

———. *A History of the Crusades*. 3 vols. Cambridge: Cambridge University Press, 1951–1954.

Said, Edward. *The Question of Palestine*. New York: Vintage Books, 1979.

Salibi, Kamal. *The Modern History of Jordan*. London: Tauris, 1998.

Sanders, James. *The Downing of TWA Flight 800*. New York: Zebra Books, 1997. Sanders and his wife have, as of April 1999, been sentenced to jail for up to ten years for having in their possession two swatches of seating material from TWA

Flight 800 which Sanders and his wife, a TWA flight attendant, believe show residue of the propellant from a missile's exhaust. The FBI contends, however, that the stains on the fabric are from glue.

Sayeed, Khalid Bin. *Western Dominance and Political Islam: Challenge and Response.* Albany: State University of New York Press, 1995.

Seabrook, William B. *Adventures in Arabia.* New York: Harcourt, Brace, 1927.

Scott, James. *Army War Heroes.* Derby, Conn.: Monarch Books, 1963.

Scott, Roddy. "Taliban Tag: SOF Rejoins the Trenches of the War without End." *Soldier of Fortune* (June 1998).

Schweitzer, Glenn E., with Carole C. Dorsch. *Super-Terrorism: Assassins, Mobsters, and Weapons of Mass Destruction.* New York: Plenum, 1998.

Segev, Tom. *One Palestine, Complete: Jews and Arabs under the British Mandate.* New York: Metropolitan Books, 2000.

Sherrow, Richard L. "Better Killing through Chemistry." *Soldier of Fortune* (September 1998).

Sivan, Emmanuel. *Radical Islam: Medieval Theology and Modern Practice.* New York: Yale, 1985.

Smail, R. C. *Crusading Warfare, 1097–1193.* Cambridge: Cambridge University Press, 1972.

Smith, Charles D. *Palestine and the Arab-Israeli Conflict,* 2d ed. New York: St. Martin's Press, 1992.

Smith, Wilfred Cantwell. *Islam in Modern History.* New York: Mentor Books, 1957.

Sprinzak, Ehud. *Brother against Brother: Violence and Extremism in Israeli Politics from Altalena to the Rabin Assassination.* New York: Free Press, 1999.

———. "The Great Superterrorism Scare." *Foreign Policy* (fall 1998).

Stein, Joel. "Digging Out," *Time,* September 24, 2001, pp. 60–66.

Stengel, Richard. "The Passionate Prosecutor: Rudolph Giuliani Snares Mobsters and Headlines," *Time,* February 10, 1986, pp. 51–53.

Sterling, Claire. *The Terror Network: The Secret War of International Terrorism.* New York: Holt, Rinehart, and Winston, 1981.

Stern, Jessica. *The Ultimate Terrorist.* Cambridge: Harvard University Press, 1999.

Stevens, Stewart. *The Spymasters of Israel.* New York: Ballantine, 1980.

Stoff, Michael B. *Oil, War, and American Security: The Search for a National Policy on Foreign Oil, 1941–1947.* New Haven: Yale University Press, 1980.

Stover, Dawn. "Nowhere to Hide." *Popular Science* (August 2001).

Talbot, John. *The War without a Name: France in Algeria, 1954–1962.* New York: Knopf, 1980.

Taylor, Edmund. *The Real Case against Nasser*. Cleveland: Zubal Books, 1956.

Tutch, Hans E. "Arab Unity and Arab Dissension." In *The Middle East in Transition*, edited by Walter Z. Laquer, New York: Praeger, 1958.

Trinquier, Col. Roger. *Modern Warfare: A French View of Counter-Insurgency*. Translated by Daniel Lee. New York: Praeger, 1964. This work carries an introduction by Bernard B. Fall, late professor at Howard University, who chronicled the French war in Indochina. Not content to write about the French experience in Indochina, Fall returned to cover the American war and died, where he would have wanted to, up front with the fighting men, a victim of a Viet Cong mortar attack.

Tuchman, Barbara. *The Guns of August*. New York: Bantam Books, 1976.

Turner, Stansfield. *Secrecy and Democracy: The CIA in Transition*. Boston: Houghton Mifflin, 1985.

Tyler, Patrick E. "British Detail bin Laden's Link to U.S. Attacks," *New York Times*, October 5, 2001, p. A1.

Uris, Leon. *Exodus*. New York: Bantam Books, 1958.

Van Creveld, Martin. *The Sword and the Olive: A Critical History of the Israeli Defense Force*. New York: Perseus/Public Affairs, 1998.

Venter, A. J. "Targeting Sudan: Why We Bombed Osama bin Laden's Shadowy World of Intrigue." *Soldier of Fortune* (December 1998).

Wallach, Janet, and John Wallach. *Arafat: In the Eyes of the Beholder*. New York: Carol Publishing Group, 1990.

Warner, Denis, and Peggy Warner. *The Sacred Warriors: Japan's Suicide Legions*. New York: Avon Books, 1984.

Wheatcroft, Andrew. *The Habsburgs: Embodying Empire*. New York: Penguin Books, 1995.

———. *The Ottomans: Dissolving Images*. New York: Penguin, 1995.

Willems, Peter. "Opium: Afghanistan's Gold." *The Middle East Magazine* (September 1997).

Woodward, Bob. *Veil: The Secret Wars of the CIA, 1981–1987*. New York: Pocket Books, 1987.

Wright, Robin. *In the Name of God: The Khomeini Decade*. New York: Simon & Schuster, 1989.

———. *Sacred Rage: The Wrath of Militant Islam*. New York: Simon & Schuster, 1986.

Xenophon. *Anabasis: The March of the 10,000*. New York: Penguin Books, 1992.

Zakaria, Rafiq. *Muhammed and the Quran*. New York: Penguin Books, 1991.

———. *The Struggle for Islam*. New York: Penguin Books, 1990.

Ziegler, Phillip. *Omdurman*. New York: Hippocrene Books, 1988.

Index

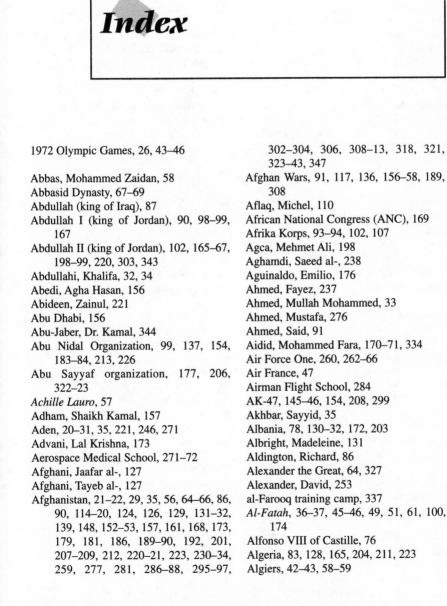

407

DATE DUE   *DAYS*

DATE DUE		
NOV 0 9 2002		
DEC 5 2002		
DEC 2 8 2002		
JAN 2 4 2003		
FEB 1 0 2003		
MAR 1 2 2003		
GAYLORD		PRINTED IN U.S.A.